Jihadists of North Africa and the Sahel

Jihadist movements have claimed that they are merely vehicles for the application of God's word, distancing themselves from politics, which they call dirty and manmade. Yet on closer examination, jihadist movements are immersed in politics, negotiating political relationships not just with the forces surrounding them, but also within their own ranks. Drawing on case studies from North Africa and the Sahel - including Algeria, Libya, Mali, Niger, Burkina Faso, and Mauritania - this study examines jihadist movements from the inside, uncovering their activities and internal struggles over the past three decades. Highlighting the calculations that jihadist field commanders and clerics make, Alexander Thurston shows how leaders improvise, both politically and religiously, as they adjust to fast-moving conflicts. Featuring critical analysis of Arabic-language jihadist statements, this book offers unique insights into the inner workings of jihadist organisations and sheds new light on the phenomenon of mass-based jihadist movements and proto-states.

ALEXANDER THURSTON is Assistant Professor of Political Science at the University of Cincinnati. He was an International Affairs Fellow at the Council on Foreign Relations between 2013–14, and has also held fellowships with the Wilson Center and the American Council of Learned Societies. He is the author of *Salafism in Nigeria: Islam, Preaching and Politics* (2016) and *Boko Haram: The History of an African Jihadist Movement* (2018) which was named by *Foreign Affairs* as one of the 'Best of Books 2018' and was a finalist for the African Studies Association's Book Prize in 2019.

Jihadists of North Africa and the Sahel

Local Politics and Rebel Groups

ALEXANDER THURSTON
University of Cincinnati

CAMBRIDGE
UNIVERSITY PRESS

CAMBRIDGE
UNIVERSITY PRESS

University Printing House, Cambridge CB2 8BS, United Kingdom

One Liberty Plaza, 20th Floor, New York, NY 10006, USA

477 Williamstown Road, Port Melbourne, VIC 3207, Australia

314–321, 3rd Floor, Plot 3, Splendor Forum, Jasola District Centre,
New Delhi – 110025, India

79 Anson Road, #06–04/06, Singapore 079906

Cambridge University Press is part of the University of Cambridge.

It furthers the University's mission by disseminating knowledge in the pursuit of
education, learning, and research at the highest international levels of excellence.

www.cambridge.org
Information on this title: www.cambridge.org/9781108488662
DOI: 10.1017/9781108771160

First published 2020

A catalogue record for this publication is available from the British Library.

Library of Congress Cataloging-in-Publication Data
Names: Thurston, Alexander, author.
Title: Jihadists of North Africa and the Sahel : local politics and rebel groups / Alexander
    Thurston.
Description: Cambridge, United Kingdom ; New York, NY : Cambridge University Press,
    2020. | Includes bibliographical references and index.
Identifiers: LCCN 2020002777 (print) | LCCN 2020002778 (ebook) |
    ISBN 9781108488662 (hardback) | ISBN 9781108726863 (paperback) |
    ISBN 9781108771160 (epub)
Subjects: LCSH: Islam and politics–Africa, North. | Islam and politics–Sahel. |
    Islamic fundamentalism–Africa, North. | Islamic fundamentalism–Sahel. |
    Terrorist organizations–Africa, North. | Terrorist organizations–Sahel. | Jihad.
Classification: LCC BP173.7 .T54 2020 (print) | LCC BP173.7 (ebook) |
    DDC 320.557–dc23
LC record available at https://lccn.loc.gov/2020002777
LC ebook record available at https://lccn.loc.gov/2020002778

ISBN 978-1-108-48866-2 Hardback
ISBN 978-1-108-72686-3 Paperback

Contents

Maps

Acknowledgments

This book emerges from more than a decade of thinking, researching, and writing about North Africa and the Sahel. Many people and institutions have helped me along the way. The book was built on their generosity.

Most proximately, the inspiration for this project grew out of my work as a research advisor at the CNA Corporation, primarily in 2016–2017. In that role, I benefited tremendously from the mentorship, collegiality, and insights of Jonathan Schroden, Julia McQuaid, Pamela Faber, and David Knoll. I also thank Patrick Johnston of the RAND Corporation and Daniel Byman of Georgetown University (and Lawfare) for giving me opportunities to present some of my early thinking on Libya in different venues during the same period.

During the 2017–2018 academic year, I was extremely fortunate to have a residential fellowship at the Woodrow Wilson International Center for Scholars, a beautiful and enriching environment in which to write and think. I thank Monde Muyangwa, Hannah Akuiyibo, Shahrazad Hired, Kimberly Conner, and Arlyn Charles for the many ways they welcomed and supported me. Members of my cohort at Wilson provided intellectual companionship and inspiration; in particular, I thank Elizabeth Stanley for her feedback on my project. Research interns at the Wilson Center, Naomi Sand and Pierre Philipps, went above and beyond in assembling and analyzing important sources for me.

During the same period, I was a nonresident fellow with the American Council for Learned Societies' Program on Religion, Journalism, and International Affairs, an opportunity made possible by the Luce Foundation. I thank John Paul Christy, Valerie Popp, and Cindy Mueller for all of their support. I was lucky to be part of another incredible cohort of scholars through the ACLS program, and participation in two rich events organized by ACLS helped shape my thinking and research. In particular, the ACLS program made clear to me how dependent I am on the work of local journalists in the Sahel and North Africa, and made me a more self-aware consumer of journalistic expertise.

Multiple institutions provided funding for the field research connected with this book. My previous employer, Georgetown University, covered research trips to Mali and Mauritania. Funding for another trip to Mali, as well as for research in Burkina Faso, came from the Rosa Luxemburg Foundation; I thank Armin Osmanovic and his staff for making those opportunities possible. ACLS provided funds that assisted with another of my trips to Mali, as well as with the purchase of other vital materials for this project. Georgetown's Mortara Center for International Studies graciously offered not only financial support but also physical space in which to host a book manuscript workshop in May 2018. I thank Alex Phelan and Moira Todd of Mortara for their work in organizing the event. And special thanks go to the colleagues who provided invaluable feedback during the workshop: Alexis Arieff, Judd Devermont, Alice Friend, Barak Mendelsohn, and Frederic Wehrey. The book you hold in your hands is much different, and better, than the draft they were shown, and much of that improvement is due to their expert advice, keen suggestions, and probing questions. Thanks also go to Garrett Hinck for his careful note-taking and valuable comments at that workshop.

Beyond the institutional support I have received, I have benefited from the mentorship and friendship of numerous colleagues. Among Georgetown colleagues, I thank Jonathan A. C. Brown, Scott Taylor, Lahra Smith, and Kennedy Opalo; and from Miami University, Patrick Haney, Bryan Marshall, Hannah Chapman, Jim Hanges, Nathan French, and Mahmud Khan. The final draft of this book was completed during my first semester at the University of Cincinnati, and I thank Richard Harknett, Laura Jenkins, Robert Haug, Elizabeth Frierson, Greg Winger, and many others for welcoming me to this fantastic institution.

I am lucky to be connected to a network of scholars whose expertise on the Sahel humbles and teaches me. Benjamin Soares, Leonardo Villalón, and Terje Østebø have been intellectual inspirations and gracious mentors; the University of Florida's Sahel Research Group as a whole, including its alumni, have profoundly shaped my thinking on northwest Africa, especially the work of Ibrahim Yahaya Ibrahim and Dan Eizenga. Other scholars and analysts of the Sahel and North

Africa have also indelibly marked the way I think about the region. I owe intellectual debts to Andy Morgan, Adam Sandor, Philippe Frowd, Yvan Guichaoua, Cédric Jourde, Geoff Porter, Fred Wehrey, Louis Audet-Gosselin, and many others. Many of these scholars also generously shared their contacts with me and gave precious advice about the logistics of field research. As with other projects, I am indebted to Aaron Zelin's meticulous collection of jihadist materials at his Jihadology website; with this project, I am also indebted to Héni Nsaibia's incredibly fine-tuned collection and analysis of materials related to armed groups in northwest Africa, much of which he curates through his MENASTREAM consultancy. Finally, I have benefited immeasurably from my ongoing conversations with Andrew Lebovich, who was also a welcome friendly face in Bamako on several occasions.

In Mali, Mauritania, and Burkina Faso, I thank the many interlocutors who gave their time and discussed controversial and grim events, bearing my questions patiently and responding thoughtfully. I thank all of those interviewees named throughout this book, as well as several not named because their particular positions necessitate anonymity. In Mauritania, special thanks go to Professor Mohamedou Meyine and the CEROS research center, the kindest hosts one could imagine. In Mali, warm thanks go to Phil Paoletta and the staff of the Sleeping Camel Hotel.

At Cambridge University Press, the editors and staff have made the publication process thorough and smooth. I thank Maria Marsh, Daniel Brown, and Atifa Jiwa for giving this project a chance and for shepherding it to completion. I thank Shaheer Husanne and Kevin Hughes for their careful work during the pre-production process. I also thank the anonymous reviewers who provided critical and important feedback at multiple points in the writing process.

Finally, I thank my beloved family. My parents, Robert Thurston and Margaret Ziolkowski, have been the greatest sources of support and kindness that anyone could ask for; Lara Thurston and Tom Bellamy remind me to have fun, which is a priceless gift; and my grandparents, Theodore and Yetta Ziolkowski, anchor me in who I am and where I come from, as do the wider Thurston and Ziolkowski clans. Josh Nelson and his family, along with Lance Steagall and his family, are family to me as well.

My son, Jack, was not yet born when this project started – and now he is my favorite conversation partner and most intrepid companion, my funniest friend and most creative playmate, and my guide to worlds of literature and imagination that I had never before known. The subject matter of this book is mostly grim; it is about people killing, hurting, and betraying one another, people in positions of power who say one thing and then do another, as well as people who threaten terrible things and then carry them out. It is my hope that by the time Jack grows up, the world will look different and better, for people in northwest Africa, for people in our own country, and for human beings around the globe. And in that hope, I dedicate this book to him.

Introduction

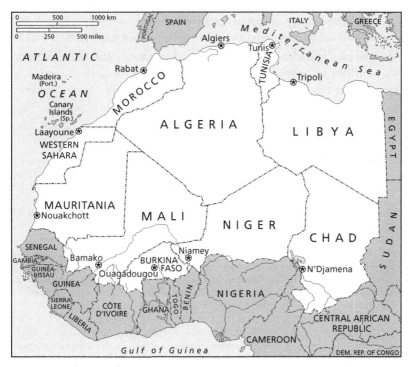

Map 1 Northwest Africa

Mass-based jihadist[1] organizations trouble different parts of the world, including areas in North Africa and the Sahel, the geographical zone

---

[1] I use the term "jihadism" to designate various movements that have arisen since the 1980s. These movements talk about jihad in ideological terms that break with the mainstream Sunni tradition's restrictions on how jihads should be conducted.

1

More complex view than "orphans"

this book covers. These organizations mobilize hundreds or even thousands of fighters. Some control territory for months or years, building "proto-states."[2]

As large organizations, they are not merely "terrorist groups" or "networks."[3] Rather, they are insurgencies and multi-dimensional bureaucracies.[4] They sometimes use terrorism, including against remote targets, but their primary context is fighting in civil wars.[5] These organizations all theoretically belong to the "global jihadist movement," but their strategic vision is largely local and regional – as, in fact, al-Qaʻida's vision was during its own formative period.[6]

Large jihadist organizations are political actors. They are political not merely in the sense that they fight in wars and have radical visions of politics. They also participate in local, national, and regional politics, and not just through intimidation but also through the management of strategic relationships. They negotiate with power-brokers, build alliances, and respond to the demands of constituencies. They are, meanwhile, prone to politicking within their own ranks. Like

---

For example, contemporary jihadists often endorse violence against civilians. All jihadist movements reject constitution-based political orders, considering them a usurpation of God's legislative prerogatives, and these movements advocate the violent overthrow of existing states.

[2] Brynjar Lia, "Understanding Jihadi Proto-States," *Perspectives on Terrorism* 9:4 (2015): www.terrorismanalysts.com/pt/index.php/pot/article/view/441/html.

[3] Studying how terrorist groups are organized gives limited insight into how jihadist groups function when they become larger entities. One of the best studies of terrorist organizations, for example, focuses on "small organizations operating somewhat secretly without the power to take and hold territory." See Jacob Shapiro, *The Terrorist's Dilemma: Managing Violent Covert Organizations* (Princeton, NJ: Princeton University Press, 2013), 2.

[4] Vera Mironova, *From Freedom Fighters to Jihadists: Human Resources of Non State Armed Groups* (New York: Oxford University Press, 2019). Mironova argues, "The groups that are the best organized internally, have less corruption, and provide more for their members become the most popular with fighters" (3). There is much to recommend this argument, but it applies only partially in northwest Africa, where both recruitment to jihadist organizations and schisms within jihadist coalitions are heavily shaped by social networks, relationships between field commanders and their superiors, and sheer contingency. I develop these arguments later.

[5] Stathis Kalyvas, "Jihadi Rebels in Civil War," *Daedalus* 147:1 (Winter 2018): 36–47, 38.

[6] Anne Stenersen, *Al-Qaida in Afghanistan* (New York: Cambridge University Press, 2017), 2. Isabelle Duyvesteyn has also argued that al-Qaʻida's "concerns can be seen as highly national and territorial." See her "How New Is the New Terrorism?" *Studies in Conflict & Terrorism* 27:5 (2004): 439–454, 444.

other rebel organizations, jihadist movements "are coalitions that depend on cooperation among differentiated, heterogeneous units."[7] The negotiations, rivalries, and conflicts between those units represent another kind of jihadist politics.

This book concentrates on jihadist politics in a triple sense, examining the politics within jihadist organizations, jihadists' engagement with the politics that surrounds them, and the interaction between these internal and external political arenas. I develop a theoretical vocabulary to describe jihadist politics. This vocabulary covers both internal political dynamics and external political postures.

To understand these forms of jihadist politics, we need to think beyond Western security paradigms. Western policymakers and analysts overwhelmingly view jihadism in terms of 9/11, assuming that jihadism is important in relation to the threat it might pose to Western soil and Western interests. Critiquing this type of analysis, Mohammed-Mahmoud Ould Mohamedou comments, "The dominant existing literature ... portrays the [Islamic State] primarily as an apocalyptic religious entity bent solely on destroying the West ... Focus on the group's extreme violence and its alienating discourse has prevented deeper examination of the political and social conditions behind its rise."[8] The political dimensions of many other jihadist groups are under-analyzed as well. As Darryl Li has commented, "Without rendering legible the political nature of jihadi projects, [terrorism studies'] focus on doctrine becomes deterministic; its analysis of propaganda tends toward voyeurism; its study of tactics redounds to incoherent moralism; and its focus on individual motivations is atomistic."[9] The political nature of jihadist projects encompasses not just their stated demands for the overthrow of existing states and the remaking of local and global orders but also their intrinsically political modes of day-to-day operation.

Many analysts prioritize either macro-level or micro-level analysis of jihadism, leaving crucial political dimensions unaddressed. Macro-level studies concentrate on the visions of ideologues and the arcs of

[7] Michael Woldemariam, *Insurgent Fragmentation in the Horn of Africa: Rebellion and Its Discontents* (Cambridge: Cambridge University Press, 2018), 6.
[8] Mohammed-Mahmoud Ould Mohamedou, *A Theory of ISIS: Political Violence and the Transformation of the Global Order* (London: Pluto Press, 2018), 1–2.
[9] Darryl Li, "A Jihadism Anti-primer," *Middle East Report* 276 (Fall 2015), www .merip.org/mer/mer276/jihadism-anti-primer.

organizations. The downside of that approach is that analysts often treat organizations as unitary actors (groups that think and move as one) and assume that well-known personalities speak for entire organizations.[10] It is a mistake, however, to treat any participant in a civil war as a unitary actor, because of the frequent gaps in aims and worldview between the leadership and the rank-and-file, or because of the frequently observed variation within a single organization on key questions and priorities.[11]

Micro-level studies of jihadism often focus on the radicalization of individual fighters, especially "homegrown terrorists" in the West and "foreign fighters" in the Middle East.[12] Yet considerable evidence suggests that people join armed organizations not as individuals but as representatives and members of groups, responding to ways that "actors within social structures, within which potential participants are embedded, collectively frame the threat posed by civil war."[13] The careers of top leaders and foreign fighters give relatively limited insight into the political forces that mobilize masses of local recruits.[14]

Western security paradigms are deeply resistant to thinking of jihadism as a form of legible politics, based on the flawed but influential assumption that taking jihadist politics seriously gives jihadists moral legitimacy. It is easier, when discussing jihadism, to speak in terms of

[10] Many of these studies are extremely useful. A sampling of the best work would include Brynjar Lia, *Architect of Global Jihad: The Life of Al Qaeda Strategist Abu Mus'ab al-Suri* (New York: Columbia University Press, 2009); Joas Wagemakers, *A Quietist Jihadi: The Ideology and Influence of Abu Muhammad al-Maqdisi* (Cambridge: Cambridge University Press, 2012); William McCants, *The ISIS Apocalypse: The History, Strategy, and Doomsday Vision of the Islamic State* (New York: St. Martin's Press, 2015); Michael W. S. Ryan, *Decoding Al-Qaeda's Strategy: The Deep Battle against America* (New York: Columbia University Press, 2016); and Brian Fishman, *The Master Plan: ISIS, al-Qaeda, and the Jihadi Strategy for Final Victory* (New Haven, CT: Yale University Press, 2016).

[11] Stathis Kalyvas, *The Logic of Violence in Civil War* (Cambridge: Cambridge University Press, 2006), 10.

[12] See, for example, Peter Neumann, *Radicalized: New Jihadists and the Threat to the West* (London: I.B. Tauris, 2016).

[13] Anastasia Shesterinina, "Collective Threat Framing and Mobilization in Civil War," *American Political Science Review* 110:3 (August 2016): 411–427, 411.

[14] The role of foreign fighters in shaping organizational trajectories has been exaggerated. For a convincing argument that foreign fighters have a limited impact, see Tricia Bacon and Daisy Muibu, "The Domestication of Al-Shabaab," *Journal of the Middle East and Africa* 10:3 (July–September 2019): 279–305.

pathologies than in terms of politics. Western policymakers and analysts often talk about "radicalization" and "extremism" as forces more akin to mass psychosis or individual deviance than as political processes; individual fighters are seen as fanatics to be killed, or as patients to be cured, rather than as socially embedded political actors.[15] If one studies the jihadist leader in isolation from his political environment, or the individual fighter without reference to the "complex webs of direct or mediated exchanges" that connect him to other people,[16] there is a risk of losing sight of the drivers of jihadists' successes and failures. Implicitly running through much of both the macro- and micro-level analysis of jihadism is the question "why do they hate us?" But the answers to that question are of limited value in answering the very different and more important question "why do jihadists accrue power in certain (wartime) contexts?"

I confront these conceptual problems by applying the *meso* level of analysis to particular organizations. An organization that may look from a macro level like an "al-Qa'ida affiliate," more or less interchangeable with other "affiliates," appears politically dynamic at the *meso* level. And micro-level studies often struggle to capture the context in which individual fighters operate. For these reasons, the *meso* or "commander-level" plane of analysis is vital for understanding jihadist politics – just as *meso*-level analysis is important to the study of conflict generally. In civil wars,[17] genocides, and other conflicts, "meso-level actors shape the process of violence."[18] The *meso*-level analysis here explores how jihadist field commanders navigate questions of politics.

Other assumptions that merit questioning have to do with how jihadist hierarchies function. Some analysts insist that jihadist field commanders merely follow orders; such analysts say that it is the

---

[15] It is not just with the study of jihadism that politics is de-emphasized. As Jacob Mundy comments, "Civil war, terrorism, and genocide ... have been increasingly theorized and studied in depoliticized ways that flatten late warfare's historical, geographical, and ideational contours." See Mundy, *Imaginative Geographies of Algerian Violence: Conflict Science, Conflict Management, Antipolitics* (Stanford, CA: Stanford University Press, 2015), 9.

[16] Marc Sageman, *Understanding Terror Networks* (Philadelphia: University of Pennsylvania Press, 2004), 137.

[17] Fotini Christia, *Alliance Formation in Civil Wars* (Cambridge: Cambridge University Press, 2012), 29–31.

[18] Evgeny Finkel and Scott Straus, "Macro, Meso, and Micro Research on Genocide: Gains, Shortcomings, and Future Areas of Inquiry," *Genocide Studies and Prevention* 7:1 (2012): 56–67, 59.

central leaderships of al-Qaʿida and the Islamic State who pull the strings in local conflicts around the world.[19] But the field commander is not, and by function of the demands placed on him cannot be, a mere conduit for the global vision of the mother organization. Politics has different meanings and applications for the locally or regionally minded field commander than for the global ideologue. Field commanders participate directly in military actions, have sustained face-to-face interactions with fighters, and broker the local arrangements that facilitate crucial initiatives such as hostage releases, governance, recruitment, and coalition-building. The fighters in mass-based jihadist organizations, moreover, are not typically operatives recruited for one spectacular attack but rather members of a wartime coalition. Field commanders, then, are essential for understanding how jihadist politics actually works.

I argue in this book that the jihadist field commander is a political entrepreneur who routinely confronts political problems for which jihadist doctrine does not provide readymade solutions. Jihadist field commanders generate diverse solutions to these problems, many of which appear to be congruent with jihadist doctrine in the eyes of the commanders and their constituencies; yet the very diversity of the solutions undertaken indicates that jihadist politics is a field of contestation and improvisation rather than a mechanical application of doctrine. Meanwhile, in his external relations the jihadist field commander possesses distinctive resources, including his status as the representative of an organization that is formally anathema (that is, blacklisted by states and the United Nations). Harnessing his ostensible pariah status, the jihadist field commander can nevertheless work to build and manage a coalition that is not just militarily but also politically and economically successful.

[19] See Bruce Hoffman, "Al Qaeda's Resurrection," Council on Foreign Relations Expert Brief, March 6, 2018, www.cfr.org/expert-brief/al-qaedas-resurrection; and Daveed Gartenstein-Ross and Nathaniel Barr, "How al-Qaeda Survived the Islamic State Challenge," *Current Trends in Islamist Ideology*, March 1, 2017, www.hudson.org/research/12788-how-al-qaeda-survived-the-islamic-state-challenge. Other analysts evaluate al-Qaʿida's record much more critically. See Daniel Byman, "Judging al-Qaeda's Record, Parts I and II," Lawfare, June 27 and 28, 2017, available at www.lawfareblog.com/judging-al-qaedas-record-part-i-organization-decline and https://www.lawfareblog.com/judging-al-qaedas-record-part-ii-why-has-al-qaeda-declined.

The jihadist field commander achieves his greatest success when the distinctive promise he offers, namely that of a counter-order, meets the needs of multiple local constituencies; it is then that the potential for a wide-ranging coalition appears, with one foot in the partly-realized jihadist counter-order and another foot still in the existing order. These coalitions and their political projects are highly unstable and vulnerable: Jihadist counter-orders can gain momentum with astonishing rapidity, but can crumble just as quickly – often due to a combination of infighting and overreach as well as the impact of the wider context, including state policies, other actors' calculations, and the positioning of rival jihadist groups. Through an analysis of these dynamics, the book aims to contribute to the study of jihadism, and also more broadly to the study of civil wars, political violence, and the trajectory of Muslim politics around the world.

Jihadist Exceptionalism, and Anathematization as a Strategic Resource

Insights drawn from political scientists' studies of conventional rebels help in explaining *meso*-level jihadist politics, and will be used throughout the book. Yet I am not convinced by political science literature that portrays jihadist leaders as cynics who calmly shop for ideologies in a supposed free market of ideas, selecting whatever best suits their material interests at a particular moment. I do not agree that the language of religion is just "cheap talk."[20] Nor do I think that because jihadists' "violence is often influenced by the context in which it unfolds and the influence of religion on it can be variable rather than constant," one should "decouple violent Islamism [sic] from ... religion."[21] There is a widespread assumption in political science that rebels generally or jihadists specifically are nothing more than survival-oriented rational actors. Yet there is a mass of empirical evidence that contradicts that assumption and points to more complicated, and often religiously inflected, decision-making processes among jihadists.

[20] Barbara Walter, "The Extremist's Advantage in Civil Wars," *International Security* 42:2 (Fall 2017): 7–39, 10.
[21] Kalyvas, "Jihadi Rebels," 37. To explain my use of "[sic]," the phrase "violent Islamism," despite wide currency, is a misnomer. Jihadism is not an extreme manifestation of Islamism but a fundamentally different project.

Perhaps in a small way, this book can even contribute to a mode of political science that is comfortable acknowledging the heavy doses of idiosyncracy, contingency, and unevenly applied ideology that shape human events, none of which are reducible to rules-bounded games played by ruthlessly rational actors.

Is is not possible, in fact, that "rational believers"[22] and "devoted actors"[23] often believe what they say? Jihadists largely appear willing to accept the consequences of their stated beliefs, rendering their talk far from "cheap." As Aisha Ahmad shows, mastering the markers and vocabularies of piety and political Islam takes time and effort. Discussing the *mujahideen* in 1980s Afghanistan, she writes, "In this cloak-and-dagger world, these arduous baseline metrics of piety [such as praying at dawn] made it labor-intensive for a nonbeliever to convincingly fake camaraderie with the mujahideen … Islam became a critical shortcut for establishing trust."[24] Given the costs and benefits of demonstrating piety, it seems plausible that a jihadist could be *both* a committed ideologue and a shrewd political actor.

At the *meso* level, religiosity intertwines with politics, facilitating experimentation and improvisation. Even if the theological–ideological tenets of Salafi-jihadism remain consistent across locales,[25] the events that confront jihadist field commanders are idiosyncratic and unpredictable. The field commander manages (or mismanages) a set of relationships that are inherently in tension; the interests of young fighters, religious hardliners, and more flexible allies are not the same. The field commander's decisions require religiously inflected explanation and legitimation, whether in advance, in the moment, or after the fact. In religious terms, the successful field commander is often one who can tell a compelling story about his violence.

---

[22] Masooda Bano, *The Rational Believer: Choices and Decisions in the Madrasas of Pakistan* (Ithaca, NY: Cornell University Press, 2012).

[23] Scott Atran, "The Devoted Actor: Unconditional Commitment and Intractable Conflict across Cultures," *Current Anthropology* 57:13 (June 2016): S192–S203.

[24] Aisha Ahmad, *Jihad & Co.: Black Markets and Islamist Power* (New York: Oxford University Press, 2017), 54.

[25] For a compelling intellectual history, see Shiraz Maher, *Salafi-Jihadism: The History of an Idea* (Oxford: Oxford University Press, 2016). See also my "Algeria's GIA: The First Major Armed Group to Fully Subordinate Salafism in Jihadism," *Islamic Law and Society* 24 (2017): 412–436.

This storytelling involves more than just the elaboration of "jihadi culture" through poetry and displays of pietistic emotion.[26] Rather, as jihadists develop their own "antipolitics" centered on a rejection of existing orders, they confront a need to express political claims, messages, and decisions without using the language of conventional politics. They deploy "shari'a politics," in the sense of "orient[ing] and legitimat[ing] their actions with reference to some representation of God's commands."[27] Islamic theology and law furnish the language of jihadist politics,[28] which only becomes comprehensible through a critical reading of jihadists' religious statements.

Aside from the particularities of jihadists' doctrines, there are other ways in which jihadist politics is exceptional in the context of rebellion and insurgency – but specifying what this exceptionalism consists of is difficult. As Li puts it, "The challenge is how to understand the distinctiveness of jihadi groups without lapsing into an all-too-often racialized exceptionalism."[29] One criterion by which jihadists are distinct is the degree to which they are anathematized – blacklisted or excluded from mainstream politics – within national and global political orders. One effect of blacklisting is that jihadists do not necessarily expect or even hope to win wars on any conventional political timeline or through conventional political bargaining. The social science mantra that rebels hope to maximize "wartime returns as anticipated in the political power sharing of the postconflict state,"[30] or even make money through the rebellion itself,[31] is hard to sustain when it comes to the very risky business of jihadism. Anathematization makes it extremely unlikely that jihadists will, *qua jihadists*, receive any

---

[26] Thomas Hegghammer, ed., *Jihadi Culture: The Art and Social Practices of Militant Islamists* (New York: Cambridge University Press, 2017).

[27] Robert Hefner, "Introduction: Shari'a Politics – Law and Society in the Modern Muslim World" in *Shari'a Politics: Islamic Law and Society in the Modern World*, edited by Robert Hefner, 1–54 (Bloomington: Indiana University Press, 2011), 10.

[28] See Daniel Lav, *Radical Islam and the Revival of Medieval Theology* (New York: Cambridge University Press, 2012).

[29] Li, "Jihadist Anti-Primer."   [30] Christia, *Alliance Formation*, 5.

[31] See Paul Collier and Anke Hoeffler, "Greed and Grievance in Civil War," *Oxford Economic Papers* 56 (2004): 563–595, 563–564.

post-conflict "returns"; and aggressive manhunts for top jihadists make wartime profits hard to enjoy.

At the same time, anathematization is a resource for jihadists. They can play on their ambiguous political position (blacklisted and therefore "outside" politics, but simultaneously enmeshed in the political fields that surround them) to offer resources to allies. Whether those allies are businesspersons, religious leaders, tribal shaykhs, or even state authorities, jihadists' partners find advantages in having one foot in the shadows and the other in the light – just as jihadists find advantages in having their allies subtly represent jihadist interests at negotiating tables and in the mainstream political arena (or the economic arena, which is crucial although not the main focus of this book). The question then becomes how different parties within jihadist coalitions tolerate, benefit from, and perpetuate the "wartime political orders" that jihadists help create.[32] In short, jihadists are different from conventional rebels partly because both their enemies and their allies treat them as different.

Jihadists are also distinct from conventional rebels and even from revolutionaries in the degree to which the counter-order they offer differs from existing orders. One RAND Corporation report states that "so far, no state or bloc of states has tried to establish a clearly defined counter-order since the end of the Cold War."[33] This is perhaps too sweeping, but the basic sentiment is correct. Not just states but also most conventional rebels do not offer truly revolutionary counter-orders. Part of the challenge of analyzing jihadist politics, however, is that jihadists often simultaneously construct counter-orders while tacitly adapting to existing orders, especially the "wartime political orders" mentioned previously. The analytical challenge, stated differently, has to do with determining when to exceptionalize jihadists and when to de-exceptionalize them.

---

[32] On the concept of "wartime political orders," where evolving conditions and relationships provide occasions for various kinds of deal-making, see Paul Staniland, "States, Insurgents, and Wartime Political Orders," *Perspectives on Politics* 10:2 (June 2012): 243–264.

[33] Michael Mazarr et al., *Measuring the Health of the Liberal International Order* (Santa Monica, CA: RAND Corporation, 2017), 148.

Jihadist Politics at the *Meso* Level

Much of jihadists' political action is improvised by "the man on the spot."[34] Even when global jihadist leaders and ideologues attempt to spell out political guidelines for field commanders, the results are inevitably generic. The infamous 2004 text *Idarat al-Tawahhush* (The Management of Savagery), written by the pseudonymous Abu Bakr Naji, has been portrayed as the blueprint for the Islamic State and other jihadists.[35] Yet the tremendous variation in the trajectories of the Islamic State's "provinces" indicate that field commanders cannot follow a manual to guide their decision-making; they improvise and compromise.[36]

Part of the reason for the gap between theory and practice is that Naji and other theorists often depict local populations as essentially passive:

The zone of *tawahhush* [savagery, or perhaps animality], before its submission to the administration, will be in a situation resembling the situation of Afghanistan before the Taliban took control: a region submitted to the law of the jungles in its primitive form. Its people, the good ones among them and even the discerning minds among the evil ones, will be thirsting for someone to administer this *tawahhush*.[37]

This is too simplistic; civilians do not simply thirst for strongmen, and chaos has its own structures that need to be navigated. Rather than simply "administering people's needs by distributing food and [medical] care, preserving security and judging between the people living in the zones of *tawahhush*," as Naji recommends,[38] many jihadist field

---

[34] This is not to say that women play no roles in jihadist organizations. For one sophisticated treatment of women's agency, see Hilary Matfess, *Women and the War on Boko Haram: Wives, Weapons, Witnesses* (London: Zed Books, 2017). Yet field commanders tend to be, so far, male.

[35] Jack Jenkins, "The Book That Really Explains ISIS (Hint: It's Not the Qur'an)," Think Progress, September 10, 2014, https://thinkprogress.org/the-book-that-really-explains-isis-hint-its-not-the-qur-an-f76a42e9a9a7/.

[36] See, for example, Niamatullah Ibrahimi and Shahram Akbarzadeh, "Intra-Jihadist Conflict and Cooperation: Islamic State–Khorasan Province and the Taliban in Afghanistan," *Studies in Conflict & Terrorism*, published online January 7, 2019,

[37] Abu Bakr Naji, *Idarat al-Tawahhush: Akhtar Marhala sa-Tamurr biha al-Umma* (self-published online, 2004), 11.

[38] Ibid., 11.

commanders find themselves in complex, give-and-take interactions with local power brokers. These are situations for which no manual could supply straightforward directives.

To take another example of the gap between jihadist theory and practice, consider the al-Qaʿida leader Ayman al-Zawahiri's 2013 strategy document "General Guidelines for Jihadist Action." This is another text that analysts widely consider a sophisticated manual.[39] One example of al-Zawahiri's guidelines was "not fighting the deviant sects [i.e., the Shiʿa and the Sufis] … so long as they do not attack [us]."[40] He urged his subordinates to minimize civilian deaths, especially of Muslims but also of non-Muslims, and to desist from "targeting enemies in mosques, markets, and rallies."[41] These are generic, commonsense recommendations, more appropriate to a small terrorist group choosing targets than to a multidimensional insurgency navigating politics; again, the guidelines leave concrete political decisions to field commanders. The guidelines give little sense of what to do with local power brokers who possess agency and may need to be bargained with, placated, or bypassed. Some recent studies have gestured to a learning process among jihadists, particularly as various jihadists take, hold, and lose territory. Yet as often as not, the lessons one group attempts to share go ignored, whether by commanders or by commanders' own subordinates.[42] In short, field commanders frequently take the initiative – sometimes without strategic guidance from their superiors and peers, sometimes to creatively execute such guidance, and sometimes despite it.

[39] This document is widely, but in my view mistakenly, considered by Western analysts to be a turning point in al-Qaʿida's thinking. See Aaron Zelin, "The Clairvoyant: The Guidelines: Measuring Zawahiri's Influence," Jihadology, March 9, 2014, https://jihadology.net/2014/03/09/the-clairvoyant-the-guidelines-measuring-zawahiris-influence/; and Katherine Zimmerman, "Al Qaeda's Strengthening in the Shadows," Statement before the House Committee on Homeland Security Subcommittee on Counterterrorism and Intelligence on "The Persistent Threat: Al Qaeda's Evolution and Resilience," July 13, 2017, https://docs.house.gov/meetings/HM/HM05/20170713/106235/HHRG-115-HM05-Wstate-ZimmermanK-20170713.pdf.
[40] Ayman al-Zawahiri, "Tawjihat ʿAmma li-l-ʿAmal al-Jihadi" (published online by Muʾassasat al-Sahab li-l-Intaj al-Iʿlami, 2013), 3.
[41] Ibid., 4.
[42] Lia, "Understanding Jihadi Proto-States." See also McCants, *ISIS Apocalypse*, ch. 3.

Field commanders' decisions affect jihadist organizations' evolution and cohesion. This is true of rebel groups more broadly: "The key actors vis-à-vis warring group alliance formation and fractionalization are often local elites, operating at a 'meso level' that links the national-level cleavages with individual-level motivations."[43] Jihadist field commanders frequently break away from their organizations, band together to overthrow central leaders, or return to the mother organization after abortive bids for autonomy. Holding jihadist organizations together requires negotiation among field commanders and between field commanders and other parties, whether local allies or their own superiors. Such negotiations are not exceptional in politics generally or within the Muslim world. As Dale Eickelman and James Piscatori have argued, "Politics, including in the Muslim world, is not simply concerned with established authority compelling obedience ... [P]olitics may have as much, if not more, to do with bargaining among several forces or contending groups."[44] Negotiation and coalition-building are constitutive elements of politics itself.

To understand *meso*-level jihadist politics, we need to analytically dissect jihadist organizations and think about their component parts. In contrast to the idea that global jihadist outfits operate more or less as hierarchies,[45] I treat jihadist organizations as political coalitions comprising relatively distinct blocs. These blocs may have doctrinal identities but their members often share some other common denominator, from shared geographical roots to ethnic solidarities to generational identities. As Paul Staniland has argued, "Insurgent groups are

---

[43] Christia, *Alliance Formation*, 5.
[44] Dale Eickelman and James Piscatori, *Muslim Politics* (Princeton, NJ: Princeton University Press, 1996), 7.
[45] For an example of this view, see Daveed Gartenstein-Ross and Nathaniel Barr, "How Al-Qaeda Works: The Jihadist Group's Evolving Organizational Design," *Current Trends in Islamist Ideology*, June 1, 2018, www.hudson.org/research/14365-how-al-qaeda-works-the-jihadist-group-s-evolving-organizational-design. Analysts have even assumed hierarchy when analyzing how jihadists relate to civilians. David Kilcullen astutely observes that many local jihadists are "accidental guerrillas" who mostly want foreign powers to leave them alone. Kilcullen's model, however, positions the relationship between transnational jihadists and local fighters as primarily vertical. See Kilcullen, *The Accidental Guerrilla: Fighting Small Wars in the Midst of a Big One* (Oxford: Oxford University Press, 2009), xiv.

built by mobilizing prewar politicized social networks."[46] These networks' differences persist inside organizations, shaping their internal politics. Rebel organizations also tend to develop internal divisions in the course of a conflict: as Fotini Christia writes, "[no] group, however homogeneous, [is] safe from internal fractionalization."[47] And as Eric Mosinger argues, "New influxes of recruits or new operational networks alter the distribution of power between rebel leaders, sometimes elevating new leaders and weakening incumbents."[48] During both their formation and their evolution, jihadist groups are prone to internal power struggles; even if everyone believes roughly the same thing, other faultlines are present.

Paths into jihadist coalitions can look very different for different actors: veterans of foreign jihads, veterans of previous domestic insurgencies, hardline religious networks, and ethnic/tribal constituencies. These blocs frequently possess different types of experiences and skills. For example, Camille Tawil discusses how, amid the emergence of the Armed Islamic Group (French acronym GIA) in Algeria in the early 1990s, "Algerian Afghans" (Algerians returning home from Afghanistan) in the group came to rely on the knowledge of younger Algerians who had not left the country: The Afghanistan veterans "were experienced fighters," but

urban guerrilla warfare required a different type of training. It called for an intimate knowledge of the narrow alleyways of Algeria's towns … and it needed those fighters to be familiar with every building in every neighbourhood, as well as with their inhabitants and their allegiances. The Afghan veterans, who had spent years overseas, were not equipped for this kind of conflict; moreover, the sudden appearance of outsiders in a given area would be sure to attract the attention of the security services. But what the Afghans could not do, the new generation of urban Islamists could.[49]

Even if one bloc is initially superior to other blocs within an organization, relationships between blocs can flatten over time; asymmetries in knowledge, skills, and popularity foster interdependence or even shift

---

[46] Paul Staniland, *Networks of Rebellion: Explaining Insurgent Cohesion and Collapse* (Ithaca, NY: Cornell University Press, 2014), 9.

[47] Christia, *Alliance Formation*, 4.

[48] Eric Mosinger, "Balance of Loyalties: Explaining Rebel Factional Struggles in the Nicaraguan Revolution," *Security Studies* 28:5 (2019): 935–975, 937.

[49] Camille Tawil, *Brothers in Arms: The Story of al-Qa'ida and the Arab Jihadists* (London: Saqi Books, 2011), 68–69.

the balance of power. In Algeria, the Afghanistan veterans who helped found and steer the GIA in 1991–1993 were somewhat sidelined within the movement by 1996. The Algerian case exemplifies a pattern where veteran jihadists, even if they are initially poised to dominate coalitions, often have relatively small constituencies of fighters who are directly loyal to them. This dynamic means that the veterans must either build broad-based support or risk facing challenges from better-connected domestic actors. Jihadist organizations are fluid and can shift in response to personalities, events, and conflict dynamics.

Alongside the internal dynamics of jihadist coalitions, there are external dynamics relating to alliances, accommodation, and collusion. Jihadists find different types of partners: local politicians, where "politician" should be understood in a broad sense that encompasses everyone from elected officials to militia commanders; state authorities, including military officers; religious leaders or movements; ethnic or tribal constituencies; businesspersons; and other jihadists. These figures' motivations for working with jihadists may vary. Contributors to the edited volume *Tribes and Global Jihadism* have shown how alliances with jihadists are attractive to tribes seeking to reposition themselves and regain influence over states and foreign powers.[50] Aisha Ahmad has examined why jihadists often attract allies among businesspersons seeking protection in black markets or turbulent environments.[51] Investigative journalists and groundbreaking scholars are exploring the murky question of how jihadists relate to and even collude with state authorities.[52]

Notably, the infamous manuals by Naji and al-Zawahiri have little to say about how to manage such relationships, particularly in terms of the compromises that these relationships entail; global ideologues may

---

[50] Olivier Roy, "Introduction" in *Tribes and Global Jihadism*, edited by Virginie Collombier and Olivier Roy, 1–13 (Oxford: Oxford University Press, 2018), 7.
[51] Ahmad, *Jihad & Co.*, xv.
[52] Maggie Michael, Trish Wilson, and Lee Keath, "Yemen: U.S. Allies Spin Deals with al-Qaida in War on Rebels," Associated Press, August 6, 2018, https://pulitzercenter.org/reporting/yemen-us-allies-spin-deals-al-qaida-war-rebels; and Evan Hill and Laura Kasinoff, "Playing a Double Game in the Fight against AQAP," *Foreign Policy*, January 21, 2015, https://foreignpolicy.com/2015/01/21/playing-a-double-game-in-the-fight-against-aqap-yemen-saleh-al-qaeda/. See also Stephen Tankel, *With Us and against Us: How America's Partners Help and Hinder the War on Terror* (New York: Columbia University Press, 2018).

even wish to deny the existence of some such relationships. Analyzing these relationships, moreover, requires care: A focus on jihadists' relationships with tribes and ethnic groups can easily devolve into crude ethnic stereotyping and devastating stigmatization (with real-world consequences), while talk of jihadists' collusion with states can devolve into conspiracy theory. If these traps can be avoided, a *meso-level* analysis can clarify the political divisions within a jihadist organization as well as the complexities of its interactions with the political forces surrounding it.

The chapters that follow represent case studies of jihadist organizations. The case studies assess jihadist coalitions' political behaviors along the following axes:

- Internal (vertical): How much discipline is there in the *vertical hierarchy* of a group, in other words between top leaders and field commanders? Possibilities include:
  o *Harmony*, where field commanders willingly carry out superiors' commands and express confidence in their superiors.
  o *Tyranny*, where field commanders carry out superiors' commands under duress or threats of violence.
  o *Autonomy*, where field commanders are partly, largely, or entirely free to carry out their own independent agendas. Autonomy may result from *delegation*, where superiors entrust field commanders with authority, or from the center's incapacity to enforce its dictates.
  o *Broken triangles*, where a superior aligns with one or more field commanders against an insubordinate field commander.
  o *Coups*, where a group of field commanders (or other second-tier actors) successfully overthrows a superior.
  o *Schisms*, where one or more field commanders breaks away from the mother organization.
- Internal (horizontal): How much cooperation is there on the *horizontal plane*, in other words among field commanders? Possibilities include:
  o *Cooperation*, where field commanders actively help one another.
  o *Rivalry*, where field commanders compete or come into conflict. This may escalate into outright fratricide.
  o *Isolation*, where field commanders operate independently of one another without conflict or cooperation.

- External: How does the group relate to the political actors around it – in other words, what is the group's external political position? Possibilities include:
  - o *Incorporation*, where the jihadist coalition formally absorbs local powerbrokers or other armed factions (jihadist or non-jihadist) into its coalition.
  - o *Merger*, where multiple units combine to form a new jihadist coalition.
  - o *Alliance*, where the jihadist coalition openly cooperates with another actor but the organizations do not merge.
  - o *Collusion*, where jihadists and another actor cooperate but maintain plausible deniability about their alliance.
  - o *Accommodation*, where the jihadist coalition reaches an explicit or tacit nonaggression pact with an external actor (jihadist or non-jihadist). A variation on this possibility is *dilution*, where the jihadist organization goes so far in accommodating other actors that it ceases to be jihadist.
  - o *Domination*, where the jihadist coalition is in a position to dictate terms to other local political actors.
  - o *Marginalization*, where the jihadist coalition is compelled – through local or external military responses, loss of alliances or support, or other factors – to retreat to the margins (geographical and political) of a territory. A variation is *failed mobilization*, where an organization begins at the margins and remains confined there. This is called "failed" in reference to the political arena, even if the group conducts terrorist attacks from the margins. Marginalization can also take the form of *collapse* (destruction or fragmentation of the organization) or *relocation* (physically moving to another territory and starting afresh).

In terms of whether jihadist coalitions succeed or fail politically, how big a factor are these internal dynamics and external political postures? It is tempting to say that the organizations with the least internal conflict and the most accommodating external postures will be the most successful at taking territory and building counter-orders. Yet so many other, external factors (including the policies of national and foreign governments) impinge on these outcomes that it would be foolish to be too schematic. Moreover, a group with sloppy and/or dictatorial leadership, riven by internal rivalries, can nevertheless conquer territory if it finds itself, so to speak, knocking on an open door amid the collapse of state authority. Political success brings its own dangers, including the danger of dilution to the point of antagonizing coalition partners (who accuse the diluters of betraying the cause) or ceasing to be jihadist and simply becoming a conventional armed group or proto-state.

What can be said with a bit more certainty are three conclusions. First, internal rivalries, if left to fester, often prove more fatal to organizations' cohesion than external interventions, although external interventions can exacerbate internal rivalries. Second, groups that accommodate internal dissent and tolerate outsiders' skepticism often prove longer-lived than their less accommodating peers. Being longer-lived, however, means only that: Longevity may translate into periodic political successes as opportunities arise, but longevity does not automatically bring cumulative political success. Third, as stated previously, the combination of infighting and overreach (in other words, uncompromising efforts to intimidate civilians) renders coalitions vulnerable to collapse.

Understanding jihadism requires analysis of jihadists' statements, but also judicious source criticism. Too often, analysts have treated jihadist documents as univocal, context-free blueprints for jihadist action. Such analysts "locat[e] agency in a discrete document/actor/ideology whose evil nature can then be referred to as a stand-alone reason for the violence observed, and thereby excise the political and historical components out of that equation."[53] My approach is to focus on statements by *meso*-level actors and read these documents with an ear to perceiving the multiple voices they contain, the debates they reflect, their limits in shaping events, and the contexts in which they are produced.

Understanding jihadism also requires triangulation between jihadist documents and other sources, including local journalism and perspectives gleaned from field research. This book is informed by field research trips to Mauritania, Mali, and Burkina Faso between 2017 and 2019.[54] The field research included interviews with prominent former members of jihadist coalitions as well as with politicians,

[53] Ould Mohamedou, *A Theory of ISIS*, 12.
[54] These trips included visits to Nouakchott, Mauritania, in September–October 2017 and April–May 2018 (partly in the context of a separate research project on contemporary Muslim scholars in the country); visits to Bamako, Mali, in

journalists, analysts, and Muslim clerics. Placing jihadist sources into context, and reading them critically, opens a window into jihadist politics. The most important such contexts are often local and regional, rather than global.

Jihadism in Northwest Africa: Localist and Regionalist Analytical Approaches

Why pursue a comparative study of jihadist politics, and why take all the cases from a single region? For one thing, jihadists' primary sphere of operations is often a limited, contiguous, and culturally bounded regional zone. There are, of course, global jihadists who advocate "indiscriminate mass-casualty out-of-area attacks."[55] For some jihadist groups, moreover, "enemy hierarchies are unclear" as they pursue both global and national-revolutionary aims.[56] Often, however, it has been the regional and local spheres that dominate jihadists' horizons.

Here is 'Abd al-Malik Droukdel of al-Qa'ida in the Islamic Maghreb (AQIM), speaking to the *New York Times* in 2008:

As far as our goals concerning the Islamic Maghreb, they are plenty. But most importantly is to rescue our countries from the tentacles of these criminal regimes that betrayed their religion, and their people. Because they are all secretions of the colonialism that invaded our country in the last two centuries, and enabled those regimes to govern. Therefore, they started governing for its account and on behalf of it. They implement its programs and protect its interests and fight Islam on its behalf. It's never going to be possible for this region to stabilize unless its people start enjoying freedom and dignity and security under Islam. The conditions of stability will not be available in the presence of these corrupt and harming models that proved for decades that they are unable to achieve the least rapprochement between their people in any of the areas. We are one nation with one religion and one

January 2018, March 2018, and June 2019; and a visit to Ouagadougou, Burkina Faso, in June 2019.

[55] Thomas Hegghammer, *Jihad in Saudi Arabia: Violence and Pan-Islamism since 1979* (New York: Cambridge University Press, 2010), 7.

[56] Thomas Hegghammer, "The Ideological Hybridization of Jihadi Groups," *Current Trends in Islamist Ideology*, 9 (November 18, 2009), www.hudson.org/research/9866-the-ideological-hybridization-of-jihadi-groups.

language. Our history is the same but our land is divided, torn apart into states by colonialism.[57]

Droukdel's primary horizon was and is regional. Moreover, as David Gutelius has commented regarding the audio version of this interview, "Droukdal uses carefully-chosen classical Arabic when explaining AQIM's Islamist credentials and goals, but inadvertently switches to his native Algerian dialect when asked about his opinions of [Algeria's then-President Abdelaziz] Bouteflika and the Algerian government. He literally could not reframe the older, familiar anti-Algerian state … rhetoric in the language of the global Jihad."[58] These observations regarding AQIM's lingering parochialism apply to other organizations. Anne Stenersen has argued that even al-Qaʻida itself, especially in the 1990s, "had a more revolutionary, Middle Eastern-focused agenda than previously assumed … al-Qaida's goal was to establish Islamic rule across the Muslim world, but with the Middle East as its main priority."[59]

Even the spread of al-Qaʻida "affiliates" after 9/11 was only global-izing in one sense. Barak Mendelsohn has shown that as al-Qaʻida collected new affiliates, "franchising neither increased the threat [of al-Qaʻida] nor enhanced al-Qaeda's political objectives – the strategy actually incurred heavy costs." Mendelsohn notes "the tendency of franchises to become entangled in local conflicts," which "distracts from the organization's general objectives."[60] One might take the Somalia-centric al-Shabab as an example.[61] With a strongly "ethno-nationalist" contingent alongside its more "internationalist" voices,[62]

[57] "An Interview with Abdelmalek Droukdal," *The New York Times*, July 1, 2008, www.nytimes.com/2008/07/01/world/africa/01transcript-droukdal.html.

[58] David Gutelius, Testimony to the Senate Committee on Foreign Relations Subcommittee on African Affairs, 17, footnote 2, November 2009, 4, www .foreign.senate.gov/imo/media/doc/GuteliusTestimony091117a1.pdf.

[59] Stenersen, *Al-Qaida in Afghanistan*, 2.

[60] Barak Mendelsohn, *The Al-Qaeda Franchise: The Expansion of Al-Qaeda and Its Consequences* (New York: Oxford University Press, 2016), 2.

[61] For histories of al-Shabab, see Stig Jarle Hansen, *Al-Shabaab in Somalia: The History and Ideology of a Militant Islamist Group* (Oxford: Oxford University Press, 2013); and Harun Maruf and Dan Joseph, *Inside Al-Shabaab: The Secret History of Al-Qaeda's Most Powerful Ally* (Bloomington: Indiana University Press, 2018).

[62] Peter Chonka, "Spies, Stonework, and the *Suuq*: Somali Nationalism and the Narrative Politics of Pro-*Harakat Al Shabaab Al Mujaahidiin* Online Propaganda," *Journal of Eastern African Studies* 10:2 (2016): 247–265.

al-Shabab's violence has concentrated on Somalia and on nearby countries, such as Kenya, that intervene in Somalia's conflicts.

Like al-Qaʻida itself, most of the actors described in this book have operated primarily at the regional level, turning their attention only intermittently to the global stage and investing most of their energy into constructing localized nodes of influence that add up to a regional military, religious, and political infrastructure. Much expert literature, fittingly, has stressed the primarily local character of northwest Africa's jihadists.[63] A localist lens helps move the analysis beyond generic questions of radicalization, permitting more contextualized analysis of "collective interaction between armed movements and their immediate social environment."[64] Moreover, given that many Salafi-jihadists are not delocalized roving predators but rather indigenes of the environments in which they operate, localization of their program is not merely a strategy but also a logical outgrowth of their core identities.

I have previously argued that in northeastern Nigeria, developments in the local political and religious fields structured and shaped the jihadist movement Boko Haram, as that movement interacted with the environment around it.[65] But this was a macro-level approach to localism. My approach treated Boko Haram as a more or less unitary actor whose trajectory could be understood by tracing the statements of its senior leaders; here, I combine a *meso*-level lens with a localist perspective to illuminate the ways in which internally divided jihadist movements interact with the environments that surround them. Adopting a comparative approach and examining multiple jihadist

---

[63] See Catriona Dowd and Clionadh Raleigh, "The Myth of Global Islamic Terrorism and Local Conflict in Mali and the Sahel," *African Affairs* 112:448 (2013): 498–509; Wolfram Lacher and Guido Steinberg, "Spreading Local Roots: AQIM and Its Offshoots in the Sahara" in *Jihadism in Africa: Local Causes, Regional Expansion, International Alliances*, edited by Guido Steinberg and Annette Weber, 69–84 (Berlin: Stiftung Wissenschaft und Politik, 2015), www.swp-berlin.org/fileadmin/contents/products/research_papers/2015_RP05_sbg_web.pdf; and Aurélie Campana, "Between Destabilization and Local Embeddedness: Jihadist Groups in the Malian Conflict Since 2015," Centre FrancoPaix, August 2018, https://dandurand.uqam.ca/wp-content/uploads/2018/08/2018_08_Campana-Report-Stabilizing-Mali.pdf.

[64] Yvan Guichaoua and Héni Nsaibia, "Comment le djihad armé se diffuse au Sahel," The Conversation, February 24, 2019, https://theconversation.com/comment-le-djihad-arme-se-diffuse-au-sahel-112244.

[65] Alexander Thurston, *Boko Haram: The History of an African Jihadist Movement* (Princeton, NJ: Princeton University Press, 2017).

organizations adds a further layer to the analysis, showing the range of options available to field commanders as they confront diverse situations and surroundings.

Northwest Africa, including both North Africa and the Sahel region, is a fruitful terrain in which to apply such analysis. North Africa began witnessing jihadist insurgencies in the 1990s.[66] The Sahel became a significant theater of jihadist operations starting in the mid-2000s, and violence there has grown markedly since Mali's collapse in 2012.[67] Key jihadist actors in northwest Africa today include AQIM, branches of the Islamic State, and more local outfits. Moreover, North Africa and the Sahel are regions where jihadist movements have often anticipated and provoked the problems that movements further east only faced later – fratricide, schisms, and territorial losses. Algeria's GIA, in particular, was a forerunner of the Islamic State to an eery extent. All of the ingredients and trends necessary to understand jihadism are present in this region.

This book sets out to map the politics of jihadism in North Africa and the Sahel, drawing on case studies from Algeria, Mali, Niger, Burkina Faso, Libya, and Mauritania. These countries offer a variety of jihadist coalitions to examine, as well as outcomes that range from violent internal disputes to broad-based coalitions to failed mobilizations. The common denominator among three of these countries – Algeria, Libya, and Mali – is civil war and the opportunities it offers for mass jihadist coalition-building, including in spillover zones of violence such as Niger and Burkina Faso. In contrast, Mauritania

---

[66] Indispensable background for understanding these movements, and their connections to trends in Afghanistan, Pakistan, and Europe, can be found in Tawil, *Brothers in Arms*.

[67] Essential readings on jihadism in the Sahel include Frederic Wehrey and Anouar Boukhars, eds., *Perilous Desert: Insecurity in the Sahara* (Washington, DC: Carnegie Endowment, 2013); Stephen Harmon, *Terror and Insurgency in the Sahara-Sahel Region: Corruption, Contraband, Jihad and the Mali War of 2012–2013* (New York: Routledge, 2016); Rahmane Idrissa, *The Politics of Islam in the Sahel: Between Persuasion and Violence* (New York: Routledge, 2017); Andrew Lebovich, "AQIM's Formalized Flexibility" in *How al-Qaeda Survived Drone Strikes, Uprisings, and the Islamic State*, edited by Aaron Zelin, 56–66 (Washington, DC: Washington Institute for Near East Policy, 2017), www.washingtoninstitute.org/uploads/Documents/pubs/PolicyFocus153-Zelin .pdf; and Ibrahim Yahaya Ibrahim, "The Wave of Jihadist Insurgency in West Africa," OECD West African Papers Number 7 (August 2017), https://people .clas.ufl.edu/abrayaim/files/The-Wave-of-Jihadist-Insurgency-in-West-Africa .pdf.

furnishes a counter-case of more limited jihadist mobilization than one might expect amid the wider regional turmoil. Morocco and Tunisia, meanwhile, have been excluded from the case selection because of their relative internal stability and security, because of the recent appearance of strong literature on jihadism and counter-jihadism in those countries,[68] and also for reasons of space and feasibility. The book covers events through 2019 but is primarily a work of history rather than an analysis of the fast-moving present.

The Structure of the Book

The chapters here follow an order that is, loosely, both chronological and geographical. Each chapter foregrounds a particular jihadist coalition and describes the evolution of its internal and external politics.

Chapter 1, "Algeria: The GIA from Incorporation to Tyranny," tells the story of shifting jihadist coalitions within Algeria's civil war in the 1990s. The GIA exemplifies dynamics at various points along the spectrum of coalition-building and coalition management. Excelling in its early history at *incorporation*, the GIA eventually succumbed to *tyranny*, leading to *schism*. The GIA case study allows for an examination of dynamics that allow jihadist coalitions to expand rapidly (namely, by absorbing other fighting units) as well as dynamics that lead to fragmentation (in the GIA's case, a collapse of trust within the organization as the central leadership lashed out at field commanders). The central leadership's tyranny was also a major factor in the GIA's fall from nascent *domination* to *marginalization*, where the wider population lost all confidence in the group.

Chapter 2, "The GSPC/AQIM: Schism, Coup, and a Broken Triangle in the Sahara," examines coalition politics within the Salafi Group for Preaching and Combat (GSPC). The GSPC, the GIA's successor group, rebranded itself as al-Qa'ida in the Islamic Maghreb (AQIM) in 2007. The GSPC's early history provides a contrast with the GIA's collapse: Whereas dissident GIA field commanders banded

---

[68] On Morocco, see Ann Marie Wainscott, *Bureaucratizing Islam: Morocco and the War on Terror* (Cambridge: Cambridge University Press, 2017). On Tunisia, see Aaron Zelin, *Your Sons Are at Your Service: Tunisia's Missionaries of Jihad* (New York: Columbia University Press, 2020); and Monica Marks, "Youth Politics and Tunisian Salafism: Understanding the Jihadi Current," *Mediterranean Politics* 18:1 (2013): 107–114.

together to pursue the *schism* that created the GSPC, within a few years dissatisfied GSPC field commanders and other officials cooperated to mount a *coup*, expelling a top leader without fragmenting the organization. Nevertheless, the GSPC's relatively decentralized character – especially as it broadened its operations in the Sahara – eventually led to the development of a *broken triangle*, as the central leadership came to align with one particular Saharan field commander amid tensions with another commander. The chapter argues that jihadist coalitions can avoid destructive schisms by empowering field commanders and tolerating a high level of dissent from them, but that this strategy has substantial costs in terms of the central leadership's ability to impose a singular vision on subordinates. Meanwhile, the GSPC/AQIM's ventures in the Sahara allowed it to move from *marginalization* within Algeria to incipient forms of *accommodation* and even *collusion* in the Sahara, especially in northern Mali. The broken triangle structure caused considerable internal tension but did not preclude external political gains.

Chapter 3, "Northern Mali: Dialectics of Local Support," describes shifting coalitions in the Malian Sahara, especially in the critical phase of 2012–2013. During this period, AQIM was a central player in the construction of a jihadist proto-state in northern Mali. AQIM transformed earlier patterns of *accommodation* and *collusion* into *alliances*. Crucially, after the French intervened militarily in 2013 to shatter the jihadist proto-state, certain northern Malian actors intensified their relationships with AQIM and elected for outright *incorporation*, while other key actors deescalated their involvement from *alliance* back to what appears to be renewed *accommodation* or perhaps *collusion*. Finally, AQIM practiced *accommodation* with schismatic field commanders, a posture that eventually facilitated a *merger* that brought together several units, including the (former) schismatics, into a new organization called Jama'at Nusrat al-Islam wa-l-Muslimin (The Society for Supporting Islam and Muslims, JNIM).

Chapters 4 and 5 provide a contrast with Chapter 3: Whereas the latter examines incorporation at the level of individual politicians and the blocs they represent, Chapters 4 and 5 discuss incorporation at the grassroots level. Chapter 4, "Central Mali: The Possibilities and Limits of Incorporation," analyzes a JNIM unit operating in the Malian regions of Mopti and Ségou. This unit, Katibat Macina or Macina Battalion, exemplifies both possibilities and limits of *incorporation*, especially along ethnic lines. Recruiting heavily among the Peul, an ethnic group that is widespread in central Mali and across the Sahel,

Katibat Macina nevertheless made virtually no inroads among Peul elites. This case differs markedly from AQIM/JNIM's relationships with certain Tuareg elites in northern Mali. Pursuing different forms of *intimidation, accommodation,* and *domination* in the center of Mali, Katibat Macina achieved remarkable political expansion but was simultaneously swept up in dynamics – including a wider "ethnicization" in the multi-sided war in central Mali – that tested its internal cohesion and seemed to limit the group's long-term political prospects.

Chapter 5, "The Mali–Niger–Burkina Faso Borderlands: Incorporation and Accommodation at the Peripheries," investigates the political career of a small Islamic State affiliate, Islamic State in the Greater Sahara (ISGS). Originating as a *schism* within a *schism,* ISGS has pursued strategies of *incorporation* even amid overall *marginalization,* positioning itself as the champion of certain pastoralist communities even as community-based militias and national governments hunt it in the borderlands. For a time, ISGS represented a case of *accommodation* between ostensibly rival jihadist organizations: ISGS and JNIM avoided fighting each other and even seemed to cooperate.

Chapter 6, "Libya: Fratricide in Derna," focuses on the northeastern coastal city of Derna, where AQIM's loose allies battled an Islamic State affiliate in 2014–2015. Echoing the discussion in Chapters 2 and 3 about AQIM and its allies, the chapter explores the limits of different strategies for jihadist coalition-building: More pragmatic strategies can alienate hardliners, but hardliners alienate civilians. Ultimately, the Libyan case shows that both *accommodation* and *intimidation* have serious drawbacks. The Libyan case also allows for an investigation of how *dilution* can creep into, and affect, jihadist calculations and coalition dynamics.

Chapter 7, "Mauritania: Post-Jihadism?" treats Mauritania as a counter-case that shows how state policies can, in specific circumstances, help prevent jihadists from expanding their coalitions. Mauritania experienced significant jihadist attacks between 2005 and 2011 as well as some jihadist recruitment for actions at home and abroad. Yet since 2011, jihadist violence in Mauritania has almost completely fallen off. Mauritania exemplifies *failed mobilization*: The enduring jihadist presence in the country did not evolve beyond small cells. Since 2011, a *"mutaraka"* (truce) has arisen between Mauritania and AQIM, reflecting a tacit agreement between the Mauritanian state and the Sahara's jihadists, as well as a tacit understanding between the Mauritanian state and Mauritanian hardliners. These understandings revolve around the state's non-intervention in northern Mali, the state's willingness to tolerate strident preaching against democracy and liberalism, the state's relatively soft treatment of local hardliners since 2010, and the state's reduction or abandonment of the use of torture against dissident clerics. The Mauritanian "model" is not easily exportable to other contexts, in part because of Mauritania's sparse population and tightly networked elites, but it does provide insights into the range of relationships that are possible between jihadists and state authorities. The chapter argues that Mauritanian policy was effective precisely because it inadvertently reduced not just individual-level recruitment but also the scope of opportunities for a nascent jihadist coalition to build *alliances*; the state helped to block jihadist alliance-building by pursuing its own forms of *accommodation* with potential jihadists and quasi-jihadists. Those Mauritanian jihadists who did not accept the terms of this accommodation were either left under the thumb of the state (i.e., in prison) or decided that *relocation* was their most viable strategy.

The conclusion critiques the War on Terror's Sahelian and global manifestations, and looks to potential futures. Despite dark predictions about a Sahel overrun with jihadists and racked by climate change, a grim future is not inevitable; if northwest Africa's jihadists have had some success in building coalitions, that does not mean that states or communities are helpless in the face of jihadism's spread. By avoiding collective punishment – and by taking advantage of whatever opportunities may exist to provide political offramps for jihadists and even to negotiate with them[69] – it may be possible to reverse the conditions that favor jihadists' political projects.

---

[69] Some recent work on this topic includes my "Political Settlements with Jihadists in Algeria and the Sahel," Organization for Economic Cooperation and Development, West African Papers Number 18 (October 2018), www.oecd-ilibrary.org/docserver/0780622a-en.pdf?expires=1559743499&id=id&accname=guest&checksum=4CF15ED4C6B0783F6230A0560DCC5817; and International Crisis Group, "'Speaking with the Bad Guys': Toward Dialogue with Central Mali's Jihadists," May 28, 2019, https://d2071andvip0wj.cloudfront.net/276-speaking-with-the-bad-guys_0.pdf.

1 | *Algeria*
The GIA from Incorporation to Tyranny

The Armed Islamic Group (GIA)[1] was a powerful force during Algeria's civil war in the 1990s. The GIA is widely seen as extremist to the point of self-destruction; later jihadists have held up the GIA as a case of "excess" gone wrong.[2] Among analysts, the GIA is now usually discussed as the precursor to al-Qaʿida in the Islamic Maghreb (AQIM). In both analyst circles and jihadist accounts, the voices – plural – of the GIA are often missing. A teleological narrative takes hold, in which the GIA's extremism becomes merely the backstory to AQIM's relative pragmatism. But the GIA itself was always a coalition, and its turn to tyranny was neither inevitable nor uncontested. Similarly, when the GIA fell apart in the late 1990s, it did so in a relatively structured way that reflected shifting internal and external politics rather than just an ideological schism.

This chapter analyzes the internal coalition politics of the GIA. I trace its formation, expansion, internal turmoil, and the 1995–1999 schism that led to the formation of the Salafi Group for Preaching and Combat (GSPC),[3] the predecessor organization of AQIM. The GIA's history reveals the agency of field commanders in changing the group's trajectory, fighting for power within the coalition, and/or striking out on their own as schismatics – themes that recur in the other case studies.

---

[1] An abbreviation for Groupe Islamique Armée. In Arabic, its name is al-Jamaʿa al-Islamiyya al-Musallaha.

[2] See, for example, "Hiwar maʿa al-Shaykh ʿAsim Abi Hayan: Mahattat min Tarikh al-Jihad fi al-Jazaʾir," Ifriqiya al-Muslima, September 2016, 26, https://azelin.files.wordpress.com/2017/01/ifricc84qicc84yyah-al-muslimah-22dialogue-with-acc84scca3im-abucc84-hcca3ayacc84n-plants-from-the-history-of-jihacc84d-in-algeria22.pdf.

[3] An abbreviation for Groupe salafiste pour la Prédication et le Combat. In Arabic, its name is al-Jamaʿa al-Salafiyya li-l-Daʿwa wa-l-Qital.

Theoretical Implications of the Case

The GIA embodies several recurring scenarios for jihadist groups. One is *incorporation*, where a jihadist coalition expands by absorbing blocs. The case clarifies the dynamics that facilitate incorporation. Why was the GIA able to absorb less ideologically extreme groups during the early phase of Algeria's civil war (1991–1994)? The answer may have something to do with "the extremist's advantage"[4] in rallying fighters and reducing commitment problems – but I think it has more to do with the ways in which the GIA became a focal point for "prewar politicized social networks."[5] The GIA drew in a wide pre-existing network of mosque-based activists and then, amid the conflict, attracted neighborhood-level networks of armed youth who either found material advantage or emotional resonance in aligning themselves with the GIA. The emotional resonance had partly to do with anathematization, which initially helped to give the GIA street-level credibility as a clear alternative to the Algerian state, as well as a romantic air attached to their outlaw posture. The GIA's wide appeal to these prewar and wartime networks made it, for a time, the center of gravity among anti-state groups. Some of the more moderate factions then joined the GIA, whether reluctantly or not, out of deference to political reality.

The case also demonstrates, however, how rapid incorporation can make a coalition unwieldy and difficult to maintain. Incorporating massive prewar networks meant that some of the early architects of the group, figures with strategic acumen and previous combat experience, were sooner or later marginalized by less experienced but more popular (and more hardline) figures. The GIA's trajectory recalls Paul Staniland's argument that prewar networks shape the organizational structures of insurgent groups.[6] The GIA also reflects what Staniland calls "mismanaged expansion."[7] Key coalition components did not trust one another. As GIA leaders and members were rapidly killed during the war, suspicions and recriminations came to plague the group amid fears of infiltration by the Algerian security services. In

---

[4] Barbara Walter, "The Extremist's Advantage in Civil Wars," *International Security*, 42:2 (Fall 2017): 7–39.
[5] Paul Staniland, *Networks of Rebellion: Explaining Insurgent Cohesion and Collapse* (Ithaca, NY: Cornell University Press, 2014), 9.
[6] Ibid., ch. 2.   [7] Ibid., 41.

an environment that fostered paranoia and mistrust, the initial drivers of incorporation quickly lost their force, giving way to internal conflict that largely proceeded along lines reflecting prewar resentments.

The lack of trust broke out into the open during a succession struggle in autumn 1994. Just months after brokering the absorption of several key units into the GIA, the group's leader, Chérif Gousmi, was killed in battle. The resulting succession struggle pitted one major coalition bloc (the most ideologically extreme but also the most powerful) against some of the recently absorbed blocs. The coalition bloc that won this succession struggle then turned to *tyranny*, purging alleged internal enemies, traitors, and heretics. The case of the GIA seems to indicate that it is difficult, in a tenuous coalition, to replace one unifying leader with another unifying leader. If rival blocs cannot agree on a compromise candidate, the stage is set for the strongest bloc to impose its candidate and in this way transform internal tension into internal violence. This tyranny led to a massive schism within the organization, as regional field commanders broke away from the coalition first on a unit-by-unit basis, and then banded together to form a rival coalition.

The GIA's internal dynamics, and the shift from coalition-building to tyranny and purges, and finally to fragmentation, track with its external political posture – the internal and external dynamics became self-reinforcing. Externally, the GIA more and more forcefully applied its tyranny to civilians during the mid-1990s, reflecting the increasingly insular and paranoid character of the leadership and exacerbating the erosion of trust within the organization. The internal and external brutality then reinforced the leadership's insularity. The GIA squandered an opportunity to achieve *domination* over portions of Algeria, and instead found itself in a position of *marginalization* – abandoned by local and international allies, and widely feared and despised by civilians. The GIA's demise was hastened along by other actors, not least of which was the Algerian state, whose amnesties for non-GIA Islamist fighters in the late 1990s helped to undercut part of the GIA's remaining appeal. Here the GIA's anathematization became a liability, as the state used amnesties to deprive the GIA of any remaining prospect of renewed coalition-building. Over the long term, the GIA fell victim to its own success: The very factors that facilitated its rapid initial expansion as a coalition ultimately contributed to its downfall. An organization that had the potential to fit Staniland's depiction of the "integrated organization" with "robust central processes [and] robust local processes" transformed itself into a "fragmented organization" possessing neither.[8]

The logic of the GIA's fragmentation also shows that it is not just prewar networks that shape armed groups' character; wars themselves generate and reconfigure networks within the organization. The units that broke away from the GIA from 1995 onward were regionally based fighting units that represented combinations of prewar networks and networks that coalesced amid the conflict. These units were cohesive enough that they broke away as blocs. As schismatic field commanders banded together to generate a new organization, the result – the GSPC – was a coalition with greater coherence than the GIA, but far fewer fighters. In this atmosphere, the remaining networks of trust sometimes correlated loosely with geographical patterns: many fighters and battalion leaders tended to mobilize and fight in and around their hometowns.[9] Under Djamel Zitouni (1964–1996) and his successor Antar Zouabri (1970–2002), the GIA's central leadership was dominated by a clique from Algiers and Blida, while the GSPC had something of an eastern and southern character.

The Background to the GIA's Emergence

The GIA began to emerge in 1991 during the lead-up to the Algerian civil war.[10] In fact, the dating of the conflict[11] could be bracketed by two events connected with the GIA: November 1991, when the proto-

[8] Ibid., 9.
[9] For example, the early GIA battalion commander 'Attiya al-Sayih, even after fighting in Afghanistan, remained largely attached to his hometown of Ksar Boukhari in Médéa Province. See Abu Rabbab Luqman Mustafa al-Qasrawi, "Safahat Matwiyya min Sirat al-Qa'id al-Sayih 'Attiya," Ifriqiya al-Muslimah, December 2016, 9, https://azelin.files.wordpress.com/2017/03/ifricc84qicc84yyah-al-muslimah-22the-series-what-makes-them-content-is-that-they-are-with-us-14-atiyah.pdf.
[10] Key works on Algeria's civil war include Martin Stone, *The Agony of Algeria* (New York: Columbia University Press, 1997); Luis Martinez, *The Algerian Civil War, 1990–1998* (New York: Columbia University Press, 2000); and Hugh Roberts, *The Battlefield: Algeria 1988–2002: Studies in a Broken Polity* (New York: Verso, 2003).
[11] For an excellent critical perspective that questions the notion of "civil war" itself, see Jacob Mundy, *Imaginative Geographies of Algerian Violence: Conflict Science, Conflict Management, Antipolitics* (Stanford, CA: Stanford University Press, 2015). Mundy prefers the term "mass violence."

GIA's first attack targeted an army barracks at Guemar, near Algeria's border with Tunisia;[12] and February 2002, when the GIA's last major leader, Antar Zouabri, was killed.

The backdrop to the civil war included rising popular dissatisfaction with the one-party state that had dominated Algeria since the country's hard-fought independence from France in 1962. A turning point came in October 1988, when mass demonstrations broke out. The demonstrations were motivated by ordinary people's economic difficulties, and also by disgust at corruption and nepotism among the country's elite.[13] The riots prompted liberalization that allowed, temporarily, for new and open challenges to state hegemony. Authorities proposed a new constitution, which nearly three-quarters of voters approved in a February 1989 referendum. The constitution allowed for the formation of new political parties.

The Islamists benefited. They had organizational advantages and a moral-political appeal that seemed to promise a break with the status quo.[14] The authorities may have also initially allowed the Islamists opportunities because authorities mistakenly calculated that they could use Islamists as bogeymen and thereby keep voters in line.[15] Islamists won numerous local seats in the June 1990 municipal elections. Islamists then dominated the first round of parliamentary elections in December 1991, winning 188 seats outright out of the 430-member body and setting themselves up to secure an absolute majority in the anticipated second round. Unwilling to tolerate an Islamist victory, the Algerian military intervened in January 1992, annulling the elections, preventing the second round from occurring, and compelling the resignation of the president, Chadli Bendjedid. This coup was followed by a full-blown conflict that eventually claimed up to 200,000 lives.

---

[12] Martinez, *Algerian Civil War*, 69.

[13] See Martin Evans and John Philipps, *Algeria: Anger of the Dispossessed* (New Haven, CT, and London: Yale University Press, 2007), ch. 4.

[14] See Mark Tessler, "The Origins of Popular Support for Islamist Movements" in *Islam, Democracy, and the State in North Africa*, edited by John Entelis, 93–126 (Bloomington: Indiana University Press, 1997).

[15] See Hugh Roberts, "From Radical Mission to Equivocal Ambition: The Expansion and Manipulation of Algerian Islamism, 1979–1992" in *Accounting for Fundamentalisms: The Dynamic Character of Movements*, edited by Martin Marty and R. Scott Appleby, 428–489 (Chicago: University of Chicago Press, 1994).

The main Islamist party during the liberalization period was the Islamic Salvation Front (French acronym FIS). The FIS included Muslim Brotherhood-style Islamists, Islamic modernists, and Salafis. Its two main leaders were Abbassi Madani (1931–2019) and Ali Belhadj (b. 1956).

On one level, Madani and Belhadj represented conflicting postures – and the resultant ambiguity about the FIS' character and intentions fueled skeptics' concerns that the FIS was covertly authoritarian. Yet, as Hugh Roberts puts it, "The relationship ... was essentially complementary."[16] Madani, a professor of education with a British doctorate, became a bridge between older Algerian Islamists and a younger, more militant generation.[17] Belhadj, the imam of al-Sunna Mosque in Algiers' Bab El Oued neighborhood, had a more eclectic background than he is sometimes credited with.[18] Yet he was more hotheaded than the other top Islamist leaders. Belhadj spoke in an exclusivist Salafi idiom, evincing anti-Shi'i and anti-Sufi views that were harsher than the stances adopted by other leading Algerian Islamists.[19] He was also connected to the proto-jihadist 1980s insurgency led by Moustafa Bouyali (1940–1987, see next section).[20]

The FIS did not rally all the Algerian Islamist leaders to its cause. The party even found advantages in shedding the intellectualism of certain leaders in favor of more populist messaging.[21] Some Islamists had an ambivalent relationship with the FIS. One key constituency was the Djaz'ara or Algerianists, whose intellectual forefather was Malek Bennabi (1905–1973). Bennabi promoted an Algerian-centric Islamism distinct from the Muslim Brotherhood. Bennabi influenced key

---

[16] Ibid., 448.

[17] For biographies of Madani and Belhadj, as well as excerpts from their writings and interviews, see *L'Algérie par ses islamistes*, edited by Mustafa al-Ahnaf, Bernard Botiveau, and Franck Frégosi (Paris: Karthala, 1991). For treatments of Algerian Islamism, see Roberts, "From Radical Mission"; and Michael Willis, *The Islamist Challenge in Algeria: A Political History* (New York: New York University Press, 1999).

[18] *L'Algérie par ses islamistes*, 70–71. Belhadj mentions reading the works of Brotherhood figures such as Hasan al-Banna and Sayyid Qutb, as well as those of Salafi forefathers such as Ibn Taymiyya and Ibn al-Qayyim.

[19] Ibid., 70–71.   [20] Willis, *Islamist Challenge*, 143.   [21] Ibid., 117–118.

Islamists, including Madani and two other figures central to this chapter: Muhammad Saïd and 'Abd al-Razzaq Redjam.[22]

Some Djaz'arists joined the FIS but were skeptical of the radicalism represented by Belhadj. After the arrests of Madani and Belhadj in June 1991, the Djaz'arists initially waxed strong within the FIS, expelling many Salafis from the *majlis al-shura* (consultation council).[23] Yet some Djaz'arists grew disenchanted with FIS efforts at making peace with the regime: Saïd and Redjam were among the FIS leaders who refused to negotiate with the government, and instead took up arms.[24] In 1994, Saïd and Redjam would both join – and then in 1995 be executed by – the GIA.

The internal divisions of the Islamist movement shaped the civil war. Actors moved in and out of coalitions. The arrests and killings of leaders heightened fluidity and uncertainty. Divisions within the Islamist movement also provided the regime with opportunities to divide and conquer, especially as the war dragged on.

The GIA's Coalition

The GIA was formalized in stages between 1991 and 1994. The proto-GIA and other armed factions constantly negotiated and renegotiated unity initiatives. The most important of these were a failed coordination meeting in September 1992 and a more successful merger in May 1994.

The GIA absorbed numerous localized militias, and it is important not to overstate the GIA's coherence, but for simplicity's sake one can point to three main constituencies that constituted the core of the GIA.[25] The first constituency was Algerians who had fought in

---

[22] George Joffé, "Trajectories of Radicalisation: Algeria 1989–1999" in *Islamist Radicalisation in North Africa: Politics and Process*, edited by George Joffé, 114–137 (London: Routledge, 2012), 126.

[23] Willis, *Islamist Challenge*, 270.

[24] 'Umar 'Abd al-Hakim (Abu Mus'ab al-Suri), *Mukhtasar Shahadati 'ala al-Jihad fi al-Jaza'ir* (self-published, June 2004), 16, available at www.cia.gov/library/abbottabad-compound/1C/1CB4B9B1633B4CF4CEB3C4E0400EA7D6_5.doc.pdf.

[25] Camille Tawil sees this as just two constituencies: Afghanistan veterans and local hardliners. I distinguish Bouyalists from the other local hardliners. See Tawil, *Brothers in Arms: The Story of al-Qa'ida and the Arab Jihadists* (London: Saqi Books, 2010), 76.

Afghanistan, either during the anti-Soviet jihad or in its chaotic aftermath. The second constituency was the remnants of Moustapha
Bouyali's Armed Islamic Movement (MIA). These MIA veterans
included the proto-GIA's first leader, Mansour Meliani. The MIA
had waged a guerrilla insurgency against the Algerian state from
1982 to 1987, "inflict[ing] serious reverses on the security forces on
several occasions" before the authorities killed Bouyali and dismantled
the group.[26] By July 1990, some of the remaining MIA leaders had
received amnesties, which "led to the gradual and clandestine reforma-
tion of various cells of the organisation."[27] These two groups – returnees and local hardliners, or "Afghan Algerians" and "Bouyalists" –
were the initial architects of the GIA. Their views and experiences
proved highly compatible.

The third key constituency was Algerian youth who were not veterans of Afghanistan or Bouyali's revolt. Their defining characteristic
was their involvement in mosque-based activist networks in the 1980s.
Some of these youth would dominate the GIA by late 1994. Ironically,
some of them were initially members of the FIS (whose relative pragmatism had been repellent to the Afghanistan veterans and Bouyalists
in the early 1990s), but then later became the most extreme members
of the GIA.

Let us now look at each constituency in more detail. The "Afghan
Algerians" brought experience in both military and ideological
matters, because they returned to Algeria as veterans of both physical
and ideological combats. Their initial reasons for going to Afghanistan
varied. Some of them were angry at the repression and defeat of
Bouyali's MIA; others were connected to the Algerian branch of the
Muslim Brotherhood.[28] The transnational Muslim Brotherhood also
played a role in recruitment, especially through the efforts of 'Abd
Allah 'Azzam (1941–1989). A Palestinian thinker, 'Azzam became an
influential recruiter around the world. He provided much of the intellectual basis for the Arab fighters' mission in Afghanistan. 'Azzam
argued that the anti-Soviet jihad was a *fard 'ayn* (individual duty,
incumbent on every Muslim) rather than a *fard kifaya* (collective duty,
or one that was fulfilled for all through the participation of some).

---

[26] Roberts, "From Radical Mission," 429.   [27] Willis, *Islamist Challenge*, 269.
[28] Tawil, *Brothers in Arms*, 33. See also 33, fn. 1.

In Peshawar, Pakistan, he created the Services Bureau (Maktab al-Khidmat) in 1984 as a focal point for donations and Arab activism.

In Algeria, 'Azzam's outreach resonated with many young militants. Perhaps the first Algerian, and one of the first Arabs, to join the Afghan jihad was Abdullah Anas (b. 1958), who came to Afghanistan after meeting 'Azzam.[29] Anas recounts one of his early encounters with 'Azzam's name and ideas:

> One day in 1983, in the city of Bel Abbès located 450 kilometers west of Algiers, I entered a bookstore that I used to frequent, seeking to find the latest world news ... But my visit to the bookstore that time was different from the previous times, for by chance that day a new issue of the Kuwaiti journal *Society* had come out. It contained a *fatwa* signed by a group of Muslim scholars from the Arab Gulf ... Its import was that the jihad in Afghanistan was an individual duty (*fard 'ayn*) upon Muslims. And among the signatories to the *fatwa* was 'Abd Allah 'Azzam. I had known that name even before he joined the Afghan mujahidin, and that was through his tapes and his books, by virtue of my belonging to the Islamic movement on the intellectual, although not the organizational, level.[30]

Anas went on to meet 'Azzam in Mecca on the 1983 pilgrimage. Through that connection, Anas headed to Afghanistan. Other Algerians heard 'Azzam's lectures or read his statements, and went to Afghanistan without meeting him personally. Even after 'Azzam was assassinated by unknown culprits in 1989, his death prompted still others to go to Afghanistan. The future GSPC/AQIM field commander Mokhtar Belmokhtar later recalled that as a teenager in the 1980s, he had become "obsessed and enamored with the Afghan jihad." But it was 'Azzam's death that pushed him to go: "The killing of the shaykh, the mujahid, the martyr 'Abd Allah 'Azzam increased this resolve of mine, for I was so influenced by that scholar-mujahid."[31]

The story of the Afghan Arabs has been recounted elsewhere;[32] what concerns us here is the impact of the Afghanistan experience on

---

[29] Ibid., 16–17.
[30] 'Abd Allah Anas, *Wiladat al-Afghan al-'Arab: Sirat 'Abd Allah Anas bayn Mas'ud wa-'Abd Allah 'Azzam* (London: Dar al-Saqi, 2017), 14.
[31] "Hiwar ma'a al-Qa'id Khalid Abi al-'Abbas – Amir al-Mintaqa al-Sahrawiyya li-l-Jama'a al-Salafiyya li-l-Da'wa wa-l-Qital," Minbar al-Tawhid wa-l-Jihad, May 25, 2006, www.ilmway.com/site/maqdis/MS_37048.html.
[32] See Mustafa Hamid and Leah Farrell, *The Arabs at War in Afghanistan* (Oxford: Oxford University Press, 2016).

Algerian militant networks. As I have argued elsewhere, the late 1980s and early 1990s became a pivotal era in differentiating Salafism from Salafi-jihadism, and in differentiating Salafi-jihadism from the Muslim Brotherhood.[33] 'Azzam was the last major Muslim Brotherhood figure to loom large within the jihadist current; other prominent jihadists are vehemently ex-Brotherhood, such as al-Qa'ida's current leader Ayman al-Zawahiri (b. 1951) and the Syrian theorist-strategist Abu Mus'ab al-Suri (b. 1958), both of whom wrote books criticizing the Brotherhood during that formative late 1980s/early 1990s phase;[34] al-Suri, notably, was for a time an adviser and propagandist for the GIA.

In the late 1980s, intra-jihadist debates gained steam in Afghanistan and Pakistan. Many jihadists, and emerging Salafi-jihadi theorists such as Abu Muhammad al-Maqdisi and Abu Qatada al-Filastini, were rejecting the Muslim Brotherhood's relatively generic Islamism and were instead giving jihadism a more thoroughly Salafi vocabulary.[35] Al-Maqdisi has written that he left 'Azzam's Sadda camp on the Pakistan-Afghanistan border over theological disagreements with 'Azzam, who in al-Maqdisi's words "considered the tomb worshippers and amulet-wearers mujahidin."[36] In other words, al-Maqdisi felt 'Azzam was too flexible with Sufis and other currents that hardline Salafis considered blameworthy innovators at best and unbelievers at worst. 'Azzam's assassination accelerated the ascendance of hardliners within the jihadist current, including al-Zawahiri. Rather than merely advocating targeted jihads against foreign powers occupying particular Muslim lands, the hardliners urged a sweeping struggle to overthrow regimes across the Middle East.

---

[33] Alexander Thurston, "Algeria's GIA: The First Major Armed Group to Fully Subordinate Jihadism to Salafism," *Islamic Law and Society* 24:4 (2017): 412–436.

[34] Ayman al-Zawahiri, *Al-Hisad al-Murr: Al-Ikhwan al-Muslimun fi Sittin Amm* (self-published, 1991); and Abu Mus'ab al-Suri, *Al-Thawra al-Islamiyya al-Jihadiyya fi Suriya* (self-published, 1991).

[35] See Joas Wagemakers, *A Quietist Jihadi: The Ideology and Influence of Abu Muhammad al-Maqdisi* (Cambridge: Cambridge University Press, 2012), especially ch. 7.

[36] Abu Muhammad al-Maqdisi, "Li-l-'Ibra min Dhakirat Afghanistan," Mu'assasat Bayan li-l-I'lam al-Islami, March 2, 2019, https://azelin.files .wordpress.com/2019/03/shaykh-abucc84-muhcca3ammad-al-maqdisicc84–22for-a-lesson-from-the-memories-of-afghanistan22.pdf. For background on the Sadda camp, see Hamid and Farrall, *The Arabs at War in Afghanistan*, 83–84.

These developments had implications for the Algerians based in South Asia: Initially recruited through Muslim Brotherhood networks, by 1989 they found the ideological ground shifting under their feet. Drawing on the thinking promoted by al-Maqdisi and al-Zawahiri, some Afghan Algerians rejected the FIS and its relatively mainstream Islamist vision even before returning home.[37] Once they arrived home, they were eager to fight the Algerian state – some of them were ready to fight even before the 1992 coup that blocked the FIS from taking power.[38] The FIS, with its willingness to enter electoral politics, was seen as too pliant and too Brotherhood-like.

The second key constituency in the early GIA was survivors of Bouyali's MIA. In the aftermath of Bouyali's death, authorities put over 200 of his followers on trial, sentencing five of them to death and acquitting only fifteen.[39] The MIA's revolt became something of a dress rehearsal for the GIA's insurgency: The MIA's violence centered on the suburbs of Algiers, just as some of the GIA's violence would several years later.

Three notable members of Bouyali's group were Ali Belhadj, later number two in the FIS, and two movers in the early 1990s Algerian uprising: Abdelkader Chebouti and Mansour Meliani. The latter, who had been condemned to death over his participation in the MIA revolt, was amnestied and released in 1989. On his release he allegedly made a temporary accommodation with the FIS, conducting paramilitary training with FIS leader Madani's support.[40] According to another account, after Belhadj's arrest in 1991, Belhadj "gave his blessing for launching armed action and appointed Chebouti as the leader of it."[41] Chebouti recreated the MIA as something of a revival of Bouyali's

---

[37] Tawil, *Brothers in Arms*, 73–74.

[38] This, for example, was 'Attiya al-Sayih's position by 1991. See al-Qasrawi, "Safahat Matwiyya," 7.

[39] Willis, *Islamist Challenge*, 71–82. For details of Bouyali's death, see *L'Algérie par ses islamistes*, 311; and Henri Lauzière, "Bouyali, Moustafa [1940–1987]" in *Encyclopedia of the Modern Middle East and North Africa*, edited by Philip Mattar, Second Edition, Volume 1, 505–506 (New York: Macmillan Reference USA, 2004).

[40] "Anciens d'Afghanistan, égorgeurs et violeurs," *l'Humanité*, December 26, 1994, www.humanite.fr/node/94028.

[41] Basir al-Za'atara, "Al-'Unf al-Musallah fi al-Jaza'ir: Min Intifadat Buy'ali [Bouyali] ila Tajawuzat 'Antar Zuwabri [Zouabri]," *Al-Hayat*, February 12, 2002, www.alhayat.com/article/1119244. See also Willis, *Islamist Challenge*, 277.

group. Initially "seen as a visionary ... Chebouti assumed heroic proportions because of the repression that thrust people who had suffered ill-treatment, injury and humiliation at the hands of the forces of order into the orbit of his movement."[42] Yet Chebouti, despite efforts to broker unity initiatives among Islamist and jihadist fighters in 1991–1992, failed to keep Algeria's militants under his banner.[43] As Luis Martinez writes, "demand exceeded supply" when it came to ambitious militant leaders seeking organizational roles in the early 1990s.[44] One of the independent-minded militants was Meliani. As Afghan Algerians returned home in the second half of 1991, they sought out Chebouti and another militant, Said Makhloufi of the Movement for an Islamic State (French acronym MEI), but soon settled on Meliani as their leader.[45] Even though the Afghan Algerians were returning with overseas combat experience, they nevertheless prized the domestic experience and credibility that Bouyali's successors had.

The proto-GIA as of 1991–1992 was headed by a Bouyalist (Meliani) with Afghan Algerians in key roles.[46] But the initial leaders of the proto-GIA were quickly removed from the battlefield: three top figures, including Meliani, were all arrested in 1992.[47] Two others were killed together in February 1994.[48] Rapid arrests and killings of veterans, either foreign or domestic, pushed a third kind of figure to the GIA's fore: young local Salafi hardliners.

The hardliners came out of mosque networks, especially in Algiers. Such networks offered opportunities for leadership at surprisingly young ages; some future GIA leaders became neighborhood imams in

---

[42] Martinez, *Algerian Civil War*, 68.   [43] Willis, *Islamist Challenge*, 270.

[44] Martinez, *Algerian Civil War*, 200.

[45] 'Abd al-Hafiz bin 'Ali, "Hakadha Bada'a al-'Amal al-Musallah didd al-Sulta fi al-Jaza'ir," *Echorouk Online*, March 30, 2009, www.echoroukonline.com/ هكذا-بدأ-العمل-المسلح-ضد-السلطة-في-الجز/. See also Tawil, *Brothers in Arms*, 47–48.

[46] These figures included Qari Saïd, Ahmad al-Wadd, Abu Layth al-Msili, Djaafar al-Afghani, and 'Attiya al-Sayih. See Bin 'Ali, "Hakadha Bada'a al-'Amal al-Musallah"; and 'Abd al-Hakim/al-Suri, *Mukhtasar Shahadati*, 16.

[47] Qari Saïd was arrested in February 1992 and was killed in 1994 following a prison break. Meliani was arrested in July 1992 and executed the following year. Ahmad al-Wadd, arrested shortly after Meliani, died in a prison mutiny in 1995. See Tawil, *Brothers in Arms*, 74–76.

[48] These were al-Sayih and Djafar al-Afghani. See "Al-Sharif Qusmi [Chérif Gousmi]: 'Al-Khalifa' Lam Yahkum Akthar min Shahr," *Al-Hayat*, October 3, 1994, www.alhayat.com/article/1875592. See also al-Qasrawi, "Safahat Matwiyya."

their twenties. Activism built wide social networks and fostered an incipient counter-order. For some youth, especially the only recently urbanized, their ideological commitments partly represented "the invention of a new identity, since by it they broke free from their former allegiances, family or regional."[49] By the early 1990s, some had organized themselves as local vigilantes. Some frequented shadowy, highly extreme groups called *takfir wa-l-hijra* (excommunication and withdrawal, in an echo of the Takfir and Hijra group in Egypt).[50] Reflecting later, one jihadist wrote unflatteringly

Some of them – according to what reached me – formed a movement that was given the name "the Salafiyya of the Capital." They used to call themselves "The Society for Commanding the Right and Forbidding the Wrong" [a core but contested notion in Islam]. From the beginning, ideas spread among them that vacillated between bigotry and *takfir* (pronouncing other Muslims unbelievers) and ignorance of the religion and the world (*al-tazammut wa-l-takfir wa-l-jahl fi al-din wa-l-dunya*). Most of them had opposed the Islamists' democratic project from the beginning.[51]

At first, the faces of this constituency were Muhammad 'Allal, better known as Moh Leveilley, and 'Abd al-Haqq Layada. Already in 1992, they had questioned the authority of older figures such as Chebouti.[52]

Both Leveilley and Layada came from the banlieu of Algiers, from the ranks of the manual laborers and unemployed.[53] Yet they brought critical advantages to the GIA. One journalist recounts that

Despite being new to armed action, and having little expertise *('ala raghm hadathatihi fi al-'amal al-musallah wa-qillat hibratihi)*, 'Abd al-Haqq Layada, an auto mechanic in Baraki ... was able to be appointed national emir of the Armed Group by virtue of his precise knowledge of popular neighborhoods in the capital, and [by virtue of] his undertaking numerous operations described as "courageous" against the security services.[54]

---

[49] Martinez, *Algerian Civil War*, 33. See also 40.
[50] Ibid., 69; Willis, *Islamist Challenge*, 227 and 268.
[51] 'Abd al-Hakim/al-Suri, *Mukhtasar Shahadati*, 12.
[52] Willis, *Islamist Challenge*, 270.
[53] Cherif Ouazani, "Des émirs plus sanguinaires les uns que les autres," *Jeune Afrique*, January 17, 2005, www.jeuneafrique.com/99278/archives-thematique/des-mirs-plus-sanguinaires-les-uns-que-les-autres/.
[54] Muhammad Muqaddam, "Rihlat al-Afghan al-Jaza'iriyyin min al-Jama'a ila Tanzim 'al-Qa'ida'," Part 3, *Al-Hayat*, November 25, 2001, www.alhayat.com/article/1070377.

As in other chaotic environments, rapid change was thrusting previously unknown figures to the forefront based on their perceived "toughness" and their ability to mobilize networks of "cohesion and trust" necessary to participate effectively in violence.[55] The Afghanistan veterans and Bouyalists knew Algeria, but the local hardliners had been on the ground continuously through the critical period 1988–1992, without being overseas or in prison. They had a surer finger on the pulse of grassroots militants – a dynamic that would come into play when Djamel Zitouni bid for the leadership of the GIA in 1994.

Leveilley and Layada's tenures at the top of the GIA were just as brief as those of their predecessors: Leveilley was killed by security forces during the above-mentioned September 1992 meeting of armed groups.[56] Layada, arrested in Morocco in June 1993,[57] was imprisoned until 2006. But the local hardliners' networks were easier to replenish than those of the Afghanistan veterans and the Bouyalists. Family networks were pulling local youth into the GIA, converting some from indifferent delinquents into extremists. Martinez profiles one figure called "Said the Sheet-Metal Worker"; after his older brother was killed, he transitioned from an apolitical youth to become the extortionist "emir" of a militant group in Les Eucalyptus, a suburb of Algiers.[58] Various other future leaders came to the GIA through their brothers, such as Antar Zouabri,[59] whose brother 'Ali was close to Leveilley and Layada.[60] Meanwhile, the local hardliners' lack of prior combat experience meant that the civil war was their first real taste of violence – they were plunged into it and their ideologies were transformed within it, unlike the Afghanistan veterans and Bouyalists who had better-formed ideas about what it meant to challenge the Algerian state, and about who the targets of violence should be.

The GIA's most politically successful leader, from the perspective of incorporating factions into the coalition, was Chérif Gousmi/Abu 'Abd

---

[55] A comparison with mafias may be apt here. See Vadim Volkov, *Violent Entrepreneurs: The Use of Force in the Making of Russian Capitalism* (Ithaca, NY, and London: Cornell University Press, 2002), 67.

[56] Willis, *Islamist Challenge*, 272.   [57] "Anciens d'Afghanistan."

[58] Martinez, *Algerian Civil War*, 96–98.   [59] Tawil, *Brothers in Arms*, 82.

[60] Camille Tawil, "'Amir al-Akhdariyya' Yakshif 'Asrar al-Jabal' wa-Tasfiyatihi al-Dakhiliyya," *Al-Hayat*, June 7, 2007, www.alhayat.com/article/1343329/
أمير-الأخضرية-يكشف-أسرار-الجبل-وتصفياته-الداخلية-عناصر-من-الجماعة-الجزائرية-تدربت-في-لبنان-فاتهم-أميرها-ب-التشيع-nbsp.

Allah Ahmad (1968–1994). Gousmi was one of the local Salafi hardliners: He began his career as an imam in his neighborhood, the Birkhadem suburb of Algiers.[61] Gousmi's short-lived tenure as GIA emir, from March–September 1994, brought an escalation of the group's violence, a bureaucratic reorganization of the GIA, and the successful May 1994 unity initiative. That initiative incorporated three other groups: Said Makhloufi's Harakat al-Dawla al-Islamiyya (the Islamic State Movement, French acronym MEI), Chebouti's MIA, and the armed FIS units led by the Djaz'arist leaders Muhammad Saïd and 'Abd al-Razzaq Redjam.[62] During the summer of 1994, the GIA's Shura Council symbolically incorporated the FIS' still-imprisoned leaders, Madani and Belhadj, as well as Makhloufi, Saïd, and Redjam.[63] The latter two were something of an ill fit for the GIA, but may have "perceived the base of popular support for Islamism to be shifting decisively away from the FIS and towards the GIA and thus feared being sidelined."[64] The only prominent refusal to join came from Madani Mezrag, emir of the FIS' armed wing, the Islamic Salvation Army (AIS).[65] Mezrag's aloofness aside, by 1994 the GIA was a massive coalition.

One jihadist's estimate, although hardly unbiased, calculates the combined strength of these factions at "more than 25,000."[66] The same source rhapsodizes about this period:

The early years were blessed (*mubaraka*). The mujahidin put forth a major effort on the preaching, military, and organizational side. The people had great sympathy and support for the mujahidin. They controlled the villages and rural areas where they were touring in their cars in broad daylight and

---

[61] "Al-Sharif Qusmi." See also "Hiwar ma'a al-Shaykh 'Asim Abi Hayan," 10.
[62] Hafid 'Uqba bin Nafi' [pseudonym], "Irshad Dhawi al-Basa'ir hawla ma Ja'a fi Maqal al-Shaykh Majid al-Rashid 'an Jihad al-Jaza'ir," 2016, 2, https://azelin .files.wordpress.com/2016/01/hcca3aficc84d-e28098uqbah-ibn-nacc84fi-22guidance-with-insights-about-what-happened-from-the-article-of-shaykh-macc84jid-al-racc84shid-about-the-algerian-jihacc84d22.pdf.
[63] "Al-Jama'a al-Islamiyya al-Musallaha...Tarikh wa-Haqa'iq," Paldf, December 10, 2007, www.paldf.net/forum/showthread.php?t=197593.
[64] Willis, *Islamist Challenge*, 325.
[65] 'Abd al-Hakim/Al-Suri, *Mukhtasar Shahadati*, 18.
[66] Abu Shu'ayb al-Jaza'iri, "Tanwir al-Basa'ir bi-Sirat al-Qa'id Abi Thumama Suwwan 'Abd al-Qadir," Ifriqiya al-Muslima, May 2017, 8, https://azelin.files .wordpress.com/2017/05/ifriqiyyah-al-muslimah-the-series-what-makes-them-content-is-that-they-are-with-us_-22-enlightenment-of-the-insights-biography-of-the-commander-abu-thamamah-sawa4.pdf.

dealing with the people on many issues, together with the presence of companies [i.e. military units], networks, and cells in the major cities. At night, they would impose their control on those cities, entering them to undertake military operations.[67]

But Gousmi's death at the hands of security forces in September 1994 split the GIA into two key camps. One was the GIA's formal leadership structure, comprising several regional field commanders and an ideologically diverse Shura Council.[68] These institutions endorsed Gousmi's deputy, Abu Khalil Mahfouz Tajin. On the other side was a coterie of Salafi hardliners from Algiers and Blida, with Djamel Zitouni as their candidate.[69] Ideology became the language of the leadership struggle: Zitouni's side accused Tajin of Djaz'arist and even Shi'i sympathies.[70] Zitouni's supporters pressured Tajin to step aside roughly a month after Gousmi's death. Yet doctrine was not the only dividing factor between the two sides: prewar networks and demography also came into play.

Zitouni's story is complex. A chicken vendor from the Algiers suburb of Birkhadem, Zitouni had a modest education.[71] He had frequented mosque study circles from at least the 1980s on.[72] He initially belonged to the FIS, but joined the armed jihadist project after his imprisonment in 1991. Although he had good relations with some of the Afghanistan veterans in the GIA, it seems that he became more extreme as he rose in the GIA's ranks.[73] According to one account, Zitouni founded the Green Battalion, whose members he was allowed to select himself;[74] another account contradicts this by saying that Zitouni's eventual successor as GIA emir, Antar Zouabri, founded the Green Battalion in his hometown of Boufarik, Blida Province, in 1993.[75] By fall 1994, Zitouni and the Green Battalion had gained widespread fame among the GIA rank and file as daring operators. Again, perceived toughness and grassroots appeal went hand in hand.

---

[67] Al-Jaza'iri, "Tanwir al-Basa'ir," 8.
[68] "Al-Jama'a al-Islamiyya al-Musallaha...Tarikh wa-Haqa'iq."
[69] These figures were Muhammad Bukabus (or Abou Kabous), Antar Zouabri, Redouane Makador, and Abu 'Adlan Rabih Ghanima. See "Hiwar ma'a al-Shaykh 'Asim Abi Hayan," 7–8.
[70] Tawil, "Amir al-Akhdariyya."   [71] Tawil, "Amir al-Akhdariyya."
[72] "Hiwar ma'a al-Shaykh 'Asim Abi Hayan," 10–11.   [73] Ibid., 12.
[74] Tawil, "Amir al-Akhdariyya."
[75] Al-Za'atara, "Al-'Unf al-Musallah fi al-Jaza'ir."

In the dispute between Zitouni and Tajin, Zitouni's grassroots support and military reputation turned the tide against the relatively more moderate members of the Shura Council.[76] Judging from the actions that Zitouni ordered after taking over the GIA – including the hijacking of an Air France flight in December 1994 and the kidnapping of seven Trappist monks at Tibhirine in March 1996 – there was some appetite (and willingness) within the GIA rank and file for broadening the war. Coalition politics followed ideological lines but also involved forms of internal public relations amid a competition for the admiration of ordinary fighters.

Zitouni's ascension was a political disaster for the GIA. During the pivotal year of 1995, Zitouni undid the coalition that Gousmi and others had forged. Here we recall Staniland's observation that mismanaged expansion threatens coalitions. In the GIA's case, Gousmi seems to have been a unique leader who could maintain the respect of hardliners such as Zitouni while opening the door to Djaz'arists and others. The GSPC/AQIM hagiographies are unanimous in their praise for Gousmi. Lest we be drawn into a "great man of history" perspective, however, one might view Gousmi as a product of the GIA's momentum through 1994, a figure thrown into the spotlight through the need for intra-coalition unity amid expansion, but who simultaneously represented the upper limit of the GIA's coalition-building prospects. Any GIA leader who reached that zenith would likely be succeeded by someone representing a faction rather than by someone capable of replicating the unifying role; perhaps, structurally, there could only be one Gousmi-like figure before the coalition turned on itself. As the prize of the emirship became more valuable, internal competition over it intensified; under these circumstances, bids by particular blocs to continue expanding the coalition were interpreted by the central leadership as particularistic power plays rather than as maneuvers that would benefit the coalition as a whole.

Zitouni moved to destroy the Djaz'ara, real and perceived. Zitouni's two most prominent victims were Muhammad Saïd and 'Abd al-Razzaq Redjam, former FIS leaders and Djaz'arists who had brought a contingent of FIS/AIS fighters with them into the GIA as part of Gousmi's May 1994 unity initiative. Saïd's presence may have

---

[76] Camille Tawil, "'Ali bin Hajar li-l-Hayat: La Ad'u al-Musallahin ila al-Nuzul min al-Jabal," *Al-Hayat*, January 18, 2004, www.alhayat.com/article/1183668.

been particularly threatening to Zitouni during the scramble to choose a new leader after Gousmi's death; Saïd had broad appeal among militants and within Algerian society.[77] Zitouni seems to have felt, even after his formal investiture as emir, that his position was threatened by the ambitions of other coalition blocs.

In 1995, as Zitouni's aggression began to antagonize many within and outside the GIA, Redjam moved to rejoin the FIS' armed wing, the AIS.[78] Saïd may have been considering a similar reversal. They were soon marked for assassination. One quasi-hagiographical (here, pro-Saïd and Redjam) account says that in October 1995, a Zitouni loyalist, a battalion commander in Boufarik, shot Saïd and Redjam in cold blood as they were making ablutions for prayer in Blida, the geographical stronghold of Zitouni's clique.[79] When rumors circulated that the two men had been killed, the GIA initially claimed that they had died fighting security forces. But in January 1996 the GIA admitted it had killed them and shifted to describing them as apostates and coup plotters.

Saïd and Redjam's murders also showed how mismanaged expansion fueled and overlapped with the growing mistrust between Zitouni and the field commanders. According to one account, Saïd and Redjam were targeted following their efforts to expand the GIA coalition by bringing in more AIS units in spring 1995. These efforts enabled a dual challenge to Zitouni: First, bringing in more AIS leaders might weaken his leadership as the coalition became more ideologically diverse; and second, Saïd and Redjam's meetings in western and central Algeria revealed mistrust of Zitouni not just within the AIS but also among at least two GIA field commanders[80] – one of whom defected later in 1995, and the second of whom was killed on Zitouni's orders.[81] After the killings, the internal purges widened to include other senior

---

[77] Gilles Kepel, *Jihad: The Trail of Political Islam*, translated by Anthony F. Roberts (Cambridge, MA: Harvard University Press, 2002), 264–266.

[78] Hassane Zerrouky, "Algérie: L'escalade meurtrière du GIA," *L'Humanité*, October 9, 1995, www.humanite.fr/node/114897.

[79] Habit Hanashi, "Al-Qissa al-Kamila l-Istishhad al-Shaykhayn Muhammad al-Sa'id wa-'Abd al-Razzaq Rajjam," Algeria Channel, February 10, 2006, www.algeriachannel.net/2008/02/القصة-الكاملة-لاستشهاد-الشيخين-محمد/.

[80] "Ali Benhadjar raconte la guerre interne au sein du GIA," Algeria Interface, December 27, 2001, https://algeria-watch.org/?p=55929.

[81] Zerrouky, "Algérie: L'escalade meurtrière du GIA."

members who were accused of either Djaz'arism, Shi'ism, or spying.[82] In late 1995, Zitouni removed the FIS leaders Madani and Belhadj from the GIA Shura Council (their presence had been symbolic, but symbols matter) and declared it licit to kill FIS leaders.[83] Threatened by the diversity of the coalition he inherited, Zitouni sought to homogenize it through violence.

The differences between Zitouni on the one hand and Saïd and Redjam on the other were not just ideological but also demographic. Saïd and Redjam, born in 1945 and 1956, respectively,[84] were significantly older than Zitouni, Zouabri, and other GIA leaders who were born in the late 1960s or the 1970s. Saïd was much closer to the outlook of the FIS' Madani (of an even older generation) than he was to that of hardliners such as Zitouni and Zouabri who were in their twenties and thirties; Saïd and Madani had known each other long before the civil war, working together in Islamist organizing since at least 1981,[85] a time when Zitouni and Zouabri were children. Saïd had personal ties to the elder statesmen of Algerian Islamism, notably Ahmed Sahnoun; and like Madani, Saïd had had a teaching career.[86] The journalist Judith Miller comments, "Secretive and elitist, Muhammad Said and his friends had only disdain for lower-class rabble rousers like Sheikh Ali Benhadj [another rendering of Belhadj]. Said, in particular, detested the young rival." Miller adds that it took Madani's personal appeal to get Saïd to join the FIS.[87] If Miller's account is correct, then Saïd may have had an even lower opinion of the chicken vendor-turned-emir, Zitouni. Geography and even ethnicity may have furthered the mistrust and enmity between Zitouni and the older men. Although Redjam was born in the capital, Saïd was from Tizi Ouzou, approximately 100 kilometers east of Algiers.[88] Saïd was, moreover,

---

[82] Other leaders were also allegedly killed on Zitouni's orders. See "Hiwar maʿa al-Shaykh ʿAsim Abi Hayan," 8, on the killing of Abu Bakr Abd al-Razzaq Zarfawi; and "GIA (Groupe islamique armé) (Armed Islamic Group)" in *The Columbia World Dictionary of Islamism*, edited by Antoine Sfeir, 45–47 (New York: Columbia University Press, 2007).

[83] "Al-Jamaʿa al-Islamiyya al-Musallaha…Tarikh wa-Haqaʾiq."

[84] Amina Qajali, *Al-Iʿlam wa-l-ʿUnf al-Siyasi* (Amman: Markaz al-Kitab al-Akadimi, 2015), 174 and 181.

[85] Ibid., 174. [86] Martinez, *Algerian Civil War*, 159, fn. 33.

[87] Judith Miller, *God Has Ninety-Nine Names: Reporting from a Militant Middle East* (New York: Touchstone/Simon and Schuster, 1996), 195.

[88] Qajali, *Al-Iʿlam wa-l-ʿUnf al-Siyasi*, 174 and 181.

ethnically Kabyle (Berber) rather than Arab.[89] In sum, the conflict
between Salafi-jihadism and Djaz'arism within the GIA encompassed
the very different profiles of the leaders of these tendencies, and the
very different things that Zitouni and Saïd offered to the rank and file.

The violence within the GIA thus reflected preexisting tensions
among coalition elements. Later GIA communications revealed that
the murders of Saïd and Redjam were part of a long rivalry between
Salafis and Djaz'arists going back to before the formation of the GIA;
there was an echo, too, of Salafis' resentment at being denied leadership of the FIS following the arrests of Madani and Belhadj in
1991 and the ensuing Djaz'arist dominance of the FIS.[90] The Salafis
who consolidated control over the GIA in 1994–1995 took revenge for
hyper-local prewar grudges, including struggles to control individual
mosques. Antar Zouabri described these bitter memories to a GIA
publication:

[The Djaz'arists] have been known for their hostility towards the Salafis since
a far-gone era, long before the jihad. They spread this accusation [that the
Salafis were Khawarij, in this context an epithet meaning non-Sunni incendi-
aries] among a number of mosques and their imams, such as the Faris
Mosque in Casbah, the Tawba Mosque in Boufarik, Al-Huda Mosque in
Blida, Al-Fath al-Mubin Mosque in El Harrach, Al-Bashir al-Ibrahimi
Mosque in Baraki, Saladin al-Ayyubi Mosque in Belkour, and others. [All
of these areas are in the vicinity of Algiers and Blida.] It was the young men
and the patrons of all these mosques who launched this jihad from the
beginning.[91]

For Zouabri, the story of the GIA was the story of young, homegrown
Salafis such as Muhammad 'Allal (Moh Leveilley) and his own slain
brother, 'Ali.[92] By the time Zitouni and Zouabri ruled the GIA, some
of the original key constituencies in the movement – Afghanistan
veterans, Bouyalists, FIS defectors, Djaz'arists, etc. – had been subordinated to young, locally radicalized hardliners from the mosque networks Zouabri came out of.

---

[89] Stone, *Agony of Algeria*, 212.   [90] Willis, *Islamist Challenge*, 270.
[91] "Hiwar ma'a Amir al-Jama'a al-Islamiyya al-Musallaha Abi Talha 'Antar
Zuwabri [Zouabri]," *Al-Jama'a* 10 (September 1996): 5–16, available at www
.algeriachannel.net/documents/gia_algeria_aljamaa_magazine_arabic_
september_1996.pdf.
[92] Al-Za'atara, "Al-'Unf al-Musallah."

Internal GIA arguments took on a highly ideological character, with Zitouni's clique accusing internal enemies of being unbelievers. These disputes filtered down through the ranks – by 1995, even the Green Battalion, out of which Zitouni and Zouabri had emerged, was a locus of fierce disputes over who was a true believer and who was not.[93] Within the battalion, Zitouni's handpicked associate began denouncing rivals to Zitouni and having them killed and arrested.[94]

GIA officials, including figures from Zitouni's inner circle, were still being killed by security forces at a rapid clip. The tide of the war had turned, as debt rescheduling and economic liberalization kicked in to benefit the regime: "this financial windfall was a trump card in the government's war strategy."[95] Meanwhile, the dissension within the GIA exposed senior members to security risks: Zitouni's key allies Muhammad Bukabus and Abu 'Adlan Rabih Ghanima, core members of the Blida clique, were killed at a checkpoint in spring 1995 while traveling to Zone 4, western Algeria, where Zitouni had appointed them as commanders following the previous zonal commander's break with the GIA central leadership.[96] The deaths, and sometimes the uncertainty over who had killed whom and why, fed an atmosphere of paranoia that in turn encouraged more internal and external violence.

Doctrinal disputes provided vehicles for genuine extremism but also cover for score-settling. Initially, the intra-Salafi loyalties forged years earlier among homegrown hardliners supplied a handhold for Zitouni and especially Zouabri – relying on those networks, they lashed out against others within the GIA, accusing opponents of Djaz'arism, an ideology the Zitouni–Zouabri clique now classified as blatant ideological deviance. Killings, however, began ricocheting in an unplanned fashion throughout the GIA, as killers (including Zitouni's and Zouabri's allies) were themselves killed.[97] The internal violence eventually claimed Zitouni's life, when fighters under a dissident field commander, Sid-Ali Benhadjar, ambushed and killed him in July 1996.

In sum, the GIA's coalition politics shifted dramatically over the course of just five years. In the early stages of the civil war, different blocs – Afghanistan veterans, Bouyalists, and homegrown Salafi hardliners – found that each constituency offered the other useful

[93] "Hiwar ma'a al-Shaykh 'Asim Abi Hayan," 19.
[94] See, for example, Al-Jaza'iri, "Tanwir al-Basa'ir," 20–21.
[95] Martinez, *Algerian Civil War*, 93.
[96] "Hiwar ma'a al-Shaykh 'Asim Abi Hayan," 22–23.   [97] Ibid., 22–23.

knowledge and expertise. The GIA's momentum even attracted, by 1994, Islamist heavyweights who were willing to subordinate themselves to Chérif Gousmi's leadership. Gousmi's death and the ensuing succession struggle, however, highlighted the tensions among these coalition blocs, particularly between the homegrown Salafi hardliners and the older, Djaz'arist leaders such as Muhammad Saïd. As the succession struggle spiraled into waves of purges and reprisals, the GIA fell apart.

The GSPC: A Field Commanders' Revolt

The contested manner of Zitouni's succession fostered major tensions between the new GIA central leadership and regional commanders. For example, the Zone 1 commander was accused of plotting to overthrow Zitouni and was killed in response.[98] Under both Zitouni and Zouabri, field commanders broke off to form splinter groups.

Here it is worth recalling Fotini Christia's explanation for why field commanders switch sides. For Christia, commanders want to win; they make and break alliances accordingly. It is debatable whether the GIA's dissident field commanders, as of 1995–1996, actually expected to win against the Algerian state. At the very least, though, the field commanders began to suspect that the GIA was doomed; if one could not win, one could still escape the death spiral the GIA had begun. The fading support within the international jihadist milieu provided another signal of how isolated the GIA central leadership was becoming.

By breaking with Zouabri, the dissidents were likely seeking to protect not just themselves but also their men. Christia writes, "Wartime commanders ... are the guardians of specific interests linked to the groups from which their men are recruited."[99] If by 1995–1996 the GIA field commanders could no longer be said to represent wide communities, they at least represented the interests of their own units. And their blocs' continued survival within the GIA was at risk. Their situation was akin to Michael Woldemariam's argument that "fragmentation is ...the preferred option for those who have survived a

[98] Ibid., 8.
[99] Fotini Christia, *Alliance Formation in Civil Wars* (New York: Cambridge University Press, 2012), 3.

power struggle, but lost it at the same time."[100] In keeping with Scott Atran's "devoted actor" framework, one can add that there is no inherent contradiction in saying that dissident field commanders were acting both pragmatically and religiously; that is, they may have been motivated both by survival interests and by pious horror at Zouabri's extremism.

The date of the GSPC's founding is commonly given as 1998, but GIA field commanders began breaking away as early as autumn 1995. Meanwhile, some accounts put the GSPC's founding as late as April 1999,[101] suggesting that it may be more accurate to view the GSPC as emergent during the period 1995–1999 rather than giving a single founding date. Reconstructing this chronology is important for avoiding the "unitary actor" fallacy and instead capturing *meso*-level shifts in GIA and GSPC coalition politics. The GSPC was not a single splinter organization but rather a new coalition comprising like-minded field commanders. The GSPC's creation was a response to fragmentation rather than a cause of it; part of the reason for taking the name GSPC in 1998 was to avoid any confusion resulting from multiple rival organizations still fighting under the GIA name.

One source says that some western battalions left the GIA in September 1995 out of disgust with Zitouni. Said Makhloufi's MEI, one of the parties to the May 1994 unity initiative, soon followed suit.[102] Another group that broke away was the Rabbaniyya Battalion, centered in Médéa Province and led by Abu Thamama 'Abd al-Qadir (1952–2004), a primary school teacher and village preacher who had been an associate of the Afghanistan veteran 'Atiyya al-Sayih.[103] In the summer of 1994, after al-Sayih's death, the Rabbaniyya Battalion joined the GIA.[104] But by late 1995/early 1996, 'Abd al-Qadir and most of the Rabbaniyya, as well as parts of the Green Battalion, broke away from Zitouni's GIA, objecting to the GIA's violence against insiders. The dissidents spent the next five years intermittently clashing

---

[100] Michael Woldemariam, *Insurgent Fragmentation in the Horn of Africa: Rebellion and Its Discontents* (Cambridge: Cambridge University Press, 2018), 49.

[101] Abu Muhammad Luqman al-Jaza'iri, "Shadha al-Nasim fi Sirat al-Qa'id Mustafa Abi Ibrahim," Ifriqiya al-Muslima, January 2017, 7, https://azelin.files .wordpress.com/2017/03/ifricc84qicc84yyah-al-muslimah-22the-series-what-makes-them-content-is-that-they-are-with-us-15-mustafa-abu-ibrahim.pdf.

[102] "Al-Jama'a al-Islamiyya al-Musallaha...Tarikh wa-Haqa'iq."

[103] Al-Jaza'iri, "Tanwir al-Basa'ir," 13–14.   [104] Ibid., 17.

with the GIA,[105] while simultaneously losing fighters and allies to the amnesty deal brokered between the Algerian government and the AIS.[106] In summer 1998, 'Abd al-Qadir's group renamed itself al-Jama'a al-Sunniyya li-l-Tabligh wa-l-Jihad, and eventually joined the GSPC in 2003.

Another group that broke with the GIA was the Islamic League for Preaching and Jihad, led by Sid-Ali Benhadjar (whose men had killed Zitouni). Officially constituted in February 1997, the League hearkened back to the FIS and Djaz'arist projects (two of its founders were former FIS parliamentarians). It proclaimed loyalty to the imprisoned FIS leaders Madani and Belhadj and invoked the memory of the slain Muhammed Saïd.[107] Field commanders displayed considerable autonomy during this period, undertaking improvised decisions at great risk.

What were the patterns in these schisms? One account relates that the GIA split into roughly four camps starting in 1996:

- "The emirship and their entourage (*al-imara wa-bitanatuha*), and with them many companies and battalions in the states of the center and west of the country."
- "Many battalions and companies among those who were far from the emirship of the group and its entourage and who were ignorant of the truth ... [but] when they knew the truth they found a connection with the reformers of the jihad (*al-muslihin li-l-jihad*)."
- "The battalions and companies close to the region of the emirship, and those people were convinced of the deviation (*ayqanu bi-l-zigh*) and rejected it, and split from the group and disavowed its name."
- Those who broke away but remained dispersed, "in the wilderness and in chaos," and who eventually accepted the government's amnesty.[108]

Meso-level actors took decisions according to the limited information they possessed, and they moved as blocs. Not just battalion commanders but also zonal emirs increasingly began to break away from the GIA.

---

[105] Ibid., 24.   [106] Ibid., 27–31.

[107] US Embassy Algiers, "New Armed Groups Joining the Old FIS?" leaked cable 97ALGIERS952, March 12, 1997, https://wikileaks.org/plusd/cables/97ALGIERS952_a.html.

[108] "Hiwar ma'a al-Shaykh 'Asim Abi Hayan," 20–21.

There was a geographical logic to some of the ruptures. There were early dissidents around Algiers and in the west, but the key breakaway commanders came mostly from zonal emirs in the east and the south – Hassan Hattab (zone 2), Mustafa Abu Ibrahim/Nabil Sahraoui (Zone 5), Abu Talha al-Janubi (zone 6), and Mokhtar Belmokhtar (zone 9). Eventually, the GSPC would draw in Zone 1 and parts of Zone 7, both in the east, as well as other battalions.[109] This eastern and southern base may have to do with geographical distance from the center and a corresponding ability to resist punishment, as well as (and here I am speculating) social networks distinct from those directly managed by Zitouni and Zouabri. Or perhaps the easterners benefited by rebelling relatively late, given that some of the rumblings of dissent began in the west and were put down while the Zitouni–Zouabri leadership still had the resources to eliminate dissidents.

According to a hagiography of Abu Ibrahim, the breakaway field commanders in the east and south initially operated without formalizing their cooperation, but in the summer of 1998 Abu Ibrahim and al-Janubi united zone 5 and zone 6 fighters under al-Janubi's leadership. Al-Janubi was soon mortally wounded in a raid, however. The unity effort then broadened at the initiative of Hattab, as well as al-Janubi's deputy Abu 'Umayr Mustafa, Mokhtar Belmokhtar, and others. This resulted in the GSPC's creation – according to this account – in April 1999.[110] The GSPC was briefly headed by Abu Mus'ab 'Abd al-Majid Dishu, who was either killed[111] or resigned,[112] after which Hattab took over.

Who were these men? In terms of age, there was little difference between most of the GSPC field commanders and the GIA's core leadership; Hattab, Abu Ibrahim, Belmokhtar, Zitouni, and Zouabri were all from the same generation. Geographically, as stated earlier, there is something of a pattern – the Zitouni–Zouabri faction's leadership included a high proportion of men from Blida and Algiers,

---

[109] Muhammad Muqaddam, "'Amir al-Jama'a al-Salafiyya' al-Jaza'iriyya Yu'akkid al-'Alaqa ma'a al-Qa'ida wa-Istimrar al-Qital Didd al-Sulta al-Jaza'iriyya," *Al-Hayat*, January 9, 2004, www.alhayat.com/article/1186250.

[110] Al-Jaza'iri, "Shadha al-Nasim," 7.   [111] Ibid., 7.

[112] Camille Tawil, "Maqtal 20 min Anasariha fi 'Amaliyyat li-l-Jaysh fi Tizi Uzu [Tizi Ouzou]," *Al-Hayat*, May 11, 1999, www.alhayat.com/article/999923/ مقتل-20-من-عناصرها-في-عمليات-للجيش-في-تيزي-وزو-الجزائر-الجماعة-السلفية-تنفي-اطاحة-حطاب-بانقلاب-nbsp.

whereas the GSPC leaders tended to come either from Algiers (Hattab
was from Rouiba, an eastern suburb of the city) or from areas further
east, such as Debdeb ('Abd al-Hamid Abu Zayd), and south, such as
Batna (Abu Ibrahim) and Ghardaïa (Belmokhtar).

One might hypothesize that the GSPC leaders tended to be somewhat less parochial than the circle around Zitouni and Zouabri –
the GSPC's leaders included men with military service (Hattab, and
the field commander Amari Saïfi who makes a longer appearance in the
next chapter); men with post-secondary degrees (Abu Ibrahim had a
degree in engineering, specializing in thermal energy,[113] while future
GSPC leader 'Abd al-Malik Droukdel had a degree in mathematics);
and men with overseas experience (Belmokhtar was an Afghanistan
veteran), or who had been close to Afghanistan veterans (Abu Ibrahim
had ties to Qari Saïd, for example).[114] Some of these men, moreover,
had been FIS members (such as Abu Ibrahim).[115] These experiences
gave them a different profile than many of the GIA hardliners whose
primary background was in mosque networks.

The GPSC leaders had also become zone commanders under
Zitouni, meaning that they were rising stars within the GIA in parallel
with him. For example, under Zitouni, Abu Ibrahim was appointed
commander for zone 5 (Batna, Oum el-Bouaghi, Tébessa, El Oued, and
Biskra).[116] Zitouni had personally appointed Hattab commander of
Zone 2.[117] They were near-peers to Zitouni in organizational terms,
and this may have disinclined them to submit to his tyranny.

Part of the reason the GSPC survived was that its leaders had the
experience and the credibility, with their own men at least, to with-
stand the dual challenge jihadists faced in the late 1990s: refocusing the
jihad on the Algerian state and not on Algerian civilians, while simultaneously attempting to talk fighters and fellow commanders out of
embracing the amnesties that the Algerian government began offering
some militants starting in 1997. And if these pressures were challenges,

[113] Al-Jaza'iri, "Shadha al-Nasim," 4–6.   [114] Ibid., 4–6.
[115] Al-Lajna al-I'lamiyya li-l-Jama'a al-Salafiyya li-l-Da'wa wa-l-Qital, "Hiwar
     ma'a Amir al-Jama'a al-Salafiyya," December 18, 2003, 2, www.cia.gov/
     library/abbottabad-compound/2D/2DF47C0A05997C12BFE19361CEE2
     5EF7_hewar_salfi.pdf.
[116] Al-Jaza'iri, "Shadha al-Nasim," 7.
[117] Camille Tawil: "Hassan Hattab: 'J'ai été forcé de prendre le maquis...',"
     Ennahar, March 15, 2009, available at www.alg24.net/hassan-hattab-jai-ete-
     force-de-prendre-le-maquis/.

they were also opportunities: The GPSC took calculated advantage of "a vacant space in the political and military landscape, given the radicalism of the GIA on the one hand and the truce declared by the AIS in October 1997."[118]

The GSPC had a further advantage: It revived some of the international support that had fled from the GIA. The GSPC's relative pragmatism was reportedly encouraged by Usama bin Laden,[119] who had been repulsed (in both senses of the word) by the GIA's leadership in the mid-1990s. By 1996, the GIA had antagonized other jihadist groups not just through its murders of Saïd and Redjam but also through its murders of a Libyan jihadist delegation and its subsequent evasiveness about the Libyans' status and whereabouts. The GIA alienated other jihadists by questioning their theological credentials. Around 1996, Zitouni wrote to Ayman al-Zawahiri (at the time a close associate of Bin Laden, though not yet his official deputy) and implied that al-Qa'ida and its jihadist peers were insufficiently committed to Salafi purity: "Regarding your relations with the other Islamic groups (non-jihadist), we think that the conditions that you pose to them hardly protect your ranks, because in this way you leave your doors wide open to groups that could subsume apostasy in their own method."[120] According to one account, one GIA emissary even vaguely threatened bin Laden, warning him not to support any other Algerian faction.[121] Bin Laden cut off his financial support to the GIA after the organization's massacres against civilians began.[122] External support appears to have followed, rather than driven, the GSPC's break with the GIA, but external support strengthened the GSPC's

---

[118] "GSPC (Group Salafite [sic] pour la Predication et le Combat) (Salafi Group for Preaching and Combat)" in *The Columbia World Dictionary of Islamism*, edited by Antoine Sfeir, 47–50 (New York: Columbia University Press, 2007), 47.

[119] 'Uthman Tizghart, "Report on History of Terrorism in Algeria," *Al-Majallah*, June 20, 1999 [inserted into FBIS June 28, 1999].

[120] Translated in Mohamed Mokeddem (Muqaddam), *Les Afghans Algériens: De la Djamaâ À la Qa'ida* (Algiers: Editions ANEP, 2002), 188. My translation here is from Mokeddem's French, because he reproduces only a fragment of the original Arabic and I have not located another copy.

[121] Interview with Abu Hafs al-Muritani, Nouakchott, April 30, 2018.

[122] Lawrence Wright, *The Looming Tower: Al-Qaeda and the Long Road to 9/11* (New York: Alfred A. Knopf, 2006), 17. According to al-Muritani (see previous note), bin Laden had been preparing to finance the GIA but never actually gave them money.

hand after the break. Once the GSPC broke away from the GIA, contact soon resumed with al-Qa'ida, paving the way for the GSPC's pledge of allegiance to al-Qa'ida in 2003 and the two groups' formal merger in 2006–2007.

Theological–Legal Vocabularies and GIA/GSPC Internal Politics

Zitouni and Zouabri responded to dissent with violence. To justify this violence, the Zitouni–Zouabri clique mobilized a theological–legal vocabulary that foregrounded issues of belief and unbelief. At its harshest, this vocabulary performed, simultaneously, the acts of deciding a person's status and deciding their fate. One GIA slogan was "no dialogue, no truce, no reconciliation, and no contract of protected non-Muslim status with the apostates (*la hiwar wa-la hudna wa-la musalaha wa-la 'aqd dhimma ma'a al-murtaddin*)."[123] Here the reference is to the Algerian authorities, deemed unbelievers whose blood could be shed – but the same logic was extended to external rivals and internal enemies.

The GIA claimed the right to legislate for all of Algeria. In his manifesto *Hiyadat Rabb al-'Alamin fi Tabyin Usul al-Salafiyyin wa-ma Yajib min al-'Ahd 'ala al-Mujahidin* (Guidance from the Lord of the Worlds in Explaining the Principles of the Salafis and What Commitment is Obligatory for the Mujahidin), Zitouni wrote, "The Armed Islamic Group considers Algeria a composite abode (*dar murakkaba*) with the two meanings present in it: for it is an abode of war and an abode of Islam (*fa-hiya dar harb wa-dar Islam*). People in it are dealt with according to their Islam or their unbelief and their loyalty or their disavowal."[124] Invoking and transforming classical vocabularies about what was considered a Muslim zone, Zitouni and Zouabri made Salafi creed and jihadist commitment the yardstick for all Algerians' status.

The language of unbelief figured prominently in the GIA's admission of responsibility for the killings of Saïd and Redjam. The writers invoked extremes of guidance and error:

---

[123] "Hiwar ma'a Amir al-Jama'a al-Islamiyya al-Musallaha," 17.
[124] Abu 'Abd al-Rahman Amin [Djamel Zitouni], *Hidayat Rabb al-'Alamin fi Tabyin Usul al-Salafiyyin wa-ma Yajib min al-'Ahd 'ala al-Mujahidin* (self-published, 1996), 8.

Following the sects that leave the Divine Law leads to discords (*fitan*) and deviation from the straight path of guidance ... just as agreeing with the people of blameworthy innovations and vapid opinions leads to opposing the people of the Prophetic model and going outside of the approach of the Prophet, may God bless him and grant him peace.[125]

Having framed the discussion thusly, the GIA depicted the Djaz'arists as deviants:

Among these blameworthy innovationist sects (*al-tawa'if al-mubtadi'a*) whose evil and harm are coming to an end is the Djaz'ara sect, or what has been called the "Students" organization. This organization had penetrated the ranks of the Armed Islamic Group (*qad ikhtaraqa sufuf al-jama'a*) ... and it tried to reach the leadership of [the group] and to take possession of it (*wa-hawala al-wusul ila qiyadatiha wa-ihtiwa'iha*) after the union [in May 1994] ... And when God Most High did not empower them to do that, and their affair came to light and their scheme came to light, they caused a schism in the Group and divided the mujahidin with the argument that the emir of the Armed Islamic Group had begun oppressing and wronging people and spilling blood with no right – according to their claim. And they decided to leave the Group.[126]

Here one can observe the rhetorical transformation of political questions – who would lead the GIA? – into theological–legal issues, even as the authors implicitly denied the political nature of the issues at stake, insisting that they had the singularly correct understanding of the "straight path of guidance" and "approach of the Prophet."

The GIA went on to say that breaking an oath of allegiance to the Group's imam was impermissible in Islamic law, and that the GIA had tired of the repeated attempts by the FIS and the Djazarists to "change the Group's Salafi approach to their heretical approach (*manhajihim al-bid'i*).[127] In light of all these events, the GIA continued, it had become necessary to kill Saïd, who "had not repented of his blameworthy innovations, his approach, and his errant organization" as well as Redjam, who while speaking in the name of the GIA had spread "unbelief" and an "errant approach." Others close to Saïd and Redjam

---

[125] Al-Jama'a al-Islamiyya al-Musallaha [GIA], "Al-Sawa'iq al-Hariqa fi Bayan Hukm al-Jaz'ara al-Mariqa," *Majallat al-Ansar* 131 (January 1996): 11–15, 11.
[126] Ibid., 12.   [127] Ibid., 12.

had been killed for "apostasy," "blameworthy innovations," and "errors."[128] This document, signed by Zitouni in January 1996, was not just a theological–legal tract but also a political assertion of his authority – as well as a milestone in the fusion of military–political and theological–legal roles in a single individual. The paradigm of internal relations that I have called *tyranny* encourages just such an intensification of the leader's claims to power; in general, more accommodating organizations make a formal separation between military–political and clerical roles.

There are multiple plausible explanations for why the GIA adopted this kind of rhetoric, and these explanations are not mutually exclusive. First, one might simply say that Zitouni and Zouabri were ideologically committed Salafi-jihadists who killed coalition partners out of belief. Yet Zitouni and Zouabri had been willing to coexist in a coalition with the Djaz'ara just months before the murders. To explain this shift, Zouabri had to insist that the Djaz'ara had misled the GIA, and that there had been a temporary ideological truce between Salafi-jihadist hardliners and Djaz'arists until the latter showed their true colors:

After all the doors were closed in their faces, they entered the Armed Islamic Group out of necessity, with the aim of reaching their polytheistic goals. They thought that the Group was a door to victory for them, so they fell silent about casting this suspicion [of being Khawarij, i.e. fanatics] on us while they were in our ranks. When our brothers discovered their scheme and killed their leaders, they left the Group.[129]

Even Zouabri had to acknowledge that a form of politics had unfolded within the GIA, a politics that had complicated (at least initially) the question of how ideology should be applied.

Second, Mohammed Hafez has argued that "rebel fratricide" is driven by multiple factions competing for the allegiances of the same broad constituency. "Ideologically extreme factions" are most prone to use violence to resolve the competition, while more centrist factions "opt for strategies that fall short of aggressively killing their rivals."[130]

---

[128] Ibid., 13.   [129] "Hiwar ma'a Amir al-Jama'a al-Islamiyya al-Musallaha," 6.
[130] Mohammed Hafez, "Fratricidal Rebels: Ideological Extremity and Warring Factionalism in Civil Wars," *Terrorism and Political Violence* (online version, 2017), 2.

One might modify this to say that the GIA's case is not necessarily fratricide in the sense of horizontally directed violence but rather violence directed downward from the leadership against subordinates; under this view the violence was partly the product of a mismatch between a hardline leadership and more accommodating field commanders and representatives of internal factions.

Third, one might say that professing a commitment to uncompromising Salafi-jihadism became a way for GIA leaders and fighters to try to forge loyalty and cohesion within the group, to transform it from a heterogeneous coalition into a homogeneous formation. This homogenizing project, however, quickly generated new forms of internal fragmentation, demonstrating that no jihadist coalition can ever function as a genuinely unitary actor. I think the violence was a result of all three of these factors; but in any case, for the GIA faction led by Zitouni and Zouabri – whether they were operating out of conviction or out of hunger for control – Salafi-jihadist ideology became a sword used against all dissent within the group or outside it.

It is no surprise, then, that those who broke away to form the GSPC became progressively more averse to disputes framed in the language of creed (see Chapter 2 as well). In its own rhetoric, the GSPC would primarily use the language of unbelief when speaking of states, and would only accuse other jihadists of deviance when speaking of the GIA itself. Yet the GSPC also worked to preserve its own theological credibility in an atmosphere suffused with competition to claim the mantle of Salafi purity.

In its founding charter, the GSPC dealt carefully with issues of creed and *takfir*. After endorsing core Salafi theological and methodological positions, such as the idea that Islam had to be understood according to the (purported) understanding of the first three generations of Muslims, the GSPC turned to more sensitive issues. It is worth quoting several points from the charter:

> Tenth: We do not declare a Muslim an unbeliever due to any major or minor sin unless he declares it lawful, and the blood and money of Muslims are safeguarded.
>
> Eleventh: Whoever falls into unbelief is not an unbeliever merely because of that, until proof is established against him. For *takfir* has conditions and contra-indications (*idh al-takfir lahu shurut*

wa-mawani'), as the imams of the community, and at their forefront Shaykh al-Islam [Ibn Taymiyya], may God have mercy on
him, have decided.[131]

The GSPC charter was silent on the subject of the GIA, but it alluded to
the GIA's extremism in *takfir*:

> Thirteenth: We take refuge in God from the opinion and thinking of
> the Khawarij, who declare Muslims unbelievers and declare their
> blood and their wealth to be legal, with no right. Those apostate
> Khawarij have taken the same view as the Takfir and Hijra Group
> [in Egypt], who declare Muslims unbelievers in general and in
> particular (*wa-qad wafaqa ha'ula'i al-khawarij al-mariqin jama'at
> al-takfir wa-l-hijra, alladhina yukaffiruna al-muslimin jumla wa-
> tafsil*). They have strayed from the path.[132]

As seen earlier, the charge of "Kharijism" or being "Khawarij" was
repeatedly hurled at the GIA – as, indeed, the charge has been thrown
at many jihadists and even non-jihadist Muslim activists by their
opponents.[133] Now it was the GSPC making the same charge. The
comparison to Takfir and Hijra was meant to reinforce this charge:
even many Salafi-jihadists considered Takfir and Hijra to lie outside
the jihadist mainstream, and there were recurring allegations that the
Algerian iteration of Takfir and Hijra had gained Zitouni's ear and
driven some of the GIA's purges. In the GSPC's charter, theological
statements transmitted political positions as well, through acts of
labeling and differentiation that sought to decenter the GIA's claims
to purity.

The GPSC, however, took care to avoid being seen by other jihadists
or by potential recruits as soft on issues of faith and unbelief. In the
charter, the GSPC explicitly rejected "Murji'ism," a theological school
that advocates postponing judgment about an individual Muslim's
faith. If Kharijism is a charge used to denounce other militants as too

---

[131] Al-Jama'a al-Salafiyya li-l-Da'wa wa-l-Qital [GSPC], "Mithaq al-Jama'a al-
Salafiyya li-l-Da'wa wa-l-Qital," undated, 6, available at http://somalimidnimo
.com/audio/balantii_jamaacada_salafiyiinta_ee_dacwada_iyo_jihaadka_ay_
ku_galeen1.pdf.

[132] Ibid., 6.

[133] On the general phenomenon of accusations of Kharijism, see Jeffrey Kenney,
Muslim Rebels: Kharijites and the Politics of Extremism in Egypt (New York:
Oxford University Press, 2006).

extreme, then Murji'ism is a charge used to denounce other militants as too permissive.[134] The GSPC positioned themselves as a middle path between Kharijism and murji'ism. They stressed their continued commitment to violence: "Fighting apostates is prioritized over fighting others among those who have always been unbelievers (*qital al-murtaddin muqaddam 'ala qital ghayrihim min al-kuffar al-asliyyin*)."[135] A politics of seeking authenticity suffused the charter, a politics largely aimed at the rank and file militants now increasingly hesitating between the GIA's vestigial image as the bannermen of the true "jihad," the appeal of government amnesties and the AIS' accommodationism, and the GSPC's bid to reform the jihadist project.

The GSPC's more accommodating views on *takfir* may have helped it to attract defectors not only from the GIA but also from the armed wing of the FIS, particularly FIS/AIS fighters who rejected the ceasefires and amnesty of the late 1990s. According to one report, the GSPC grew from around 700 fighters at their founding to as many as 3,000 less than a year later, primarily because of these dual streams of defectors. The GSPC also attracted recruits because of its emphasis on renewing the fight against military installations.[136]

Even as the GSPC competed with the GIA, the GSPC largely avoided mentioning their former comrades – an essentially political decision, given that theological imperatives would arguably necessitate a more full-throated denunciation of "deviation." When discussing the GIA later, figures such as Belmokhtar were uncomplimentary but terse. Belmokhtar later said

After the killing of the Group's emir, Abu 'Abd al-Rahman Amin [Djamel Zitouni, in 1996], may God have mercy on him, and the appearance of the deviation in the operational approach of the Group (*zuhur al-inhiraf fi manhaj al-jama'a al-'amali*), we decided to cease our allegiance to the emirate of the Group along with our adoption of the moniker of the "Armed Islamic Group," after we had offered them suggestions and an explanation.[137]

---

[134] For a discussion of how different Salafis, Islamists, and jihadists have discussed murji'ism, see Daniel Lav, *Radical Islam and the Revival of Medieval Theology* (New York: Cambridge University Press, 2012).

[135] Al-Jama'a al-Salafiyya li-l-Da'wa wa-l-Qital, "Mithaq," 6.

[136] Tizghart, "Report."   [137] "Hiwar ma'a al-Qa'id Khalid Abi al-'Abbas."

The choice of words was careful: Belmokhtar sought, first, not to inadvertently undermine his own credentials by dating the "deviation" to the time of Zitouni, when Belmokhtar and others were still fighting under the GIA. Second, Belmokhtar did not say "the appearance of unbelief," but rather implied that Zouabri had deviated more in strategic terms than in creedal ones. Belmokhtar, it seemed, wanted to condemn the GIA but without pronouncing a form of *takfir* against them. The closest GSPC leaders came to pronouncing *takfir* was in discussing the massacres of Algerian villagers in the late 1990s, which Abu Ibrahim called "horrible crimes that no Muslim who testifies 'There is no god but God and Muhammad is the Messenger of God' would accept." Abu Ibrahim, however, went on to assert that almost all of the massacres were committed by regime forces.[138] Elsewhere, Abu Ibrahim even called the GSPC "an extension of the Armed Islamic Group, committed to its approach before the aberration and deviation (*al-zaygh wa-l-inhiraf*)."[139] As with Zouabri's politicized narratives about the Djaz'ara, asserting control over the historical narrative was a key form of jihadist politics: GSPC politics involved trying to tell a plausible story about the GIA that would condemn Zouabri without implicating the GSPC in that very condemnation.

Other GSPC/AQIM leaders would later reflect on the GIA in similar terms. One AQIM official used the same term, "deviation (*inhiraf*)," to discuss the GIA's leadership. He acknowledged that the diversity of opinions within the GIA contributed to its internal power struggles. But he attributed the "deviation" primarily to what he called the GIA leaders' shortcomings – "conceit and arrogance," as well as "ignorance of morals of disagreement (*jahl bi-adab al-khilaf*)."[140] Another AQIM leader named Hisham Abu Akram, in a 2015 document, again used the word "deviation" to describe what happened to the GIA – and to exonerate those who broke away to form the GIA:

By the grace of God and His mercy for the Algerian jihad, the deviation was limited to only the circle of those found in the leadership of the Group, whereas the leaders of most of the regions avoided that deviation and announced their withdrawal and their disavowal of that errant leadership

---

[138] Muqaddam, "'Amir al-Jama'a al-Salafiyya' al-Jaza'iriyya."
[139] Al-Lajna al-I'lamiyya li-l-Jama'a al-Salafiyya li-l-Da'wa wa-l-Qital, "Hiwar ma'a Amir al-Jama'a al-Salafiyya."
[140] "Hiwar ma'a al-Shaykh 'Asim Abi Hayan," 5.

that opposed the method of the Truth. Then their effort bore fruit in the unifying of the ranks under the banner of the Salafi Group for Preaching and Combat.[141]

Abu Akram undertook the same balancing act that Belmokhtar did when discussing the GIA. Abu Akram went so far as to call the slain Djaz'arist leader Muhammad Saïd a "martyr" (implicitly rebuking not just Zouabri, but also Zitouni). For Abu Akram, the GIA's high point was embodied not in Zitouni but in Chérif Gousmi.[142] Abu Akram spelled out the devastating political consequences that followed the GIA leadership's behavior after Gousmi's death. He noted that many GIA field commanders and units were immune to the "deviation" and that some ordinary Algerian Muslims continued to differentiate between mujahidin they trusted and the GIA's most brutal extremists. Nevertheless, he said,

Since the deviation occurred at the top of the command pyramid, and the role of the command is very important, their effect on the jihad was very big. They completely destroyed tourism to the point that the tyrants regained their strength because of their actions at a time when they were about to fall ... Regarding the people's distinguishing between the people of excess and other Mujahideen, we can conclude with certainly that the crimes of the extremists, their mischief and their corruption had an impact on public sympathy with and their support for the Mujahideen. Support greatly receded. In fact, some sects joined the tyrants and carried arms to fight the Mujahideen. They did not differentiate between a true and committed Mujahid and a mischievous and criminal outsider. For them, they have all become identical.[143]

Even here, however, Abu Akram – like Belmokhtar – did not refer to Zouabri and his core followers as unbelievers, but rather used the language of "deviation," "excess," and "extremism." Within the

---

[141] Abu Akram Hisham, "Al-Shaykh Abu Muhammad al-Yamani: Rihlatuhu ila al-Jaza'ir wa-Qissat Istishhadihi," Ifriqiya al-Muslima, December 2015, 3, https://azelin.files.wordpress.com/2016/03/abucc84-akram-hishacc84m-e2809cmessages-from-the-mujacc84hid_s-notebook-2-shaykh-abucc84-muhcca3ammad-al-yamanicc84-his-trip-to-algeria-and-the-story-of-his-martyrdom22.pdf.

[142] "Exclusive Interview with Shaykh al-Mujahid Hisham Abu Akram," *Al-Risalah*, January 2017, 3, https://azelin.files.wordpress.com/2017/01/al-risacc84lah-media-22exclusive-interview-with-al-qacc84_idah-in-the-islamic-maghribs-shaykh-hishacc84m-abucc84-akram22.pdf.

[143] Ibid., 4.

GSPC, meanwhile, internal conflicts continued – but now they would be framed as divisions over strategy and decision-making, rather than as issues of belief and unbelief.

Conclusion

The GIA was one of the most complex jihadist coalitions ever assembled, and for a time one of the most successful. Yet the distinct blocs within the coalition – the Afghanistan veterans, the Bouyalist militants, and the local hardliners, as well as Djaz'arist and ex-FIS figures who joined later – clashed bitterly. Rapid leadership turnover destabilized the GIA's internal politics, and preexisting tensions reared their heads soon after the coalition reached its largest point.

The GIA's most hardline leaders, Djamel Zitouni and Antar Zouabri, attempted to discipline and homogenize the coalition through tyranny and internal violence. Amid purges, these emirs advanced an uncompromising theological–legal vocabulary that tarred all dissenters and rivals as unbelievers who deserved death. The internal violence proved so destabilizing that the Zitouni–Zouabri faction suffered a disparate but widespread revolt by field commanders, many of whom eventually united to form the GSPC as a formal schism. The GSPC put forth an alternative theological–legal vocabulary that still cast the Algerian state as unbelieving tyrants, but that softened the application of unbelief against other Algerians, even the remnants of the GIA.

2 | The GSPC/AQIM
Schism, Coup, and a Broken Triangle in the Sahara

As the previous chapter discussed, the Salafi Group for Preaching and Combat (French acronym GSPC) originated as a field commanders' revolt against the central leadership of the Armed Islamic Group (French acronym GIA). The GSPC was significantly smaller than the GIA at its peak but was more cohesive. It was this very cohesion, as well as the formalization and empowerment of bureaucratic structures within the organization, which allowed the bulk of the GSPC leadership to mount a coup against their leader – a former regional field commander himself – in 2003. The GSPC rebranded as al-Qa'ida in the Islamic Maghreb (AQIM) in 2007.

Nevertheless, the organization remained at heart a coalition of field commanders, some of them quite independent-minded. If bureaucratization facilitated a smoothly executed coup at the top, it did not allow for the total enforcement of superiors' dictates to subordinates. The GSPC's decentralized character persisted despite repeated centralizing efforts. This was partly due to internal cuture: The group's founders, in their prior roles under the GIA, had learned to fear "deviation . . . at the top of the command pyramid."[1] Geography also made the GSPC's own field commanders prone to assert independence. In the early 2000s, the GSPC made a growing investment in its deep Saharan activities, adding a new dimension to coalition politics. Saharan field commanders repeatedly bucked the authority of the central leadership based in northern Algeria. The GSPC evolved into a coalition of far-flung political–military units, rather than the kind of mass movement that the GIA had originally aspired to become.[2]

---

[1] "Exclusive Interview with Shaykh al-Mujahid Hisham Abu Akram," *Al-Risalah*, January 2017, 4, https://azelin.files.wordpress.com/2017/01/al-risacc84lah-media-22exclusive-interview-with-al-qacc84_idah-in-the-islamic-maghribs-shaykh-hishacc84m-abucc84-akram22.pdf.

[2] For one important treatment of internal GSPC/AQIM conflicts, see Adib Bencherif, "From Resilience to Fragmentation: Al Qaeda in the Islamic Maghreb

Theoretical Implications of the Case

The GSPC case allows for a study of how varying levels of trust, cohesion, and alliance at the horizontal and vertical levels can produce different outcomes: In the latter half of the 1990s, the GIA was simply too riven with mistrust and division for dissident field commanders to feel that they had a chance at reorienting the organization, and so they left; in contrast, in the early 2000s the GSPC field commanders and top personnel had sufficient confidence in each other and in the organization that they could simply remove the top leader and carry on.

The example of the GSPC's jihadist coup parallels Naunihal Singh's observation that with military coups, "coups from the top" are successful more often than coups spearheaded by lower-ranking officers. Singh adds that coups from the top "are likely to be shorter and less bloody." Senior officers often know and trust one another, and "can use their bureaucratic prerogatives to lay considerable groundwork for a coup before they strike."[3] The comparison has limits, of course: The GSPC resembled a standing military to the extent that it was relatively cohesive and bureaucratized by the time the coup occurred in 2003, although the GSPC did not resemble a standing army in the sense that the GSPC's cohesion at the top was not matched by integration of all field commanders into a disciplined hierarchy.

The GSPC's next iteration, as AQIM, affords an opportunity to study the type of internal political pattern that I call the *broken triangle*. In this metaphor, the vertices of the triangle are a superior and two subordinates, in this case a jihadist emir and two field commanders. A triangle can be broken on just one side, indicating either tension between the emir and one of his subordinates, or tension between the two subordinates that does not involve the emir. In the case of AQIM, we have a triangle with two broken sides, a formation where the emir aligned with one field commander against another. Broken triangles can be produced by multiple factors; in this case, the

and Jihadist Group Modularity," *Terrorism and Political Violence*, published online August 2017. Here my contribution is to delve more deeply into both the coalition politics and the theological–legal vocabularies the group used in these conflicts.
[3] Naunihal Singh, *Seizing Power: The Strategic Logic of Military Coups* (Baltimore: Johns Hopkins University Press, 2014), 79–80.

breaks reflected geographical distance, disputes over resource allocation, tensions over strategy, and personality conflicts.

A notable feature of broken triangles is that they can persist for a
surprisingly long time – in the case of AQIM, for at least five years. By
definition, the broken triangle falls short of more dramatic scenarios
such as schism, fratricide, or assassination; the broken triangle hangs
by a thread, but can hang for a long time as actors seek to avoid a total
rupture. The endemic tensions can influence the trajectory of the
organization as a whole, including through repeated attempts by the
central leadership to discipline (but not alienate) the wayward field
commander, as well as through the direct and indirect effects of rivalry
between field commanders.

The broken triangle within AQIM was ultimately a remarkably
stable structure. In a sense it survived even the ultimate break in the
relationship. Eventually, the dissident field commander struck out on
his own – but then returned to the fold within three years. Indeed, the
persistence and flexibility of the broken triangle and the eventual
reconciliation reflect lessons that GSPC/AQIM figures learned from
their prior experience in the GIA; the GSPC/AQIM leadership repeatedly opted for accommodation (even of schisms) rather than tyranny.

At the theological–legal level, even within the broken triangle, the
different players hewed to an unwritten rule that *takfir* (declarations of
excommunication) would not be used in internal debates. In 2011, the
Mauritanian news outlet Agence Nouakchott d'Information (ANI)
interviewed the AQIM field commander Mokhtar Belmokhtar
(1972–2016?), the focal point of tension within the broken triangle.
Among other topics, the interview covered internal disagreements
within the organization:

ANI: It is said that after you, personally, separated yourself from
the Saharan emirate [of AQIM] and after it was
entrusted to its present emir, Yahya Abu 'Ammar, a
conflict (*khilaf*) broke out between you on one side,
and Abu 'Ammar and 'Abd al-Hamid Abu Zayd
[another Sahara-based AQIM field commander] on
the other side.

Belmokhtar: As you know, a dispute can take the form of contradiction
(*'ala wajh al-tadadd*) or it can take the form of diversity (*'ala wajh al-tanawwu'*). All of this goes back to
the difference in conceptions and how each person

understands them according to his experience and the
conditions that surround his activities, and the manner
of engaging with different events and stances. And the
dispute that you mentioned does not go beyond being
one of diversity. In it our rule is morals, and good
Islamic manners, and mutual respect without defam-
ation and speaking evil of others, as is the case with
people of empty opinions and ugly politics (*ahl al-
ahwa' wa-l-siyasat al-khabitha*). And this type of dispute, whose guiding precept is the orthodox law,
occurred even in the time of Abu Bakr and 'Umar [the
first two Caliphs], and they were the most eminent of
the Companions in dealing with the contentious legal
issues of that age (*huma ashraf al-sahaba fi al-ta'amul
ma'a nawazil dhalika al-'asr*).[4]

These words may sound like a dodge. But Belmokhtar's answer reflects
a keen desire on the part of multiple voices within AQIM to keep intra-
jihadist disagreements within the bounds of political and strategic,
rather than creedal, difference.

Perhaps even more surprisingly, AQIM's internal difficulties did not
prevent it from achieving a significant degree of success in rebuilding.
The GSPC's schism with the GIA, as well as the overall trajectory of
Algerian conflict and politics in the late 1990s, left both the GSPC and
the GIA in a position of *marginalization*. Subsequent events allowed
the GSPC to reposition itself. The GSPC's repositioning involved a
twin strategy of *relocation* and *accommodation*; relocation into the
Sahara, and accommodation of the business, tribal/ethnic, and political
interests that the GSPC (and then AQIM) encountered, especially in
northern Mali. These political deals were more complex, it should be
noted, than the so-called crime-terror nexus that figures in some super-
ficial analyses of AQIM.[5]

[4] "Amir 'Katibat al-Mulaththamin' Khalid Abu al-'Abbas fi Muqabala Muthira
ma'a 'Akhbar Nuwakshut'," Agence Nouakchott d'Information, November 9,
2011, https://azelin.files.wordpress.com/2011/11/khc481lid-abc5ab-al-
abbc481s-mukhtc481r-bin-mue1b8a5ammad-bilmukhtc481r-interview-with-
nouakchott-news-ar.pdf.
[5] Richard Chelin, "From the Islamic State of Algeria to the Economic Caliphate of
the Sahel: The Transformation of Al Qaeda in the Islamic Maghreb," *Terrorism
and Political Violence*, published online June 7, 2018.

The central leadership seemed to bless field commanders' dealmaking, yet that central leadership, still ensconced in northern Algeria, left much of the execution of the approach to field commanders – a decision that positioned field commanders as powerful voices within the organization and that allowed field commanders to construct locally situated political and economic networks. External accommodation mirrored a degree of internal accommodation.

Field commanders benefited substantially from their formal anathematization as they generated these patterns of accommodation. Even as the Francophone press decried one GSPC/AQIM figure after another as the "Bin Laden of the Sahara," the field commanders took on leading roles in political and economic networks – particularly the Saharan kidnapping economy that flourished from 2008 to 2012 – that connected them directly or indirectly to crucial figures at the local and national levels, from criminals to heads of state. If certain rumors and reports are to be believed, moreover, some of the same heads of state who held up the jihadist threat as a means of securing massive counterterrorism assistance from the West were simultaneously benefiting from the kidnapping economy itself. Local politicians, meanwhile, found that having allies and partners in the shadows could produce multiple political and economic benefits, including by leveraging those alliances to affect the balance of their own rivalries with other politicians.

In a fundamental way, AQIM's approach tests the coherence of the jihadist project. As Belmokhtar's answer in the previous extract shows, after Algerian jihadists pulled back from a politics of mutual recrimination and violence, they worked to confine differences of opinion to the level of strategy, viewpoint, and perspective. Yet if differences are merely "diversity," how can that diversity be managed and adjudicated without sacrificing the jihadist claim to be the sole representatives of a pure Islam?

Indeed, the diversity tells us something about the limits of jihadism as a form of politics. In accommodating contradictory approaches to jihadism while insisting on broad unity, AQIM unwittingly demonstrated that none of those approaches offered a particularly promising path to the group's stated objective of overthrowing regimes and installing jihadist governance across northwest Africa. If jihadists can never achieve that objective, then any given approach – conducting spectacular attacks, using kidnappings to make political statements and demands, temporarily seizing territory, slowly building popular support, or imposing harsh visions of shari'a – are all both equally enticing and equally futile. AQIM's internal politics revolve partly around refusing to acknowledge the elephant in the room, namely the ultimate impossibility of their overall project. In the shadow of that elephant, the group's internal politics have much to do with the ways that different leaders both see the weaknesses in each other's approaches but also find continued need of each other.

From GSPC to AQIM: Coalition Politics, Internal Structures, and Clerical Authority

Chapter 1 discussed the formation of the GSPC between 1995 and 1999 as a field commanders' revolt within the GIA. After the death of two early movers in the GSPC initiative, a field commander named Hassan Hattab became the group's emir. As one of four zonal commanders and several other prominent field commanders who formed the GSPC,[6] Hattab appears to have been something like first among equals, with less than absolute authority over men who had very recently been his peers.

A fault line developed within the GSPC over the question of formally joining al-Qa'ida, with Hattab on the skeptical side. His opponents have been vocal about the split in contrast to Hattab's relative discretion about it. One of Hassan's critics writes that "signs of defeatism (*'alamat al-inhizam*) had appeared in him for a while, especially after the events of September 11."[7] After leaving the GSPC in 2003, seemingly involuntarily, Hattab eventually surrendered to Algerian authorities. Since then, he has lived under heavy surveillance, working with the authorities on efforts to convince other jihadists to surrender.[8]

In vague comments made after his surrender, and perhaps using remarks vetted by authorities, Hattab said that as the GSPC's emir,

[6] Abu Rabbab Luqman Mustafa al-Qasrawi, "Safahat Matwiyya min Sirat al-Qa'id al-Sayih 'Attiya," Ifriqiya al-Muslimah, December 2016, 7, https://azelin .files.wordpress.com/2017/03/ifricc84qicc84yyah-al-muslimah-22the-series- what-makes-them-content-is-that-they-are-with-us-14-atiyah.pdf.
[7] 'Abd al-Malik Droukdel, "Bara'a min Af'al 'Hasan Hattab'," Minbar al-Tawhid wa-l-Jihad, February 10, 2005, www.ilmway.com/site/maqdis/MS_1664.html.
[8] Farid Alilat, "Algérie: qu'est devenu Hassan Hattab, le fondateur du GSPC?" *Jeune Afrique*, March 4, 2014, www.jeuneafrique.com/134366/politique/alg-rie- qu-est-devenu-hassan-hattab-le-fondateur-du-gspc/.

he had "categorically refused to join the al-Qaʻida organization." He suggested that his reasons were largely strategic. He was concerned that the move "would bring huge problems including suicide operations, which I reject, the tarnishing of the image of the exegetes among the youth, as well as the kidnapping of foreigners which harms the national interest and invites the interference of foreign countries."[9] The GSPC/AQIM denounced Hattab's surrender in very harsh terms, as a "betrayal of God and His Messenger" and as "selling the blood of the martyrs," but stopped short of pronouncing *takfir* against him.[10]

In the period 1999–2003, Hattab's debate partners included some of the key field commanders who had helped set up the GSPC. One was Mustafa Abu Ibrahim or Nabil Sahrawi (1966–2004), another was Mokhtar Belmokhtar, and a third was ʻAbd al-Malik Droukdel, also known as Abu Musʻab ʻAbd al-Wadud (b. 1970). After Hattab was sidelined, Abu Ibrahim briefly succeeded Hattab until his own death in battle, whereupon Droukdel became the GSPC's emir and has remained the leader up to the time of writing.

The GSPC's internal debate over affiliating with al-Qaʻida has often been analyzed as an ideological or strategic dispute rather than in terms of coalition politics.[11] Hattab's role, when discussed, is seen as that of an individual who was hesitant about globalizing the Algerian conflict. But there was a political structure to the internal divisions and to the eventual coup. For one thing, there was a political rivalry between Hattab and Abu Ibrahim. The rivalry reflected the structure and history of the GSPC. Hattab had arguably been less important to the GSPC's creation than Abu Ibrahim. According to one account, the nucleus of the GSPC's coalition was an agreement between Abu Ibrahim, then the GIA's Zone 5 commander, and his counterpart in Zone 6; Hattab only joined later. Hattab seems to have recognized the political importance of giving Abu Ibrahim key positions within the early GSPC, first assigning him a military command, then placing him

[9] Mustapha Ferhat and Zineb A., "Hassan Hattab: Il n'y a pas de Qaida en Algérie," *Echorouk*, July 6, 2009, https://algeria-watch.org/?p=26673.

[10] Droukdel, "Baraʾa."

[11] For another analysis, see Pierre Pahlavi and Jérôme Lacroix Leclair, "L'institutionnalisation d'AQMI dans la nébuleuse Al-Qaida," *Les Champs de Mars* 24:2 (2012): 9–28. Their analysis, I think, overemphasizes Afghanistan veterans' roles in the GSPC's affiliation to al-Qaʻida, and oversimplifies Belmokhtar's role.

in charge of external relations, then asking him to reorganize and reinvigorate the jihadists in Zone 2, and finally appointing him head of the newly constituted Council of Notables (Majlis al-A'yan).[12]

Interestingly, the same account says that the Council of Notables was intended to "correct disequilibrium and prevent pitfalls," a reaction to the GIA experience. Politically, however, the Council mobilized against Hattab; after Hattab either resigned or was expelled, the Council designated Abu Ibrahim as the new GSPC emir.[13] Droukdel states that Hattab resigned at a summer 2003 Council meeting and was immediately replaced by Abu Ibrahim.[14] The coup against Hattab was organized by the very structures meant to ensure that the organization ran smoothly; it was, to borrow military phraseology, a senior officers' coup and as such it followed the pattern alluded to by Singh – methodical and bloodless. On September 11, 2003, the GSPC pledged allegiance to al-Qa'ida.[15]

Alongside the rivalry between Hattab and Abu Ibrahim, there was another political dynamic that has appeared in multiple jihadist groups: the question of pledging allegiance to an external jihadist actor. This decision can have different ramifications depending on where one sits in an organization's hierarchy. In contrast to prevailing wisdom that affiliating with a global actor boosts the fortunes of an entire organization, my own view is that for the top leader of a local or national organization, the advantages of new material and resources may actually be outweighed by fears of losing power and prestige. For secondary figures in an organization, however, cultivating transnational ties can boost their status both internally and externally. Belmokhtar, for example, personally shepherded the extended visit of an al-Qa'ida envoy to Niger, Mali, and Algeria in 2000–2001; the exercise ended badly in that the envoy was killed in battle with the Algerian security forces, but the episode reinforced Belmokhtar's status as an intermediary between al-Qa'ida and the GSPC (he does not seem to have been blamed for the envoy's death). The coup against Hattab was thus not only about the GSPC's interests as a corporate entity; it

---

[12] Al-Qasrawi, "Safahat Matwiyya," 7–8.   [13] Ibid.
[14] Droukdel, "Bara'a."
[15] "Algerian Extremists Pledge Allegiance to Al Qaeda," AFP, October 22, 2003, www.abc.net.au/news/2003-10-23/algerian-extremists-pledge-allegiance-to-al-qaeda/1497716.

also served the ambitions of particular field commanders, who could leverage their own ties to external actors to boost their own positions.

The pro-al-Qaʻida GSPC leaders may also have been responding to the mood of the rank and file. Barak Mendelsohn writes that the GSPC's "jump on the al-Qaeda bandwagon appears to have been motivated primarily by organizational interest – above all, fear for the group's survival."[16] Hattab, who admittedly had reasons to be jaded, later described the decision in these terms. In a 2009 interview, Hattab commented, "The affiliation of the GSPC to al-Qaʻida was done to save face and lift the troops' morale because, frankly, the Salafi Group had lost its legitimacy and credibility following my departure. By announcing the affiliation, the GSPC threw itself in a way into the arms of al-Qaʻida to keep within the Group the elements that were beset with doubt."[17] This statement is self-aggrandizing, but it may also give insight into the GSPC's internal dynamics before and after Hattab's departure. The GSPC had been struggling to talk fighters out of surrendering even before its own top leader accepted the government's amnesty offer (in the interview, Hattab says he began negotiating with the regime in 2003). Affiliating with al-Qaʻida may have been a way to signal to the rank and file not just that the GSPC had international jihadist credibility but also that now there was no turning back. Hattab's successors attempted a careful balancing act during the period from roughly 2003–2008, empowering young hardliners but also maintaining space for other constituencies. "Fearful of alienating a large contingent of older GSPC members, Droukdal renewed tactically familiar hit and run attacks on Algerian military targets even while younger members of the AQIM blew themselves up in the hopes of gaining martyrdom."[18] The coup against Hattab thus also reflects the field commanders and senior officials' effort to mediate between the demands of the rank-and-file, the hesistancy of some remaining Hattab-esque figures in the organization, and the strategic orientation of the organization as a whole.

---

[16] Barak Mendelsohn, *The Al-Qaeda Franchise: The Expansion of Al-Qaeda and Its Consequences* (Oxford: Oxford University Press, 2016), 130–131.

[17] Ferhat and Zineb A., "Hassan Hattab: Il n'y a pas de Qaida en Algérie."

[18] David Gutelius, Testimony to the Senate Committee on Foreign Relations Subcommittee on African Affairs, November 17, 2009, 4, www.foreign.senate .gov/imo/media/doc/GuteliusTestimony091117a1.pdf.

Bureaucratization helped enable the coup; after the coup, bureaucratization progressed still further, at least at the center of the organization. The removal of Hattab confirmed and extended the power of
the Council of Notables, not just in terms of Abu Ibrahim's succession
but also in laying the foundation for what seems to have been a smooth
transition after Abu Ibrahim's unexpected death in 2004. Droukdel,
Abu Ibrahim's successor, essentially followed Abu Ibrahim up the
ranks. A mathematics student from Meftah in Blida Province, Droukdel joined armed action in Algeria in the early 1990s as a member of
Saïd Makhloufi's Movement for the Islamic State, parts of which were
absorbed into the GIA in its 1994 unity initiative. Within the jihadist
milieu, Droukdel distinguished himself first as a bombmaker and then
as a battalion commander; ultimately, as Zone 2 commander, he was
asked to join the GSPC's Council of Notables in 2003. When Abu
Ibrahim replaced Hattab as GSPC emir, Droukdel became head of the
Council.[19] And when Droukdel succeeded Abu Ibrahim as emir, it
appears to have been one of the most orderly successions that any
GIA or GSPC iteration had experienced in the preceding decade; the
GSPC, especially after Hattab's exit, solidified an orderly bureaucratic
structure at the top.

The Council has retained its importance to the GSPC/AQIM since the
early 2000s. In recent years, the Council's current head, Abu 'Ubayda
Yusuf al-'Annabi, has been one of AQIM's most prominent spokesmen,
especially when it comes to commenting on macro political developments in Algeria, North Africa, and beyond.[20] Bureaucratization also
helps AQIM with the strategic management of religious authority.
Droukdel, as emir, seems to have borne in mind the negative lesson
embodied by the GIA's last two major leaders, Djamel Zitouni and
Antar Zouabri – namely, the lesson that conflating military–political
and religious–legal authority in a single person makes that leader highly
vulnerable to internal critiques and perhaps highly prone to autocratic
behavior. Droukdel seeks religious credibility in his own right:

---

[19] Abu Mus'ab 'Abd al-Wadud ('Abd al-Malik Droukdel), "Hiwar ma'a Amir
    'Al-Jama'a al-Salafiyya li-l-Da'wa wa-l-Qital'," Minbar al-Tawhid wa-l-Jihad,
    2005, www.ilmway.com/site/maqdis/MS_27385.html.
[20] For one example, see Yusuf al-'Anabi, "Fakku Hisar Banghazi," Ifriqiya
    al-Muslima, June 2016, https://jihadology.net/2016/06/26/new-video-message-
    from-al-qaidah-in-the-islamic-maghribs-shaykh-abu-ubaydah-yusuf-al-anabi-
    lift-the-siege-on-binghazi/.

He drenches his rhetoric in religious vocabulary and is regularly referred to in jihadist circles as a "shaykh." Yet Droukdel often delegates the task of detailed religious–legal explication, in other words of giving *fatawa*, to explicitly clerical figures. Two prominent GSPC/AQIM clerics were Abu al-Bara' Ahmad (1963–2006) and Abu al-Hasan Rashid al-Bulaydi (d. 2015), who had deeper histories of religious learning than did Droukdel or other field commanders. According to one AQIM hagiography of al-Bulaydi:

> The shaykh grew up attending circles of knowledge, purification, and subtleties. After he had folded up his knees with some of the people of knowledge and righteousness, learning knowledge and good behavior from them, he became an imam and sermon-giver in the mosque of his village … [his neighbors] had recourse to him (despite his young age) to reconcile between quarreling parties, conclude marriage contracts, and to deliver preaching at holidays and on the day of funerals.[21]

Al-Bulaydi's rise within the jihadist milieu was based on his clerical profile, and his role was "as a preacher and a teacher of [the Prophet's] biography, jurisprudence, and Islamic consciousness several times a week" for many years.[22] As a clerical and legal voice within the organization, he conceived his role in contradistinction to the GIA's approach to theological–legal issues under Zitouni and Zouabri. Al-Bulaydi's hagiographer comments, "He used to speak to us a lot about the Armed Islamic Group, and what was the chief reason leading to the obliteration of the extremists (*fana' al-ghulat*)." In the cleric's view, Zitouni and Zouabri were deeply ignorant of the shari'a and lacked the requisite credentials for making statements and decisions.[23] This perspective obviously comes from someone who broke with the GIA, but it also reflects the GSPC's effort to present its leadership as comprising both commanders and clerics.

Al-Bulaydi was ultimately tapped to head both the GSPC/AQIM's Legal Committee (al-Lajna al-Shar'iyya) and its Judicial Group

---

[21] Abu Qatada al-Tayyib al-Wahrani, "Ma Istafadtu min al-Shaykh Abi al-Hasan fi Ayyam al-Fitan," Ifriqiya al-Muslima, January/February 2016, 3. https://azelin.files.wordpress.com/2016/02/abucc84-qatacc84dah-al-tcca3ayyicc84b-al-wahracc84nicc84–22what-i-benefited-from-shaykh-abucc84-al-hcca3asan-during-the-times-of-strife-by-his-disciple22.pdf.

[22] Ibid., 4.   [23] Ibid., 11.

(al-Hay'at al-Qada'iyya).[24] When detailed legal pronouncements need to be made, Droukdel has routinely turned to figures such as al-Bulaydi, thereby avoiding putting his personal credibility on the line with every dispute. For example, it was al-Bulaydi who corresponded with dissidents in the Nigeria-based Boko Haram who, in 2011, sought AQIM's legal advice (and political support) amid their plans to break with Boko Haram and start a rival jihadist outfit.[25] The GSPC/AQIM epitomizes the ways that jihadist organizations elevate clerics as political voices – on multiple occasions, al-Bulaydi's *fatawa* had political implications for AQIM's internal coalition politics and external alliance-building efforts.

One liability of these organizational structures, including both the Council of Notables and the religious-legal organs of the GSPC/AQIM, is that they have been overwhelmingly headed and staffed by men from northern Algeria. Droukdel is from Meftah in Blida. Al-Bulaydi was from Blida as well.[26] The Council of Notables' chairman Yusuf al-'Annabi, if his surname is any indication, is from 'Annaba in northeastern Algeria near the border with Tunisia. Abu Ibrahim, Droukdel's predecessor, was from Batna, also in the northeast.[27] Substantial differences in geographical origins, life experiences, and militant careers separate the northern Algerians from some of the most prominent battalion commanders operating in the Sahara – and the northern Algerian leadership has struggled in its efforts to discipline subordinates in the desert. Bureaucracy played a key role in AQIM's internal politics, but the authority of bureaucratic structures waned as one moved from the organization's political center to the peripheries.

[24] Ibid., 4–5.
[25] Abu al-Hasan Rashid al-Bulaydi, *Nasa'ih wa-Tawjihat Shar'iyya min al-Shaykh Abi al-Hasan Rashid li-Mujahidi Nayjiriya* (Mu'assasat al-Andalus li-l-Intaj al-I'lami, 2017), https://azelin.files.wordpress.com/2017/04/shaykh-abucc84-al-hcca3asan-rashicc84d-22sharicc84ah-advice-and-guidance-for-the-mujacc84hidicc84n-of-nigeria22.pdf.
[26] Al-Wahrani, "Ma Istafadu," 3.
[27] Al-Lajna al-I'lamiyya li-l-Jama'a al-Salafiyya li-l-Da'wa wa-l-Qital, "Hiwar ma'a Amir al-Jama'a al-Salafiyya," December 18, 2003, 1, www.cia.gov/library/abbottabad-compound/2D/2DF47C0A05997C12BFE19361CEE25EF7_hewar_salfi.pdf.

GSPC/AQIM in the Sahara: Rivalries and a Broken Triangle, 2003–2011

In 2006, the GSPC renewed its pledge of allegiance to al-Qa'ida and, in January 2007, renamed itself al-Qa'ida in the Islamic Maghreb or AQIM (one factor in this process was the relationship between Droukdel and Abu Mus'ab al-Zarqawi,[28] but the Algeria–Iraq connection lies beyond the scope of this chapter.) The group retained a presence in northern Algeria, where its leadership was based and where it periodically carried out attacks – including bombing a United Nations building in December 2007. But the group's real opportunity for political momentum was in the Sahara.

On a surface level, the Saharan turn was symbolized by a spate of kidnappings in the southeastern Algerian Sahara in 2003. Led by a GSPC operative named 'Amari Saifi or 'Abd al-Razzaq "Al-Para" (b. 1966), a former paratrooper, the kidnappers seized a total of thirty-two European tourists between February and April of that year. The net result was a boon for the GSPC: It is estimated that the German government paid a total of five million euros for some of the hostages.

On another level, the 2003 kidnappings were not the real indicator of the Saharan turn. The individual kidnappings were amateurish, partly because, according to the hostages themselves, "their leaders came from Algeria's northern coastal region and were not used to driving in the sands of the Sahara."[29] Saifi himself was reportedly from Guelma in far northeastern Algeria. He came up through the GIA as part of the same "Green Battalion" out of which Zitouni and Zouabri had emerged, and had been close to Zitouni. After Zitouni's death, Saifi had joined Hattab in breaking the Zone 2 fighters away from the GIA. As part of the GSPC, Saifi was given command of Zone 5, in eastern Algeria. Saifi pursued ambitious operations, including an

---

[28] "An Interview with Abdelmalek Droukdal," *New York Times*, July 1, 2008, www.nytimes.com/2008/07/01/world/africa/01transcript-droukdal.html. See also Pahlavi and Leclair, "L'institutionnalisation d'AQMI"; and Jean-Pierre Filiu, "The Local and Global Jihad of al-Qa'ida in the Islamic Maghrib," *Middle East Journal* 63:2 (Spring 2009): 213–226, 221.

[29] Rukmini Callimachi, "Anatomy of an Abduction," *New York Times*, July 29, 2014, www.nytimes.com/2014/07/30/world/africa/militant-kidnapping-video.html.

attack in January 2003 that killed forty-three Algerian soldiers, and
then the kidnapping of the Europeans.[30]

The combination of these factors – Saifi's preference for spectacular
attacks and his own relative unfamiliarity with the Sahara, both topo-
graphically and politically – caused his downfall. The 2003 kidnappings made him, almost overnight, internationally infamous, soon
dubbed (as at least two other GSPC/AQIM field commanders would
be, later) "the Bin Laden of the Sahara." As the hostages were being
rescued and ransomed, Saifi was pursued across the desert. In Chad, he
clashed with both government forces and rebels, losing men and falling
into rebel hands in March 2004. He was repatriated to Algeria, where
he remains in prison.

If Saifi's career demonstrates how a Saharan operation could
spin out of control for a field commander from northern Algeria, two
other field commanders demonstrate the inverse. Mokhtar Belmokhtar
and 'Abd al-Hamid Abu Zayd both had Saharan roots, and both of
them built long and politically sophisticated careers deep in the desert.
Belmokhtar was from Ghardaïa, in central Algeria, while Abu Zayd's
family members were desert dwellers by background. Abu Zayd
spent part of his childhood in the small town of Zaouia El-Abidia, in
the Touggourt commune of eastern Algeria.[31] Both men would eventually gravitate much further southward in the Sahara, especially to
northern Mali.

My point here is not to essentialize Saharans or argue that being
born in Ghardaïa automatically confers knowledge of how to navigate
politics in, say, Gao. And Abu Zayd, who participated in the 2003
kidnappings, did not necessarily professionalize the operation, nor did
he prevent Saifi's disastrous end. One should not overstate the
"Saharan-ness" of either Belmokhtar or Abu Zayd. At the same time,
however, the two men developed a comfort with Saharan operations
that had eluded Saifi, as well as formidable political networks that the
northerner had not had the time, or perhaps the skill, to build. Later,
some northern Algerians (particularly Yahya Abu al-Hammam,

---

[30] Muhammad Muqaddam (Mokeddem), "Qissat Su'ud Qiyadi 'Al-Jama'a
al-Salafiyya' al-Jaza'iriyya wa-Suqutihi 'Abd al-Razzaq 'al-Bara'," *Al-Hayat*,
November 8, 2004, www.alhayat.com/article/1910707.

[31] Alfred de Montesquiou, "Abou Zeid veut être le Ben Laden du Sahara," *Paris
Match*, September 30, 2010, www.parismatch.com/Actu/International/Abou-
Zeid-otages-francais-Areva-Niger-154423.

discussed later) would also build formidable political presences in the Sahara, but only after lengthy processes of relationship-building and political maneuvering. One could not simply enter the Sahara, conduct a big operation, and expect to succeed.

Belmokhtar and Abu Zayd came to jihadism by different paths. Belmokhtar was an Afghanistan veteran who quickly gravitated to the GIA after his return home in 1993. Abu Zayd's journey went by way of the Muslim Brotherhood in the late 1980s, then the Islamist party the Islamic Salvation Front (FIS). He only joined the GIA after his brother was killed by Algerian security forces in 1996.[32] Neither man was part of the Zitouni–Zouabri network of northern Algerian Salafi hardliners, the network that eventually dominated (and divided) the GIA.

By the mid-1990s, Belmokhtar had distinguished himself as a terrorist in the area around Ghardaïa. Belmokhtar stole vehicles from oil companies and involved himself in cross-border smuggling between Algeria and Mali. These activities allowed him not just to finance his own battalion but also to supply weapons to other GIA units. Belmokhtar extended his reputation through violence: After the May 1995 murder of five expatriates working for Algeria's national hydrocarbons company Sonatrach, the GIA rewarded Belmokhtar by declaring him the group's Saharan emir.[33] Significantly, Belmokhtar choose a deputy who also hailed from Ghardaïa, emphasizing how shared geographical affiliations could strengthen trust within jihadist ranks; the deputy, Ibrahim Abu Ishak, would fight at Belmokhtar's side until dying in a raid on Mauritanian territory in 2005.[34] A combination of perceived toughness, local connections, and financial acumen propelled Belmokhtar's rise within the GIA, GSPC, and AQIM.

By the mid-1990s, Belmokhtar was using the Sahara and the Sahel as a conduit for different types of activities, including transit for returning fighters and foreign emissaries. One Algerian jihadist later recalled that after he himself left Sudan (where he had been staying with Bin Laden) in late 1995, "I entered the Niger desert, where I met the brother

---

[32] Ibid.

[33] Lemine Ould M. Salem, *Le Ben Laden du Sahara: Sur les traces du jihadiste Mokhtar Belmokhtar* (Paris: Éditions de la Martinière, 2014), 41–46.

[34] U.S. Embassy Nouakchott, "GSPC Announces 'Names' of Five Members Killed in Attack on Mauritania," leaked cable 05ALGIERS1525, July 19, 2005, https://search.wikileaks.org/plusd/cables/05ALGIERS1525_a.html.

[Belmokhtar] and his group. I went into Algeria with them in the same year to the ninth region [i.e., the desert of southern Algeria, where Belmokhtar was the regional commander]."[35]

Belmokhtar's familiarity and comfort with Saharan territory was already apparent in summer 2001 when, as mentioned previously, he welcomed an emissary from al-Qaʻida, Abu Muhammad al-Yamani. The emissary flew to Niger's capital, Niamey, and then traveled into the Nigerien desert, "where the brothers were awaiting him, with [Belmokhtar] at their head." The party then traveled into northern Mali, and from there into Algeria.[36] During al-Yamani's visit, the GSPC established its first training camp in northern Mali in early 2002, again with Belmokhtar's involvement.[37] Overall, the visit not only elevated Belmokhtar's reputation but also reflected his ability to navigate the Sahara in a geographical and political sense.

In Mauritania and especially in northern Mali, Belmokhtar worked systematically to build local ties. One well-known aspect of his strategy was marriage. The Mauritanian journalist Lemine Ould M. Salem has related that one of Belmokhtar's earliest Malian marriages, probably his first in the country, was to an Arab woman of noble birth but modest circumstances. Her family lived in the area of Lerneb far to the west of Timbuktu, near Mali's border with Mauritania. This marriage must have occurred by 2003, because his in-laws and other local connections played a role in helping Belmokhtar to negotiate ransoms for the Europeans kidnapped in Algeria that year. One notable in-law, his wife's uncle, was Oumar Ould Hamaha, who later became a relatively prominent Malian jihadist.[38] At that time, Belmokhtar's local relationships may have been more crucial to his project than direct local recruitment. One 2006 estimate calculated that he had "over 60" fighters, a relatively small number[39] – yet he had already

---

[35] "Exclusive Interview with Shaykh al-Mujahid Hisham Abu Akram," 2.
[36] Abu Akram Hisham, "Al-Shaykh Abu Muhammad al-Yamani: Rihlatuhu ila al-Jaza'ir wa-Qissat Istishhadihi," Ifriqiya al-Muslima, December 2015, 4, https://azelin.files.wordpress.com/2016/03/abucc84-akram-hishacc84m-e2809cmessages-from-the-mujacc84hid_s-notebook-2-shaykh-abucc84-muhcca3ammad-al-yamanicc84-his-trip-to-algeria-and-the-story-of-his-martyrdom22.pdf.
[37] Ibid., 5.   [38] Ould M. Salem, *Le Ben Laden du Sahara*, 56–61.
[39] U.S. Embassy Niamey, "More on Bultmeier Murder and GSPC," leaked cable 06NIAMEY1296, December 4, 2006, https://search.wikileaks.org/plusd/cables/06NIAMEY1298_a.html. I believe the cable's reference to "Bin Lawarr" is a

made himself into a political figure of some importance in the Mali–Mauritania borderlands. Belmokhtar is one of the paradigmatic cases in this book of the jihadist field commander as a political entrepreneur.

The 2003 kidnappings challenged Belmokhtar's dominance of the Saharan jihadist scene. This was due not only to the episode itself but also to the way it empowered Abu Zayd. Abu Zayd and his Tariq ibn Ziyad Battalion were key participants alongside al-Para in the kidnappings.[40] When al-Para was captured, Abu Zayd was effectively promoted. Belmokhtar later complained that al-Para and Abu Zayd, who had been part of the "eastern" rather than "southern" emirate of the GSPC, had crowded in on his territory uninvited. Others in AQIM claimed that Belmokhtar had solicited that unit's involvement.[41] Belmokhtar's internal position may also have been weakened by Hattab's departure; as late as summer 2007, before Hattab's surrender became public, Belmokhtar referred to the departed emir with respect and expressed nostalgia for the bygone times "when they used to gather weapons, with El Para, in Morocco, Mali, Niger, and Chad."[42] Under Hattab, it seems, Belmokhtar had had a warmer relationship with the central leadership and a freer hand in the Sahara than was the case after Droukdel took over; if Belmokhtar had participated in the 2003 coup against Hattab, perhaps he came to regret it.

Whatever the truth, 2003–2004 brought upheaval for the internal coalition dynamics of the GSPC. With Hattab expelled, Abu Ibrahim dead, and Saifi in prison, by the end of 2004 there were three major poles of authority within the coalition: Droukdel and his clerical allies in northern Algeria; Belmokhtar; and Abu Zayd. In theory, Droukdel had the final word over decisions taken within AQIM's "Saharan emirate,"

mistake, and that Embassy officials misheard "Belaour," one of Belmokhtar's nicknames.

[40] Callimachi, "Anatomy of an Abduction."

[41] Letter from the Shura Council of al-Qaʻida in the Islamic Maghreb to the Shura Council of the Veiled Men Battalion, October 3, 2012, 28, http://hosted.ap.org/specials/interactives/_international/_pdfs/al-qaida-belmoktar-letter-english.pdf [dead link]. A 2007 cable from U.S. Embassy Algiers depicts Belmokhtar as an ally of both al-Para and Hattab and as a skeptic about the GSPC decision to affiliate with al-Qaʻida. See "Mokhtar Belmokhtar and AQIM: Is One-Eye on His Last Leg?" 07ALGIERS904, June 27, 2007, https://search.wikileaks.org/plusd/cables/07ALGIERS904_a.html.

[42] Mohamed Mouloudj, "El-Qaïda Maghreb s'étiole," *La Dépêche de Kabylie*, June 17, 2007, www.depechedekabylie.com/evenement/41412-el-qaida-maghreb-setiole/.

but in reality, he often struggled to impose his will, especially over Belmokhtar. Rumors of tension between Droukdel and Belmokhtar were circulating by 2007.[43]

In order to counterbalance Belmokhtar, Droukdel repeatedly leaned on Abu Zayd and his bloc, creating a broken triangle that would shape AQIM coalition politics for a decade. One of Droukdel's first steps was to demote Belmokhtar, in 2007,[44] from the emir of the Saharan region to a mere battalion commander (for the Veiled Men Battalion, which would later constitute the core of Belmokhtar's temporarily independent faction). Droukdel dispatched a series of northern Algerians to the Sahara, beginning with the new Saharan emir, Yahya Abu 'Ammar/ Yahia Djouadi (b. 1967 in Sidi Bel Abbès, northeastern Algeria), in 2007.[45] According to one analyst, Belmokhtar had been so outraged over Abu Zayd's activities that Belmokhtar had even considered ceasing terrorist activities in the Sahara and brokering a truce with Algerian authorities; in response, Droukdel considered killing Belmokhtar in the event that Belmokhtar refused to resume attacks.[46] Yet none of these parties were willing to take such drastic steps, which is part of what allowed the broken triangle to endure for years.

Around 2009, Droukdel appointed a new Saharan emir, Nabil Makhlufi/Nabil Abu Alqama. But Makhlufi also failed to control Belmokhtar. Makhlufi died in a car accident in September 2012 on the road between Gao and Timbuktu.[47] He was succeeded by Yahya

---

[43] U.S. Embassy Algiers, "Mokhtar Belmokhtar and AQIM."

[44] Andrew Wojtanik, "Mokhtar Belmokhtar: One-Eyed Firebrand of North Africa and the Sahel," Combating Terrorism Center Jihadi Bios Project, March 1, 2015, 15, https://ctc.usma.edu/app/uploads/2018/01/CTC_Mokhtar-Belmokhtar-Jihadi-Bio-February2015–2.pdf.

[45] Mohammed Mahmoud Abu al-Ma'ali, "Al-Qaeda and Its Allies in the Sahel and the Sahara," Al Jazeera Center for Studies, May 1, 2012, 3, http://studies .aljazeera.net/ResourceGallery/media/Documents/2012/4/30/ 2012430145241774734Al%20Qaeda%20and%20its%20allies%20in%20the %20Sahel%20and%20the%20Sahara.pdf. See also U.S. Department of the Treasury, "Treasury Targets Al Qaida-Affiliated Terror Group in Algeria," July 17, 2008, www.treasury.gov/press-center/press-releases/Pages/hp1085.aspx.

[46] "Al-Hudur al-Muritani fi al-Qa'ida sa-Yazdad ma'a Taqallus 'Adad al-Jaza'iriyyin fi Far' al-Sahra'," France24, September 30, 2010, www.france24 .com/ar/20100930-algeria-sahel-al-qaeda-Othmane-lahyani-journalist.

[47] "Nord-Mali: Nabil Makloufi, un chef d'Aqmi, se tue au volant de sa voiture," *Jeune Afrique*, September 10, 2012, www.jeuneafrique.com/174378/societe/ nord-mali-nabil-makloufi-un-chef-d-aqmi-se-tue-au-volant-de-sa-voiture/.

Abu al-Hammam (1978–2019).[48] A northern Algerian who had come to the Malian Sahara in the early 2000s, Abu al-Hammam had fought alongside Belmokhtar before joining Abu Zayd's circle and basing himself in the Timbuktu region.[49]

When the AQIM-driven, Saharan kidnapping economy really kicked off in 2008, Belmokhtar and Abu Zayd were positioned to dominate it – and to compete with each other. Abu Zayd was the more financially successful kidnapper. His men perpetrated AQIM's two most lucrative kidnappings: the seizure of five French nationals along with a Togolese and a Malagasy in Arlit, Niger, in September 2010;[50] and the capture of two Swiss and one German in remote northern Mali in January 2009. According to an investigation by the *New York Times*, AQIM may have obtained a combined ransom of $70.5 million for those hostages. That sum represents the bulk of the estimated $91.5 million in ransoms that AQIM received between 2008 and 2013. Belmokhtar, in contrast, may have earned less than $10 million in ransoms for AQIM, through his men's kidnapping of three Spanish aid workers in Mauritania in November 2009, which brought AQIM an estimated $5.9 million; and the snatching of two Canadian diplomats in Niger in December 2008, which brought an estimated $1.1 million.[51]

The rivalry between Belmokhtar and Abu Zayd was exacerbated by the absence of a clear demarcation of geographical zones of influence. In a rough sense, Belmokhtar was the more dominant figure in Mauritania, and Abu Zayd the more prominent kidnapper in northern Niger. Yet Belmokhtar's reach extended into Niger, particularly the capital Niamey and its environs, where Belmokhtar's group staged at least two kidnappings. Both men used northern Mali as a place to keep hostages,

---

[48] "Abu al-Hammam fi Awwal Muqabala Lahu ba'd al-Tadakhkhul al-Faransi bi-Mali," *Al-Akhbar*, January 10, 2016, https://alakhbar.info/intrep/interv/13563-2016-01-10-18-02-56.html [dead link].

[49] On Abu al-Hammam's career, see Alex Thurston, "Timbuktu: A Laboratory for Jihadists Experimenting with Politics," War on the Rocks, January 23, 2019, https://warontherocks.com/2019/01/timbuktu-a-laboratory-for-jihadists-experimenting-with-politics/.

[50] Jean-Philippe Rémy, "Les quatre otages enlevés au Niger libérés," *Le Monde*, October 29, 2013, www.lemonde.fr/afrique/article/2013/10/29/les-otages-francais-enleves-au-niger-ont-ete-liberes_3503622_3212.html.

[51] Rukmini Callimachi, "Paying Ransoms, Europe Bankrolls Qaeda Terror," *New York Times*, July 29, 2014, www.nytimes.com/2014/07/30/world/africa/ransoming-citizens-europe-becomes-al-qaedas-patron.html.

train fighters, and plan operations. Abu Zayd gravitated toward the Timbuktu region, which meant that he too had interests extending into Mauritania. Meanwhile, not everything was competition: Fighters moved back and forth between the two battalions, and the battalions coordinated their operations to some extent.[52]

And yet, the tension remained. The competition concerned not just money and power but also strategy. Of the hostages kidnapped by AQIM between 2008 and 2012, it was Abu Zayd who ordered and perhaps even personally carried out the sole confirmed, premeditated execution of a hostage for political reasons – the beheading of British national Edwin Dyer in May 2009.[53] Abu Zayd may have killed Dyer because of the British government's refusal to pay a ransom (three other Europeans kidnapped along with Dyer, two Swiss and one German, were released, likely after being ransomed). Yet the reason AQIM gave for killing Dyer was that the British government was refusing to grant AQIM's demand for the release of Abu Qatada al-Filastini, the Salafi-jihadist cleric and theoretician who had, long before, issued *fatawa* on the GIA's behalf.[54] Abu Zayd's unit may have also executed French national Michel Germaneau in July 2010, although the circumstances of Germaneau's death are unclear; some reports hold that the aged Germaneau died of a heart attack in AQIM custody. In any case, AQIM claimed that Germaneau was executed out of revenge for a Franco-Mauritanian raid that had killed six AQIM fighters in a failed rescue bid.[55] In February 2010, Abu Zayd not only made a political statement but achieved an operational goal, exchanging French national Pierre Camatte (kidnapped in Ménaka, northern

---

[52] Andrew Lebovich, "A Look Inside AQIM," *The Wasat*, January 15, 2012, https://thewasat.wordpress.com/2012/01/15/a-look-inside-aqim/.

[53] "Algerian Named in Briton Killing," BBC News, June 4, 2009, http://news.bbc .co.uk/2/hi/africa/8083099.stm.

[54] Ibid.; Helen Pidd, "Background: The kidnapping of Edwin Dyer," *The Guardian*, June 3, 2009, www.theguardian.com/world/2009/jun/03/edwin-dyer-hostage-killed-al-qaida.

[55] "Un élu malien déclare que Michel Germaneau a été 'décapité'," *L'Express*, July 25, 2010, www.lexpress.fr/actualite/monde/un-elu-malien-declare-que-michel-germaneau-a-ete-decapite_908484.html. The assertion that Germaneau died of a heart attack comes from the Algerian journalist Mohamed Mokeddem. See "Aqmi: Abou Zeid ne serait pas celui qu'on croit, selon Mokeddem," *Jeune Afrique*, October 27, 2010, www.jeuneafrique.com/183947/politique/aqmi-abou-zeid-ne-serait-pas-celui-qu-on-croit-selon-mokeddem/.

Mali, in November 2009)[56] for four AQIM members who had been imprisoned in Mali.[57] The idea of using hostages for political leverage rather than financial gain fit with the wishes of al-Qa'ida central, which had attempted (unsuccessfully) to order AQIM to use hostages, especially the workers kidnapped in northern Niger in 2010, to pressure European governments to withdraw soldiers from Afghanistan.[58] In contrast to Abu Zayd and Droukdel's use of hostages as political tools, Belmokhtar (despite obtaining smaller ransoms) seemed more interested in ransoming them.

At least once, a dispute over what to do with hostages brought a vivid, face-to-face confrontation between Belmokhtar and Abu Zayd. The Canadian diplomat Robert Fowler (held by Belmokhtar's men in 2008–2009) recalled that just before the moment of his and his colleague's release – which was to occur simultaneously with the release of two European women held by Abu Zayd – a dispute broke out. After the released hostages and the negotiators drove away from the assembled AQIM fighters, the negotiators informed Fowler that

In those last moments Belmokhtar, by word and deed, had indicated he was taking the decision to free all four of us out of Abou Zeid's hands; the deal for his hostages (Louis and me) had been done for almost two weeks and he would not abide seeing the two women left behind to die while Abou Zeid haggled over details. I suppose, too, that it was a matter of face. First was the fact that he had made his deal and would see it honoured, and second was the issue of whose vision, value system, and authority would prevail among AQIM forces in the southern Sahara. Moreover, this struggle was being played out before the eyes of the assembled clans, and Belmokhtar could not blink.[59]

---

[56] "Moi, Pierre Camatte, otage d'Al-Qaïda pendant 89 jours," *Jeune Afrique*, March 30, 2010, www.jeuneafrique.com/197799/politique/moi-pierre-camatte-otage-d-al-qaeda-pendant-89-jours/.

[57] "La libération de quatre islamistes en échange de l'otage français," RFI, February 23, 2010, www.rfi.fr/contenu/20100223-liberation-quatre-islamistes-echange-otage-francais.

[58] See "Gist of Conversation," recovered from Usama bin Laden's compound in Abbottabad and declassified by the Office of the Director of National Intelligence. The file is available in English and Arabic at www.dni.gov/files/documents/ubl/english/Gist%20of%20conversation%20Oct%2011.pdf; and www.dni.gov/files/documents/ubl/arabic/Gist%20of%20conversation%20Oct%2011%20-%20Arabic.pdf.

[59] Robert Fowler, *A Season in Hell: My 130 Days in the Sahara with Al Qaeda* (New York: HarperCollins, 2011), 266.

Fowler does not specify what "details" concerned Abu Zayd, but it is tempting to conclude that Abu Zayd was considering the idea of using the women in another attempt at political leverage. Additionally, Abu Zayd and Belmokhtar differed over how to treat hostages. According to Fowler, Abu Zayd adopted a harsher approach and employed greater coercion in pressuring hostages to accept Islam.[60]

Droukdel largely took Abu Zayd's side in these disputes. Droukdel later reprimanded Belmokhtar over his management of the Fowler kidnapping, accusing Belmokhtar of not only cutting AQIM's leadership out of the decision-making but also of ignoring al-Qa'ida central's wishes. AQIM and al-Qa'ida central, Droukdel said, would have preferred to use the Canadian hostages to secure releases of imprisoned AQIM members and to pressure Western forces to leave Afghanistan. Droukdel further complained that Belmokhtar had let the Canadians go free "for the most trifling price (*bi-abkhas thaman*)."[61]

As Abu Zayd enriched AQIM and sought to leverage some hostages for wider political impact, Belmokhtar pursued local political alliances in northern Mali and particularly in Mauritania. In the Mauritanian capital, Nouakchott, and elsewhere, Belmokhtar cultivated young Mauritanians who were interested in jihadism (see Chapter 7). The composition of Belmokhtar's bloc differed in some ways from Abu Zayd's. Belmokhtar's close lieutenants and allies included Mauritanian and Malian Arabs, such as the Mauritanian national Al-Hasan Ould Khalil or Jouleybib (1981–2013), whereas Abu Zayd favored Algerians such as Abu al-Hammam and Malian Tuareg elites such as Iyad ag Ghali (see later in the chapter). These constituencies were not necessarily mutually exclusive, but it appears that the divisions between Abu Zayd's network and Belmokhtar's were not just strategic but also ethnic.

Belmokhtar was increasingly dissatisfied with the direction of the organization. Above all, he was eager to escalate ambitious military attacks at the regional level. Growing schisms within AQIM, epitomized by the emergence of the Movement for Tawhid/Unity and Jihad in West Africa (abbreviated as MUJWA in English and MUJAO in

---

[60] Ibid., 264–265.

[61] Letter from the Shura Council of al-Qa'ida in the Islamic Maghreb to the Shura Council of the Veiled Men Battalion, 22. See also Mathieu Guidère, "The Timbuktu Letters: New Insights about AQIM," *Res Militaris* (2014), https://hal .archives-ouvertes.fr/hal-01081769/document.

French) in 2011, positioned Belmokhtar to strike out on his own. These schisms widened, ironically, during the 2012–2013 jihadist occupation of northern Mali, a time when AQIM briefly had the chance to realize some of its political designs for the Muslim societies of northwest Africa.

AQIM, MUJWA, Ansar al-Din, and the Occupation of Northern Mali: The Politics of Coalitions and Alliances, 2011–2013

The period from January 2012 to January 2013 saw some of AQIM's greatest successes. As northern Mali slipped out of the central government's control, AQIM moved from the shadows to center stage. AQIM initially acted as a supporting actor in other groups' bids for control. Then AQIM co-managed the jihadist emirate that took power. Yet these developments intensified disagreements within AQIM, particularly within the broken triangle between AQIM's emir 'Abd al-Malik Droukdel and his two leading Saharan field commanders, Mokhtar Belmokhtar and 'Abd al-Hamid Abu Zayd. All three nodes of the triangle were affected by the way the two field commanders leveraged Mali-centric alliances to advance their own interests and visions, often against Droukdel's stated preferences and to the detriment of AQIM's cohesion.

This triangular relationship also, as so often in jihadist coalition politics, had a geographical component. As noted earlier in the chapter, prior to 2012 Belmokhtar and Abu Zayd did not have a clear demarcation of territory within the Sahara. During 2012, however, geographical demarcations became clearer as a rough division of labor emerged in Mali: Belmokhtar and MUJWA dominated in Gao, northeastern Mali; Abu Zayd and the more hardline part of the Mali-centric, jihadist-leaning movement Ansar al-Din (see later) dominated in Timbuktu, northwestern Mali; and the more "jihadist lite" portion of Ansar al-Din dominated in Kidal, far northeastern Mali, where they sidelined AQIM. The geographical divisions within the jihadist emirate reflected and deepened other political tensions. These events are revisited in more detail, and from Ansar al-Din's perspective, in Chapter 3.

By late 2012, Droukdel's inability to control his Saharan commanders had undermined the jihadist state-building project in northern

Mali. Belmokhtar, openly frustrated with Droukdel and Abu Zayd, temporarily broke away from AQIM at the end of 2012. Abu Zayd, although not as openly defiant, disregarded Droukdel's advice to move slowly with the implementation of AQIM's brand of shari'a and with the territorial expansion of the jihadist proto-state. In this sense, Abu Zayd contributed to provoking a French-led military intervention in northern Mali. By February 2013, the jihadist emirate was crushed, AQIM was more fragmented than ever, Abu Zayd and other commanders were dead, and Belmokhtar had struck out on his own in the most dramatic fashion possible.

Yet the conditions under which these ruptures occurred ultimately permitted, over the long term, a reconciliation: Still influenced by the GIA's negative example, none of the leading actors in AQIM called each other unbelievers. In late 2015, Belmokhtar formally returned to AQIM. In early 2017, his lieutenants and allies were reincorporated into a Sahara-wide hierarchy – either with Belmokhtar's permission or as a means of coping with his death. AQIM accommodationism kept relations from fraying completely and eventually permitted reconciliation. Before discussing those later developments, however, it is worth reviewing the events of late 2011 to early 2013 and the disagreements they provoked.

In fall 2011, a development occurred that would shape the jihadist occupation of northern Mali while creating a new path for Belmokhtar within AQIM's coalition politics. A bloc within AQIM broke away, calling itself MUJWA. Analysts have advanced various theories for understanding MUJWA. One early theory was that MUJWA represented a rebellion by black African AQIM members against the Algerians in the group. Yet MUJWA's leaders hailed from racial and ethnic groups – especially from various Mauritanian and Malian Arab tribes – that understand themselves as white.[62] One example is the Mauritanian Arab Hamada Ould Mohamed Kheirou, MUJWA's official leader. Additionally, MUJWA's first major operation was the October 2011 kidnapping of three European aid workers in Tindouf, Algeria – a strange target for a group purportedly seeking to wage jihad in West, rather than North, Africa. Moreover, AQIM and MUJWA largely

---

[62] On notions of whiteness and blackness in the Sahara, see Bruce Hall, *A History of Race in Muslim West Africa, 1600–1960* (Cambridge: Cambridge University Press, 2011).

cooperated during the jihadist takeover of northern Mali, which again suggests that racial antagonisms were not decisive.

Another early theory was that MUJWA represented a front for Malian and Mauritanian Arabs who had major stakes in smuggling and kidnapping; this could be seen as an ethnic division within AQIM, but more between different kinds of "whites" than between "whites" and "blacks." The sums of money involved in smuggling and kidnapping were substantial – the Tindouf kidnapping alone may have brought MUJWA nearly $11 million.[63] Major figures in MUJWA, especially the Malian Arab-Tuareg named Sultan Ould Badi,[64] have been accused of deep involvement in drug trafficking, especially around Gao (Ould Badi's home region).[65] MUJWA could thus be seen as a powerful economic vehicle as well.

Whatever MUJWA's aims, its leaders were closer to Belmokhtar than to the rest of AQIM, reflecting Belmokhtar's success in building relationships with Saharan Arab communities over nearly two decades. Belmokhtar, increasingly alienated from Droukdel, took a central role in mediating between MUJWA and AQIM in 2012.[66] Here, too, Belmokhtar's approach angered the central AQIM leadership. In a later missive, Droukdel complained

[Belmokhtar] committed an error in his effort with the brothers in Tawhid and Jihad [i.e., MUJWA]. That was when he gave his effort with them precedence over the calls of the Emirate [i.e., Droukdel's circle] to hold preliminary sessions with the battalions of al-Qaʻida, in order to put the internal affairs of the house in order (*li-ajl tartib al-bayt al-dakhili*), and then after that to widen the efforts with the brothers in Ansar al-Din and in Tawhid and Jihad.[67]

Here was a core question in jihadist politics: who was a coalition member, and who a mere ally? Belmokhtar did not just ignore Droukdel's preferences for how to deal with MUJWA; he also implicitly challenged Droukdel's understanding of how the concentric

[63] Callimachi, "Paying Ransoms."
[64] Lamhar Arab on his father's side and Idnan Tuareg on his mother's side.
[65] Andrew Lebovich, "Trying to Understand MUJWA," The Wasat, August 22, 2012, https://thewasat.wordpress.com/2012/08/22/trying-to-understand-mujwa/.
[66] Abu al-Maʻali, "Al-Qaeda and Its Allies," 5.
[67] Letter from the Shura Council of al-Qaʻida in the Islamic Maghreb to the Shura Council of the Veiled Men Battalion, 25.

circles of AQIM's political relationships worked: Belmokhtar privileged what one might call a "second circle" bloc (MUJWA) over what
Droukdel considered the core coalition. Notably, Belmokhtar flatly
refused to pursue reconciliation within AQIM, even declining to attend
a multi-battalion meeting that Makhloufi/Alqama attempted to hold.[68]

Frustrated by often losing out within AQIM's internal coalition
politics, Belmokhtar positioned himself as a political broker between
the core coalition and a close ally. He even scored a rare political
victory against Abu Zayd when it came to the issue of demanding that
MUJWA offer repentance (*tawba*) for having broken with AQIM.
This theological–legal matter brings us back to the question of how
AQIM uses Islamic vocabularies within coalition politics. One implication of making *tawba* can be that one is returning to the fold of true
Islam. Belmokhtar's ability to convince Droukdel to drop this demand
for MUJWA displayed, once more, how AQIM continued to react
against the GIA by avoiding framing internal disputes as matters of
belief and unbelief. Yet the affair also showed the limits of Droukdel's
power over Belmokhtar and the way that the MUJWA issue was not
just about MUJWA and AQIM as organizations but also about rivalries between Belmokhtar and the other top AQIM leaders. The emergence of MUJWA shifted relations within the broken triangle and
strengthened Belmokhtar's position within that structure.

By the fall of 2012, Belmokhtar was criticizing Droukdel and
looking for the exit; Belmokhtar's own political base had grown strong
enough that he needed no longer to endure the tension implicit in the
long-running broken triangle with Droukdel and Abu Zayd. In October, a letter from AQIM's Shura Council to the Shura Council of the
Veiled Men Battalion (effectively, a letter from Droukdel to Belmokhtar) laid out a set of organizational disputes. The letter from AQIM
leadership quoted extensively from, and worked to rebut, a letter that
Belmokhtar had earlier sent to them. Belmokhtar was dissatisfied both
with his own position and with the direction of AQIM. Belmokhtar
alleged that the central leadership had sidelined him and mismanaged
the Sahara, particularly through what he saw as over-centralization.
He also complained about targets: "Over the course of a decade, we
have not seen a major military attack (*'amal 'askari naw'i*), despite
formidable material capabilities. Our work has been limited to the

[68] Ibid.

routine of kidnappings, with which the mujahidin have become bored."[69]

The establishment of the Malian jihadist enclave did not placate Belmokhtar's appetite for "major attacks." Nor, apparently, had he been satisfied with his own raids (such as in Mauritania in 2005) or with the periodic attacks carried out by AQIM in northern Algeria, most dramatically the bombing of a United Nations building in 2007 and a 2011 attack on a major military academy.[70] It would be tempting to read Belmokhtar's complaints as a mere pretext for breaking with Droukdel, were it not for the fact that after the break, Belmokhtar immediately staged several major attacks. These attacks included the January 2013 mass hostage-taking at In Aménas, eastern Algeria, an incident discussed later.

In November 2012, Belmokhtar formally broke with AQIM and declared that his Veiled Men Battalion would report directly to al-Qaʻida central. This was not an impulsive decision but an act structured by political relationships. Belmokhtar's Mauritanian and Malian Arab ties greatly strengthened his hand. Even some figures who owed major debts to Abu Zayd – such as MUJWA's leader Ould Kheirou himself, who had likely been freed by Malian authorities as one of the then-AQIM members traded for Pierre Camatte[71] – backed Belmokhtar in his dispute with AQIM. In comparison with Abu Zayd, Belmokhtar had built the deeper and more extensive Saharan political network, and it was that network that enabled his bid for independence.

As Belmokhtar's relationship with Droukdel deteriorated, Abu Zayd's relationship with Ansar al-Din also complicated Droukdel's goals for the Malian venture. Ansar al-Din's own internal politics are the subject of Chapter 3, but here we are concerned with how Ansar al-Din functioned as an ally of AQIM, and how that alliance affected AQIM's internal disputes. Ironically, it was not just Belmokhtar's

---

[69] Ibid., 26.
[70] Andrew Lebovich, "AQIM Returns in Force in Northern Algeria," *Combating Terrorism Center Sentinel* 4:9 (September 2011), https://ctc.usma.edu/posts/aqim-returns-in-force-in-northern-algeria.
[71] Laurent Touchard, Baba Ahmed, and Chérif Ouazani, "Mali: Hamada Ould Mohamed Kheirou, le cerveau du Mujao," *Jeune Afrique*, October 3, 2012, www.jeuneafrique.com/139880/politique/mali-hamada-ould-mohamed-kheirou-le-cerveau-du-mujao/.

growing political power in Mali but also that of Abu Zayd – ostensibly Droukdel's counterweight and ally against Belmokhtar – that changed dynamics within the triangle, limiting Droukdel's ability to influence events in northern Mali.

Led by the Malian national and ethnic Tuareg politician Iyad ag Ghali (b. 1958), Ansar al-Din represented a vehicle for the ambitions of several actors. For ag Ghali, surveying the political landscape of northern Mali in late 2011, creating Ansar al-Din offered a chance to reclaim leadership over the brewing Tuareg separatist rebellion. According to many accounts, ag Ghali had been refused the leadership of the main Tuareg-led separatist rebel movement, the National Movement for the Liberation of the Azawad (French acronym MNLA). Creating Ansar al-Din was also a way ag Ghali could pursue his relatively recent, possibly sincere and possibly cynical commitment to Salafism. For other Malian Tuareg elites, Ansar al-Din represented a way to participate in the rebellion while hedging their bets against the MNLA and remaining close to ag Ghali. For AQIM, meanwhile, Ansar al-Din represented an entry point into the rebellion. Once relations between the MNLA and Ansar al-Din broke down in April–June 2012 and the jihadists emerged as the stronger power in the north, the connection to Ansar al-Din allowed AQIM to openly take a role in administering the nascent jihadist emirate.

AQIM's participation in the rebellion brought Abu Zayd and ag Ghali closer together, and their vision for how to manage and expand the emirate caused friction not just with Belmokhtar but also with Droukdel. For his part, Droukdel feared that his field commanders were antagonizing northern Malian populations and politicians by moving too quickly to implement a Salafi-jihadist version of Islamic law. In a letter to his Mali-based field commanders, Droukdel evoked the near-certitude that there would be an external military intervention or a totalizing blockade against the jihadist emirate. One possible outcome was that the pressures on the emirate would "arouse the people against us as a result of being starved and of having their supplies and salaries cut off."[72] Droukdel argued that "we should not overdo things or be reckless in our decisions (*an la nubaligh*

---

[72] Letter from 'Abd al-Malik Droukdel to Saharan field commanders in al-Qa'ida in the Islamic Maghreb, 2012, 12, http://hosted.ap.org/specials/interactives/_international/_pdfs/al-qaida-manifesto.pdf [dead link].

wa-la nujazif fi qararatina)."[73] Looking further into the future, Droukdel added,

This is also an auspicious and important opportunity to extend bridges to different sections and components of Azawadi [i.e., northern Malian] society – Tuareg, Arab, or black – with the aim of removing the state of social, political, and intellectual separation between the mujahidin and those [social] segments, to the extent possible. And foremost are the major tribes, the principal rebel movements with their different orientations, and the notables of Azawadi society, the scholars, and the eminent assemblies, personalities, and forces. If we are only able to accomplish this limited, positive measure during our short experience and then the project of the state (*mashru' al-dawla*) fails for one reason or another, it would be enough for us.[74]

Droukdel saw northern Mali's populations not as subjects to be either ruled or rebuked, but as a political audience whose sympathies for jihadism could be strategically cultivated. He spoke bluntly to his correspondents: "Among the mistaken policies that we have seen you fall into is rushing to apply the *shari'a*." Droukdel objected to "destroying tombs," and "applying the Divine punishment for extramarital sex (*tatbiq hadd al-zina*)"[75] – in other words, he rejected the very acts that made northern Mali's jihadists so infamous in the global media in 2012. Given that such acts were most prominent in Timbuktu, where Abu Zayd was based, it seems that Droukdel was rebuking Abu Zayd in particular.

Many of the harsher acts that jihadists undertook in Timbuktu, such as destroying tombs, reflected decisions taken locally rather than due to orders from Droukdel. For example, the International Criminal Court later brought a case against Ahmad al-Faqi al-Mahdi, a Malian national, and convicted him of destroying protected heritage sites in Timbuktu. One court document described the decision-making process as follows:

8. AL MAHDI was also in direct contact with the leaders of Ansar Dine and AQIM (continuously or intermittently present in Timbuktu), such as Iyad AG GHALY (the leader of Ansar Dine), Abou ZEID (the "Governor" of Timbuktu under the armed groups), Yahia Abou AL HAMMAM (the future emir of AQIM for the Sahel), and Abdallah AL CHINGUETTI (a religious scholar within AQIM).

---

[73] Ibid., 13.   [74] Ibid., 13.   [75] Ibid., 14.

9. Prior to overseeing the attack in question against historic monuments and buildings dedicated to religion, AL MAHDI was consulted about their destruction. Subsequently, in about late June 2012, Iyad AG GHALY took the decision to destroy the mausoleums, in consultation with Abou ZEID, Yahia Abou AL HAMMAM, and Abdallah AL CHINGUETTI. Their common plan was to attack and destroy buildings dedicated to religion, which were also historic monuments.[76]

If Droukdel often relied on Abu Zayd (and Abu al-Hammam) to counterbalance Belmokhtar, the Timbuktu-based field commanders nevertheless pursued political agendas of their own. Significantly, Droukdel is not named as a key decision-maker when it came to destroying tombs.

One final reason for the tensions between Droukdel, Belmokhtar, and Abu Zayd is that all three men appear to have been frustrated with the limitations that jihadist politics imposes on its bearers; the tensions in the broken triangle were not just personality conflicts but also the result of built-in dilemmas in jihadists' political projects. Jihadism does not represent a "failure of political Islam"[77] in the sense that it has died out, but it has failed to generate a viable methodology for achieving its own stated goals. Either jihadists seize territory and implement an uncompromising version of their agenda, inviting Western military intervention and alienating the local population; or they launch massive attacks that may galvanize a bit of support but do not add up to any program for taking power; or they seek a more pragmatic middle course that cannot satisfy hotheads and that risks "diluting" jihadism itself. Abu Zayd inclined toward the first option, Belmokhtar endorsed the second, and Droukdel the third – yet none of them had a genuine long-term vision for success. Each simply demanded more of what he himself advocated.

Thus Abu Zayd was one of the front-line commanders in the jihadists' push into central Mali in January 2013 (the event that provoked the French-led military intervention that ultimately destroyed the jihadist enclave, confirming Droukdel's fears). For his part, Droukdel

---

[76] International Criminal Court, "Decision on the confirmation of charges against Ahmad Al Faqi Al Mahdi," March 24, 2016, 23, www.icc-cpi.int/CourtRecords/CR2016_02424.PDF.
[77] A phrase made famous by Olivier Roy. See *The Failure of Political Islam*, translated by Carol Volk (Cambridge, MA: Harvard University Press, 1994).

advocated caution and patience with the goal of building broader political and social ties, although he did not (perhaps could not) articulate what such ties would be used for. And Belmokhtar, rejecting Droukdel's mix of admonishments and exhortations, may have even viewed the Malian enclave as a distraction from the broader goals of shaking the foundations of regional states' power, especially in Algeria. Finally, Belmokhtar may have been operating from a partly reactive position, caught between Droukdel's demands and the restlessness of his own fighters. None of the three key figures, however, had a solution for the core futility that seems hard-wired into the jihadist project.

Realignments and Reconciliations after the Fall of the Malian Emirate

After the French-led military intervention began in January 2013, AQIM and its jihadist allies scattered. Many were killed. Abu Zayd and 'Abd Allah al-Shinqiti (Abdullah al-Chinguetti), a Mauritanian national and AQIM battalion commander, died together in February 2013, fighting French-led forces in remote mountains in northern Mali.[78] For his part, the now-independent Belmokhtar headed north. At the head of his own organization, he was free to pursue his own brand of violent politics. He soon launched the type of spectacular attack he had called on AQIM to perpetrate: the January 2013 mass hostage-taking at the Tigentourine gas facility in In Aménas, eastern Algeria.

Belmokhtar framed the Tigentourine attack in intensely political terms, presenting it as a strike against multiple enemies: "Western corporations," "neo-colonialism (*al-isti'mar al-jadid*)," "the global Zionist project," "the traitorous rulers [of Muslim-majority countries],"[79] and the "Western Crusader Zionist alliance (*al-tahaluf al-gharbi al-salibi al-sihyuni*)."[80] In Belmokhtar's telling, the

---

[78] "Al Qaeda Group Confirms Death of Abou Zeid and Another Leader," Reuters, June 16, 2013, www.reuters.com/article/us-mauritania-aqim/al-qaeda-group-confirms-death-of-abou-zeid-and-another-leader-idUSBRE95F0DQ20130616.

[79] Mokhtar Belmokhtar (Khalid Abu al-'Abbas), "Al-Muqaddima" from Al-Murabitun, *Tigentourine: Al-Harb 'ala Wukala' Faransa fi al-Jaza'ir* (self-published, 2014), 4.

[80] Ibid., 7.

Tigentourine gas facility stood at the political intersection of all these forces. Tigentourine symbolized the interwoven political and economic relationships that, in his view, allowed Western powers and North African regimes to oppress Muslims in Algeria, Mali, and around the world. "Neo-colonialism" was the thread connecting these forms of oppression: Belmokhtar simultaneously described the attack as revenge for the "new French invasion" of Mali, which signaled "the beginning of the return of yesterday's colonialist,"[81] and as revenge for the straitened circumstances of ordinary Algerians. If jihadism promises equitable justice to ordinary people, here was Belmokhtar's version of justice.

In this vein, Belmokhtar told a story:

One day in Ramadan, it happened that we met with some of the residents in one of the regions of Algeria no more than 550 kilometers from the capital. They offered us their *iftar* [the meal that ends the daily fast in Ramadan] – out of hospitality for us – and do you know what it was? It consisted of a few measures of pasta (macaroni) ... We were astonished then and we asked the head of that family about his work. He said: 'I walk through these tracks on foot, gathering camel dung, and I sell it to some of the peasants' ... And we saw for ourselves sacks of that dung in his house. Had you seen his contemptible state, and his worn-out clothing and sandals, it would have grieved you. And the worst of all this – by God – was that you could see, from the site of his house, a giant corporation for extracting petroleum!!![82]

Belmokhtar framed the attack as a military and symbolic action that positioned him and his men on the side of the Algerian people, the northern Malian people, and Muslims worldwide against their (alleged) oppressors. Belmokhtar stressed how swiftly the attack followed the French-led invasion of northern Mali (just four days) but also stressed that his forces had adopted a long-term perspective on how to conduct a jihad against stronger foes.

There was a flavor here of the jihadist posture I have called accommodation, or what Belmokhtar presented as a forgiving attitude toward Muslim civilians who were ill-disposed toward the jihad. In his treatise on Tigentourine, Belmokhtar prescribed

mercy for the masses of Muslims who do not grasp the reality of the existing conflict, nor the requirements of the testament "There is no God but God

[81] Ibid., 5.   [82] Ibid., 4.

and Muhammad is the Messenger of God" due to their distance from the necessary legal understanding and their obliviousness to it, or even their alienation (*li-bu'dihim 'an al-fahm al-shar'i al-wajib wa-taghyibihim 'anhu bal taghribihim*), as is the case of many people in Muslim countries. [So it requires] gradualism on our part in addressing people and calling to them.[83]

Here, then, was Belmokhtar's answer to Droukdel and Abu Zayd: greater ambition in the military sphere, but tempered by something akin to Droukdel's conciliatory attitude toward ordinary Muslims. In Belmokhtar's telling, this combination represented a path to success for the jihadist project. Gradualism, but a gradualism punctuated by spectacular attacks. There was even something of an ambition to recreate something perhaps not seen in Algeria since the early days of the GIA: a self-presentation as romantic heroes and Robin Hood-esque figures, not just accommodating but also championing the ordinary Muslim. Belmokhtar was never able to seriously deliver on that ambition, however; his unit remained essentially a strike force.

In terms of intra-jihadist politics in the Sahara, Belmokhtar was working to merge his own battalion with MUJWA. Belmokhtar had already taken with him, into his independent battalion, some of the figures who moved with ease between AQIM and MUJWA, notably his relative Oumar Ould Hamaha.[84] MUJWA, too, showed an appetite for spectacular attacks. In May 2013, MUJWA and Belmokhtar's men, supervised by Belmokhtar, carried out simultaneous raids and shootings in two major northern Nigerien cities, Agadez and Arlit.[85] In August 2013, Belmokhtar's Signers in Blood Battalion formally merged with MUJWA, forming a new unit called al-Murabitun. Named for a medieval northwest African Muslim empire, al-Murabitun proclaimed the same themes that Belmokhtar had sounded after Tigentourine: unity among Muslims, targeting France and its allies in northwest Africa, and avenging the French-led attack on northern Mali. Regarding the mother organization – AQIM – from which both Belmokhtar and MUJWA had broken, al-Murabitun's founding statement was silent; it neither mentioned AQIM nor insinuated that AQIM was afflicted with unbelief.[86] The call for

---

[83] Ibid., 6–7.   [84] Ahmed, "Leader of al-Qaida Unit."

[85] "Mokhtar Belmokhtar 'Masterminded' Niger Suicide Bombs," BBC, May 24, 2013, www.bbc.com/news/world-africa-22654584.

[86] "Hallat Jama'atay 'al-Mulaththamun' wa-'Al-Tawhid wa-l-Jihad' wa-Ittihaduhuma fi Tanzim 'Al-Murabitun' bi-Amir 'Jadid'," Agence Nouakchott

intra-jihadist unity represented a kind of competition with AQIM, but the door remained open to reconciliation.

By 2015, relations were warming between Belmokhtar and AQIM. After a major joint operation, the November 2015 assault on the Radisson Blu Hotel in Mali's capital Bamako, Droukdel announced the formal reintegration of al-Murabitun into AQIM.[87] The mother organization was conciliatory in explaining this reintegration. In a 2016 interview, AQIM's Yahya Abu al-Hammam said simply that al-Murabitun "announced that they were [re-] joining the organization, and may God reward them well, after it became clear to them that it is not proper for the Muslims to be fighting the armies of the Cross with scattered ranks and discordant hearts."[88] Abu al-Hammam did not argue that al-Murabitun had come back to the right creed after having fallen into unbelief, or that al-Murabitun had needed to repent – he did not even argue that al-Murabitun had had no basis for their disagreements. Rather, Abu al-Hammam simply insisted that unity was best from the pragmatic point of view for the success of the jihad. The Sahara's jihadists, it seemed, needed each other.

One reason Belmokhtar may have needed AQIM – and here my analysis is admittedly speculative – is that al-Murabitun had a relative lack of clerical authority. In both components of al-Murabitun, namely Belmokhtar's own Veiled Men Battalion and his partners in MUJWA, field commanders were prominent. Belmokhtar put himself forward as the champion of ordinary Muslims who were suffering, in his view, under the boots of tyrants; yet Belmokhtar never attempted the kind of maneuver that the GIA leaders did in the mid-1990s, that of centralizing clerical and military authority in a single figure. The leaders of al-Murabitun and MUJWA were fluent in basic Salafi-jihadi discourses,[89]

---

d'Information, August 22, 2013, https://web.archive.org/web/20130824180342/http://ani.mr/?menuLink=9bf31c7ff062936a96d3c8bd1f8f2ff3&idNews=22616.

[87] Andrew Lebovich, "The Hotel Attacks and Militant Realignment in the Sahara-Sahel Region," Combating Terrorism Center *Sentinel* 9:1 (January 2016), https://ctc.usma.edu/posts/the-hotel-attacks-and-militant-realignment-in-the-sahara-sahel-region.

[88] "Abu al-Hammam fi Awwal Muqabala Lahu."

[89] It is striking, however, how generic MUJWA's doctrinal statement was. See Al-Lanja al-Shar'iyya li-Jama'at al-Tawhid wa-l-Jihad fi Gharb Ifriqiya, "Hadhihi 'Aqidatuna," Mu'assasat al-Murabitin, January 2013, https://jihadology.net/2013/01/09/al-murabitin-foundation-for-media-production-presents-a-new-statement-from-jamaat-at-tawḥid-wa-l-jihad-fi-gharb-ifriqiyyas-shariah-committee-this-is-our-aqidah/.

and both blocs had their own legal structures. Yet they had no clerics of note. Perhaps it dawned on Belmokhtar that al-Murabitun, as essentially a glorified strike force, had limited political horizons without the broader bureaucratic structures that AQIM offered – especially in the face of the internal and external challenge that the Islamic State presented to al-Murabitun starting in 2015 (see Chapter 5). Belmokhtar had the political networks necessary to sustain a fighting force with a regional military posture, but not to build a shadow state.

Additionally, by 2015–2016 Belmokhtar was the most hunted man in northwest Africa, and particularly in Libya (even the Islamic State's Libya branch put out a call for his death). A recurring target of Western airstrikes, he was reported dead in June 2015 and again in November 2016. The latter strike may have succeeded, although at the time of writing AQIM has not yet confirmed his death.

Belmokhtar's death or incapacitation, along with the deaths of other leaders from al-Murabitun and the former MUJWA, accelerated AQIM's drive toward intensified internal unity. In March 2017, AQIM released a video announcing a new structure for the Sahara, a unit called Jama'at Nusrat al-Islam wa-l-Muslimin, or the Group for Supporting Islam and Muslims (JNIM). Formally part of AQIM's hierarchy and formally subject to Droukdel's authority, JNIM was led by Iyad ag Ghali, who was shedding the last shred of plausible deniability about his deep involvement with AQIM. In the announcement video, ag Ghali appeared flanked by four others: Amadou Kouffa of Ansar al-Din's "Macina Battalion" (see Chapter 4); Yahya Abu al-Hammam, AQIM's Saharan emir; Abu Abd al-Rahman al-Sanhaji, AQIM's Saharan judge; and Al-Hasan al-Ansari, deputy leader of al-Murabitun (and a stand-in for the missing Belmokhtar). The dominant theme of the announcement video was, once again, the need for intra-jihadist unity.

JNIM has called for letting bygones be bygones. In a 2017 interview, ag Ghali made accommodating statements about al-Murabitun's return to AQIM:

Difference (*al-khilaf*) is a natural matter between humans for many well-known reasons, but [for] the people of religion (*ahl al-din*) – no matter how far their difference reaches or how much their perspectives multiply – the religion; and the fear of God the Blessed and Exalted; and advancing His

right, to Him the Glory and Power, over their own fortunes; and looking to
the interest of Islam and Muslims (*maslahat al-Islam wa-l-muslimin*) remains
their incentive for every good and their reason for overcoming all barriers.[90]

Here, then, matters had come full circle. In 2011, Belmokhtar told a
Mauritanian interviewer that "the dispute that you mentioned does
not go beyond being one of diversity." Nearly six years later, AQIM
had weathered the schism, eventually returning to a point where
ag Ghali could categorize all those difficulties as mere "difference"
that remained bounded by a shared religious viewpoint. After breaking apart completely, the broken triangle was eventually quietly
buried.

Internal and even external accommodation, in short, was AQIM's
method for dealing with one broken triangle and later for attempting
to prevent the emergence of other such triangular tensions. AQIM has
even left the door open to Islamic State defectors who change their
minds. AQIM has suffered two relatively minor defections to the
Islamic State: the defection of parts of several northern Algerian battalions in fall 2014, who formed the ill-fated Jund al-Khilafa (Soldiers
of the Caliphate); and the more consequential defection of part of al-
Murabitun, under the command of Adnan Abu al-Walid al-Sahrawi, in
May 2015. Whereas Jund al-Khilafa was largely dismantled by Algerian security forces, al-Sahrawi's "Islamic State in the Greater Sahara"
(ISGS) remains a small but potent force up through the time of
writing.[91] The relationship between JNIM and ISGS is revisited in
Chapter 5.

Like other affiliates of al-Qa'ida that have remained loyal to the
central organization and to the brand, AQIM has formally rejected
the Islamic State. For example, in a 2016 interview, Yahya Abu
al-Hammam said:

We do not recognize the legality of this "caliphate" and we do not consider
it legitimate to pledge allegiance to it (*la na'tarif shar'iyyat hadhihi "al-
khilafa" wa-la nara mashru'iyyat bay'atiha*). We do not think that it is

---

[90] "'Al-Masra' Tuhawir al-Shaykh Aba al-Fadl Iyad Ghali," *Al-Masra* 45, April 3,
2017, 4, https://azelin.files.wordpress.com/2017/04/al-masracc84-newspaper-45
.pdf.

[91] For background on ISGS, see Jason Warner, "Sub-Saharan Africa's Three 'New'
Islamic State Affiliates," Combating Terrorism Center *Sentinel* 10:1 (January
2017), https://ctc.usma.edu/sub-saharan-africas-three-new-islamic-state-
affiliates/.

following the Prophetic method (*minhaj al-nubuwwa*) for "the Prophetic method" is the method of consultation and the method of mutual consent among the Muslim community, the method of mercy and compassion (*minhaj al-rahma wa-l-ra'fa*) with the believers, the method of practicing justice and wisdom. "The Prophetic method" is not the path of killing the people of Islam, and the best of the people of Islam among the jihadist groups. "The Prophetic method" is not "dividing the ranks (*shaqq al-sufuf*)" and splitting "the groups working to support the religion."[92]

Here, Abu al-Hammam worked to refute a number of Islamic State talking points, especially the idea that the Islamic State was a unifying force for jihadists.

Yet, in keeping with broader AQIM approaches to intra-jihadist conflict (and in contrast to the Islamic State), Abu al-Hammam did not refer to Islamic State members as unbelievers or apostates. Accommodation has been the rule, and open debate the exception. Abu al-Hammam said that AQIM had initially stayed silent about the intra-jihadist conflicts in Syria, and only spoke out once the Islamic State's proclamations began to elicit questions from the younger members in AQIM. He framed local AQIM–Islamic State clashes as a problem between Muslims, rather than a contest between a believing sect and an errant one:

We think that these [clashes] are a great disruption (*fitna 'azima*) by which God is testing us, and these [clashes constitute] fighting between Muslims, especially at this time when the enemies of Islam are rushing in from every place and banding together against our Muslim community. And in this time when the mujahidin are supposed to unify their efforts and aim their guns at the breasts of the enemies of the religion, we see things that sadden us and pain us, and God is the one whose help we ask ... What we say in the greater Sahara is that we implore God to spare the blood of Muslims and mujahidin, and to reunite them and repair their discord. I ask Him, may He be glorified, to lift the tribulation from our community. As for our relationship with the group of Abu al-Walid al-Sahrawi, which announced its allegiance to the [Islamic] State, it is, up to now, a normal relationship and we are in communication with them. We pray to God for their sake that He may guide them in a beautiful way back to the truth.[93]

At the time of writing, al-Sahrawi still remains a rebel against AQIM – but AQIM's hand remains open to him, and press rumors periodically

---

[92] "Abu al-Hammam fi Awwal Muqabala Lahu."   [93] Ibid.

predict a rapprochement.[94] The long shadow of the GIA's fratricidal self-destruction continues to shape AQIM's accommodationism toward internal debates and even toward external rivals.

Conclusion

Since the Islamic State seized headlines in 2014, it has been well-known that jihadists debate and disagree with each other, sometimes to the point of violence. Less discussed has been the nature of intra-jihadist disagreement within a single organization. This chapter has suggested that it matters a great deal how jihadists disagree. For the Islamic State, and long before them the GIA, any major disagreement inevitably centered on the issue of creed and belief, with dissenters cast as unbelievers. The end result of such a politics is violence and rupture.

The GSPC and its successor, AQIM, have taken a more conciliatory approach. From 2003 through the (likely) death of Mokhtar Belmokhtar in 2016, the Sahara was an arena of bitter, long-running disagreements between various figures in AQIM. But these leaders, partly reacting against the disastrous trajectory of the GIA, worked to confine disagreements to the level of strategy. From the time of the GSPC's break with the GIA onward, GSPC/AQIM leaders were reluctant, and often unwilling, to bring issues of creed and belief into debates about strategy. Mindful of what happens when a central leadership declares dissenters unbelievers and then kills them, AQIM tolerated an internal culture of autonomy and disagreement, a long-running broken triangle. In public and private statements, AQIM leaders credited their rivals with being Muslims. This approach left the door open to reconciliation, not just in theoretical but in practical terms, as AQIM's reintegration of Belmokhtar's men shows.

What do these different styles of debate tell us about jihadist politics? For starters, they suggest that jihadists are affected by the same banalities of intra-organizational politics that beset any team, from corporations to political campaigns. Yet there are also specificities to jihadist politics. On the one hand, the vast extent of the Islamic tradition, and even the internal diversity of the jihadist tradition,

---

[94] "Mali: deux importants groupes jihadistes opèrent un rapprochement," RFI, December 14, 2017, www.rfi.fr/afrique/20171214-mali-deux-importants-groupes-jihadistes-operent-rapprochement.

furnishes multiple models for disagreement; AQIM leaders' statements suggest that they take those models seriously. On the other hand, the ultimate futility of jihadist action hangs over the actors' heads, setting the stage for disagreement over strategy but also producing a fatalism that other types of organizational politics lack, or at least do not possess in the same degree. The leader who offers his followers a form of jihadist politics that exudes ambition, as Belmokhtar did in 2012–2013, has a significant short-term advantage in these internal political fights. In the long term, however, perhaps the ultimate advantage lies with the most pragmatic: of Abu Zayd, Belmokhtar, and Droukdel, it is only the latter who is confirmed to be alive at the time of writing. Jihadist politics is thus beset with a push and pull between those who call for more action and those who call for more prudence, those who advocate schisms in the name of ambition and those who call for unity in the name of patience. Ultimately, however, one wonders if Droukdel could say, in 2020 more than what he said in 2008 when asked about his organization's great success and its greatest failure: "We believe that our greatest achievement is that the jihad is still continuing in the Islamic Maghreb ... If it is necessary to have a failure, then surely our failure is that we are for a long time unable to win martyrdom and join our brothers who preceded us on the road of sacrifice and martyrdom."[95] For all that jihadists had endured in the Sahara, they had achieved nothing lasting.

[95] "An Interview with Abdelmalek Droukdal."

3 | Northern Mali
Dialectics of Local Support

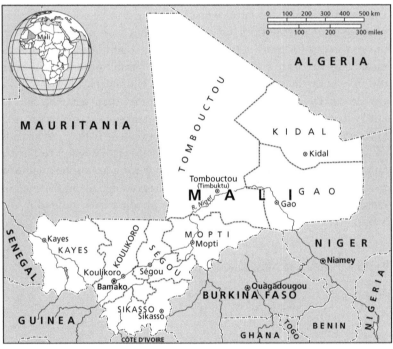

Map 2 Northern Mali

Chapters 1 and 2 concentrated on coalition politics within a series of Algeria-born jihadist organizations: the GIA, the GSPC, and AQIM. Chapter 2 included analysis of AQIM's alliances in northern Mali, but from an AQIM-centric perspective. In this chapter I look at the period 1990–2017 from the perspective of northern Malian actors, jihadist and non-jihadist.

The central characters in this chapter are the leaders of Ansar al-Din ("Defenders of the Faith"), a key actor in the northern Malian rebellion of 2012. Ansar al-Din was led by the Tuareg politician Iyad ag Ghali (b. 1958). When France intervened militarily in northern Mali in January 2013, ag Ghali deepened his commitment to AQIM. Yet other Tuareg politicians in Ansar al-Din, including some of his longtime companions, made the opposite choice and shed their jihadist affiliations in order to return to mainstream politics.

Why did ag Ghali become more committed to jihadism than his Tuareg peers? Ag Ghali's personal religious transformation likely influenced his choice. Yet contextual and political factors are also crucial to consider. Viewed against the backdrop of northern Malian history from 1990 onwards, by 2013 ag Ghali's political position was distinctly tenuous. Ag Ghali's position as a "broker" between AQIM and the Tuareg politicians in his home region of Kidal elevated his influence amid the 2012 rebellion,[1] but the requisite balancing act proved unsustainable as France's intervention destroyed the AQIM/Ansar al-Din jihadist proto-state. Hitching his star to AQIM in 2013 made ag Ghali "public enemy number one" in the Sahara,[2] but it also represented his most promising path to continued political relevance.

Ag Ghali's case highlights mechanisms through which jihadists can pick up crucial allies in wartime. The contrasting choices of ag Ghali's one-time allies in Ansar al-Din, however, reveal other mechanisms in jihadist politics. Various reductionist analyses assert that jihadists, and particularly al-Qaʻida, adroitly exploit civil wars.[3] Yet jihadists do not simply prey on passive and disoriented populations; rather, jihadist implantation evolves through dialectics with local conditions. Jihadists' prospects for enlarging their coalitions and building alliances

[1] Olivier Walther and Dimitris Christopoulos, "Islamic Terrorism and the Malian Rebellion," *Terrorism and Political Violence* 27:3 (2015): 497–519.
[2] Baba Ahmed, Benjamin Roger, Christophe Boisbouvier, and Farid Alilat, "Sahel: Iyad Ag Ghaly, l'insaisissable ennemi public n°1," *Jeune Afrique*, March 19, 2018, www.jeuneafrique.com/mag/540964/politique/sahel-iyad-ag-ghaly-linsaisissable-ennemi-public-n1/.
[3] See United States Institute of Peace Task Force on Extremism in Fragile States, "Preventing Extremism in Fragile States: A New Approach," February 2019, www.usip.org/sites/default/files/2019-02/preventing-extremism-in-fragile-states-a-new-approach.pdf. The authors write (3), "Extremism both preys on fragile states and contributes to chaos."

are shaped by the opportunities presented by local politics and "wartime political orders."[4]

In northern Mali, as Thomas Hüsken and Georg Klute have written, the political order is increasingly characterized by "heterarchy," meaning "the mutable as well as unstable intertwining of state and nonstate orders and the plurality of competing power groups."[5] Amid heterarchy, local politicians can exercise considerable agency when relating to jihadists. Strikingly, politicians who identify "off-ramps" can even extricate themselves from jihadist alliances relatively unscathed. The case of northern Mali shows that jihadist coalitions and alliances have internal logics reflecting the contexts in which they emerge and the multiple options available to the leaders of political-military blocs.

This framing of the Malian case breaks with some previous accounts of the conflict. Influential accounts have depicted northern Malian jihadists, especially Ansar al-Din, as pawns of AQIM. A right-wing think tank, the Foundation for the Defense of Democracies, has called Ansar al-Din "the local face of AQIM in Mali." The Foundation described AQIM as having "stood up" Ansar al-Din.[6] The United Nations Security Council reached similar conclusions, writing, "AQIM wanted to create an ostensibly independent movement that would hide its true roots by abandoning the name 'Al-Qaida'."[7] But dismissing Ansar al-Din's complexity and attributing agency primarily to AQIM cripples understanding of the group's "circumstantial jihadists" – whose equivalents are found in many contemporary civil wars and who are never merely pawns of al-Qa'ida.

Theoretical Implications of the Case

The northern Malian case highlights how involvement by local politicians in jihadist projects can escalate from *accommodation*

[4] Paul Staniland, "States, Insurgents, and Wartime Political Orders," *Perspectives on Politics* 10:2 (June 2012): 243–264.

[5] Thomas Hüsken and Georg Klute, "Political Orders in the Making: Emerging Forms of Political Organization from Libya to Northern Mali," *African Security* 8 (2015): 320–337, 321.

[6] Thomas Joscelyn, "Analysis: Al Qaeda Groups Reorganize in West Africa," *Long War Journal*, March 13, 2017, www.longwarjournal.org/archives/2017/03/analysis-al-qaeda-groups-reorganize-in-west-africa.php.

[7] United Nations Security Council, "Ansar Eddine," version as of February 3, 2015, www.un.org/securitycouncil/sanctions/1267/aq_sanctions_list/summaries/entity/ansar-eddine.

to *collusion* to *alliance* to *incorporation*. Ag Ghali also exemplifies how local politicians can exert substantial influence within jihadist coalitions' internal politics, as well as influence over the trajectories of those coalitions. As local politicians enter into jihadist coalitions they affect internal balances of power – in this case, reinforcing the "broken triangle" structure of AQIM as discussed in the last chapter. Local politicians can become prominent voices within jihadist coalitions, especially when (as in Mali) such support is essential for helping jihadists move from *marginalization* to *domination*.

Even more interestingly, the case of northern Mali shows that some jihadist coalitions acquiesce to local politicians who want to de-escalate their involvement. Often it is a combination of factors – financial, military, and political incentives; duress and the deterioration of an earlier political status quo; and/or changing religious viewpoints and topographies – that draws politicians into various degrees of involvement with jihadists. Yet local politicians are not merely flies trapped in the jihadists' spiderweb; they maintain agency, as shown by the divergent paths that ag Ghali and some of his peers took. Even in chaotic conditions, local politicians appear to carefully assess their options – although, it should be pointed out, it is difficult to fully reconstruct their decisions and the relative weight of belief, self-interest, and social ties in shaping those decisions.

These dynamics also foreground jihadists' agency. Within a coalition, some field commanders may gravitate toward or strike up partnerships with local politicians even as other field commanders develop tensions with those same figures. Meanwhile, jihadists face complex choices when allies want to step away. Trying to enforce compliance through violence, up to and including assassination, could be a means of discouraging allies from breaking off. Yet such violence could have unpredictable effects, including a broader loss of local support. Perhaps for these reasons, AQIM acquiesced when some of its Malian allies decided to de-escalate their involvement after France's military intervention in 2013. And perhaps AQIM perceived advantages in that very de-escalation, as all parties adapted to a new status quo, where accommodation and collusion could actually be more useful to the organization than open alliance.

The Lifeworld of Iyad ag Ghali

Iyad ag Ghali was born in the Kidal region in 1958,[8] sixty-five years after the French colonial conquest of Timbuktu and the ensuing French conquest of all of northern Mali. Ag Ghali belongs to the Iriyaken clan of the Ifoghas, the "noble" clan cluster of the Kel Adagh, which is itself a tribal confederation within the larger Tuareg people. Although being Iriyakén made ag Ghali a noble, it did not position him to obtain hereditary leadership of the Kel Adagh, which is reserved for the Kel Afella clan.[9]

Unlike other Tuareg confederations in Mali and Niger, the Kel Adagh did not violently resist French colonialism. The Kel Adagh's long-serving paramount ruler, or *aménokal*, Attaher ag Illi (d. 1962, in office 1913–1914 and 1915–1962) was a favorite of the colonial administration. The French reshaped the office of *aménokal* into a more permanent, powerful, and patrilineal position than it had ever been before[10] – a transformation that would later frustrate ag Ghali's own bid to sideline or supplant the *aménokal* of his era.

Despite the Kel Adagh's quietism under French rule, the transition from colonialism to independent Mali in 1960 provoked a rebellion in the Kel Adagh heartland of Kidal. The 1963–1964 rebellion had multiple causes, ranging from ambiguous French gestures toward the possibility of creating a Saharan polity in the 1950s, to the racism and contempt that Tuareg "whites" felt for the "blacks" in southern Mali, to the centralizing and authoritarian policies of the administration of Mali's first President Modibo Keïta (in office 1960–1968).

The rebellion was short-lived. The rebels were outmatched, militarily and politically. The *aménokal* – now Intalla ag Attaher (in office 1962–2014), one of Attaher ag Illi's sons – remained loyal to the Malian state. Within a short time, the Malian military regained control of the Kidal region. Malian government forces imposed draconian collective punishments, poisoning wells, destroying livestock, and

---

[8] "'Al-Masra' Tuhawir al-Shaykh Aba al-Fadl Iyad Ghali," *Al-Masra* 45, April 3, 2017, 4, https://azelin.files.wordpress.com/2017/04/al-masracc84-newspaper-45 .pdf. 1958 is the date Ag Ghali gives, although many sources give the date as 1954.

[9] Pierre Boilley, *Les Touaregs Kel Adagh. Dépendances et révoltes: du Soudan français au Mali contemporain* (Paris: Karthala, 1999), 47.

[10] Ibid., 165–174.

in what ways are descriptions of
Tuareg different Above?

publicly humiliating captured rebels. The rebellion exposed fault-lines
in Kel Adagh politics, as the *aménokal*'s own brother Zeid joined the
rebels.[11] The theme of rebellions exposing and exacerbating intra-
Ifoghas tensions would reappear throughout ag Ghali's career. The
rebellion also directly and tragically affected ag Ghali's life. According
to some accounts, his father, Ghali ag Babaker, was fatally shot by
rebels in 1963. The incident was accidental – ag Babaker had been
coerced into guiding a column of soldiers, and he was wearing a coat
that hid his identity from the rebel sniper.[12] Amid the many losses that
the Kel Adagh suffered in 1963–1964, ag Ghali experienced a deeply
personal loss.

In the 1970s, as a young man, ag Ghali became part of a generational cohort called the *ishumar*. The word derives from the French
chômeur, meaning "unemployed." The *ishumar* were young Tuareg
migrants who headed for Algeria, Libya, and elsewhere seeking work
amid the Saharan-Sahelian drought that began in 1968. Outside Mali,
and particularly in Libya, the *ishumar* forged a unique, hybrid culture
as well as a sharpened sense of Tuareg political identity. They found a
mercurial patron in Libya's ruler Muammar Qadhafi (in power
1969–2011). Qadhafi recruited Tuareg to fight in his foreign ventures
in the 1980s but proved unreliable when it came to helping the Tuareg
advance their own political goals. Ag Ghali became a central figure in
the *ishumar* generation and in the cohort's relationship with Qadhafi.
He served in Qadhafi's Islamic Legion, fighting in Lebanon and perhaps also in Chad. By the early 1980s, then identifying as a sort of
"leftist nationalist,"[13] he was a leader among Tuareg who planned to
return to Mali and launch an uprising.

The *ishumar* experience, as Georg Klute has written, generated two
basic competing understandings of Tuareg identity. On the one hand,
the *ishumar* and the wider Tuareg diaspora in North Africa developed
an egalitarian, pan-Tuareg "feeling of national unity" that transcended

[11] Baz Lecocq, *Disputed Desert: Decolonisation, Competing Nationalisms and
Tuareg Rebellions in Northern Mali* (Leiden: Brill, 2010), 197.

[12] Boilley, *Les Touaregs Kel Adagh*, 327–328; this episode also came up in my
interview with MNLA representative Saïd Ben Bella, Nouakchott, October
2017. Ag Ghali's longtime but now estranged friend Manny Ansar questioned
the story and said he had never heard ag Ghali mention it or express any "spirit
of vengeance." Interview with Manny Ansar, Bamako, March 13, 2018.

[13] Interview with Mohammed Mahmoud Abu al-Ma'ali, Nouakchott, April
28, 2018.

older notions of tribal and clan identity. On the other hand, there was
the continued pull of the "customary framework of the society,"
rooted in tribal differences and social hierarchies.[14] The competition
between those two understandings of identity reverberated through the
rebellion of 1990 and afterwards.

In June 1990, ag Ghali's Mouvement populaire de libération de
l'Azawad (Popular Movement for the Liberation of Azawad, MPLA)
initiated a rebellion in northern Mali. The rebellion took impetus from
a combination of factors: the politicization of the *ishumar*; memories
of the 1963–1964 rebellion; drought; widening economic inequality;
and government corruption.[15] Better armed, better organized, and
more politically sophisticated than their forebears, the MPLA generated military and political momentum, eliciting wide popular support
among Kel Adagh Tuareg.[16] The MPLA did not, however, attract the
support of the *aménokal*, Intalla ag Attaher, who remained loyal to the
Malian state.[17]

In 1991, multiple factors broke the momentum of the MPLA, which
dropped "liberation" from its name to become the MPA. Negotiations
between the MPA and the state positioned ag Ghali as the state's key
interlocutor in the north, but caused dissensions among the rebels. The
MPA fragmented into factions that assumed a tribal and sectional
character,[18] as the ethic of a pan-Tuareg rebel project collapsed. The
MPA signed two agreements with the Malian government, the January
1991 Tamanrasset Accords and the 1992 National Pact. Yet conflict
continued in the north amid competition among armed groups. These
trends foreshadowed similar ones following the 2012 rebellion.

Some of the groups that emerged out of ag Ghali's MPA not only
challenged the MPA's leadership of the rebellion but also the social
hierarchy of the Kel Adagh Tuareg, namely the dominance of the
"noble" Ifoghas within the confederation. These fissures drew on a
longer history, running from roughly the 1940s to the 1990s. Deep
social transformations had occurred, first as colonial authorities eman-
cipated slaves and then as postcolonial droughts upended hierarchies.
By the 1970s and 1980s, some Tuareg "nobles" found themselves

[14] Georg Klute, "Hostilités et alliances: Archéologie de la dissidence des Touaregs
au Mali," *Cahiers d'Études Africaines* 35:137 (1995): 55–71, 56.
[15] David Gutelius, "Islam in Northern Mali and the War on Terror," *Journal of
Contemporary African Studies* 25:1 (January 2007): 59–76, 60-61.
[16] Boilley, *Les Touaregs Kel Adagh*, 481.   [17] Ibid., 492.   [18] Ibid., 495–521.

[handwritten annotation: "more agency – highly stratified"]

scraping by in North Africa, West Africa, Europe, or in Mali's capital Bamako. Such predicaments led to relationships (marriage, employment, etc.) with other Tuareg who had previously been seen as social juniors.[19] The accumulating effects of these changes surfaced amid the rebellion. As Baz Lecocq writes, "An unknown number of bellah [slaves or former slaves] took sides against their former masters, which inaugurated new political balances and more tense social relations in the post rebellion period."[20]

Not just the bellah but also the Imghad, a social category of "free" but "non-noble" or "vassal" Tuareg, asserted themselves. Imghad self-assertion drew on a history dating back to colonial rule, which "despite the intentions of most French officials and many Tuareg leaders ... tended to undermine the bases for social hierarchy that colonial and noble writers found so natural."[21] One outspoken group was the Armée révolutionnaire de libération de l'Azawad (Revolutionary Army for the Liberation of Azawad, ARLA). Whereas the MPA was dominated by Ifoghas, ARLA proclaimed a sweeping egalitarianism and elevated members of the Imghad.[22] In 1994, ARLA kidnapped the *aménokal* himself in a show of discontent with power structures it saw as outmoded and oppressive.

The *aménokal*'s sons, meanwhile, were increasingly stepping into the political spotlight – and their activities would both reconfigure their family's authority and challenge the role that ag Ghali sought. The brothers – Mohamed, Alghabass, and Attayoub – were rivals to ag Ghali but sometimes also his allies, even if he seems to have nursed a longstanding ambition to displace the Intalla family as paramount leaders of the Kel Adagh Tuareg. The *aménokal*'s sons had taken a different path than ag Ghali; none of them were members of the *ishumar*, the young Tuareg who sought work in Algeria and Libya during the desperate decades of the 1970s and 1980s. Alghabass went to Libya only at the end of the *ishumar* period, from 1988 to 1990, in

[19] Ibid., 384–386.
[20] Baz Lecocq, "The Bellah Question: Slave Emancipation, Race, and Social Categories in Late Twentieth-Century Northern Mali," *Canadian Journal of African Studies* 39:1 (2005): 42–68, 43.
[21] Bruce Hall, *A History of Race in Muslim West Africa, 1600–1960* (Cambridge: Cambridge University Press, 2011), 174.
[22] Boilley, *Les Touaregs Kel Adagh*, 513–521.

order to help prepare the rebellion of 1990.[23] Even during the rebellion, the *aménokal*'s sons limited their participation.

As the rebellion wound down, the *aménokal*'s sons and ag Ghali had different forms of political capital. Mohamed, Alghabass, and Attayoub ag Intalla were recasting themselves as politicians, while ag Ghali drew on his image as a warrior and power broker. Both of these postures were vulnerable to challenges from multiple other power centers within Kel Adagh society – a dynamic that would intensify both the rivalry and the interdependence between the Intalla brothers and ag Ghali in the years to come.

In March 1996, northern Malian fighters ceremonially burned weapons in a "flame of peace," formally ending the rebellion. Yet the Malian state's half-hearted efforts to decentralize power in the north created new opportunities for political maneuvering. Reinforcing these political changes at the local level were political upheavals at the national level: In 1991–1992, Mali transitioned away from military rule and entered a new, multi-party civilian system. By 1996, Tuareg leaders faced new arenas of competition. The *aménokal*'s sons entered electoral politics, showing that hereditary authority on its own was no longer sufficient to guarantee their power. From 1999 to 2002, Alghabass ag Intalla served as mayor of Kidal,[24] and then from 2002 to 2012 he represented Kidal as a deputy in the Malian National Assembly. His brother Mohamed became a deputy for Tin-Essako, while Attayoub became mayor of Kidal. Both Mohamed and Alghabass ag Intalla belonged to the dominant party of the era, ADEMA, although both were rarely seen in Bamako or at the legislature.[25]

Controlling the Kidal region's legislative seats had less to do with shaping national policy than with local politics and relations between Kidal and Bamako. Even that control was difficult to sustain. By the 2000s, Imghad politicians – representing the demographic majority in many places – were winning elections across the north. The rise of Imghad politicians revealed the declining prospects for continued Ifoghas electoral hegemony, even in Kidal. Alghabass ag Intalla estimated that while he won his first National Assembly election in

---

[23] Interview with Alghabass ag Intalla, Washington, January 13, 2018.

[24] Lecocq, *Disputed Desert*, 328.

[25] U.S. Embassy Bamako, "All in the Family: Legislative Politics in Kidal," leaked cable 07BAMAKO594, June 1, 2007, https://wikileaks.org/plusd/cables/07BAMAKO594_a.html.

2002 with some 70 percent of the vote, he received only 55 percent of the vote for his reelection in 2007. Had he run again in 2012, he calculated that he might have lost.[26] The rise in Imghad political consciousness placed the Ifoghas on the defensive; as one representative of an Imghad-led militia told me, "The Imghad's candidate will always win [in Kidal] because [the Imghad have] an absolute majority."[27]

Ag Ghali took a different, less public path than the ag Intalla brothers during the period 1996–2006. Unlike some of his lieutenants from the MPA, such as Ibrahim ag Bahanga (1970–2011), ag Ghali did not join the Malian army. Nor did he seek elected office, whether out of what former friends describe as shyness or to avoid openly challenging the *amenokal*'s family – something that both sides wanted to avoid. Ag Ghali preferred to be "the chief alongside the chief," wielding informal authority.[28] From approximately 2007–2010, he served as Mali's consul in Jeddah, Saudi Arabia, although he would ultimately be recalled (or perhaps expelled) under a cloud of suspicion concerning his contacts there.[29] He also became an advisor to Malian President Amadou Toumani Touré and a negotiator with both Tuareg rebels and the GSPC/AQIM. Over time, however, ag Ghali's reputation as an honest broker began to suffer, a dynamic that likely contributed to his eventual embrace of jihadism.

In the late 1990s, religious changes were also occurring in northern Mali. These changes affected ag Ghali, the Intalla brothers, and the society around them. An overwhelmingly Muslim society, northern Mali had long been committed to the particular form of Sunni Islam – Maliki in terms of legal school, Ash'ari in terms of theology, and infused with Sufism – that has long predominated in northwest Africa. Yet by the 1970s, other currents were gaining strength. By the 1990s, these changes were affecting Kidal.

---

[26] Interview with Alghabass ag Intalla.

[27] Interview with Fahad ag Mohamed, Bamako, June 21, 2019.

[28] Interview with Manny Ansar.

[29] This period of Ag Ghali's adult life is the most weakly documented. Notably, ag Ghali does not discuss this period in his interview with *Al-Masra*, cited previously. For a brief description of his activities in Jeddah, see Al-Sheikh Mohamed, "Iyad Ag Ghali: Mali's Desert Fox," *Asharq al-Awsat*, February 15, 2013, https://eng-archive.aawsat.com/al-sheikh-mohamed/features/profiles/iyad-ag-ghali-malis-desert-fox. According to Abu al-Ma'ali in the previously cited interview, ag Ghali was deputy consul, and not consul, in Jeddah.

Economic and political changes fed religious transformations. Structural adjustment, liberalization of media and civil society, and the advent of civilian multi-party politics had a quadruple effect. First, the influence of Islamic nongovernmental organizations and private donors increased: as Susan Rasmussen wrote in 2007, "the Pakistani *da'wa* [see below] and Saudi Arabian mosques, clinics, and schools in Niger and Mali fill gaps in economic assistance left in the wake of IMF and World Bank restructuring policies."[30] Second, local Islamic voices asserted themselves in new ways, including by taking staff positions in international Islamic NGOs.[31] Third, northern voices defined themselves against what they saw as southern forms of politics and religiosity. And fourth, intra-Muslim competition grew within the north. As David Gutelius writes, "While this increasingly public, but specifically northern, discourse arose in part to counter other Muslim leaders' claims to religious authority (and by extension political clout and access to economic opportunities), it showed growing intracommunal rivalries and competition on Islamic orthodoxy and orthopraxy."[32] It may also be the case that by the 1990s, mechanisms for reproducing classical Islamic scholars were beginning to break down,[33] creating a vacuum into which other Islamic currents, including Salafism and Salafi-jihadism, would increasingly enter.

One such current was Jama'at al-Da'wa wa-l-Tabligh (the Society for Preaching and Spreading the Message). Founded in India in 1926, Tabligh counts adherents around the world. Tabligh's followers cultivate personal piety and conduct missionary tours where they enjoin other Muslims to become more pious. Known in Mauritania and Mali

---

[30] Susan Rasmussen, "Re-Formations of the Sacred, the Secular, and Modernity: Nuances of Religious Experience among the Tuareg (Kel Tamajaq)," *Ethnology* 46:3 (Summer 2007): 185–203, 189.

[31] Jonathan Benthall, "Islamic Aid in a North Malian Enclave," *Anthropology Today* 22:4 (August 2006): 19–21.

[32] Gutelius, "Islam in Northern Mali," 63.

[33] One can easily identify prominent Muslim clerics based in southern Mali: the Chérif of Nioro du Sahel, the former High Islamic Council President Mahmoud Dicko, and the current Council President Ousmane Madani Haïdara. It is more difficult to identify prominent clerics in the north, although it should be noted that Dicko is originally from the Timbuktu region, as is the Islamic scholar and former Ambassador to Saudi Arabia Mahmoud Zouber.

simply as "Da'wa," Tabligh arrived in Kidal between the mid and the late 1990s.[34] In 2002, a French journalist reported:

The city of Kidal has thus become a hotspot for proselytism by the "bearded ones" of the Da'wa sect, suspected of preparing the bed for a more radical Islam, which [Kidal's] inhabitants dispute. "Certainly we open our broadcasts every day with the reading of the Qur'an. But that does not mean that we are succumbing to the sirens of religious fundamentalism," protests Moussa ag Itjimit, presenter on the local radio [station] Tizias.[35]

According to his own account, ag Ghali participated in Tabligh from 1998–2011:

God inspired us – to Him be praise and thanks – to join Jama'at al-Da'wa wa-l-Tabligh. This was a beneficial phase in which God Most High facilitated [my] completion of the memorization of the Holy Qur'an, and [my] visits to God's Muslims and [my] acquaintance with many of them in many places, such as [Saudi Arabia], the Gulf, Mauritania, India, Pakistan, Nigeria, Niger, Togo, and Benin. [I] even [visited] Muslim communities in the West, in France and other countries.[36]

And there was more to ag Ghali's relationship with Tabligh. If ag Ghali was "fascinated by their message" and "disillusioned by the fractiousness of Touareg tribal politics," he was also maneuvering for "legitimacy as a religious figure."[37]

The flourishing of Islamic activism within northern Mali had repercussions for inter-ethnic relations. Formerly low-status groups challenged the groups that had traditionally wielded religious leadership. "Bellah and Songhay imams openly criticised Kel Ifoghas Tuareg and [Arab] Kunta leaders in terms of their orthopraxy."[38] For an Ifoghas figure like ag Ghali to meet such challenges required new religious and

[34] Lecocq puts the date at Ramadan 1419 or December 1998/January 1999. See *Disputed Desert*, 322 and Baz Lecocq and Paul Schrijver, "The War on Terror in a Haze of Dust: Potholes and Pitfalls on the Saharan Front," *Journal of Contemporary African Studies* 25:1 (January 2007): 141–166, 148–151.

[35] Christine Holzbauer, "Les inquiétants émirs du Sahel," *L'Express*, November 28, 2002, www.lexpress.fr/actualite/monde/les-inquietants-emirs-du-sahel_497478.html.

[36] "'Al-Masra' Tuhawir al-Shaykh Aba al-Fadl Iyad Ghali."

[37] Andy Morgan, "What Do the Touareg Want?" Andy Morgan Writes, February 1, 2013, www.andymorganwrites.com/what-do-the-touareg-want/.

[38] Gutelius, "Islam in Northern Mali," 64.

symbolic capital – such as a stronger command over the content of the Qur'an – which Tabligh helped him to acquire.

Ag Ghali may have seen Tabligh as a vehicle not just for reinforcing his authority among the Kel Adagh but also for defending his status within northern Mali more broadly. As late as November 2009, by which time northern Malian interest in Tabligh had declined considerably, ag Ghali continued to use the movement to elevate his visibility in Kidal. Organizing an "international conference" for Tabligh in the city, ag Ghali appeared to some Kidal leaders as "a polarizing element and a potential threat to both the traditional leadership and the local population's current desire for calm." Such leaders also saw ag Ghali as someone keen to appear "in grand form to reinforce his relevance to the Kidal leadership after over a year spent in Jiddah."[39] Tabligh gave him new international connections but also new local platforms. These were modes of conducting politics, but with plausible deniability in the form of spirituality.

As ag Ghali elevated his religious credentials, the potential challenge did not go unnoticed by the ag Intalla family, all of whom joined Tabligh for a short time.[40] Just as ag Ghali sought religious legitimacy through Tabligh, so the *aménokal*'s sons sought a re-legitimation. Considered *shurafa'*, or descendants of the Prophet Muhammad, the *aménokal*'s family has long cultivated a hybrid religious–hereditary–political leadership profile.[41]

Then, in 2006, another rebellion broke out. Ag Ghali took charge, helming the Alliance Démocratique pour le Changement (Democratic Alliance for Change, ADC). Alongside ag Ghali were veterans of the 1990 rebellion and ag Ghali's old MPA. These figures included two prominent Tuareg officers who defected from the Malian army, Hassan ag Fagaga and Ibrahim ag Bahanga, as well as two long-time associates of ag Ghali, Ahmada ag Bibi and Mohamed ag Aharib. The initial rebellion lasted only from May to July 2006 before the ADC accepted a preliminary accord brokered by Algeria. By March 2007, ag Ghali was essentially co-hosting a development forum in Kidal with President Amadou Toumani Touré and Prime Minister Ousmane Issoufi Maiga. Such events kept ag Ghali in the political spotlight, as

---

[39] U.S. Embassy Bamako, "Dawa Meeting in Kidal Not Much to Talk About," leaked cable 09BAMAKO822, December 21, 2009, https://wikileaks.org/plusd/cables/09BAMAKO822_a.html.
[40] Ibid.   [41] Lecocq, *Disputed Desert*, 328.

the government's designated interlocutor for the interests of Kidal and even the entire north.[42]

Yet, in a foretaste of the difficulty he would have imposing himself as leader of the 2012 rebellion, during the 2006–2009 uprising some of ag Ghali's own commanders bucked his authority.[43] Ag Bahanga launched his own rebellion in 2007 as the Alliance touareg Nord-Mali pour le Changement (Northern Mali Tuareg Alliance for Change, ATNMC), which rejected the Algerian-brokered peace process. As in the 1990s, clan differences shaped the fragmentation of the 2006 rebellion; ag Bahanga and some of the other ATNMC leaders came from the Ifergoumessen clan of the Ifoghas, rather than from ag Ghali's Iriyaken.

Ag Bahanga's activities posed dilemmas for ag Ghali. As US diplomats in Bamako wrote in a 2008 cable,

The Tuareg position on Bahanga is somewhat ambiguous. Nearly all Tuareg leaders, excepting Iyad ag Ghali, have staunchly condemned Bahanga's decision to resort to violence. No Tuareg leaders, however, have denounced Bahanga's demands regarding a military withdrawal from northern Mali, increased development and the implementation of the Algiers Accords. A very small percentage of Tuaregs, said Azaz [ag Doudagdag, an Imghad politician then reportedly an informal advisor to then-President Touré], just three or four fractions, are currently in rebellion. Azaz claimed the rebels' objectives, however, are shared by one hundred percent of Malian Tuaregs.[44]

Ag Ghali positioned himself as a broker, traveling to Algeria and Libya to negotiate a settlement. Yet his ability to act as the key spokesman for the north, already challenged after the compromises of 1991–1992, now seemed even weaker. The same 2008 cable conveyed Imghad politicians' skepticism about ag Ghali's motives:

If Tuareg leaders' response to Bahanga is ambiguous, the role of ADC leader Iyad ag Ghali is inscrutable. Azaz, [Ghoumar] ag Intaha and [Mohamed Issouf] ag Ghallas laughed when asked if ag Ghali – who is currently in Libya

---

[42] "ATT A LA CLOTURE DU FORUM DE KIDAL: 'L'appel au développement ne se fait pas par la voie des armes, qui est, et restera inacceptable'," *Nouvel Horizon*, March 27, 2007, www.maliweb.net/category.php?NID=17184.

[43] Interview with Manny Ansar.

[44] U.S. Embassy Bamako, "Tuareg Leaders from Gao and Timbuktu: Time for Peace Running Out," leaked cable 08BAMAKO339, April 7, 2008, https://wikileaks.org/plusd/cables/08BAMAKO339_a.html.

negotiating with the Malian government and members of Bahanga's Northern Mali Tuareg Alliance for Change (ATNMC) – represented the interests of Tuaregs from the regions of Gao and Timbuktu. There is apparently no communication between ag Ghali and non-Kidal Tuaregs. When asked if ag Ghali was negotiating on behalf of northern Malians, Malian Tuaregs, Tuaregs from Kidal or just members of the ADC, Azaz said ag Ghali negotiated for ag Ghali and no one else.[45]

Compounding ag Ghali's challenges was the fact that he was posted to Jeddah during much of this period; often now, he was seeking to shape Tuareg politics from afar.

Ag Ghali was managing a web of relationships: Tuareg politicians, the ADC, ag Bahanga's ATNMC, the Malian state, and neighboring governments. The 2006–2009 rebellion seems to have represented the last occasion when it was possible for ag Ghali to present himself as a wise elder statesman. Another 2008 cable provides a snapshot of how he approached the late stages of the rebellion. One passage flags the challenge that Alghabass ag Intalla posed for ag Ghali's long-term role in Kel Adagh politics:

[Ag Ghali] remains in telephone contact with many Tuareg rebel leaders, including ADC spokesman Ahmada ag Bibi, the two Intallah brothers [i.e., Alghabass and Mohamed], Bahanga and Fagaga. Of the four National Assembly Deputies from th[e] region of Kidal (ag Bibi, Alghabass ag Intallah, Mohamed ag Intallah, and Deity ag Sidamou), only Alghabass appears to have the bearing, charisma and intelligence needed to rival ag Ghali. As the second son of the Kidal Tuareg's tradition[al] leader, Alghabass has the pedigree needed to assume a larger leadership role. He is, however, only in his mid-30s and lacks ag Ghali's military and political credentials.[46]

According to one expert, ag Ghali and ag Bahanga were coordinating with one another during this time, and ag Bahanga was quietly drifting toward a more Islamist outlook.[47] But ag Ghali was also struggling to maintain his position as the top power broker.

Alghabass ag Intalla declined to join the rebel ADC and its offshoots, feeling that they were badly organized.[48] Instead, he moved

[45] Ibid.
[46] U.S. Embassy Bamako, "Follow Up on Tuareg Insurgents in Mali (C-AL8–00949)," leaked cable 08BAMAKO824, October 3, 2008, https://wikileaks.org/plusd/cables/08BAMAKO824_a.html.
[47] Interview with Mohammed Mahmoud Abu al-Ma'ali.
[48] Interview with Alghabass ag Intalla.

into the politics of mediating peace, with nongovernmental organizations as his vehicle. One organization was the Alliance inter-régionale pour la paix et le développement du nord (Inter-Regional Alliance for Peace and Development, AIR-NORD), created in 2005 with ag Intalla as president. AIR-NORD met with rebels in June 2006,[49] and later negotiated releases of hostages held by ag Bahanga.[50] In 2009, ag Intalla formed another organization, the Réseau pour le Plaidoyer, la Paix, la Sécurité et le Développement dans les trois régions Nord du Mali (Network for Petitioning, Peace, Security and Development in the Three Regions of Northern Mali).[51] Ag Ghali did not join the Network, but he helped host the meeting in Kidal where it was created, suggesting that he felt a need to influence both the warmaking and peacemaking arenas. The Network became a lobbying group – according to one of its former leaders, the Network tried to pressure the Malian government to do more to stop drug trafficking, jihadism, and the erosion of the tourism and security in the north. The group attracted the support of many parliamentarians and hereditary rulers.[52]

These roles helped Alghabass ag Intalla to reinforce his status as a power broker among the Tuareg, a status that implicitly threatened ag Ghali. Yet at the same time, ag Intalla felt that the Malian government viewed his organizations as political rather than peacemaking bodies, and that the government hampered some of his activities.[53] Some observers, meanwhile, questioned his intentions. In an interview from the period, ag Intalla had the following exchange with a journalist:

---

[49] Chahana Takiou, "Me Harouna Toureh, vice-président de Air-nord à propos de la crise qui secoue le mali dans sa partie septentrionale," *L'Indépendant*, September 28, 2007, www.maliweb.net/la-situation-politique-et-securitaire-au-nord/me-harouna-toureh-vice-president-de-air-nord-a-propos-de-la-crise-qui-secoue-le-mali-dans-sa-partie-septentrionale-4750.html.

[50] B. Daou, "8 otages à libérer et trêve pour le reste du Ramadan," *L'Indépendant*, September 20, 2007, http://afribone.com/spip.php?article8015; and U.S. Embassy Bamako, "Bahanga Releases Last Three Malian Soldiers," leaked cable 09BAMAKO58, January 28, 2009, https://wikileaks.org/plusd/cables/09BAMAKO58_a.html.

[51] "Manifeste pour la creation d'un reseau de plaidoyer en faveur de la paix, de la securite et du developpement au Nord Mali," November 3, 2009, www.eda.admin.ch/content/dam/countries/countries-content/mali/fr/resource_fr_196456.pdf.

[52] Interview with Mohamed Ould Mahmoud, Bamako, March 12, 2018.

[53] Interview with Alghabass ag Intalla.

Are narcotrafficking and al-Qa'ida your targets?
Absolutely, that is the raison d'être of our movement [meaning the Network].

Can it be possible that there is not a single narcotrafficker among you?
If by chance there is one and we find out, we will hand him over ourselves to justice.

And al-Qa'ida, how will you bring them to justice?
We will support the State in its efforts and we will raise awareness among our communities.
    Be more specific, because what you say is what everyone says.
Our plan for the near term is to set up a delegation of experts to go and see al-Qa'ida wherever they are found, and ask them to leave our territory, or otherwise we will fight them.
    Lift your right hand and say, "I swear it."
I swear it.[54]

The presence of jihadists had already cast a shadow over the rebellion and over leading Kel Adagh politicians. These dimensions of the conflict foreshadowed the difficult choices ag Intalla would face in 2011–2013, when he found himself only one step removed (if that) from AQIM through his role in the more pragmatic wing of Ansar al-Din. By then, the balance of power was shifting in key ways back toward ag Ghali and toward AQIM. If ag Ghali and ag Intalla came to Ansar al-Din for different motives, they were both nevertheless responding to the same core issue: Political fragmentation in the north had thrown the Ifoghas on the defensive.

AQIM's Implantation in Northern Mali: Tuareg and Arab Interests

When discussing the GSPC/AQIM's arrival and implantation in northern Mali, analysts tend to emphasize the Algerian jihadists' agency while depicting the northern Malian population as passive recipients of jihadist outreach. But northern Malian Tuareg and Arab leaders strategically engaged the jihadist presence, especially in political, economic, and religious terms. As International Crisis Group has written,

[54] Adam Thiam, "Alghabass Ag Intalla: Nous irons dire aux Salafistes de quitter notre pays!" *Le Républicain*, December 9, 2009, www.maliweb.net/category .php?NID=54061.

"AQIM is a political and social object, not a pathology."[55] Other actors made use of AQIM just as AQIM made use of them.

Let us begin with the economic context of AQIM's implantation. Even by 2001–2002, Malian and Algerian observers were concerned about the "traffic of weapons, stolen vehicles, or underground migrants heading for Europe" in northern Mali. The alleged role of the GSPC/AQIM field commander Belmokhtar in that traffic was already a cause of particular worry. By then, the region had been effectively abandoned by the Malian military.[56]

One should not overstate the so-called drug-terror nexus.[57] Nor should one overstate the involvement of AQIM in the smuggling of even licit goods, such as cigarettes.[58] Yet AQIM did benefit from changes that overlapped with its implantation. The longstanding "regional connectivity" of northwest Africa has been inflected in new ways as trans-Saharan smuggling has changed since the 1990s: "Saharan smuggling, or the most illegal and most valuable part of it, is increasingly controlled by 'mafias,' centralising agencies that function 'just like a state' and that are locally much resented."[59] Julian Brachet has even argued that amid the criminalization of irregular cross-border movement since the early 2000s, "smugglers, as a category of actors playing a specific part in the global migration process, are directly manufactured by the migration policies put in place to stop them."[60] In this sense, the GSPC's arrival in northern

---

[55] International Crisis Group, "Mali: Avoiding Escalation," July 18, 2012, 5, https://d2071andvip0wj.cloudfront.net/189-mali-avoiding-escalation.pdf.

[56] Holzbauer, "Les inquiétants émirs du Sahel."

[57] Wolfram Lacher, "Challenging the Myth of the Drug-Terror Nexus in the Sahel," West Africa Commission on Drugs, Background Paper Number 4, 2013, www.globalcommissionondrugs.org/wp-content/uploads/2017/02/Challenging-the-Myth-of-the-Drug-Terror-Nexus-in-the-Sahel-2013-09-12.pdf.

[58] A *Jeune Afrique* article mentions that it is difficult to tell who gave Mokhtar Belmokhtar the nickname "Mr. Marlboro" – and that the nickname may have come from the intelligence services. Laurent Touchard, Baba Ahmed, and Cherif Ouazani, "Aqmi: Mokhtar Belmokhtar, le trafiquant," *Jeune Afrique*, October 3, 2012, www.jeuneafrique.com/139882/politique/aqmi-mokhtar-belmokhtar-le-trafiquant/.

[59] Judith Scheele, *Smugglers and Saints of the Sahara: Regional Connectivity in the Twentieth Century* (Cambridge: Cambridge University Press, 2012), 239.

[60] Julien Brachet, "Manufacturing Smugglers: From Irregular to Clandestine Mobility in the Sahara," *The Annals of the American Academy of Political and Social Science*, published online February 21, 2018, 30.

Mali coincided with shifts in the nature of smuggling in ways that favored the GSPC/AQIM economically and politically.

Competition over smuggling routes and turfs factored into the 2006 rebellion, especially in conflicts between rebels and pro-government militias. Meanwhile, the influx of profits from cocaine smuggling in the mid-2000s disrupted social hierarchies; "involvement in the drug trade can be seen as a strategy for social mobility that appears especially attractive to subordinated groups seeking social recognition in the face of traditional and religious norms."[61] In this context, AQIM became implicated in northern Malian smuggling not just as a participant but perhaps more importantly as an armed faction that some smugglers found useful to align with amid their struggles with other smugglers and other factions. In parallel, a kidnapping economy developed in which AQIM became the central but not the only participant. The smuggling economy and the kidnapping economy intersected with each other and with the wider political field. Those dynamics drew some northern Malian actors into the jihadist milieu while antagonizing others.

One of the key actors who drew closer to the jihadists during this time was, of course, Iyad ag Ghali. From 2003 to 2009, ag Ghali went through what he later called "the stage of getting to know the mujahidin and beginning to make ties with them."[62] The date 2003 reflects ag Ghali's involvement in negotiations with the GSPC over their mass hostage-taking of European tourists in southern Algeria that year. Ag Ghali became an intermediary between the German government, the Malian government, and the GSPC, eventually transmitting a reported $6.7 million ransom payment to the GSPC in exchange for the release of fourteen hostages, ten of them Germans.[63]

Ag Ghali also had family ties to AQIM. He was related to Hamada ag Hama (better known as 'Abd al-Karim al-Tarqi or Abdelkrim al-Targui, d. 2015). Al-Targui reportedly joined the GSPC/AQIM in the late 1990s, becoming a protégé of the field commander 'Abd al-Hamid

---

[61] Luca Raineri and Francesco Strazzari, "State, Secession, and Jihad: The Micropolitical Economy of Conflict in Northern Mali," *African Security* 8 (2015): 249–271, 257.

[62] "'Al-Masra' Tuhawir al-Shaykh Aba al-Fadl Iyad Ghali."

[63] "'Lion of the Desert': Ex-Partner of Germany Leads Malian Islamists," Der Spiegel, January 21, 2013, www.spiegel.de/international/world/leader-of-malian-islamists-once-helped-german-government-a-878724.html.

Abu Zayd and participating in the negotiations around the European hostages seized in 2003. Al-Targui later commanded his own battalion, Katibat al-Ansar ("Battalion of the Supporters").[64] Family ties reinforced ag Ghali's position as a "broker" in the networks connecting the Kel Adagh Tuareg elite and AQIM. Indeed, AQIM needed brokers and partners; an AQIM kidnapping in 2008, at least according to one account, intensified "local nomadic populations' fear of being 'collateral damage' were Mali or Algeria to take military action against AQIM."[65] Amid such fears, AQIM needed negotiators who could not just obtain ransoms but also manage the politics surrounding the disruptions caused by high-profile kidnappings.

If ag Ghali was ready to act as AQIM's broker and ally, other voices within the Kel Adagh were more ambivalent. This ambivalence came to the fore in the 2006 rebellion by the ADC. According to one ADC leader, the ADC directly fought AQIM in 2006.[66] A leaked US Embassy Bamako cable states that the ADC "attack[ed] AQIM twice in 2006."[67] According to another cable, however,

In late 2006 the ADC engaged with elements of what is now AQIM in northern Mali. ADC members who participated in the AQIM attacks later reported that ag Ghali had quietly directed fellow Ifogas to pull back just as the ADC prepared to attack AQIM. This forced the ADC's Idnane and Taghat Melet members to face AQIM alone. Afterwards, Ifogas reportedly refused to help fellow Idnanes and Taghat Melets negotiate for the release of prisoners captured by AQIM. One disaffected ADC member, who said he was eventually forced to speak with AQIM leader [Belmokhtar] directly to

---

[64] "Qui sont les deux jihadistes abattus par l'armée française au Mali?" RFI, May 21, 2015, www.rfi.fr/afrique/20150521-mali-mort-abdelkrim-al-targui-amada-ag-hamal-ibrahim-ag-inawalen-bana-barkhane/. "Al-Ansar" or "the supporters" refers to the idea that the Malian Tuareg jihadists were the equivalent of the early Muslims in Medina who welcomed the Prophet Muhammad and his closest Companions.

[65] U.S. Embassy Bamako, "The Liberation of AQIM's Austrian Hostages: An Inside View," leaked cable 08BAMAKO888, November 14, 2008, https://search.wikileaks.org/plusd/cables/08BAMAKO888_a.html.

[66] Interview with Ahmada ag Bibi, Bamako, March 13, 2018.

[67] U.S. Embassy Bamako, "Berabiche and AQIM in Northern Mali," leaked cable 08BAMAKO371, April 17, 2008, https://wikileaks.org/plusd/cables/08BAMAKO371_a.html.

win the release of a captured relative, described the ADC as weakened to the point of dissolution following this episode.[68]

If this account is correct, then by 2006 the GSPC/AQIM represented both a party to the conflict and an external lever that ag Ghali used to affect intra-Tuareg rivalries, to the advantage of the Ifoghas but also to the disgust of some of its members.

Relationships between the Tuareg and the GSPC/AQIM remained somewhat limited through the 2000s. One American cable concluded that the Tuareg in northern Mali were open to collaborating with AQIM on logistical and smuggling issues, but rejected AQIM's religious vision and considered the Algerians "a foreign extremist group trespassing on Tuareg land." The cable added that ADC attacks on the GSPC/AQIM had prompted the jihadists to withdraw to Timbuktu and invest in relationships with Arabs, particularly from the Berabiche confederation. "In addition to linguistic links, Malian Berabiche are culturally closer to southern Algerian Arabs, like Moctar bel Moctar who is an ethnic Chaamba, than they are to non-Arab Tuaregs." The cable cautioned against overstating any cultural ties between the Berabiche and AQIM. Yet the authors also suggested that the Berabiche presence along the Mauritanian–Malian border positioned those Malian Arabs to involve themselves in AQIM kidnapping and smuggling. "If one is able to enlist the support of the right Berabiche, one could conceivably circumvent the Tuareg zone entirely. AQIM likely pays taxes to cross some zones and receives payments from others crossing AQIM territory."[69]

As in Kidal, ambivalence developed around AQIM's activities in Timbuktu. In June 2009, AQIM assassinated Lamana Ould Bou, a Malian colonel, Berabiche Arab, and former 1990s-era rebel faction leader. The incident raised questions about the politics of AQIM's implantation in northern Mali and its relationship with local state authorities. The BBC's headline proclaimed, "Malian Al-Qaeda Hunter Shot Dead," framing Ould Bou as a key intelligence figure

---

[68] U.S. Embassy Bamako, "Tribal Fault Lines within the Tuareg of Northern Mali," leaked cable 08BAMAKO239, March 6, 2008, https://wikileaks.org/plusd/cables/08BAMAKO239_a.html. See also U.S. Embassy Bamako, "Details on Recent Hostages Release and Next Steps for Mali-Tuareg Negotiations," leaked cable 08BAMAKO712, August 7, 2008, https://wikileaks.org/plusd/cables/08BAMAKO712_a.html.
[69] U.S. Embassy Bamako, "Berabiche and AQIM in Northern Mali."

investigating AQIM.[70] Yet Mali's *L'Indépendant* reported that some of Ould Bou's colleagues saw him as a "double agent" who had colluded with AQIM in drug trafficking.[71] *Jeune Afrique* commented that "his perfect knowledge of the Sahel and the peoples who live there and who cross it made him indispensable in the management of the Northern Malian portfolio within the [State Security]," adding that he had become the "privileged interlocutor of the Salafists [i.e, AQIM]" in ransom negotiations.[72] In 2008, American diplomats had classified Ould Bou and other Berabiche officers as "go-betweens" in negotiations involving AQIM and the government of Libya over kidnapped Europeans. The diplomats added that Ould Bou was "believed to have fed information to criminal and terrorist organizations in the past."[73] The analyst Andrew Lebovich comments that "according to one Arab notable and businessman from north of Timbuktu, Ould Bou's illicit activities and dealings with AQIM were made possible precisely because he had helped constitute groups of Arab fighters to oppose Tuareg rebels after 2006."[74]

Ould Bou's case illustrates the complex relationships operating in the north. As *Jeune Afrique* wrote concerning the wider context of his murder, "Songhaïs against Tuareg, Salafists against spies, Tuareg against Arabs, militias against residual rebels ... Timbuktu is living a veritable nightmare."[75] All of the major actors, directly or indirectly, were interacting with AQIM. The jihadists represented not just a new pole of influence in northern Mali but also a tool that some actors used to advance their own interests. When those actors engaged AQIM,

[70] "Malian Al-Qaeda Hunter Shot Dead," BBC, June 11, 2009, http://news.bbc.co .uk/2/hi/africa/8095040.stm.
[71] Saouti Labass Haidara, "Le lieutenant-Colonel Lamina Ould Bou exécuté par al Qaïda: Le héros et le barbouze," *L'Indépendant*, June 15, 2009, www.maliweb .net/category.php?NID=46065.
[72] "Meurtres au Sahel," *Jeune Afrique*, June 23, 2009, www.jeuneafrique.com/ 202753/politique/meurtres-au-sahel/.
[73] U.S. Embassy Bamako, "Berabiche and AQIM in Northern Mali"; see also Wolfram Lacher, "Organized Crime and Conflict in the Sahel-Sahara Region," Carnegie Endowment for International Peace, September 2012, 12–13, https:// carnegieendowment.org/files/sahel_sahara.pdf.
[74] Andrew Lebovich, "Reconstructing Local Orders in Mali: Historical Perspectives and Future Challenges," Brookings Institution, July 2017, 9, footnote 24, www.brookings.edu/wp-content/uploads/2017/08/lebovich_mali .pdf.
[75] "Meurtres au Sahel."

they provoked counter-reactions, including from AQIM when deals went sour.

One other micro-case study emphasizes these trends. Amid the 2006–2009 rebellion, the Gao region saw multi-sided conflicts and intrigues. Not just inter-ethnic but also intra-ethnic tensions operated. These included tensions between the Kounta Arabs and the Tilemsi Arabs; the latter were "historically subjects of the Kounta."[76] Part of the context was a proxy war: As a response to ag Bahanga's ATNMC and its prolongation of the 2006 rebellion even after ag Ghali made peace, authorities in Bamako sponsored pro-government northern militias. Bamako saw these militias as a counterweight to Tuareg rebels. Meanwhile, the militias and their business allies leveraged government support to "protect their business interests," including in drug smuggling.[77] One militia was led by the Tilemsi Arab Major Colonel Abderahmane Ould Meydou,[78] and it furnishes a noteworthy micro-case of jihadist politics and alliances.

Tarkint, a town in northern Gao region, was a node in various economic and political competitions. In a May 2009 cable, US diplomats discussed a disputed local election in the town. On the April 26 election day, diplomats reported, Ould Meydou's Tilemsi Arab militiamen "descended on Tarkint with 15 vehicles" and engaged in what their rivals, namely Kounta Arabs and Tuareg, decried as "ballot stuffing and intimidation."[79] The Tilemsi fighters reportedly included figures tied to AQIM, most prominently a man named Sultan Ould Badi.[80] US diplomats wrote, "Although northern Mali's Kounta and

---

[76] Judith Scheele, "Tribus, États et fraude: la région frontalière algéro-malienne," *études rurales* 184 (2009): 79–94, 84, fn. 18.

[77] Lacher, "Organized Crime," 12.

[78] Grégory Chauzel and Thibault van Damme, "The Roots of Mali's Conflict: Moving beyond the 2012 Crisis," Clingendael, March 2015, 33, www .clingendael.org/sites/default/files/pdfs/The_roots_of_Malis_conflict.pdf.

[79] U.S. Embassy Bamako, "Electoral Tensions in Tarkint: Where AQIM, Arab Militias, and Tuaregs Meet," leaked cable 09BAMAKO280, May 8, 2009, https://wikileaks.org/plusd/cables/09BAMAKO280_a.html.

[80] Another Tilemsi Arab with even longer ties to the GSPC/AQIM was Ahmed al-Tilemsi/'Abd al-Rahman Ould al-'Amar (d. 2014), who joined 'Abd al-Hamid Abu Zayd's Tariq bin Ziyad Battalion in the mid-2000s. United Nations Security Council, "Abderrahmane Ould El Amar," version as of September 9, 2014, www.un.org/securitycouncil/ar/sanctions/1267/aq_sanctions_list/ summaries/individual/abderrahmane-ould-el-amar. See also David Thomson, "Ahmed al-Tilemsi: portrait d'un 'des principaux financiers du Mujao'," RFI,

Telemsi communities are both of Arab origin, conflict between the two is not a new phenomenon. What is new, however, is the proximity of Arab militias, disgruntled Tuareg rebels, and newly affluent Arab AQIM intermediaries."[81] US diplomats discussed suspicions that Ould Badi and other Tilemsi Arabs had perpetrated the 2008 kidnapping of two Canadian diplomats in Niger (see Chapter 2); American officials even mentioned the possibility that the ransoms paid for the Canadians had been reinvested by the kidnappers into elections in Tarkint and elsewhere.[82] AQIM did not just prey on passive Malians; Malians used AQIM's resources to advance their own, often hyper-local political interests.

In Tarkint, the Tilemsi Arabs' preferred candidate, Baba Ould Cheikh, won the 2009 mayoral election. He became progressively infamous as an alleged AQIM collaborator. A long-time smuggler, Ould Cheikh was reputedly involved in both the hostage negotiations of 2003 and in later episodes, such as Belmokhtar's ransom of the two Canadian diplomats.[83] Later in 2009, Ould Cheikh would be central to the "Air Cocaine" scandal, where the wreckage of a drug-laden plane was found in the desert north of Gao; Ould Cheikh was accused of involvement in the ill-fated shipment, which may have passed through Tarkint.[84] Ould Cheikh embodied the intersection of various forces in northern Malian politics – smuggling, ethnic mobilization, elected office, and the influence that could accrue from connections to AQIM.

December 11, 2014, www.rfi.fr/afrique/20141211-mali-ahmed-al-telemsi-portait-principaux-financiers-mujao.

[81] U.S. Embassy Bamako, "Electoral Tensions in Tarkint."

[82] U.S. Embassy Bamako, "A Familiar Name Surfaces in Search for Canadian Diplomats' Kidnappers," leaked cable 09BAMAKO106, February 23, 2009, https://wikileaks.org/plusd/cables/09BAMAKO106_a.html; U.S. Embassy Bamako, "Electoral Tensions in Tarkint"; and Mamadou Makadji, "Cheibani aux mains de la justice américaine: Le présumé meurtrier de diplomates extradé par le gouvernement malien," *Le Républicain*, March 18, 2014, https://maliactu.net/cheibani-aux-mains-de-la-justice-americaine-le-presume-meurtrier-de-diplomates-extrade-par-le-gouvernement-malien/.

[83] Vincent Hugeux, "Mali: la double vie du caïd déchu Baba Ould Cheikh," *L'Express*, April 11, 2013, www.lexpress.fr/actualite/monde/afrique/mali-la-double-vie-du-caid-dechu-baba-ould-cheikh_1239465.html.

[84] Andrew Lebovich, "Mali's Bad Trip," *Foreign Policy*, March 15, 2013, https://foreignpolicy.com/2013/03/15/malis-bad-trip/; and Lacher, "Organized Crime," 12.

Typically, AQIM's local alliances began as economic arrangements, then grew into more broadly political alliances (and rivalries). This is not to say that genuine religious convictions did not coexist with more prosaic interests. Some of AQIM's allies, for example ag Ghali and Ould Badi, would be speaking the language of Salafi-jihadism by 2012. Whether one interprets that choice cynically or not, such actors invested time and effort into making themselves religiously compatible with AQIM. At a more grassroots level, AQIM had access to some mosques in the north during the 2000s; one report on the assassination of Colonel Lamana Ould Bou in 2009 mentioned that in the period before his murder, Ould Bou had been leading a crackdown against AQIM in Timbuktu, "in which the final episode was the arrest, in the mosque of Abaradjou [a Timbuktu neighborhood] of an individual who presents himself, according to the circumstances, as Mauritanian, Malian, or Nigerien."[85] In addition to whatever overt or covert presence they had in mosques, AQIM (from its GSPC days) undertook outreach and charity; Morten Bøås and Liv Torheim state that the GSPC/AQIM "bought themselves goodwill, friendship and networks by distributing money, handing out medicine, treating the sick and buying SIM cards and airtime for people ... In many ways AQIM was acting as an Islamic charity, with the exception that its members carried arms and did not hesitate to use them." The authors further state that AQIM cultivated relationships with local shaykhs in Timbuktu.[86]

In short, the scene-setting for AQIM's alliances amid the 2012 rebellion took years to unfold. AQIM's implantation in northern Mali was not a one-sided wooing of a passive population by a cunning terrorist force, but rather a dialectic in which the Algerian jihadists and their local allies saw strategic advantages in collaborating. Some alliances were tactical and temporary, and could even end violently, as Ould Bou's assassination possibly demonstrates. Other alliances drew

---

[85] Haidara, "Le lieutenant-Colonel Lamina Ould Bou exécuté par al Qaïda."

[86] Morten Bøås and Liv Elin Torheim, "The Trouble in Mali – Corruption, Collusion, Resistance," *Third World Quarterly* 37:4 (2013): 1279–1292, 1287; and Bøås, "Guns, Money, and Prayers: AQIM's Blueprint for Securing Control of Northern Mali," Combating Terrorism Center *Sentinel* 7:4 (April 2014), https://ctc.usma.edu/guns-money-and-prayers-aqims-blueprint-for-securing-control-of-northern-mali/. It is unclear to me, however, what the sources for these assertions are.

northern Malian actors into AQIM's orbit in a more lasting way. Each alliance, moreover, touched off reactions shaped by the wider context of tribal and ethnic histories, economic competition, and Bamako's divide-and-rule policies. These shifting dynamics recall Fotini Christia's argument that rebel field commanders – or here, we might say, political actors generally – will shift alliances for tactical reasons as they calculate their long-term opportunities for post-conflict gain (or here, we might say, medium-term economic and political advantage). Ag Ghali's somewhat anomalous case, however, remains central to the inquiry. Unlike most other prominent northern Malian actors, he would eventually shift permanently into the jihadist camp, a decision that requires further analysis.

The Rebellion of 2012: The Politics of Jihadist Coalitions and Alliances

Much has been written about the Malian rebellion of 2012, and Chapter 2 already alluded to some of the main dynamics. Rather than analyzing the rebellion as a whole, here I emphasize what the rebellion revealed about jihadist politics.

To give a brief overview of the conflict, key northern rebels included the separatist Mouvement national de libération de l'Azawad (National Movement for the Liberation of the Azawad, MNLA) and the jihadist-leaning Ansar al-Din. The MNLA launched its revolt in January 2012. The MNLA initially received assistance from Ansar al-Din, AQIM, and the AQIM offshoot the Movement for Unity and Jihad in West Africa (MUJWA). These forces soon controlled major cities and towns in northern Mali, including the regional capitals Kidal, Timbuktu, and Gao. The MNLA's rebellion was facilitated by the weakness of the Malian military. The state's strength was further undercut by endemic corruption combined with officials' negligence and even collusion vis-a-vis criminality in the north. In March 2012, a military coup against Mali's civilian president threw Malian national politics into chaos and let the rebels take more territory.

The MNLA proclaimed an independent state of "Azawad" in April 2012. But by May, cooperation between the MNLA and Ansar al-Din was breaking down. In June, Ansar al-Din and its jihadist allies expelled the MNLA from the northern regional capitals. The jihadist proto-state controlled by Ansar al-Din, AQIM, and MUJWA lasted until January 2013. That month, jihadists' attempt to expand into central Mali prompted a French-led military intervention called Operation Serval. That intervention broke jihadists' control over major cities and sent them fleeing into the desert.

Ansar al-Din was led by Iyad ag Ghali, but creating a new movement was not his first choice. In October 2011, ag Ghali met the MNLA's leaders in Zakak, far northeastern Mali; according to one MNLA leader, ag Ghali was there as "an emissary from the Malian government." According to the same account, ag Ghali did not initially seek to lead the MNLA, but he changed his mind when he saw where events were heading.[87] Yet in an ironic reversal of the dynamics at work in 1990, ag Ghali was now the older, more conservative Tuareg leader whose authority was challenged by younger, idealistic Tuareg rebels – some of whom had just returned from Libya, although the bulk of the attendees were reportedly defectors from the Malian army.[88] The MNLA's political spokesmen were his juniors by decades,[89] and were plugged into diasporic and online networks of Tuareg who dreamed of a revitalized "Azawadi" nationalism. Some of the MNLA's military leaders were ag Ghali's contemporaries and even his former subordinates, but they now claimed center stage – to ag Ghali's political detriment.[90]

At Zakak, ag Ghali failed to convince the MNLA to allow him to reprise the role he had played in 1990 and 2006 as leader of those uprisings; the problems that ag Ghali had faced circa 2006–2009 in reining in Ibrahim ag Bahanga now resurfaced even more forcefully. Some MNLA fighters – too young to have fought in 1990 or even in 2006 – admired the recently deceased ag Bahanga more than they did ag Ghali.[91] Some of the founders of the MNLA, such as Bilal ag Achérif, had remained in contact with ag Bahanga after the ADC made its peace agreement with the Malian government in 2006, an accord that ag Achérif and other Azawadi nationalists had rejected.

---

[87] Interview with Bilal ag Achérif, Bamako, June 21, 2019.   [88] Ibid.

[89] Bilal ag Achérif, Moussa ag Assarid, and Moussa ag Acharatoumane were all born in the mid-1970s or after.

[90] I am thinking here of Mohamed ag Najem, the MNLA's military head.

[91] Jérôme Pigné, "Nord-Mali, qui était Ibrahim Ag Bahanga?" *Les Carnets du Sahel*, 2r3s, September 2018, https://medium.com/@Sahel2R3S/nord-mali-qui-était-ibrahim-ag-bahanga-256d34067bc6.

Ag Achérif met ag Bahanga in Libya in 2009 and three more times in the Malian desert in 2011 to intensify their cooperation.[92]

It was thus the more uncompromising side of the 1990 and 2006 rebellions whose torch the MNLA sought to take up. Skeptical of ag Ghali's history of repeatedly negotiating with the Malian government, some MNLA leaders even considered ag Ghali a traitor.[93] Many MNLA fighters also saw ag Ghali, in his incarnation as a Tablighi activist and budding jihadist, as too religiously conservative for the nationalist, "Azawadi" project they envisioned. The MNLA's leadership and its rank-and-file – which was multi-clan and multi-caste – rejected ag Ghali.[94]

This was an "affront" ag Ghali could not accept.[95] According to some accounts, after his political defeat at Zakak, ag Ghali then presented himself at a meeting of Tuareg nobles in Abeibara, Kidal region. There he sought a formal position within the chiefly system, perhaps as heir to the *aménokal*. But that mantle was given, for the time being, to his rival Alghabass ag Intalla, the *aménokal*'s prominent son.[96] The designation of ag Intalla as "executive chief" appeared to ratify his status as a kind of crown prince, while reinforcing his position as a central Ifoghas politician and negotiator. The timing also suggests that the MNLA made not just ag Ghali but also the Ifoghas nobles more broadly quite nervous.

Rebuffed by the MNLA and disappointed by the Ifoghas aristocracy, ag Ghali created Ansar al-Din. He turned to two constituencies to assemble the movement. The first was committed jihadists, including

---

[92] Interview with Bilal ag Achérif.

[93] Interview with Mohamed ag Aharib, Bamako, 24 January 2018. See also David Lewis and Adama Diarra, "Insight: Arms and Men out of Libya Fortify Mali Rebellion," *Reuters*, 10 February 2012, https://www.reuters.com/article/us-mali-libya/insight-arms-and-men-out-of-libya-fortify-mali-rebellion-idUSTRE8190UX20120210.

[94] Interview with Manny Ansar.

[95] Interview with Mohamed Ould Mahmoud.

[96] For various accounts of these events, see Jean-Cristophe Notin, *La Guerre de la France au Mali* (Paris: Tallandier, 2014), 63; "Nord-mali: modernisation de la tribu des Ifoghas: Alghabas ag intalla, le nouveau chef," *Le Combat*, November 23, 2011, www.maliweb.net/non-classe/nord-mali-modernisation-de-la-tribu-des-ifoghas-alghabas-ag-intalla-le-nouveau-chef-35814.html; and Morten Bøås "Northern Mali: Criminality, Coping and Resistance along an Elusive Frontier" in *The Politics of Conflict Economies: Miners, Merchants and Warriors in the African Borderland*, 86–98 (New York: Routledge, 2015), 91.

people who had long been in AQIM and MUJWA's orbit. The second constituency was Ifoghas nobles. These were men such as Mohamed ag Aharib, who had lived and fought at ag Ghali's side for decades and for whom ag Ghali "had always been our leader."[97] Another was Ahmada ag Bibi, who was (like Alghabass ag Intalla) still an elected deputy in Mali's National Assembly at the time of the 2012 uprising.[98] Yet another was Cheikh ag Aoussa (d. 2016), another longtime associate of ag Ghali. Ag Aoussa reportedly played a key role in recruiting major Ifoghas clans such as the Ifergoumessen to Ansar al-Din, and also in recruiting some of the remnants of ag Bahanga's fighters.[99] According to one MNLA leader, ag Ghali worked to convince many locals that he had no ties to AQIM, even as he worked with AQIM from at least January 2012 on, with AQIM fighters present at an early battle in Aguelhok. The same MNLA leader said that AQIM entered into Ansar al-Din like a "sickness" and then spread through the organization.[100]

Ag Ghali scored a political triumph in recruiting Alghabass ag Intalla, who joined Ansar al-Din around February 2012 after initially belonging to the MNLA. He became the "Number Two" of the movement,[101] a position reflecting his status in Kel Adagh society. Explaining his choices, he later said,

Yes, right at the start we were with the MNLA. But afterwards we joined Ansar ud-Dine. We thought that this was how we could defend religion in our society and at the same time defend our territory. And protect our entire culture, right here. I found that Ansar ud-Dine were fairly strong compared to the MNLA, in their actions against the enemy. So, we preferred to go with Ansar ud-Dine. But after that, we saw that Iyad went too far, one might say.[102]

[97] Interview with Mohamed ag Aharib.
[98] "Les hommes influents d'Ansar Dine: Qui sont-ils?" *La Dépêche*, July 23, 2012, http://maliactu.net/les-hommes-influents-dansar-dine-qui-sont-ils/.
[99] Interview with Mohammed Mahmoud Abu al-Ma'ali.
[100] Interview with Bilal ag Achérif.
[101] Tarek Hafid, "Alghabass ag Intalla, Vice-Président du Haut Conseil pour l'Unité de l'Azawad: 'Nous n'avons jamais été des extrémistes'," *Le Soir d'Algérie*, July 6, 2013, www.lesoirdalgerie.com/articles/2013/07/06/article.php?sid=151079&cid=2.
[102] Andy Morgan, "Alghabass ag Intalla: Interview with the Head of the MIA," Andy Morgan Writes, January 31, 2013, www.andymorganwrites.com/interview-with-alghabass-ag-intalla-head-of-the-islamic-movement-of-azawad-mia/.

This explanation satisfies few observers. Morten Bøås speculates that perhaps "his father [the *aménokal*] placed him there to prevent Ag Ghaly from leading the Ifoghas and the people of the Kidal area into an alliance with the Islamist forces that, if carried through to its ultimate conclusion, would make any future negotiated settlement with the Malian state impossible."[103] In an interview with me, ag Intalla said that he joined Ansar al-Din because it was better organized militarily than the MNLA. His father, he said, had not approved of Ansar al-Din and had felt that the movement's brand of Islam would destabilize life in Kidal; preferring the older, tribal structure of authority, his father had favored the MNLA.[104] Bøås' theory about a family strategy of political diversification, however, cannot be ruled out.

In any case, ag Intalla – and possibly Intalla himself – did not see Ansar al-Din and its proximity to AQIM as politically toxic. This observation reinforces one of this book's central contentions, namely that jihadist politics appears fundamentally different at the local level than in the (often crude) assumptions generated by analysts in Washington, London, and Paris. At the same time that ag Ghali was taking advantage of AQIM's anathematized status to recover from the political blows dealt to him by the MNLA, the Intalla family (or parts of it) were confident enough in their political standing that they could risk working with an anathematized faction.

A final theory posits that with the MNLA's rise – a movement headed by the Ifoghas separatist Bilal ag Achérif, but comprising many Idnan and Imghad Tuareg fighters – the Ifoghas felt the need to close ranks. Ag Ghali became the focal point of Ifoghas discomfort with the MNLA.[105] One of the Ifoghas who became a leader in Ansar al-Din, the politician Ahmada ag Bibi, told me that he and others never believed in the "Azawadi" project. "There will never be an Azawad," he said. According to ag Bibi, other communities in the north, whether in Gao, Ménaka, or Timbuktu, never cared about the Azawadi dream and even resented it. In ag Bibi's view, since 1990 the Ifoghas had always fought to force the Malian state to give a special political status to Kidal, rather than to the north as a whole.[106] Ansar al-Din's

---

[103] Bøås, "Northern Mali: Criminality, Coping and Resistance," 92.
[104] Interview with Alghabass ag Intalla.   [105] Interview with Manny Ansar.
[106] Interview with Ahmada ag Bibi.

disavowal of separatism may have appealed to the Ifoghas nobles, at least in comparison with the MNLA.

Some northern leaders also assert that Algerian authorities pressured Ifoghas nobles to join Ansar al-Din. According to this view, Algerian leaders saw Ansar al-Din as a counterweight to the MNLA and the threat that Tuareg secessionism could pose to Algerian interests.[107] The MNLA's ag Achérif, without naming Algeria, told me pointedly that "some regional powers" had backed Ansar al-Din in order to stamp out the MNLA's revolution.[108]

Whatever their motivations for joining, the Ifoghas nobles elicited – at least at first – some concessions from ag Ghali. Alghabass ag Intalla said that he secured ag Ghali's agreement that Ansar al-Din would not use suicide bombings.[109] Another well-informed observer suggests that ag Intalla and the others reached a two-part agreement with ag Ghali: The armed struggle would be confined to northern Mali, and Ansar al-Din would not take hostages or plant mines.[110] This agreement broke down later, but in early 2012 some version of a deal won Tuareg nobles' support.

These compromises underscore the political nature of the jihadist project. Later on, the Tuareg nobles would be called on to explain and disavow their relationship with jihadists. Yet in 2012 it was the jihadists who felt obliged to publicly justify their willingness to work with professional politicians. In an interview with an online jihadist forum, the Ansar al-Din hardliner Sanda Ould Bouamama said:

The Ansar al-Din group is a movement that was founded after its leaders had been absorbed in bitter experiences in the past in the path of reforming the society, reclaiming its rights, and removing injustice and disgrace from it. Among [the leaders] were those who had followed the path of armed nationalist revolution. Among them were those who chose to enter government positions, with the aim of steering the reins of government from up close. Another group tried out the route of da'wa (calling) to God and making change in accordance with the Islamic methodology. Some of them joined Jama'at al-Da'wa wa-l-Tabligh, and it left a good mark on them in terms of religiosity and adherence to Islam. Some of them tried out da'wa according to the methodology of the Islamic organizations that follow the methodology of scholarly Salafism. Some of them melted away into ordinary

---

[107] Interview with Mohamed Ould Mahmoud.
[108] Interview with Bilal ag Achérif.   [109] Interview with Alghabass ag Intalla.
[110] Interview with Mohamed Ould Mahmoud.

life and were occupied with themselves, either out of fatigue and despair at the change of circumstance, or to await another opportunity. Then God decreed that a small group would become conscious of the reality of the disease, and God guided them to knowledge of the religion of Islam and understanding of the foundations of reform in accordance with the Prophetic methodology. This group applied themselves to calling those from whom good was expected to the path of jihad and implementing God's law, calling people to God, and waging war on unbelief, [blameful] innovation, and corruption, by means of proof, explanation, the sword, and the spear. They were helped in this by their connection to the jihadist vanguard posted in the frontier of the greater Sahara for more than ten years. When the collective realized the futility or deficiency of the methodologies they were on, they decided to correct their analysis [literally, fix their probe/sounder] and proceed to form an armed, organized entity in which the Muslims of these zones could take refuge, to be the foundational core for launching the Islamic project.[111]

Ansar al-Din became a coalition of jihadists and politicians who were open to working with one another. The jihadists could claim that their newfound Tuareg allies were people who had finally seen the light, while the Tuareg politicians could use vague language about religious authenticity to explain their involvement.

"Shariʿa politics" in the early Ansar al-Din coalition was largely generic, because of the breadth of the coalition. Amid the initial military momentum, it was easy to downplay internal divisions. The Ifoghas nobles might have been latecomers to Salafi-jihadism, but they were all lifelong Muslims. Some of them possessed respectable levels of religious learning; for example, as a young man in the 1970s and 1980s, Alghabass ag Intalla received a classical Islamic education "in the brush" around Kidal. He attended a Qur'an school and studied Islamic jurisprudence up to the level of the *Risala*,[112] a medieval text that one might call "intermediate" within the classical northwest African Islamic legal curriculum.

Yet preexisting divisions persisted within the coalition. In a social network analysis of the 2012 northern Malian rebel groups, Olivier

[111] Shabakat Ansar al-Mujahidin, "Al-Liqa' al-Maftuh ma'a al-Shaykh Sanda Wuld Bu 'Amama," 2012, 5–6, https://jihadology.net/wp-content/uploads/_pda/2012/08/ane1b9a3c481r-ad-dc4abn-open-meeting-with-sandah-c5abld-bc5ab-amc481mah.pdf.
[112] Interview with Alghabass ag Intalla.

Walther and Dimitris Christopoulos show that most of the Ifoghas nobles in Ansar al-Din were only weakly integrated into the hardcore jihadist scene. Ag Ghali was the central broker between the other Ifoghas, the hardline Ansar al-Din jihadists, and AQIM. Individuals such as ag Intalla and ag Bibi were directly connected to ag Ghali but not to AQIM's Saharan field commanders, Belmokhtar and Abu Zayd.[113]

In the beginning, the Ifoghas politicians in Ansar al-Din saw ag Ghali as "very moderate." He consulted them regularly.[114] But as 2012 progressed, the politicians lost influence over ag Ghali as the jihadist influences on him grew. Ag Ghali drew close to AQIM's Abu Zayd, who was more useful to ag Ghali than was Belmokhtar; Belmokhtar was already having disputes with the rest of AQIM (see Chapter 2). Ag Ghali differed with Belmokhtar and Belmokhtar's allies in MUJWA over key decisions, including MUJWA's kidnapping of several Algerian diplomats in Gao in April 2012.[115] The rivalry between Belmokhtar and Abu Zayd began to shape not just AQIM's but also Ansar al-Din's evolution, especially after the final break between Ansar al-Din and the MNLA in May–June 2012.

As with jihadist coalition dynamics discussed in previous chapters, geographical factors came into play alongside ideological ones. Amid the 2012 establishment of a jihadist "proto-state," something of a Timbuktu–Kidal split occurred: AQIM waxed dominant in Timbuktu while the Ifoghas nobles kept their own counsel in Kidal. Ifoghas politicians distanced themselves, geographically and ideologically, from the most intimate contacts between Ansar al-Din and AQIM. Gao, meanwhile, was in the hands of MUJWA and Belmokhtar.

AQIM had a representative in Kidal, the Algerian national Nabil Abu Alqama. Yet despite being AQIM's "Saharan Emir,"[116] and

---

[113] Walther and Christopoulos, "Islamic Terrorism," 507. I would also highlight Cheikh ag Aoussa's role as a broker. See "Portrait de Cheick Haoussa: Le vrai chef de la rébellion au nord," *Le Procès Verbal*, July 9, 2012, http://maliactu .net/portrait-de-cheick-haoussa-le-vrai-chef-de-la-rebellion-au-nord/.

[114] Interview with Mohamed ag Aharib.

[115] Interview with Mohammed Mahmoud Abu al-Ma'ali.

[116] "Nord-Mali: Nabil Makloufi, un chef d'Aqmi, se tue au volant de sa voiture," *Jeune Afrique*, September 10, 2012, www.jeuneafrique.com/174378/societe/ nord-mali-nabil-makloufi-un-chef-d-aqmi-se-tue-au-volant-de-sa-voiture/.

despite having helped Ansar al-Din during the January 2012 battle at Aguelhok,[117] Abu Alqama found himself rebuffed by Kidal's elites. When he tried to buy up abandoned soldiers' houses, he had to back down due to local objections.[118] Ultimately, at a meeting at Alghabass ag Intalla's house, Ansar al-Din's ag Bibi asked Abu Alqama and AQIM to leave Kidal.[119] In September 2012, while driving between Timbuktu and Gao, he died in a car crash.[120] Perhaps an accident, or perhaps not – as with the iconoclastic Tuareg rebel leader Ibrahim ag Bahanga's death in a car accident in August 2011, the possibility of assassination is substantial. Perhaps wisely, Abu Alqama's successor as AQIM's "Saharan Emir," Yahya Abu al-Hammam, based himself in Timbuktu and not Kidal.

Ag Ghali circulated frequently between the northern cities,[121] but Timbuktu became the preeminent site of intra-jihadist negotiations. It was in Timbuktu that ag Ghali and Abu Zayd attempted to broker a formal unity initiative involving Ansar al-Din, AQIM, and MUJWA.[122] Moreover, as the AQIM leaders in Timbuktu acquired a greater say in ag Ghali's decisions, emblematic moves were made, for example stripping the Ifoghas politician Mohamed ag Aharib of his position as Ansar al-Din's spokesman in favor of the hardline jihadist Sanda Ould Bouamama.[123] A Berabiche Arab from the Timbuktu region, Ould Bouamama's elevation signaled the layering of ideological, geographical, and ethnic distinctions within Ansar al-Din.

In 2012, the two main components of Ansar al-Din pursued divergent political strategies. Later, Alghabass ag Intalla commented, "My role in Ansar al-Din consisted in opening the organization toward the world and preventing its radicalization."[124] At critical junctures, the

---

[117] Interview with Mohammed Mahmoud Abu al-Ma'ali.
[118] Interview with Aminetou ag Bibi, Bamako, March 10, 2018. The sister of Ahmada ag Bibi, she was and remains an MNLA member.
[119] Ibid.
[120] "Nord-Mali: Nabil Makloufi, un chef d'Aqmi, se tue au volant de sa voiture."
[121] Interview with Mohamed ag Aharib.
[122] Letter from the Shura Council of al-Qa'ida in the Islamic Maghreb to the Shura Council of the Veiled Men Battalion, October 3, 2012, 25, http://hosted.ap.org/specials/interactives/_international/_pdfs/al-qaida-belmoktar-letter-english.pdf [dead link].
[123] Interview with Mohamed ag Aharib. Or perhaps it is accurate to say that both men presented themselves as spokesmen for Ansar al-Din.
[124] Hafid, "Alghabass ag Intalla, Vice-Président du Haut Conseil pour l'Unité de l'Azawad."

Ifoghas politicians represented the movement in negotiations with outsiders. Ag Intalla visited Algeria amid the early hostilities between the rebels and the Malian state: "My role involved reassuring the neighboring countries, notably Algeria, and saying that we had no unwholesome objective."[125] This negotiator role also concerned internal northern Malian politics: in spring 2012, ag Intalla represented Ansar al-Din in negotiations with the MNLA over the nature of the Azawadi project and the possibilities for cooperation between the two groups.[126]

During the second half of 2012, ag Intalla, ag Aoussa, and ag Aharib represented Ansar al-Din in talks mediated by the Economic Community of West African States through the offices of the government of Burkina Faso.[127] As part of these negotiations, Burkina Faso's Foreign Minister Djibril Bassolé even met ag Ghali in Kidal in August.[128] Burkinabè authorities sought to convince Ansar al-Din to cut ties with AQIM and MUJWA and to instead "inscribe its action in the Tuareg demands."[129] Regional states hoped that Ansar al-Din would henceforth function as an ethnic rather than a jihadist movement. In all this, the Ifoghas nobles functioned as the faces of Ansar al-Din in intra-Tuareg politics and vis-à-vis neighboring governments. Militarily, they benefited from their alliance with the anathematized AQIM but politically, this faction of Ansar al-Din remained viable in the mainstream.

At the same time, other faces of Ansar al-Din were becoming notorious in northern Mali and in the international media. Hardliners, such

---

[125] Ibid.

[126] "Mali: 'Azawad al-Islamiyya' Tanshaqq 'an 'Ansar al-Din' wa-Tad'u li-'Hall Silmi'," *Asharq al-Awsat*, January 25, 2013, http://archive.aawsat.com/details .asp?section=4&article=714529&issueno=12477#.Wil7YztrxaQ.

[127] Ursula Soares, "Nord du Mali: première rencontre entre Ansar Dine et le médiateur Blaise Compaoré," RFI, June 18, 2012, www.rfi.fr/afrique/ 20120618-nord-mali-premiere-rencontre-entre-ansar-dine-le-mediateur-compaore; and "Mali: Ansar Dine se divise," BBC Afrique, January 24, 2013, www.bbc.com/afrique/region/2013/01/130124_mali_ansardine_scission.shtml. See also "Interview de Mohamed Aharib, porte-parole d'Ansar Dine," AFP, November 16, 2012, www.youtube.com/watch?v=D1xkpqxiOiE.

[128] Adam Nossiter, "Burkina Faso Official Visits Mali in Effort to Avert War," *New York Times*, August 8, 2012, www.nytimes.com/2012/08/08/world/ africa/burkina-faso-official-visits-mali-in-effort-to-avert-war.html.

[129] Soares, "Nord du Mali: première rencontre."

as Ould Bouamama, presented a grim face to journalists. Ould Bouamama claimed responsibility for destroying mausoleums in Timbuktu in June 2012, saying starkly, "All of this is *haram*. We are all Muslims. UNESCO is what?"[130] In another interview, Bouamama called al-Qaʿida "our Islamic brothers" and described the group's intentions in black and white terms: "When you accept that there is Islam, you have to accept that there is Shariah."[131]

Speculating about what was going on within Ansar al-Din during this time suggests several possibilities, not all of them mutually exclusive. First, some observers – such as German intelligence – stated "that [ag Ghali] had boasted to his associates that the negotiations were a sham, and that he was merely trying to buy time to prepare his military offensive against the south."[132] Yet the negotiations do not seem to have been a sham from the perspective of the other Ifoghas politicians, given the effort they expended and the fact that they continued negotiating after the French intervention. Another possibility is that ag Ghali was hedging his bets, weighing the advantages of different paths: a negotiated settlement with the Malian government and other groups, or a definitive commitment to jihadist action. Amid this bet-hedging, different members of his coalition were useful to him in different ways – ag Intalla and others were palatable to ECOWAS and the Malian government, while Ould Bouamama had credibility on the jihadist scene.

Even some voices in AQIM were open to flexible arrangements involving Ansar al-Din: In a letter to his Mali-based field commanders, AQIM's emir ʿAbd al-Malik Droukdel proposed various kinds of organizational structures in which Ansar al-Din would officially rule northern Mali, while AQIM would carry out independent, external jihadist actions under its own name. Droukdel directed his field commanders to consult ag Ghali about this point.[133] Droukdel appeared

---

[130] "Timbuktu Shrines Damaged by Mali Ansar Dine Islamists," BBC, June 30, 2012, www.bbc.com/news/world-africa-18657463.

[131] Adam Nossiter, "In Timbuktu, Harsh Change under Islamists," *New York Times*, June 3, 2012, www.nytimes.com/2012/06/03/world/africa/in-timbuktu-mali-rebels-and-islamists-impose-harsh-rule.html.

[132] "Lion of the Desert."

[133] Letter from ʿAbd al-Malik Droukdel to Saharan field commanders in al-Qaʿida in the Islamic Maghreb, 6, http://hosted.ap.org/specials/interactives/_international/_pdfs/al-qaida-manifesto.pdf [dead link].

open to some bet-hedging and strategic, localized branding on ag Ghali's part. Droukdel favored expanding the coalition rather than foreclosing political avenues.

A third possibility is that different segments of Ansar al-Din were competing to gain ag Ghali's ear while also competing to shape external perceptions of the movement in ways that would constrain other blocs. The Ifoghas were advocating a compromise that would preserve some of Ansar al-Din's far-reaching Islamist and Salafi agenda but would frame it in terms that still permitted negotiations; had they succeeded in convincing ag Ghali to accept a negotiated outcome, the Ifoghas would have marginalized the hardliners or provoked them into leaving the group. The hardliners, meanwhile, were pushing for more aggression that would then foreclose the possibility for negotiated settlements. Negotiations became an object of contestation in intra-coalition power struggles.

December 2012–January 2013 proved the turning point for Ansar al-Din's cohesion. According to ag Intalla and ag Aharib, the Ifoghas leaders in Kidal were excluded as ag Ghali and Abu Zayd decided to advance into central Mali. Ag Intalla, in Burkina Faso at the time, advised against the plans, but he was outweighed by Timbuktu-based jihadists such as Abu Zayd and the rising jihadist star Amadou Kouffa (see Chapter 4).[134] The Ifoghas considered the administrative district of Douentza, located in the northeast part of the Mopti Region and captured by jihadist forces in August 2012, the furthest southern limit of "Azawad." They had no interest in extending the fight deeper into the Mopti Region, much less into southern Mali.[135] The Ifoghas were negotiating with the Burkinabè and Malian governments up to the last moment. Ignoring their negotiations and their reservations, ag Ghali joined Abu Zayd and Kouffa in personally directing the jihadist advance on the town of Konna in January 2013. That action immediately provoked what the Tuareg nobles (and AQIM's emir Droukdel) had feared: a French reaction. The intervention not only reversed the entire jihadist project but also splintered the Ansar al-Din coalition back into its prewar components, with the important exception that ag Ghali fully committed to jihadism.

[134] Interview with Alghabass ag Intalla.
[135] Interview with Mohamed ag Aharib.

Ansar al-Din after Operation Serval: Diverging Paths

The French-led military intervention of January 2013, Operation Serval, drastically accelerated the Ifoghas politicians' calculation that Ansar al-Din, once assumed to be a vehicle for protecting their political relevance and containing ag Ghali's radicalism, was now a liability. Splitting with ag Ghali, the politicians formed a new group, the Mouvement Islamique de l'Azawad (Islamic Movement of Azawad, MIA), under the leadership of Alghabass ag Intalla.

In public comments, ag Intalla attributed the split to ag Ghali's intransigence on several issues. The Ifoghas had wanted to continue negotiating with other armed movements and with the Malian government, and they wanted to sever connections with AQIM; the latter's anathematization, once a strategic resource for these northern Malian politicians, was now the worst type of association one could have amid the French intervention. Ag Intalla commented, "We had it out with [ag Ghali] the other day and we said, really, we want to talk with the rest of the world."[136] The MIA framed itself as emanating "from the moderate wing (*min al-janah al-mu'tadal*)" of Ansar al-Din.[137] "For us," ag Intalla said in another interview, "it is possible to struggle against Mali. But we could not survive in the face of the implication of France, the United Nations, the African Union. So it was necessary to find a way out. The internationalization of the conflict was going to be fatal for our people."[138] The reference to "our people" was not idle. Driving ag Intalla's decision to form the MIA, it seems, was a feeling that his own constituency's (i.e., Kidal's and the Ifoghas') survival was at stake. It is even possible that ag Ghali supported the MIA's move in order to remove the Ifoghas from France's crosshairs.[139]

One of the first groups the MIA wanted to talk to was the MNLA. The separatists were now more or less openly backed by France, which considered the MNLA an anti-jihadist counterweight. The MNLA arrived in Kidal in late January 2013 and immediately constituted a

---

[136] Morgan, "Alghabass ag Intalla."
[137] "Mali: 'Azawad al-Islamiyya' Tanshaqq 'an 'Ansar al-Din'."
[138] Hafid, "Alghabass ag Intalla, Vice-Président du Haut Conseil pour l'Unité de l'Azawad."
[139] Interview with Mohammed Mahmoud Abu al-Ma'ali.

"Transitional Council of the State of Azawad."[140] They soon reached an understanding with ag Intalla and his men.[141] This rapprochement set the stage for more far-reaching unity initiatives in northern Mali, at least among Tuareg and Arab nobles.

In May 2013, Mohamed ag Intalla formed an umbrella organization for non-jihadist Tuareg rebel groups. This organization was eventually called the Haut conseil pour l'unité de l'Azawad (High Council for the Unity of the Azawad, HCUA). This generic-sounding name was chosen partly because the "Islamic Movement of Azawad" moniker had drawn criticism for sounding too akin to a jihadist organization.[142] At a May 19 meeting in Kidal, Mohamed ag Intalla and his father, the *aménokal*, formally incorporated Alghabass ag Intalla and his followers into the HCUA; Alghabass announced the MIA's dissolution.[143] Led by the *aménokal* and his sons, the HCUA tacitly advanced the notion that leadership of the Kel Adagh still came from the confederation's leadership, rather than from any particular ideology.

Alghabass ag Intalla had – with his family's assistance – created an off-ramp for himself and others from jihadism. The international community, Malian national authorities, and neighboring governments acquiesced to this act of political rehabilitation. Peace, after all, would require a broad spectrum of participants. By June 2013, ag Intalla was representing the HCUA at the Ouagadougou accord, an initial ceasefire between the Malian state and the non-jihadist armed groups in the north.

In 2014, some of the major non-jihadist, Tuareg- and Arab-led rebel and political formations in northern Mali banded together to create the Coordination des mouvements de l'Azawad (Coordination of the Movements of the Azawad, CMA). The major components of the CMA were the MNLA, the HCUA, and part of the Mouvement arabe de l'Azawad (Arab Movement of the Azawad, MAA). Again, Alghabass ag Intalla became part of a broad umbrella coalition of armed actors whom the Malian government and the Western powers saw as politically legitimate (meaning, they were willing to listen to their demands and

[140] Mouvement National de Libération de l'Azawad, "C.T.E.A.," January 25, 2013, www.mnlamov.net/actualites/34-actualites/244-ctea.html.
[141] Morgan, "Alghabass ag Intalla."   [142] Interview with Mohamed ag Aharib.
[143] "Mali: Le Haut Conseil de L'Azawad met en place ses instances," RFI, May 20, 2013, www.rfi.fr/afrique/20130520-mali-haut-conseil-azawad-instances-intalla-ag-attaher-alghabass-ag-intalla.

to negotiate with them). Ag Intalla served as the CMA's president from December 2016–September 2017, as part of an agreement within the coalition to rotate the presidency among the member groups.[144]

The CMA has periodically leveraged relatively soft forms of Islamism as a political tool. For example, CMA authorities declared the imposition of shariʻa in Kidal in early 2019, in what I see as a bid to test Malian authorities' willingness to completely cede control of Kidal to the CMA; after pushback came from the Malian state, the CMA softened their decree, but the episode showed how the language of shariʻa politics remains relevant and even mainstream in the north.[145] Yet ag Intalla is, for all intents and purposes, widely and probably fittingly treated (including by European and American actors) as a prominent politician rather than as a former jihadist.

To return to early 2013, after the departure of the MIA, the remainder of Ansar al-Din was now considered fully jihadist and completely politically anathema within Malian politics and the international system. In February 2013, the United States government declared Iyad ag Ghali a "Specially Designated Global Terrorist."[146] He was simultaneously blacklisted by the United Nations' Al-Qaida Sanctions Committee.[147] The following month, the United States government designated Ansar al-Din a "Foreign Terrorist Organization."[148] Again, the United Nations' Al-Qaida Sanctions Committee did the equivalent.[149] Blacklisting ag Ghali and Ansar al-Din, but not ag Intalla and the MIA (or the HCUA), followed an essentially political logic. The rationale for the designations evoked incidents from 2012 and thus

---

[144] "Kidal: Sidi Brahim Ould Sidatt du MAA succède à Alghabass Ag Intalla à la tête de la CMA," Kibaru, September 12, 2017, http://malijet.com/actualte_dans_les_regions_du_mali/rebellion_au_nord_du_mali/194181-kidal-sidi-brahim-ould-sidatt-du-maa-succede-a-alghabass-ag-inta.html.

[145] Alex Thurston, "Mali: Sharia in Kidal?" Sahel Blog, February 20, 2019, https://sahelblog.wordpress.com/2019/02/20/mali-sharia-in-kidal/.

[146] U.S. Department of State, "Terrorist Designations of Iyad ag Ghali," February 26, 2013, www.state.gov/j/ct/rls/other/des/266576.htm.

[147] United Nations Security Council, "Security Council Al-Qaida Sanctions Committee Amends One Entry on Its Sanctions List," September 23, 2014, www.un.org/press/en/2014/sc11576.doc.htm.

[148] U.S. Department of State, "Terrorist Designations of Ansar al-Dine," March 21, 2013, www.state.gov/j/ct/rls/other/des/266575.htm.

[149] United Nations Security Council, "Security Council Al-Qaida Sanctions Committee Adds Ansar Eddine to Its Sanctions List," March 19, 2013, www.un.org/press/en/2013/sc10947.doc.htm.

could have applied equally to all past and present Ansar al-Din leaders,[150] but foreign powers chose not to treat the MIA as terrorists. The divergent paths taken by Ansar al-Din's leaders after Serval show that involvement with jihadism in 2012 was not in and of itself an obstacle to mainstream political legitimacy afterwards. The start of Serval was effectively do-or-die time for one's role in northern Malian politics: At that point no more strategic ambiguity about one's identity and intentions was possible.

Or was it? Various journalists and Malian politicians have suggested that ag Ghali maintained political ties with his former colleagues even after they defected from his movement. In early 2015, *Jeune Afrique* speculated that ag Ghali was working behind the scenes to shape the Algiers peace process, in which the HCUA had a major role. *Jeune Afrique* labeled Alghabass ag Intalla and Cheikh ag Aoussa as two key, unofficial conduits between ag Ghali and the Algiers talks. The magazine cited an anonymous French intelligence officer who claimed that ag Ghali and ag Intalla were in contact, and quoted an anonymous Malian official who commented, "It is very difficult to believe that there are no longer any connections between these people."[151] Or as one of ag Ghali's detractors put it, even more strongly, "the true leader of the CMA is Iyad."[152] If one accepts such accounts, then the fragmentation of Ansar al-Din as a coalition led to two realignments. First, ag Ghali and the Ifoghas politicians went from full-fledged coalition partners to mere allies (or even more minimally, interlocutors) of each other; second, ag Ghali went from a mere ally of AQIM to a full-fledged member of AQIM's own coalition.

Why did ag Ghali not make the same choice that ag Intalla and the other Ifoghas politicians did in January 2013? Why not avoid blacklisting, a seeming political death sentence that undermined over two decades of careful positioning and repositioning within northern Malian and national Malian politics? Certainly, it would have been harder for ag Ghali, in comparison with the other Ifoghas, to extricate himself from his jihadist associations – after all, ag Ghali led the assault on Konna personally. And yet it would not have been impossible for ag

[150] "Terrorist Designations of Iyad ag Ghali."
[151] Benjamin Roger, "Mali: l'ombre d'Iyad Ag Ghali plane sur les négociations d'Alger," *Jeune Afrique*, February 18, 2015, www.jeuneafrique.com/225445/politique/mali-l-ombre-d-iyad-ag-ghali-plane-sur-les-n-gociations-d-alger/.
[152] Interview with Fahad ag Mohamed, Bamako, June 21, 2019.

Ghali to reinvent himself: He had done so before, more than once. Meanwhile, regional powers had been keen to pry ag Ghali away from AQIM up until the eve of the jihadist advance into central Mali. Even France might have quietly celebrated ag Ghali's return to the fold and the ensuing political quarantining of AQIM within the northern Malian context. Yet ag Ghali did not make this choice.

One factor was that ag Ghali was not alone in remaining with the jihadist forces. Even after most of the Ifoghas left Ansar al-Din for mainstream politics, some Tuareg stayed inside AQIM and the now thoroughly jihadist remnant of Ansar al-Din. AQIM offered some inducements in this direction. Late 2012 saw a flurry of shifts within the Saharan jihadist milieu, as Mokhtar Belmokhtar broke with AQIM (see Chapter 2). AQIM began to restructure its Saharan battalions, spinning off a new battalion ("Yusuf bin Tashfin," named for a medieval Saharan conqueror) under Malian Tuareg leadership.[153] AQIM was reeling – the prominent Saharan field commander Abu Zayd died battling French forces in February 2013, and other leading figures were killed as well – but AQIM still had resources to offer its friends.

Additionally, ag Ghali might have felt that mainstream politics now held little advantage for him, at least in the short term. If he returned to the fold, it would not be the same as it was for ag Intalla, the son of the aged *aménokal*. Ag Intalla was granted leadership positions in post-Serval political configurations. Yet when it came to ag Ghali, various other actors – the Malian government, the French, the MNLA, and others – might have demanded concessions and even humiliations. Notably, the MNLA's Bilal ag Achérif told me that he himself had urged ag Ghali to break with AQIM in order to get international support for an independent Azawad. In response, ag Ghali had told him that international powers would not be satisfied with a mere break – they would also, ag Ghali argued, have asked him to fight AQIM but would not have given him enough support to do so, thus leaving him in an impossible position.[154]

Meanwhile, as other Ifoghas politicians left Ansar al-Din and transitioned into the MIA, then into the HCUA, the power of both the *aménokal*'s family and the MNLA grew correspondingly. What role

[153] "Tanzim al-Qa'ida Tilin [sic] 'an Katiba bi-sm 'Yusuf bin Tashfin'," *Azzaman*, November 28, 2012, http://azzaman.info/?p=849.

[154] Interview with Bilal ag Achérif.

would have been available to ag Ghali within these configurations? He had already tried virtually every option, from rebel politics to nonviolent religious activism to bidding for the position of *aménokal* to advising presidents to serving as an overseas diplomat. Running for office, as discussed previously, held little appeal for him. And how would young fighters and activists perceive him now? By 2013, ag Ghali may have felt that there was no path available to him in mainstream politics.

Additionally, the national political landscape and ag Ghali's potential place in it were now very uncertain. Ag Ghali had negotiated, partnered with, and even worked for the departed president Amadou Toumani Touré for more than two decades, from Touré's 1991 military coup through the 2012 coup against Touré. But in January 2013, who knew what was on the cards? Ag Ghali may have doubted whether he could trust the interim authorities in Bamako, or their successors, to enforce and respect any deals he struck with them. Perhaps in this climate, ag Ghali considered it better to remain in the shadows, preserving a political role through attention-grabbing terrorism and by maintaining backroom communications with his interlocutors in the mainstream. Once a broker between the anathematized and the mainstream, ag Ghali may now have felt that his own anathematization was the best political outcome he could envision.

Ideological factors cannot be ruled out: "There is no more Iyad today," ag Intalla told me in an interview. In ag Intalla's opinion, the practical politician had disappeared, leaving behind a hardened jihadist.[155] Yet such comments are hard for me to accept at face value, especially if it is true that ag Ghali and ag Intalla remain in contact to discuss and shape political developments in northern Mali. Perhaps ag Ghali is both ideologically committed to jihadism and strategically savvy when it comes to positioning himself for the future.

By 2017, all of the challenges that existed before the 2012 rebellion remained. Some challenges had increased, including the overall level of violence in the north and center of Mali. Did ag Ghali, as many Malians felt, hold the keys to resolving these problems? In March–April 2017, Mali's official "Conference of National Understanding" recommended that the government talk to ag Ghali and the central Malian jihadist leader Amadou Kouffa. Strikingly, however, at that

---

[155] Interview with Alghabass ag Intalla.

same moment ag Ghali was announcing that Ansar al-Din had formally joined AQIM. Ansar al-Din merged with several other jihadist groups to create Jama'at Nusrat al-Islam wa-l-Muslimin (The Group for Supporting Islam and Muslims, JNIM). Ironically, ag Ghali's importance to making peace in Mali seemed to move in lockstep with the difficulties of imagining an actual dialogue with him.

As JNIM's name suggested, the group's ambitions were not just military and ideological but also political. In an April 2017 interview, ag Ghali said that JNIM sought not just to "exhaust the enemy by targeting him in every place where he is found" but also to "strive to gain popular support (*al-hirs 'ala kasb al-hadina al-sha'biyya*)."[156] Whether out of fanaticism or political calculation (or both), and whether he wanted to rebuild a jihadist enclave or to be invited back to the negotiating table (or both), ag Ghali confirmed his status as Mali's preeminent jihadist leader. And ironically, even though in 2012 he had been close to the hardline AQIM field commander Abu Zayd, he now sounded like the more politically accommodating Droukdel. JNIM would be an aggressive terrorist organization, but it would also be a vehicle for political outreach to different northern Malian constituencies.

Conclusion

Northern Malian politics from 2003 to the present reveals a great deal about how jihadist coalitions and alliances work. The GSPC/AQIM cultivated a wide range of local allies, but these allies were not merely dupes for the Algerian jihadists; rather, northern Malian politicians moved strategically within a web of relationships and rivalries, leveraging the resources represented by AQIM. During the 2012 rebellion, aligning with AQIM advanced the ambitions of certain Ifoghas Tuareg politicians. Not only did Ansar al-Din allow these politicians to carve out a major place for themselves within the rebellion, it also positioned them to have a considerable say in the post-rebellion negotiations.

Yet figures such as Alghabass ag Intalla knew when it was time to exit that vehicle. In turn, local, national, and international authorities allowed them to do so without political consequences. The experiences of ag Intalla and his peers, especially when contrasted with the

---

[156] "'Al-Masra' Tuhawir al-Shaykh Aba al-Fadl Iyad Ghali."

experience of Iyad ag Ghali, show that jihadism is not just driven by fanatics who want to establish an emirate at any cost. Rather, jihadist movements become implicated in broader local political struggles. At key moments, local politics can help determine how jihadist formations shift. Crises drive some actors to drop their formal alliances with jihadists, while driving other actors to move from alliances into full-fledged coalitions with jihadist organizations.

4 | Central Mali

The Possibilities and Limits of Incorporation

Map 3 Central Mali

Chapter 3 discussed jihadist coalition politics in northern Mali. There, coalition-building involved intra-elite positioning. AQIM's Mali-centric subsidiary Jama'at Nusrat al-Islam wa-l-Muslimin (The Group for Supporting Islam and Muslims, JNIM), formed in 2017, counts a heavy portion of local elites among its leaders and allies, above all its top leader the Malian national Iyad ag Ghali.

Despite its northern leadership, much of the violence carried out in JNIM's name has affected central Mali. Indeed, ag Ghali's home turf, the Kidal region in northeastern Mali, became the least violent region within the conflict zone. Rather, the central region of Mopti emerged as Mali's most dangerous place. Between 2012 and early 2019, 52 percent of the total violence in Mali occurred in Mopti; in terms of numbers killed, this meant 896 people, 64 percent of whom were killed after 2017. Jihadist groups, moreover, had likely perpetrated less violence (354 confirmed victims) than community-based militias (669 confirmed victims).[1] Central Mali also led the estimates in terms of militia violence. The structure of political violence was fundamentally different in the center than in the north.

The divergence between the north and the center was highlighted by the 2018 presidential elections. During the first round of voting, in July, 871 polling sites had to close, many of them due to violence and intimidation; over 700 of those sites were in Mopti. During the second round, in August, 493 polling sites closed, of which 444 were in Mopti. In contrast, Kidal reported no closures during the second round. In the north, ex-rebels (including some of ag Ghali's former allies) brokered agreements with the Malian government to secure and administer the elections. In Mopti, in contrast, jihadists essentially prevented an election from taking place.[2]

This chapter argues that the different patterns of violence in the north and the center of Mali reflect the very different structures of jihadist coalitions in those areas. In terms of jihadist leadership, the north was dominated by JNIM's leader, ag Ghali, and his deputy, the Algerian national and AQIM Saharan Emir Yahya Abu al-Hammam

[1] José Luengo-Cabrera, visualization of casualties in Mali drawing on ACLED data, March 29, 2019, available at https://twitter.com/J_LuengoCabrera/status/1111571427310911488. After Mopti, Gao was next in terms of casualty figures, with 450 deaths in this period, then Ségou with 156, Timbuktu with 86, and Kidal with 76.

[2] Alex Thurston, "Mali's Elections Saw Some Islamist Militant Violence. Here's What These Patterns Suggest," *Washington Post* Monkey Cage blog, September 7, 2018, www.washingtonpost.com/news/monkey-cage/wp/2018/09/07/malis-elections-saw-some-jihadist-violence-heres-what-these-patterns-suggest/?utm_term=.c6589fbeb2b8.

(1978–2019). These men focused on targeting foreign forces and wooing the prominent individuals – militia commanders, politicians, and clerics – who represented important blocs. In central Mali, however, Amadou Kouffa has functioned both as a JNIM field commander and as the architect of a very different kind of coalition. Kouffa's coalition-building strategy plays ambiguously and dangerously with the increasingly fraught issue of ethnic identity for the Peul, a historically pastoralist group spread across West Africa. Drawing support from young Peul shepherds and benefiting from authorities' ethnic profiling and collective punishment of the Peul, Kouffa's "jihadism from below" contrasts markedly with ag Ghali's "jihadism from above."

Theoretical Implications of the Case

When jihadists apply a bottom-up instead of top-down method of coalition-building, processes of incorporation look much different than they do at the elite level. In fact, the processes of coalition formation become much harder to reconstruct. Bottom-up incorporation involves deal-making among little-known, relatively junior figures who speak for small blocs of fighters. These blocs may be community-level networks or fragments of other jihadist coalitions; they are, as with other blocs discussed in this book, prewar networks or networks forged and reforged in wartime, but their composition is likely to be more fluid than elite-directed networks and their outlines are harder for the outside observer to perceive.

The conditions that facilitate bottom-up incorporation can be identified with some clarity, although they are heavily context-dependent. Crudely put, bottom-up incorporation is most successful when the jihadist coalition positions itself as the defender of multiple group-specific interests, including those related to resource allocation and ethnic identity. This mode of positioning can demand rhetorical ambiguity on jihadists' part, as jihadists attempt to speak to multiple and potentially mutually exclusive projects. For example, an unambiguous statement of ethnic particularism risks *dilution* of the jihadist project, while potentially alienating other constituencies; it is difficult to function as an ethnic nationalist or self-defense movement and as a multi-ethnic jihadist project at the same time. The rhetorical ambiguity that Katibat Macina deploys in central Mali, regarding the question of ethnicity, is thus a logical outcome of the makeup of its coalition and the strategies it has used for incorporation. At the same time, such ambiguity has become harder for Katibat Macina to sustain over time; as the "ethnicization" of the conflict in central Mali intensified, some coalition blocs within Katibat Macina started pushing the leadership to direct its violence along more explicitly ethnic lines.

An additional theoretical takeaway from these processes is that bottom-up incorporation may render the incorporation of elites and prominent power-brokers more, rather than less, difficult. Katibat Macina's wide recruitment among young herders is matched by its failure (or perhaps unwillingness) to attract a single prominent politician to its banner, a marked contrast with the trajectory of jihadists in northern Mali. When jihadists incorporate constituencies in a bottom-up way without needing local politicians as intermediaries, those politicians can be threatened rather than attracted by the group's power. And in certain contexts, bottom-up and top-down incorporation can become mutually exclusive; Katibat Macina's bottom-up incorporation has been driven partly by many young herders' rejection of local elites and power-brokers, and so a pivot to recruiting elites could end up antagonizing the coalition's primary constituencies of fighters. This dynamic helps explain why Katibat Macina, in its external political relations, has blended patterns of intimidation (against local elites and communities who do not defer to the group's demands), accommodation (of certain elites and communities that do defer), and outright domination (of areas where combinations of intimidation and accommodation culminate in direct jihadist control).

A Biographical Sketch of Amadou Kouffa

Compared with ag Ghali, Amadou Kouffa's biography is less well known.[3] Born between the early 1950s and the early 1960s,[4] Kouffa's surname comes from the village of Kouffa or Koufa in the Niafunké

---

[3] Kouffa's first name is rendered in different ways in the Malian and international media: Amadou, Hamadoun, Mamadou, Muhammad, etc.

[4] One source puts Kouffa's birth date around 1953: See B. Daou, "Attaques de Tenenkou: L'ombre de Hammadoun Koufa avec un Mouvement de Libération du Macina plane," *Le Républicain*, January 23, 2015, http://malijet.com/a_la_une_du_mali/121613-attaques_de_tenenkou_l_ombre_de_hammadoun.html. Another source puts the birth date at 1961: International Federation for Human Rights/Malian Association for Human Rights (FIDH/AMDH), "In Central Mali, Civilian Populations Are Caught between Terrorism and Counterterrorism,"

cercle (administrative district) of the Timbuktu region, just north of the
Mopti region. As a child, he became an itinerant Qur'an student – a
relatively common path in Mopti. He also earned repute as a singer,
customizing songs for clients or to mock girls who spurned him. This
dual career as student and singer gave Kouffa a wide knowledge of
Mopti, its villages, and its people.[5]

By the early 2000s, Kouffa had converted his local renown into a
career as an anti-establishment preacher.[6] Kouffa rose amid broader
shifts in Mali's religious field.[7] From the 1930s on, and particularly
by the 1980s, new and sometimes underground Muslim activist
movements emerged, challenging the Maliki–Ash'ari–Sufi model
described in the previous chapter. In the 1990s, liberalization and
multi-party democracy allowed activism to flourish openly, generating a flurry of new Islamic associations, publications, and radio
outlets.

Amid the rise of activist clerics, traditionalists lost some ground. Not
completely, of course: Today, Mali's preeminent Muslim cleric is the
Chérif of Nioro du Sahel, Mohamed Ould Cheickna, who leads a
branch of the Tijaniyya Sufi order. But nontraditionalist, activist clerics
have also become prominent; these figures may reject or downplay
Sufism, and their authority is not primarily genealogical. By the 2000s,
nontraditionalist clerics such as Ousmane Madani Haïdara and the
Salafi preacher Mahmoud Dicko made their weight felt in politics. In
2009, Dicko and Haïdara (who are often at odds with one another,
although not in this case) helped mobilize opposition against the

---

November 2018, 27, www.fidh.org/IMG/pdf/fidh_centre-of-mali_population-
sized-between-terrorism-and-counter-terrorism_727_en_november2018.pdf.
[5] Interview with Boubacar Cissé, Bamako, January 25, 2018.   [6] Ibid.
[7] For background on these shifts, see Louis Brenner, *Controlling Knowledge:
Religion, Power, and Schooling in a West African Muslim Society* (Bloomington:
Indiana University Press, 2001); Benjamin Soares, *Islam and the Prayer
Economy: History and Authority in a Malian Town* (Ann Arbor: University of
Michigan Press, 2005); International Crisis Group, "Islam et politique au Mali:
entre réalité et fiction," July 18, 2017, https://d2071andvip0wj.cloudfront.net/
249-islam-et-politique-au-mali-entre-realite-et-fiction.pdf; and Ibrahim Yahaya
Ibrahim, "Islamisme dans le Sud, jihadisme dans le Nord: pourquoi l'activisme
islamique au Mali s'est-il exprimé différemment?" *Bulletin FrancoPaix* 2:10
(December 2017), https://dandurand.uqam.ca/wp-content/uploads/2018/01/
Bulletin-FrancoPaix-vol-2_no-10_FR.pdf.

proposed revisions to Mali's family code.[8] In this atmosphere, it was not impossible for someone from humble origins, like Kouffa, to make a name for himself as a preacher.

In Mopti, recent decades have also brought challenges to the political-religious establishment. The activist and researcher Dougoukolo Alpha Oumar Ba-Konaré has argued that, ironically, the families descended from nineteenth-century jihad leaders in Peul areas (see later) saw their influence diminish over time. "Today, these families have no political weight in Mali. It is an Islam of intellectuals, of writing. They do not even have a seat on the High Islamic Council of Mali and there are only three on the Council of the Tijaniyya."[9] In 2006, a riot in Djenné, Mopti, revealed young Muslims' dissatisfaction with how local politicians and imams were managing the town's mosque – which is arguably the most powerful symbol of Islam in Mali. An anthropologist who has worked in Djenné concluded that the riot "was the manifestation of a widespread sense of impotence and exclusion from the centres of power and decision-making that directly affects the homes people live in and the buildings where they pray and socialise and which they maintain as a community."[10] Hereditary religious authorities were losing popularity in some quarters.

Around the late 2000s, perhaps channeling some of the frustrations in his society, Kouffa became more hardline.[11] Some of this trajectory may have been influenced by travels outside Mali. One account suggests that Kouffa traveled widely in Africa during the 1990s, and "contributed ... to financing and founding mosques and schools in

[8] On the family code debate, see Benjamin Soares, "Family Law Reform in Mali: Contentious Debates and Elusive Outcomes," in *Gender and Islam in Africa: Rights, Sexuality, and Law*, edited by Margot Badran, 263–290 (Washington, DC, and Stanford, CA: Woodrow Wilson Center Press/Stanford University Press, 2011).

[9] Claire Meynial, "Alpha Oumar Ba-Konaré: 'Les djihadistes utilisent la fragilité des bergers peuls'," *Le Point Afrique*, December 7, 2017, www.lepoint.fr/afrique/alpha-oumar-ba-konare-les-djihadistes-utilisent-la-fragilite-des-bergers-peuls-07-12-2017-2178017_3826.php.

[10] Trevor Marchand, "The Djenné Mosque: World Heritage and Social Renewal in a West African Town" in *Religious Architecture: Anthropological Perspectives*, edited by Oskar Verkaaik, 117–148 (Amsterdam: University of Amsterdam Press, 2013), 134.

[11] Several accounts put the change in 2008–2009. See, for example, Morgane Le Cam, "Mali: Ousmane Bocoum, l'homme qui dialogue avec les djihadistes," *Le Monde*, April 12, 2019, www.lemonde.fr/afrique/article/2019/04/12/mali-ousmane-bocoum-l-homme-qui-dialogue-avec-les-djihadistes_5449578_3212.html.

Algeria, Mauritania, Libya, and Mali"[12] – although such accounts
should be treated with caution, given the journalistic propensity to
sensationalize and internationalize the backgrounds of jihadists. By the
early 2000s, Kouffa had reportedly fallen in with Jama'at al-Tabligh
(see Chapter 3), the global Muslim missionary movement.[13] Reportedly traveling to Afghanistan and the Middle East, he seems to have
abandoned his Sufi-Maliki background and gravitated, via Tabligh,
toward Salafism. Back in Mali, the debate over proposed revisions to
the family code angered him, and he became a vocal opponent of the
reforms.[14] He joined in the opposition helmed by Dicko and Haïdara.
Yet he also outflanked them in his rhetoric, criticizing not just this
individual law but also the wider political system. Meanwhile, through
Tabligh, Kouffa met Iyad ag Ghali.[15] According to one account, ag
Ghali systematically toured central Mali between approximately
1998 and 2010, extending his political and religious influence;
according to the same interlocutor, both ag Ghali and Kouffa participated in an international Tabligh conference held in Sévaré, Mopti
Region in 2011.[16]

At some point during 2012, Kouffa rallied to ag Ghali's side. He
favored the jihadist push into Mopti in January 2013, participating in
taking the town of Konna. On the night of the jihadist conquest,
Kouffa reportedly announced at the main mosque, "There is no more
prefect, no more sub-prefect, no more mayor, never again duties and
taxes, no more national identity card ... Women [must] stay in the
house, not leaving unless veiled. There is no more law other than the
shari'a and it is the imam of Konna [presumably he meant himself]
who will be in charge of applying it."[17] If this report is accurate, then
Kouffa already had in mind the project he would pursue starting in

[12] Khalid Yayamut, "Mamadu Kufa wa-l-Irhab fi al-Sahil wa-l-Sahra',"
Asharq al-Awsat, March 25, 2019, https://aawsat.com/home/article/
1649036/ممادو-كوفا-والإرهاب-في-الساحل-والصحراء.
[13] "Mali: qui est Amadou Koufa, ce prêcheur radical qui inquiète?" RFI, July 6,
2015, www.rfi.fr/afrique/20150706-mali-amadou-koufa-precheur-radical-
inquiete-mopti-iyad-ag-ghali-dawa/.
[14] Yayamut, "Mamadu Kufa."
[15] One credible source states that Kouffa and ag Ghali's relationship began by
"at least 2008." FIDH/AMDH, "In Central Mali, Civilian Populations Are
Caught," 7.
[16] Interview with Malian NGO official, Bamako, June 2019.
[17] Daou, "Attaques de Tenenkou."

2015: the expulsion of state authorities down to the municipal level, combined with a shari'a politics that promised transformative justice. The French intervention that came in response to the events at Konna, however, evicted the jihadists – and, for a time, appeared to have killed Kouffa, who disappeared from the public eye until he resurfaced in 2015.

A Sketch of Kouffa's Coalition

In building his coalition, Kouffa has recruited heavily among his own ethnic group, the Peul. Yet the coalition is not limited to the Peul. For starters, Kouffa benefits from the resources offered by AQIM and JNIM's Tuareg and Arab leaders. In addition to relying on Tuareg logisticians who help bring arms and ammunition from the north,[18] Kouffa has used the branding opportunities that JNIM makes possible: He has "frequently alternated between his role as a regional jihadist commander under Iyad Ag Ghali … and that as a Peul leader. In this, he was attempting to create and organise a transnational ethnic Peul militant movement embedded within a larger al-Qaeda affiliate."[19] Speaking in one 2018 video, Kouffa said in the Peul language, Fulfulde, "I call the Peul in every place, in Senegal, in Mali, in Niger, in Burkina, in Cote d'Ivoire, in Ghana, in Nigeria, and Cameroon … to jihad in the path of God." He added, "Because they raised up the flag of 'There Is No God But God' and called the people to rule by the Law of God, France incited its followers and armed them to kill the Peul people."[20] As the violence in Mopti has escalated, including inter-communal violence and Malian military crackdowns that routinely target the Peul, Kouffa has positioned himself as the defender and religious voice

---

[18] On the career of one Tuareg logistician, Alhousseyni ag Assaleh, see "Arrestation d'un présumé proche d'Amadou Koufa par Barkhane: Des incohérences sur la véritable identité du détenu," Kibaru, July 24, 2017, https:// kibaru.ml/fr/art/arrestation-d-un-présumé-proche-d-amadou-koufa-par-barkhane-des-incohérences-sur-la-véritable-identité-du-détenu-.

[19] Andrew Lebovich, "The Death of a Jihadist: A Chance to Curb Mali's Conflict," European Council on Foreign Relations, December 13, 2018, www.ecfr.eu/ article/commentary_the_death_of_a_jihadist_a_chance_to_curb_malis_conflict.

[20] My translation is from the Arabic subtitles. See Jama'at Nusrat al-Islam wa-l-Muslimin, "Infarru Hifafan wa-Thiqalan: Kalima Mar'iyya li-l-Shaykh al-Mujahid Muhammad Kufa Amir Mintaqat Masina," Mu'assasat al-Zallaqa, November 2018, https://archive.org/details/isololo_13.

of his ethnic community – a defender against multiple enemies, from the hyperlocal to the world stage.

To add further context, the Peul are an ethnic group dispersed across the Sahel and the northern parts of several coastal West African countries. They number perhaps 25 million. Within Mali, the Peul constitute an estimated 15 percent of the population, making them the country's second-largest ethnic group. The Peul are subdivided into numerous sections and communities, including groups that no longer speak Fulfulde. The Peul have internal hierarchies based on lineages and membership in particular subgroups, "castes," or what might be better called "socio-professional categories."[21] Traditionally pastoralists, the Peul have a regional history that reverberates in complex ways today. Narratives of past glory (in some eyes) compete with criticisms of that same past. In the nineteenth century, Peul religiopolitical leaders established theocratic polities in various parts of the greater Sahel. These polities included the Macina Empire or *diina*, which lasted from 1818–1862 in present-day central Mali.[22]

What the *diina*'s legacy means for Kouffa's forces is hotly debated. When organized jihadist violence resurfaced in the central Malian regions of Mopti and Ségou in 2015, Western (and some Malian) media coverage immediately dubbed Kouffa's group the "Macina Liberation Front." Some Peul intellectuals and politicians have been outraged by this designation. As one commentary in a Malian newspaper read,

For your information, Kouffa is not from Macina [perhaps a reference to Kouffa being from southern Timbutku] and is not of the same tariqa (Sufi order) as the people of Macina: the Qadiriyya and Tijaniyya ... Kouffa is a Wahhabi (Qatar, Arabia, and the countries of the Gulf). Then and now, Kouffa's people call themselves the people of the brush; they have never had the name of a liberation front, never called for an ethnic jihad, and the victims of Kouffa are more numerous among the Peul than among the others. Reducing the terrorizing jihadism of Kouffa to a Peul reconquest or domination is a discourse that is simply clumsy and hypocritical. You can listen to the recordings attributed to Kouffa – since their appearance, you will never find the name front nor liberation of Macina. They always say jihadism

---

[21] Interview with a Burkinabè historian, Ouagadougou, June 2019.
[22] For a classic history of Macina, see Amadou Hampâté Bâ and Jacques Daget, *L'Empire Peul du Macina (1818–1853)* (Abidjan: École Pratique des Hautes Études, 1984 [1962]).

while mainly citing the international forces they call occupiers and people of the cross; the government of Mali is accused of submitting to Crusaders and infidels. He calls for fighting all those who collaborate with these forces and allies (states). [All parenthetical asides are in the original text.][23]

Such voices call Kouffa an upstart Salafi (or "Wahhabi") and a foreign puppet whose violence not only clashes with the spirit of the nineteenth-century empire but also trashes Macina's legacy, and not just figuratively: Kouffa's forces were widely blamed for an incident in May 2015 where dynamite was set off at the mausoleum of Seku Amadu (d. 1845), the *diina*'s founder. The explosion came just a few days before the annual mass visitation of Amadu's grave was due to take place. As the Malian journalist Adam Thiam wrote at the time, the act was "a provocation for the hundreds of thousands of local Muslims and a gesture marked by Salafist fundamentalism to the detriment of an identity-based Islam in which Seku Amadu, beyond the saint and admirer of God, also embodied the Peul influence."[24] Kouffa's Salafi-jihadist project is difficult to square with the Sufism-infused jihad of Seku Amadu – or, at the very least, "Macina" means something very different to Kouffa's followers than to his detractors, including the many Muslims (including Peul Muslims) who oppose him.

What to call the group – Macina Liberation Front versus Katibat Macina – is not just a semantic point, but more importantly has to do with how Kouffa and his fighters understand their project. One member of the Peul elite told me that he does believe that Kouffa wants to impose a version of shari‘a in central Mali, but that Kouffa does not aim to recreate the theocratic state of Macina, nor to separate from Mali.[25] This is debatable: Kouffa's influence across the border in Burkina Faso (see Chapter 5) may gesture toward regionalist ambitions. Yet Kouffa does not take explicitly secessionist postures. In this way, Kouffa differs from the Islamic State, which famously proclaimed

[23] Amadou Sallah Cisse, "Kouffa n'a jamais travaillé à la réhabilitation du Macina," *Le Reporter*, January 9, 2019, https://malijet.com/actualite-politique-au-mali/flash-info/221758-kouffa-n'a-jamais-travaillé-à-la-réhabilitation-du-macina.html.

[24] Adam Thiam, "Signature du jihadiste Hamadoun kouffa? Le mausolée du saint Sekou Amadou dynamité vers Mopti," *Le Républicain*, May 5, 2015, www.maliweb.net/editorial/signature-du-jihadiste-hamadoun-kouffa-le-mausolee-du-saint-sekou-amadou-dynamite-vers-mopti-947542.html.

[25] Interview with Amadou Mody Diall, Bamako, March 9, 2018.

"The End of Sykes-Picot" (i.e., the dissolution of the Iraqi-Syrian border),[26] and from Boko Haram, which has long rejected the existence and legitimacy of Nigeria as a political and territorial entity.

As the Peul critiques of Kouffa suggest, there are intra-Peul conflicts at stake in his project. Within the Peul and beyond, the makeup of Kouffa's coalition has favored social juniors and "people who are excluded" from local power structures because they come from a low-ranking social category.[27] All of this has facilitated wide recruitment.

Kouffa's coalition formed in several waves.[28] First, there were jihadists with prior experience, who came into the group in batches. Some of these were fighters, reportedly mostly Peul, who were already loyal to Kouffa during the 2012 rebellion.[29] Others were former members of the Movement for Unity and Jihad in West Africa (MUJWA), an AQIM offshoot that played a key role in the 2012–2013 jihadist occupation of northern Mali. The ex-MUJWA fighters sometimes took circuitous routes into Kouffa's camps. Some of them passed through "self-defense" associations that arose after 2013, such as the Dewral Pulaaku ("Peul Harmony") association, which has been accused of "laundering former MUJWA fighters."[30]

The second broad constituency to join came in after 2015 on a basis that was partly ethnic and partly religious but also heavily material. This constituency included Peul villagers and herders (or rather, shepherds and goatherds, who care for but do not own their animals)[31]

---

[26] Islamic State of Iraq and Syria, "The End of Sykes-Picot," June 2014, available at http://jihadology.net/2014/06/29/al-%E1%B8%A5ayat-media-center-presents-a-new-video-message-from-the-islamic-state-of-iraq-and-al-sham-the-end-of-sykes-picot/.

[27] Interview with Ali Tounkara, Bamako, June 20, 2019.

[28] My list here builds on Adam Thiam's sketch of Kouffa's coalition. See "Centre du Mali: Enjeux et dangers d'une crise négligée," Centre pour le dialogue humanitaire/Institut du Macina, March 2019, 38–39, https://sahelresearch.africa.ufl.edu/files/Centre20HD20–20Etude20sur20le20Centre20du20Mali20–20mars202017.pdf.

[29] FIDH/AMDH, "In Central Mali, Civilian Populations Are Caught," 26.

[30] Rémi Carayol, "Mali: l'histoire du chef du village de Boulikessi, contraint de négocier avec le Mujao," *Jeune Afrique*, December 29, 2016, www.jeuneafrique.com/mag/384784/politique/mali-lhistoire-chef-village-de-boulikessi-contraint-de-negocier-mujao/. See also Boukary Sangaré, "Le Centre du Mali: épicentre du djihadisme," GRIP, May 20, 2016, 9–10.

[31] FIDH/AMDH, "In Central Mali, Civilian Populations Are Caught," 28.

seeking access to the redistributive policies and "equitable justice" offered by the jihadists. Various Peul recruits also sought revenge and protection after they or their communities were abused by Malian soldiers and ethnic militias. The largest pool of recruits may be those who sought protection (economic or physical) and revenge, in line with findings from previous research in Mali and in other African contexts.[32] As one former Katibat Macina fighter told researchers in 2016, "Since the state left, we have had to protect ourselves as best as we can."[33] There appears to be variation within Kouffa's coalition in terms of where and to what extent hardcore jihadists overlap with local self-defense groups – a self-defense group that talks about the deficiencies of the state and calls for the application of shari'a may be only loosely a part of the coalition, and Kouffa's forces and allies do not always self-identify as jihadists.[34]

Third, there are non-Peul who found a home in Kouffa's movement for reasons that seem to be somewhat individualistic and idiosyncratic. Such recruits may have been motivated either by social vulnerability and a need for protection, or by the desire to make money. In this category too might be placed those who have benefited from prison breaks staged by Kouffa's forces,[35] and who found joining the group to be their best post-escape option.

Fourth, Kouffa may have found support among certain Qur'an school students and their masters who share Kouffa's vision. The role of Qur'an students is particularly murky, and here the analyst should be especially careful: In diverse conflicts in West Africa, outsiders have often thrown cruel and unsupported accusations at Qur'an schools and their students, especially in the context of the Boko Haram crisis in the

---

[32] Mercy Corps, "'We Hope and We Fight': "Youth, Communities, and Violence in Mali," September 2017, www.mercycorps.org/sites/default/files/Mercy%20Corps_Mali_Hope%20and%20Fight_Report_Eng_Sept%202017_0.pdf. See also United Nations Development Program, "Journey to Extremism in Africa: Drivers, Incentives and the Tipping Point for Recruitment," 2017, https://journey-to-extremism.undp.org/content/downloads/UNDP-JourneyToExtremism-report-2017-english.pdf.

[33] Lori-Anne Théroux-Bénoni et al., "Mali's Young 'Jihadists': Fuelled by Faith or Circumstance?" Institute for Security Studies, August 2016, 5, https://issafrica.s3.amazonaws.com/site/uploads/policybrief89-eng-v2.pdf.

[34] Interview with Ali Tounkara.

[35] "Katibat 'Masina' Tatabanna Hujum Niunu [Niono]," Kibaru, December 7, 2016, https://kibaru.ml/ar/art/b9uwx.

Lake Chad Basin.[36] Nevertheless, in Mopti and Ségou the Qur'an schools seem to be one element in the conflict, in multi-faceted ways. Kouffa reportedly draws little support from the Qur'an teachers themselves, but he may derive recruits from Qur'an schools (as a former, and well-networked, former Qur'an school student himself).[37] It should be noted that while Qur'an schools are found throughout Mali, their concentration is highest in Mopti, the sole region in Mali where Qur'an schools outnumber government primary schools.[38]

Kouffa may also accrue popularity from closing government schools – indeed, there are long legacies of resistance to Western-style education in the region, dating back to the colonial period. Community-led efforts to close government schools in Mopti predate Kouffa's own efforts in that direction.[39] By March 2019, some 513 schools were closed in Mopti, or 62 percent of the total number of schools then closed in Mali.[40] Kouffa's men benefit from fault lines around education in the region; by closing government schools, they activate and intensify "ideological competition."[41] Finally, although the fighters are overwhelmingly male, women have "multi-faceted supporting roles as wives of 'men of the bush' and as informants in informal surveillance mechanisms that pass on information and contribute to maintaining jihadists' version of law and order. Moreover,

---

[36] For a rebuttal to such accusations, see Hannah Hoechner, *Quranic Schools in Northern Nigeria: Everyday Experiences of Youth, Faith, and Poverty* (Cambridge: Cambridge University Press, 2018), ch. 2.

[37] Mathieu Pellerin, "Les trajectoires de radicalisation religieuse au Sahel," IFRI, February 2017, 27–28, www.ifri.org/sites/default/files/atoms/files/pellerin_radicalisation_religieuse_sahel_2017.pdf.

[38] *Autoportrait du Mali: Les Obstacles à la Paix* (Bamako: Institut Malien de Recherche Action Pour la Paix, 2015), 44. See also Diarah Bintou Sanankoua, "Les écoles 'Coraniques' au Mali: problèmes actuels," *Canadian Journal of African Studies* 19:2 (1985): 359–367.

[39] Olivier Dubois and Boubacar Sangaré, "Au centre du Mali, c'est le Far west," *Journal du Mali*, January 5, 2017, www.journaldumali.com/2017/01/05/centre-mali-cest-far-west/.

[40] United Nations Security Council, "Situation in Mali: Report of the Secretary-General," March 26, 2019, 11, https://reliefweb.int/sites/reliefweb.int/files/resources/S_2019_262_E.pdf.

[41] Boubacar Sangaré, "Au Centre du Mali, les extrémistes décrètent l'école 'haram'," *Sahelien*, June 7, 2017, https://sahelien.com/au-centre-du-mali-les-extremistes-decretent-lecole-haram-2/.

women are more likely to actively participate when they are bonded to the insurgency through familial ties."[42]

Unlike ag Ghali's forces and the top-down structure of JNIM in the north, Kouffa's style of "jihadism from below" means that many of the field commanders and clerics in his coalition are difficult to identify and seem to have limited prior experience in politics. The names of these figures typically appear only fleetingly in the Malian press when they are killed or captured, and their biographies remain sketchy at best. For example, the unit commander Bekaye Sangaré was reportedly killed by Malian gendarmes in the village of Mounga on July 13, 2017.[43] Malian journalists who contacted local sources described Sangaré as having been a man in his thirties, a "native of Youwarou, in the region of Mopti," who had been outraged by "arrests in the Peul community, which he judged arbitrary."[44] Of the names floated as possible successors to Kouffa when it was thought that French forces had killed him in late 2018, most seemed unknown even to Malian journalists.[45] Propaganda from "Katibat Macina" has sometimes foregrounded figures other than Kouffa, but it is difficult to glean much information about personalities such as the "Shaykh Yahya" who speaks in one early video.[46]

[42] Natasja Rupesinghe and Yida Diall, "Women and the Katiba Macina in Central Mali," Norwegian Institute of International Affairs, September 3, 2019, 1, https://nupi.brage.unit.no/nupi-xmlui/bitstream/handle/11250/2612965/NUPI_Policy_Brief_13_2019_RupesingheDiall51413.pdf?sequence=2&isAllowed=y.

[43] "Un chef jihadiste abattu par l'armée au Mali," Voice of America, July 14, 2017, www.voaafrique.com/a/un-chef-jihadiste-abattu-au-mali-par-l-armee/3944027.html.

[44] "Mali: ce que l'on sait de Bekaye Sangaré, ce proche d'Amadou Kouffa abattu dans le centre," ESJ-Bamako Actu, July 14, 2017, https://mussoya.wordpress.com/2017/07/14/mali-ce-que-lon-sait-de-bekaye-sangare-ce-proche-damadou-kouffa-abattu-dans-le-centre/.

[45] Jérôme Pigné, "Sahel: Quelle recomposition après l'élimination d'Hamadou Kouffa dans le centre du Mali?" Institut Thomas Moore, November 27, 2018, http://institut-thomas-more.org/2018/11/27/sahel--quelle-recomposition-apres-lelimination-dhamadou-kouffa-dans-le-centre-du-mali/#_ftn7.

[46] Ansardin Katiba du Macina (Ansar al-Din, Katibat Masina), "Awwal Maqtaʻ Fidiyu Yazhur Fihi Ahad Qadat al-Maydaniyyin li-Katibat Ansar al-Din bi-Mintaqat Masina," May 2016, available at https://jihadology.net/2016/05/18/new-video-message-from-jamaat-anṣar-al-din-first-video-of-katibat-macina/. Another name that has surfaced is Boukary Petal, said to be another important preacher in the Katiba. See Moodi, "Nous ne sommes pas des Peuls mais des djihadistes/Nous sommes des Peuls et pas des djihadistes," Nomade Sahel,

The non-elite, even anti-elite nature of Kouffa's project makes his movement somewhat faceless. International Crisis Group has sketched what it calls a hierarchical structure of the movement, featuring an advisory council (*majlis shura*) and dispersed units (each called a *markaz*) that "repor[t] decisions taken at the local level to the Katiba's central command."[47] Yet other analysts have commented that the organization appears "loosely structured," with bands of 30–50 fighters that "appear fairly autonomous and whose hierarchy is difficult to determine."[48]

Kouffa's ability to recruit young Peul fighters serves the wider interests of JNIM and AQIM. Some observers have even suggested that Peul recruits are simply "cannon fodder" for Iyad ag Ghali and the Arab leaders of AQIM and JNIM.[49] Peul fighters have helped stage some of the most prominent terrorist attacks in Sahelian capitals in recent years, including the 2015 assault of the Radisson Blu hotel in Bamako.[50]

Kouffa's coalition-building strategy has limited if not outright foreclosed the possibility for replicating the kind of recruitment of elites that ag Ghali pursued when creating Ansar al-Din in 2011–2012. At the village level, Peul elites – village heads, pasture managers, and even clerics – have become targets for Kouffa's men. At the national level, Peul politicians and civil society leaders have urged Malian authorities to open a dialogue with Kouffa, but Peul politicians have not been drawn into Kouffa's coalition; there is no equivalent, among the Peul, to the Tuareg politicians discussed in Chapter 3. I revisit that issue later, discussing not only who has joined Kouffa's coalition but also who has deliberately not joined. Before that, however, some wider context is in order.

June 21, 2018, http://nomadesahel.org/nous-ne-sommes-pas-des-peuls-mais-des-djihadistes-nous-sommes-des-peuls-et-pas-de-djihadistes/.

[47] International Crisis Group, "Speaking with the 'Bad Guys': Toward Dialogue with Central Mali's Jihadists," May 28, 2019, 5, https://d2071andvip0wj .cloudfront.net/276-speaking-with-the-bad-guys%20(1).pdf.

[48] FIDH/AMDH, "In Central Mali, Civilian Populations Are Caught," 36.

[49] Benjamin Roger, "Mali: Amadou Koufa, le visage peul d'Al-Qaïda," *Jeune Afrique*, November 20, 2018, www.jeuneafrique.com/mag/665565/politique/mali-amadou-koufa-le-visage-peul-dal-qaida/.

[50] Andrew Lebovich, "The Hotel Attacks and Militant Realignment in the Sahara-Sahel Region," Combating Terrorism Center *Sentinel* 9:1 (January 2016), https://ctc.usma.edu/the-hotel-attacks-and-militant-realignment-in-the-sahara-sahel-region/.

Mopti and Ségou: Jihadism and Intra-Peul Tensions in a Wider Conflict Matrix

The conflict in central Mali – in other words, the regions of Mopti and Ségou, although the lines between "north" and "center" blur in places such as southern Timbuktu – involves at least five different axes of violence. First, there is jihadist violence against the state and its representatives, as well as against foreign forces. Second, there is violence within Peul communities, especially concerning resources and localized, even individual grievances. Third, there is violence between the Peul and other ethnic communities such as the Bambara and the Dogon. Those communities' men, including hunters' groups, have organized themselves into formal or informal "self-defense" militias. Fourth, there is collective punishment meted out by the Malian armed forces, often targeting the Peul. Finally, there is banditry, which targets travelers, livestock, and communities. Underlying these forms of violence are multiple causes. As one Malian researcher told me, it is, "the connection between the factors" that drives the violence.[51]

These overlapping and competing forms of violence create ambiguity about who the perpetrators are, fostering an atmosphere of suspicion and uncertainty.[52] As *Jeune Afrique*'s Rémi Carayol wrote in 2016,

Fear of the other is what everyone shares in what was the Macina of Seku Amadu, where today a war is playing out behind closed doors. From Ségou to Timbuktu, from Bankass to Nampala, the other could be a jihadist who is working underground, an army informer or a simple somebody who, because someone promised him 150,000 FCFA if he comes to lay a mine and if it produces victims among the Blue Helmets or the Malian soldiers, has taken on the characteristics of a killer.[53]

Meanwhile, the different axes of violence reflect layers of contested history. There are long-term historical conflicts over land, power, and

---

[51] Interview with Ali Tounkara.
[52] Jacob Mundy has argued that the question "who kills whom?" haunted Algeria in the 1990s. See *Imaginative Geographies of Algerian Violence: Conflict Science, Conflict Management, Antipolitics* (Stanford, CA: Stanford University Press, 2015).
[53] Rémi Carayol, "Mali: dans le Macina, un jihad sur fond de révolte sociale," *Jeune Afrique*, June 20, 2016, www.jeuneafrique.com/mag/332806/politique/reportage-mali-macina-tombait-aux-mains-jihadistes/.

memory, juxtaposed with short-term triggers for violence. These triggers involve the way that the 2012 rebellion in the north, the 2013 military intervention in the north and center, and ongoing military campaigns against jihadists since 2015 prepared the ground for multi-directional hostilities to break out.

Of the different axes of violence, the intra-Peul conflicts are the most vital for understanding Kouffa's coalition. In central Mali, intra-ethnic conflicts among the Peul have partly run along what might crudely be called class lines. Peul society in central Mali has different, hierarchically and professionally organized groupings marked by surnames and geographical homelands. Peul society is also marked by the legacies of past slavery (formally banned by French authorities in 1905 and again at independence in 1960) and ongoing structures of dependence, subservience, and hierarchy.[54] These economic hierarchies and class distinctions shape access to land. Among Malian researchers who study the conflicts in Mopti and Ségou, there is recurring talk of "rackets" and oligarchies.[55] Or as one researcher told me, in both Peul and Dogon zones, local governance has been in the hands of an "ultra-minority" that used power to control and exclude.[56] Peul elites control key offices, including hereditary positions at the village level (such as chief and imam) as well as elected and administrative offices at various levels. Peul elites use these offices to advance and entrench their control over resources, particularly grazing areas.

Historically, when herders wished to access such an area, known as the *bourgoutière*, they had to pay the guardians either in cash or livestock. Disputes over access, or over land, water, and animals more broadly, could be referred to politicians and judges. Such authorities, however, were prone to take bribes and side with local elites. One interlocutor from central Mali said that corruption grew after the military dictator Moussa Traoré (in office 1968–1991) left power, as discipline and accountability withered within the civil service and civil servants from outside Mopti came to see their postings as opportunities to amass funds for building houses back in Bamako.[57] Even when

---

[54] On these dynamics, see Salif Togola, "L'esclavage dans la region de Mopti" in *L'Esclavage au Mali*, edited by Naffet Keita, 47–77 (Paris: L'Harmattan, 2012).

[55] Thiam, "Centre du Mali: Enjeux et dangers," 36.

[56] Interview with Ali Tounkara.

[57] Interview with Yoby Guindo, Bamako, June 18, 2019.

judgments favored the poor, they might go unapplied by local power-brokers.[58] As of 2019, most Malians felt that the judiciary was Mali's most corrupt institution; in one survey, 58 percent of respondents (and in Mopti, 65 percent) held that view.[59]

The conflicts in the region are heavily shaped by local geography. In Mopti, some lands are not fertile, leaving the fertile lands intensely "coveted."[60] Mopti encompasses the inner Niger Delta (not to be confused with the Niger Delta of southeastern Nigeria). The inner Delta, around the confluence of the Niger and Bani Rivers, comprises a wide floodplain. This flooded zone (*zone inondée*) includes four of Mopti's eight *cercles* – that is, subregional administrative districts. These *cercles* are Tenenkou, Youwarou, Djenné, and Mopti, the western *cercles* of the Mopti Region. The region's four eastern *cercles* – Douentza, Bandiagara, Koro, and Bankass – constitute the nonflooded zone (*zone exondée*). One expert believes that the majority of Kouffa's fighters were/are pastoralists from the nonflooded zone who resented paying duties to access the flooded zone.[61] The flooded zone was originally the epicenter of the conflict.[62] Violence has also occurred in northern Ségou Region, namely the region's northernmost *cercles* of Niono and Macina, which immediately border Youwarou, Tenenkou, and Djenné.

Conflict over the management of pastures reaches back centuries. In the early nineteenth century, Seku Amadu redrew the boundaries of certain *leyde* (singular *leydi*), or pastoral territories, and created as many as five new *leyde*.[63] The manager or *jowro* of each pasture is,

---

[58] Interview with Amadou Mody Diall.

[59] Morgane Le Cam, "Mali: ' J'ai reçu tellement de pressions et de menaces de mort…'," *Le Monde*, April 11, 2019, www.lemonde.fr/afrique/article/2019/04/11/mali-j-ai-recu-tellement-de-pressions-et-de-menaces-de-mort_5448976_3212.html.

[60] Interview with Ali Tounkara.

[61] Thiam, "Centre du Mali: Enjeux et dangers," 36.

[62] Interview with Boubacar Cissé.

[63] Olivier Barriere and Catherine Barriere, *Le Foncier-Environment: Pour un egestion viable des ressources naturelles renouvelables au Sahel: Approche interdisciplinaire dans le delta intérieur du Niger (Mali)* (Paris: Mission Française de Coopération, 1995), 48 (see also footnote 69), available at http://horizon.documentation.ird.fr/exl-doc/pleins_textes/divers09–08/010004194.pdf.

in theory, selected by the society as a whole and is not a hereditary position.[64] Yet in practice, colonial authorities made the *jowro* into a fixed, hereditary office where the *jowro* became the de facto owner of the pasture.[65] By the postcolonial period, the *jowro* office often became the preserve of elite families. That dynamic marginalized other families and sometimes engendered conflicts within office-holding families; for example, the son and brother of a deceased *jowro* might engage in a long-term dispute over the succession. When the state's courts tried to adjudicate such disputes, a door was opened to bribery, favoritism, and ill will.[66] Meanwhile, "the superimposition of state laws on these traditional modes of regulation has been a powerful factor in the reduction of their legitimacy."[67]

Over time, the fees imposed by the *jowros* increased, especially for nonlocal herders – fueling conflict and resentment. As the concentration of wealth grew, droughts led some poor herders to sell their animals under duress, reducing them to "mere shepherds."[68] At the same time, even the *jowros* were losing power to farmers amid the conversion of some pastures into rice fields. Alongside tensions between the *jowros* and the herders, farmer–herder conflicts also broke out. Local authorities' interventions and corruption tended to exacerbate rather than resolve matters.[69]

Central Mali is subject to increasing demographic and economic strain. The population has grown rapidly, with fertility reaching roughly seven children per woman in Mopti and Ségou. Demographic pressures have been exacerbated by drought (in the 1970s and 1980s), climate change, and, more recently, falling tourism due to insecurity and kidnapping in the north. As Adam Thiam comments, "It must be remembered that peace in the Delta has been and remains possible only

---

[64] Ibid., 48–51; interview with Amadou Mody Diall.

[65] Interview with Boubacar Cissé.

[66] Lorenzo Cotula and Salmana Cissé, "A Case Study: Changes in 'Customary' Resource Tenure Systems in the Inner Niger Delta, Mali" in *Changes in 'Customary' Land Tenure Systems in Africa*, edited by Lorenzo Cotula, 81–101 (International Institution for Environment and Development, 2007), 96.

[67] Aurélien Tobie, "Central Mali: Violence, Local Perspectives and Diverging Narratives," SIPRI, December 2017, 9, www.sipri.org/sites/default/files/2018-02/sipriinsight_1713_mali_3_eng.pdf.

[68] FIDH/AMDH, "In Central Mali, Civilian Populations Are Caught," 21.

[69] Tor Benjaminsen and Boubacar Ba, "Farmer-Herder Conflicts, Pastoral Marginalisation and Corruption: A Case Study from the Inland Niger Delta of Mali," *Geographical Journal* 175:1 (March 2009): 71–81.

due to compromises and equilibria among the three systems of production (agriculture, herding, fishing) found by the producers themselves, who cohabit in a decreased space."[70] But these equilibria have been tested by "intensive agriculture and expansive pastoralism," as well as conflicts involving fishermen – both internal conflicts, between those who take the small fish out of desperation and those who fear the long-term impacts of overfishing, and conflicts between fishermen and the representatives of other economic sectors.[71] Land problems affect many residents of Mopti.[72]

Amid these pressures, resource-based conflicts occurred in central Mali throughout the colonial and postcolonial periods. One locally famous episode was the December 1993 clash between two neighboring villages, Sosobé and Salsalbé, in Tenenkou *cercle*. Resource-based conflicts reverberated within the localized violence that later became part of the matrix of central Malian jihadism.

Resource pressures have contributed to rapid social changes and micro-level tensions. Within living memory, communities' lives have changed dramatically. The anthropologist Claudine Sauvain-Dugerdil's decades-long fieldwork among Dogon populations found that as wild game and plants disappeared and as harvests suffered from the 1970s onward, many Dogon youth began migrating to cities, such as Mopti *ville*, seeking work. "Young people's mobility," she wrote in a 2013 article, "is part of a broader phenomenon of the diversification of livelihoods, which is linked to decreasing natural resources, demographic pressures, and the entrance into a cash economy."[73] Sauvain-Dugerdil expalined that youth mobility led to the rise of more individualistic lifestyles, noting that "the current youth generation is the first generation with personal belongings: bikes, radios, watches, but also their own livestock."[74] These dynamics, in turn, contributed to the rise of greater Islamic piety among youth who had worked outside their villages and then returned home. The resulting changes also

[70] Thiam, "Centre du Mali: Enjeux et dangers," 19.

[71] Interview with Brema Ely Dicko, Bamako, January 22, 2018.

[72] HiiL, "Justice Needs and Satisfaction in Mali 2018: Legal Problems in Daily Life," March 2019, 103, www.hiil.org/wp-content/uploads/2018/07/HiiL-Mali-JNS-report-EN-web.pdf.

[73] Claudine Sauvain-Dugerdil, "Youth Mobility in an Isolated Sahelian Population of Mali," *Annals of the American Academy of Political and Social Science* 648 (July 2013): 160–174, 167.

[74] Ibid., 169.

affected gender relations and sparked greater assertiveness (on the part of boys *and* girls) about challenging their parents' ability to select spouses for them. Throughout the region, respect for parents and elders has reportedly declined, as youth contest traditional hierarchies and refuse to submit to them.[75]

Gender dynamics may play a substantial role in the conflict. As in northeastern Nigeria and other conflict theaters,[76] jihadism's effects on gender relations at first seem paradoxical: Jihadists enforce veiling and even seclusion for women, but simultaneously offer women opportunities to gain power and status as wives, camp helpers, recruiters, and informants.[77] By reducing dowries, jihadists also tap into longstanding tensions surrounding gender, marriage, social status, and the ability to build an independent family in the "post-slavery" society of central Mali.[78] Even more broadly, part of jihadism's appeal may lie in its promise to restructure a social order that some youth see as outmoded and faltering. On the one hand, Katibat Macina has coerced women into leaving off cultural and economic activities that jihadists reject; on the other hand, one of the Katiba's female preachers reportedly proclaimed that "we women can rise up" by participating in the counter-order that Kouffa's forces offer.[79]

The 2012–2013 Northern Malian Rebellion and Its Impact on Mopti and the Peul

When the Tuareg-led rebellion broke out in January 2012, it theoretically concerned "the Azawad" – which meant, according to some understandings, the regions of Kidal, Timbuktu, and Gao. Other

---

[75] Interview with Ali Tounkara.

[76] Valerie Hudson and Hilary Matfess, "In Plain Sight: The Neglected Linkage between Brideprice and Violent Conflict," *International Security* 42:1 (Summer 2017): 7–40. See also Matfess, *Women and the War on Boko Haram: Wives, Weapons, Witnesses* (London: Zed Books, 2017).

[77] For some discussion of these dynamics, see Ibrahim Yahaya Ibrahim and Mollie Zapata, "Regions at Risk: Preventing Mass Atrocities in Mali," United States Holocaust Memorial Museum, April 2018, 13, www.ushmm.org/m/pdfs/Mali_Report_English_FINAL_April_2018.pdf.

[78] See Lotte Pelckmans, "Stereotypes of Past-Slavery and 'Stereo-styles' in Post-Slavery: A Multidimensional, Interactionist Perspective on Contemporary Hierarchies," *International Journal of African Historical Studies* 48:2 (2015): 281–301.

[79] Rupensinghe and Diall, "Women and the Katiba Macina in Central Mali," 3.

understandings of Azawad, however, encompassed two of the north-ernmost *cercles* in Mopti: Douentza and Youwarou.[80] The MNLA attacked Youwarou in February 2012, and AQIM used the chaos of the rebellion to settle a score with the mayor of one Douentza town, Hombori, where AQIM had perpetrated a kidnapping of two French geologists in November 2011.[81] The MNLA came to Douentza as early as April 2012.[82]

As jihadist influence increased in northern Mali during the course of 2012, the MNLA lost influence to MUJWA in Gao and northern Mopti. After MUJWA captured Gao from the MNLA in June, the MNLA fell back. Multiple forces were present in Douentza, including MUJWA and the Songhai-Peul self-defense militia Ganda Izo. After the kidnapping of an Arab fighter linked with MUJWA in late July 2012, MUJWA blamed Ganda Izo. The crisis allowed MUJWA to escalate its intimidation of other forces, splitting Ganda Izo and opening the door for MUJWA to take full control of Douentza in September.[83] Mean-while, the state withdrew from the north and much of the center, while unofficially tolerating certain militias there.[84]

MUJWA was discussed in Chapter 2 and mentioned in Chapter 3, but here it is worth revisiting MUJWA's internal coalition structure. MUJWA was close to the Algerian AQIM field commander Mokhtar Belmokhtar and was formally headed by a Mauritanian national, Hamada Ould Mohamed Kheirou. Yet many of its members in Gao were Malians, including Tilemsi Arab politicians and smugglers such

[80] Tobie, "Central Mali," 3 (see also fn. 8).
[81] Abdoulaye Diakité, "Nord-Mali: Youwarou attaqué, le chef de village de Hombori tué," *L'Indicateur du Renouveau*, February 20, 2012, http://malijet.com/actualte_dans_les_regions_du_mali/rebellion_au_nord_du_mali/39052-nord-mali-youwarou-attaque-le-chef-de-village-de-hombori-tue.html; and "Mali: Youwarou attaquée par la rebellion," Mali Actu, March 15, 2012, http://maliactu.net/mali-youwarou-attaquee-par-la-rebellion/.
[82] NeïmatouNaillé Coulibaly, "Occupation de Douentza: Elle ne date pas du 1er septembre 2012," *Le Combat*, September 20, 2012, www.maliweb.net/armee/occupation-de-douentza-elle-ne-date-pas-du-1er-septembre-2012-93286.html.
[83] Ibid. See also "Mali: les nouveaux maîtres de Douentza restent discrets," RFI, September 4, 2012, www.rfi.fr/afrique/20120904-mali-nouveaux-maitres-dounetza-restent-discrets; Moussa Dagnogo/Boukary Daou, "Occupation de Douentza par le Mujao: Le Pr Ali N. Diallo explique les vraies raisons," *Le Républicain*, September 4, 2012, www.maliweb.net/la-situation-politique-et-securitaire-au-nord/occupation-de-douentza-par-le-mujao-le-pr-ali-n-diallo-explique-les-vraies-raisons-89448.html.
[84] Tobie, "Central Mali," 11–12.

as Sultan Ould Badi and Ahmed al-Tilemsi.[85] The group also recruited within ultra-conservative Salafi villages, particularly one named Kadji, close to Gao.[86]

MUJWA's rule in Gao in 2012–2013 tapped into and transformed intra-ethnic tensions in the city and surrounding areas. On one level, many of the "black" Songhai and Peul residents of the area were deeply suspicious of the Arabs in the movement; "local Songhais, Peuls, and Bellas [former slaves of the Tuareg]," the analyst Hannah Armstrong wrote in early 2013, "now view the words 'Arab' and 'trafficker' as synonyms." At the same time, these "black" inhabitants of Gao also

preferred [MUJWA] rule to the reign of terror that preceded it, when Tuareg rebels, having joined with jihadis to chase out state forces, descended like furies upon the northern Malian territory they claimed to be liberating. Tuareg rebels looted, murdered, raped, pillaged, and shot into crowds of demonstrators, targeting state symbols and dark-skinned ethnic groups, setting the stage for jihadis to grab power by restoring civil order and a simulation of justice. For the darker-skinned ethnicities like the Peul, the Songhai, and the Bella, rebel crimes were magnified by their shared history with the Tuareg: they had traditionally been subjected to slavery by the lighter-skinned Tuareg. Rebel control of the northern territory thus portended a return to white-on-black slavery.[87]

The Arab-led MUJWA thus recruited among the Songhai and the Peul, although there was resistance to MUJWA among these populations as well.[88]

---

[85] Andrew Lebovich, "The Local Face of Jihadism in Northern Mali," Combating Terrorism Center *Sentinel* 6:6 (June 2013), https://ctc.usma.edu/the-local-face-of-jihadism-in-northern-mali/; and François Soudan, "Mali: le chef militaire du Mujao est un Malien," *Jeune Afrique*, July 27, 2012, www.jeuneafrique.com/140645/politique/mali-le-chef-militaire-du-mujao-est-un-malien/.

[86] Interview with Modibo Galy Cissé, Bamako, June 17, 2019; Antoine Malo, "Mali: à Kadji, des islamistes sous surveillance," *Le Journal de Dimanche*, August 10, 2013, www.lejdd.fr/International/Afrique/Mali-a-Kadji-des-islamistes-sous-surveillance-623497-3198245.

[87] Hannah Armstrong, "Winning the War, Losing the Peace in Mali," *The New Republic*, February 28, 2013, https://newrepublic.com/article/112539/malis-ethnic-tensions-fester-after-fighting.

[88] Christian Eboulé, "Au Mali, l'histoire oubliée de la résistance des populations de Gao face à l'invasion djihadiste," TV5 Monde, https://information.tv5monde.com/afrique/au-mali-l-histoire-oubliee-de-la-resistance-des-populations-de-gao-face-l-invasion.

In Mopti, the 2012 rebellion evoked bitter memories of past northern rebellions and abuses. In the 1990s, communities in Mopti had suffered raids by northern Tuareg- and Arab-led groups. Perhaps counterintuitively, in 2012 these memories of past victimization prompted some men from Mopti to join northern armed groups, including the MNLA. Some such recruits felt a short-term need for self-protection, while others wanted to acquire skills and training that would facilitate communal self-defense.[89] For example, the once and future Peul militia leader Hama Founé joined the MNLA in 2012.[90]

Other Peul joined MUJWA – for example, Peul from villages in Douentza considered MUJWA an ally against nearby farmers from the Dogon and other ethnic groups.[91] The maxim that "the enemy of my enemy is my friend" came into play with MUJWA's recruitment of Peul, as MNLA raids in Douentza pushed some herders into MUJWA's arms. In Douentza, MUJWA previewed some of the styles of control that would later help Kouffa attract recruits: MUJWA offered protection and "equitable justice" to young Peul herders.[92] The state, meanwhile, supported some ethnic-based community armed groups in non-jihadist zones, hoping to counter the MNLA and the jihadists – but generating long-term consequences.[93]

For several months in 2012, Douentza marked the southern limit of jihadist expansion. In late 2012, as talks proceeded in Burkina Faso between Iyad ag Ghali's Ansar al-Din and the Malian government, most of central Mali was still under formal government control. But in January 2013, jihadists pushed further into Mopti. On January 10, Ansar al-Din and AQIM took Konna, approximately 114 kilometers west of Douentza and inside the *cercle* of Mopti. The capture of Konna positioned the jihadists to advance on Mopti city and the adjacent

[89] Interview with Aba Cissé, former mayor of Soosoobé village, Bamako, January 24, 2018.
[90] Rémi Carayol, "Mali: Hama Foune Diallo, mercenaire du delta," *Jeune Afrique*, July 18, 2016, www.jeuneafrique.com/mag/340339/politique/mali-hama-foune-diallo-mercenaire-delta/; see also Thiam, "Centre du Mali: Enjeux et dangers," 15.
[91] Thiam, "Centre du Mali: Enjeux et dangers," 20. See also Camille Dubruelh, "Mali: 25 Burkinabè tués dans un village lors d'affrontements intercommunautaires," *Jeune Afrique*, May 25, 2012, www.jeuneafrique.com/175957/politique/mali-25-burkinab-tu-s-dans-un-village-lors-d-affrontements-intercommunautaires/.
[92] Sangaré, "Centre du Mali," 4–5.   [93] Interview with Ali Tounkara.

town of Sévaré. A near-simultaneous bid by Malian soldiers to recapture Douentza faltered.[94] These events triggered an immediate response from France in the form of Operation Serval, which began on January 11.

Operation Serval expelled MUJWA from Gao and triggered the fragmentation of MUJWA's coalition along both ideological and geographical lines. The Arab-led, regionally minded jihadists close to MUJWA, especially Mokhtar Belmokhtar's forces, began launching spectacular attacks on targets across northwest Africa (see Chapter 2). But the more locally minded elements of MUJWA's coalition concentrated on their own homes or adopted homes. Part of the former MUJWA based itself in the eastern Gao/Ménaka region (see Chapter 5), where they recruited heavily among Peul on both sides of the Mali–Niger border. Meanwhile, other former Peul elements of MUJWA returned to Mopti and formed part of Kouffa's early forces. Such dynamics could be extremely complex at the hyper-local level: One mayor who sent young men to fight with MUJWA in 2012 as a means of self-protection would later find himself repeatedly detained in Mali and Burkina Faso, accused of being a jihadist and disavowed by the very herd owners who had originally encouraged him, reportedly, to seek out MUJWA's help.[95] The 2013–2015 period was one of rapid micro-level realignments. Kouffa was eventually positioned to absorb various fragments of earlier coalitions.

During France's Operation Serval (January 2013–July 2014), the state returned to Mopti. This return was deeply problematic. Accusations that the Malian army was killing and collectively punishing the Peul began immediately, with MUJWA alleging in January 2013 that the army had killed forty Peul as a reprisal for suspected Peul collaboration with jihadists.[96] Other locals also accused authorities of abuses, especially when it came to the unsolved case of some twenty, mostly

---

[94] Tiemoko Diallo, "Mali Islamists Capture Strategic Town, Residents Flee," Reuters, January 10, 2013, www.reuters.com/article/us-mali-rebels/mali-islamists-capture-strategic-town-residents-flee-idUSBRE90912Q20130110?feedType=RSS&feedName=worldNews.

[95] Carayol, "Mali: l'histoire du chef du village de Boulikessi."

[96] "Mali: Le MUJAO accuse l'armée malienne d'avoir massacré 40 Peuls," Alakhbar, January 13, 2013, http://fr.alakhbar.info/5772-0-Mali-Le-MUJAO-accuse-larmee-malienne-davoir-massacre-40-Peuls-.html. See also Andrew Lebovich, "Mali's Sleeper Cell," African Arguments, May 30, 2013, https://africanarguments.org/2013/05/30/malis-sleeper-cell-by-andrew-lebovich/.

Peul, civilians killed near Doungoura, a village in Tenenkou, in March 2013. In the aftermath of that massacre, Peul civilians and leaders decried the state's unresponsiveness.[97]

The redeployment of civilian authorities evoked resentment. By the end of May 2014, "99 percent of State officials [had] been redeployed" in the Mopti Region, at least officially.[98] Yet "some agents recycled past practices, engaging in racketeering and bribery. For some residents, the withdrawal of the State in 2012, synonymous with the end of taxation, predation and other harassment, had been perceived as a blessing."[99] Even before the jihadist resurgence in central Mali in 2015, intermittent violence was forcing some local authorities to flee.[100]

The Launch of Kouffa's Project and Its "Ethnicizing" Effects on Violence in Central Mali

In early 2015, jihadist violence began to increase in central Mali. Attacks in January and February targeted northern Ségou as well as the Tenenkou and Youwarou *cercles* of Mopti. The initial targets were state authorities and soldiers.[101]

If there is a start date to the current jihadist conflict in the center, it would be the January 5, 2015 attack on Nampala, Ségou, where "men on motorbikes seized the town ... and made the black flag fly there." Amid attacks on other villages, the area's gendarmes, mayors, and hereditary leaders fled for Bamako. One journalist wrote,

---

[97] "Le charnier de Doungoura," *L'Aube*, April 20, 2015, http://news.abamako
.com/h/88603.html. See also International Crisis Group, "Central Mali: An
Uprising in the Making?" July 6, 2016, 9, https://d2071andvip0wj.cloudfront
.net/central-mali-an-uprising-in-the-making.pdf.

[98] United Nations Security Council, "Report of the Secretary-General on the
Situation in Mali," June 9, 2014, 6, https://minusma.unmissions.org/sites/
default/files/n1441729_eng_0.pdf. See also International Crisis Group,
"Central Mali," 8, fn. 44.

[99] FIDH/AMDH, "In Central Mali, Civilian Populations Are Caught," 25.

[100] United Nations Security Council, "Report of the Secretary-General on the
Situation in Mali," September 22, 2014, 6, https://minusma.unmissions.org/
sites/default/files/n1453676_eng.pdf.

[101] United Nations Security Council, "Report of the Secretary-General on the
Situation in Mali," March 27, 2015, 8, https://minusma.unmissions.org/sites/
default/files/n1508173.pdf.

"The men on motorbikes" sow terror by distributing tracts in which they call for not collaborating with the army; by disseminating, thanks to mobile phones, the speeches of a man presented as being Amadou Kouffa; or by imposing aggressive sermons in the villages. They appear suddenly out of nowhere, violently interrupting marriage ceremonies, threatening to kill the family members of those who enlist in the army, and leaving as quickly as they came.[102]

It was difficult to determine the identity of the attackers in Nampala and Tenenkou, but residents told journalists that the gunmen were local youths who said that they were fighting the state in the name of Islam. The young fighters disseminated Kouffa's recorded messages. Residents said that the young fighters found a reception among populations who felt abandoned by the state, including amid the lingering bitterness left by the unresolved 2013 massacre of Peul civilians at Doungoura.[103]

For some ordinary people, jihadist attacks brought not a decrease but an *increase* in security. Some locals credited the jihadists with reducing the banditry that had been endemic in Tenenkou since the Tuareg-led rebellion of the early 1990s. This dynamic affected different ethnic communities differently: as Peul reported less victimization by bandits, Dogon charged that their own communities were suffering an increase in Peul banditry, jihadist and non-jihadist.[104]

As Kouffa's forces gained momentum, the state and the traditional hierarchy retreated. Peul elites at the village level became frequent targets for violence. For example, the mayor of Dogo, Youwarou, was killed in April 2015. The violence prompted other local authorities to flee, leaving some localities without government authorities.[105] Chiefs, imams, and administrators were assassinated for their alleged collaboration with the military and the regional and national authorities.[106] Another early assassination, in August 2015, targeted the imam of Barkerou village, three kilometers east of Nampala. The imam

---

[102] Rémi Carayol, "Mali: dans le Macina, un jihad sur fond de révolte sociale."
[103] Daou, "Attaques de Tenenkou."
[104] Human Rights Watch, "Mali: Abuses Spread South," February 19, 2016, www .hrw.org/news/2016/02/19/mali-abuses-spread-south.
[105] "Mali: Boni: L'assassinat louche du maire," *L'Indicateur du Renouveau,* January 25, 2017, http://maliactu.net/mali-boni-lassassinat-louche-du-maire/.
[106] Thiam, "Centre du Mali: Enjeux et dangers," 13.

was killed at or near his home by two youths who knew where he lived.[107] The imam's murder followed his public denunciations of Kouffa's forces,[108] as well as his alleged assistance to authorities in identifying one of Kouffa's men in the village.[109] Jihadist violence created a permissive environment that encouraged other forms of violence against local elites. Under the cover of social panic, locals pursued revenge, score-settling, or banditry.[110]

The Malian army reinforced its presence in major towns in western Mopti (Sévaré, Tenenkou, Douentza).[111] Yet the weak state security presence in rural areas meant that security degraded as one moved down the administrative hierarchy: Mopti city (and adjacent Sevaré) was safer and better controlled than *cercle* centers such as Tenenkou town. Then, in turn, many villages were more dangerous than the *cercle* centers – or were beyond the reach of the authorities.[112]

In this atmosphere, the Malian military defaulted to a knee-jerk reaction: ethnic profiling of the Peul. Collective punishment of the Peul reportedly began as early as one week after the jihadist attack at Nampala in January 2015. One local official later told the Malian Association of Human Rights that

FAMa [Malian armed forces] returned a few days later. They said that the Fulani [Peul] were responsible. They arrested suspects and beat them up. Some were brought to Bamako and released after being made to pay money. After that, the population stopped collaborating with them. The jihadists benefited from this. They came to the villages and said, "We ask nothing of you except to not report us." They executed army informants.[113]

---

[107] "Attaque à la 'Gare de Sogoninko': le gouvernement privilégie la piste 'd'un acte terroriste'," Studio Tamani, August 14, 2015, https://webcache .googleusercontent.com/search?q=cache:OdymYHyWKQ4J:https://www .studiotamani.org/index.php/politique/4795-attaque-a-la-gare-de-sogoninko-le-gouvernement-privilegie-la-piste-d-un-acte-terroriste+&cd=9&hl=en&ct= clnk&gl=us&client=safari.

[108] Emma Farge and Adama Diarra, "Mali's Islamist Conflict Spreads as New Militant Group Emerges," Reuters, August 19, 2015, www.reuters.com/article/ us-mali-violence/malis-islamist-conflict-spreads-as-new-militant-group-emerges-idUSKCN0QO19320150819.

[109] Human Rights Watch, "Mali: Abuses Spread South."

[110] Thiam, "Centre du Mali: Enjeux et dangers," 13.

[111] International Crisis Group, "Central Mali," 16.

[112] Interview with Boubacar Sangaré, Bamako, January 21, 2018.

[113] FIDH/AMDH, "In Central Mali, Civilian Populations Are Caught," 30.

Even as collective punishment backfired, security forces continued making arbitrary arrests, especially of ethnic Peul. Military interrogators beat, tortured, and humiliated detainees, sometimes conducting mock executions to terrify them.[114] Since 2015, Malian journalists and activists have repeatedly denounced the tendency of the armed forces, foreign journalists, and others to "*faire l'amalgame entre* (conflate)" the jihadists and the Peul.[115]

Meanwhile, Kouffa's recordings in Fulfulde circulated throughout Mopti and beyond, traveling by WhatsApp and other platforms to reach a wide audience. Kouffa adapted his messaging to political developments and to the concerns of ordinary people. His movement highlighted security force abuses and government corruption, promising to deliver a new social order.[116]

Amid the crackdown, the violence spread into eastern Mopti, the non-flooded zone. In the *cercles* of Djenné, Koro, Bandiagara, and Bankass, jihadists replicated the methods they had used to the west, assassinating mayors and other local elites.[117] Many of the jihadists' victims were Peul, as in western Mopti, but Peul civilians were also being victimized by the Malian armed forces. In October 2015, the Malian military launched Operation Séno (Fulfulde for "plain" or "savanna"), which brought a new round of abuses. Operation Séno concentrated on Dogon country in eastern Mopti Region,[118] but the violence there was already so intricately layered that the campaign could do little to reverse the trends. As one Dogon leader told Human Rights Watch, "Yes, the jihadists are in our zone, but the situation is very complex: an Islamist can also be a bandit, and a bandit a jihadist." As jihadists targeted the Dogon and then the Dogon began to lash out against the Peul as a whole, the jihadists in turn positioned themselves

---

[114] Human Rights Watch, "Mali: Abuses Spread South."

[115] For an analysis that disentangles various threads of analytical conflation and confusion, see Dougoukolo Alpha Oumar Ba-Konaré, "Entre faux djihadistes et faux chasseurs traditionnels, les civils piégés dans le centre du Mali," The Conversation, October 22, 2018, https://theconversation.com/entre-faux-djihadistes-et-faux-chasseurs-traditionnels-les-civils-pieges-dans-le-centre-du-mali-105181.

[116] Interview with Boukary Sangaré, Bamako, January 20, 2018.

[117] "Mali: Boni: L'assassinat louche du maire."

[118] International Crisis Group, "Central Mali," 16; and "Mali: début d'une opération militaire anti-jihadiste en pays Dogon," RFI, October 27, 2015, www.rfi.fr/afrique/20151027-mali-operation-militaire-seno-jihadistes-pays-dogon-bandiagara-koro-mopti.

as defenders of Peul herders.[119] One illustration of these tensions was two deaths – the killing of an AQIM senior official by Dogon hunters in May 2016, followed by the assassination of a prominent Dogon hunter and militia leader, Théodore Somboro, that October. These incidents elevated tensions between Dogon and Peul overall.[120] Jihadism spread in Mopti not just due to jihadists' political acumen, but due to the choices that other actors were making and the ways that each actor's violence reverberated through communities.

The years 2016–2017 saw a proliferation of militias in northern and central Mali, most of them with a sectional or ethnic character. In Mopti and Ségou, this dynamic extended to the Peul, the Dogon, and the Bambara. Often, the Dogon and Bambara militias were extensions of local hunters' networks, using hunting weapons and receiving support and encouragement from their own communities. Creating militias also allowed village-level elites to reassert their authority amid crisis. As Adam Thiam writes, some militias are "formed by elected officials or traditional authorities." Thiam continues: "This can be done without the state … or with its assent."[121]

The Bambara hunters are more a network than a single organization. Among the Dogon, the most formidable militia was Dan Na Ambassagou, a coalition of hunters that came together in late 2016.[122] Credible observers accused the Malian government of "informally sub-contracting some of its defense responsibilities to these groups."[123] Peul voices accused the Malian army of directly commanding a Bambara militia in Tenenkou.[124] The murkiness of these dynamics further undermined some communities' confidence in the state.

Eventually, micro-level and *meso*-level truces were struck between different ethnic communities, particularly in eastern Mopti. In August

---

[119] Human Rights Watch, "Mali: Abuses Spread South."
[120] Thiam, "Centre du Mali: Enjeux et dangers," 43.   [121] Ibid., 42.
[122] Human Rights Watch, "'We Used to Be Brothers': Self-Defense Group Abuses in Central Mali," December 2018, 27, www.hrw.org/sites/default/files/report_pdf/mali1218_web.pdf.
[123] Ibid., 23.
[124] Rémi Carayol, "Mali – Oumar Aldjana: 'Nous avons créé un mouvement pour mettre fin aux exactions contre les Peuls'," *Jeune Afrique*, June 20, 2016, www.jeuneafrique.com/335206/politique/mali-oumar-aldjana-avons-cree-mouvement-mettre-fin-aux-exactions-contre-peuls/.

2018, Peul and Dogon leaders signed an agreement in Koro *cercle*.[125]
In September 2018, Dan Na Ambassagou's leader, Youssouf Toloba,
signed a unilateral ceasefire at a ceremony in Sévaré. The ceasefire was
intended to reduce Dogon–Peul conflict in eastern Mopti.[126] Yet truces
were hard to sustain amid recurring disputes, provocations, and
reprisals. Most dramatically, in March 2019 armed men – likely from
Dan Na Ambassagou – massacred at least 157 mostly Peul villagers in
Ogassagou and Welingara, Bankass *cercle*.

By the time of the Ogassagou massacre, Dan Na Ambassagou had
grown powerful enough that the Malian government had difficulty
controlling it. Following the massacre, the government ordered the
militia to disband – but when Malian soldiers attempted to arrest one
of Dan Na Ambassagou's commanders in Koro in mid-April 2019,
militia fighters forced the soldiers to withdraw.[127] As the government
pursued "Disarmament, Demobilization, and Reintegration" initiatives, Dan Na Ambassagou and others refused to disarm. "Us
disarming would be exposing our people to carnage," one Dan Na
Ambassagou spokesman said in early 2019.[128] Dan Na Ambassagou
sometimes spoke in extremely harsh terms against the Peul; one
spokesman told me that in his view, the Peul wanted the entire plain
in Dogon country for themselves. The spokesman argued that Dan Na
Ambassagou was not primarily fighting jihadists but rather what he

[125] Centre pour le dialogue humanitaire, "Signature d'un accord de paix entre les
communautés Peulh et Dogon de Koro dans le region de Mopti au Mali,"
August 29, 2018, www.hdcentre.org/fr/updates/fulani-and-dogon-
communities-from-koro-sign-a-peace-agreement-in-the-mopti-region-of-mali/.
[126] Centre pour le dialogue humanitaire, "Youssoufou Toloba et son group armé
Dan Na Ambassagou signent un engagement en faveur d'un cessez-le-feu au
centre du Mali," September 28, 2018, www.hdcentre.org/fr/updates/youssouf-
toloba-and-his-dan-nan-ambassagou-armed-group-sign-a-commitment-
towards-a-ceasefire-in-central-mali/.
[127] Aaron Ross, "Mali Struggles to Disarm Ethnic Militia Suspected of Massacre,"
Reuters, April 19, 2019, www.reuters.com/article/us-mali-security-militia/mali-
struggles-to-disarm-ethnic-militia-suspected-of-massacre-idUSKCN1RV0T2.
See also Marcelin Guenguere, "Communiqué Dana Ambassagou sur les faits de
Koro," Dan Na Ambassagou, April 14, 2019, available at http://bamada.net/
communique-dana-amassagou-sur-les-faits-de-koro.
[128] Morgane Le Cam, "Au Mali, le difficile désarmement des milices," *Le Monde*,
April 10, 2019, www.lemonde.fr/afrique/article/2019/04/10/au-mali-le-
difficile-desarmement-des-milices_5448506_3212.html.

suggested was a broader, organized Peul menace. "The Peul," he said, "have become the terrorists."[129]

The ethnicization of violence in central Mali became both an effect of escalation and a cause for it; whatever government support existed for anti-Peul militias created dynamics that the government could not control. It is worth recalling how thin the Malian military's presence is, in Mopti and nationally; as of early 2019, there were only 1,316 Malian defense and security personnel deployed to Mopti.[130]

To return to the events of 2016, as Kouffa's forces increasingly drew political impetus from Bambara and Dogon violence against the Peul, the jihadists outcompeted the ethnic Peul militias that formed during this period. One Peul militia that appeared in 2016 was l'Alliance nationale pour la sauvegarde de l'identité peule et la restauration de la justice (The National Alliance for Safeguarding Peul Identity and Restoring Justice, ANSIPRJ). Led by the half-Peul, half-Tuareg commander Oumar Aldjana, the ANSIPRJ claimed to have 700 fighters at the moment of its formation in June 2016.[131] Aldjana, originally from Niafunké *cercle* in Timbuktu region, had fought with the MNLA during the 2012 rebellion. Another Peul fighter who had been with the MNLA in 2012, Hama Founé Diallo of Tenenkou, formed another militia, the Movement for the Defense of the Homeland (MDP), in July 2016.[132]

Both militia leaders, and particularly the considerably older Diallo, brought military and political credentials to bear. Yet in relatively short order, both men were reabsorbed into wider currents within Mali's militia politics, with northern rather than central Malian politics as their center of gravity. By fall 2016, Aldjana's ANSIPRJ had fragmented. Aldjana aligned himself with the ex-rebel, Tuareg-led Coordination of Azawad Movements (CMA) bloc in the north. Meanwhile, his estranged vice-president aligned with the rival, pro-

---

[129] Interview with Marcelin Guenguéré, Bamako, June 22, 2019.
[130] United Nations Security Council, "Situation in Mali: Report of the Secretary-General," March 26, 2019, 5.
[131] "Un nouveau mouvement politico-militaire peul créé au Mali," RFI, June 20, 2016, www.rfi.fr/afrique/20160620-mali-mouvement-politico-militaire-peul-alliance.
[132] Carayol, "Mali: Hama Foune Diallo."

government militia bloc called the Plateforme.[133] By spring 2017, Aldjana proclaimed that his portion of the ANSIPRJ was joining the MNLA (one of the constituent parts of the CMA), and Aldjana was basing himself in the north.[134] Here, the fact that Mopti was not covered by the Algiers Accord of 2015 came into play: Ambitious militia commanders who wanted to position themselves within the political dynamics engendered by the Accord needed a northern affiliation. As International Crisis Group noted in 2016, some Peul politicians felt that "peace [was] being built without them if not against them. Many believe[d] that 'you need to take up arms to be heard'."[135]

Jihadist mobilization among the Peul was shutting out potential competitors. Aldjana openly acknowledged that there was no viable political niche for him in Mopti. The jihadists on the one side and Bamako-based Peul elites on the other side had become the two main forces in intra-Peul politics. In May 2017, an interviewer had the following exchange with Aldjana:

Interviewer: Why have you decided to stop defending the Peul community?
Aldjana: I decided that after having analyzed the situation of the Peul community, in Bamako and on the ground. I am stopping the fight because the Peul are not united. In Bamako, they only carry on political struggles, which are struggles over earnings, not for general earnings, but for individual or group earnings . . . I will not be a pawn of the virus that is striking my community. I wanted to contribute to the Peul cause and not to create disorder. But I will continue, as an observer, to support the Peul cause 100%.
Interviewer: How have your men reacted to your decision?
Aldjana: You know, on the ground, many Peul are engaged in carrying on a struggle, which is the jihad. Me, I am in my region and I practice my religion, but I am not ready to convert myself or to convert my men to join the ranks of the mujahidin. The Peul who have embraced this cause

[133] Rémi Carayol, "Mali: le mouvement peul de l'ANSIPRJ dépose les armes," *Jeune Afrique*, November 22, 2016, www.jeuneafrique.com/376208/politique/mali-mouvement-peul-de-lansiprj-depose-les-armes/.
[134] Olivier Dubois, "Oumar Aldjana: 'L'ANSIPRJ va complètement intégrer le MNLA'," *Journal du Mali*, October 5, 2017, www.tamoudre.org/geostrategie/resistance/oumar-aldjana-lansiprj-va-completement-integrer-mnla/.
[135] International Crisis Group, "Central Mali," 17.

> refuse to have another Peul force on the ground, a force
> that may not be jihadist. I do not wish to fight these
> people, and my means do not permit me to fight them.[136]

With this blunt explanation, Aldjana suggested that several trends were
interacting in central Mali. First, Kouffa's forces had a growing monop-
oly over the claim to be defenders of the Peul, leaving other would-be
"self-defense" militias with the grim choice of either killing Peul jihadists
(and hence undermining their own claim to represent Peul interests) or
surrendering to the pull of jihadism. Second, Aldjana's words implied
that in the matrix of violence in central Mali, being a successful
political–military actor required some kind of external patronage,
whether from Kidal or Bamako. Kouffa had the backing of JNIM, the
Dogon and Bambara militias (likely) had the national government's
backing, and so the logical patron left to Aldjana was the Peul elite in
Bamako. Peul politicians may have given some support to Hama Founé
Diallo in an effort to stem Peul recruitment to jihadism,[137] but Diallo
was "not very well-connected."[138] In any event, the Peul elite seemed to
decide that investing heavily in militias was unwise. Without external
support, Peul self-defense militias faltered, and Kouffa benefited.

Meanwhile, Kouffa's forces were moving from hit-and-run attacks
into more abiding forms of political influence. According to the Malian
Association for Human Rights, by late 2018 "dozens of villages" were
under jihadist control. Where jihadists felt strong enough, Kouffa's
forces gave villagers the choice to accept jihadist rule, flee to a non-
jihadist zone, or face blockades, kidnappings, and assassinations. Jihadists killed villagers whom they believed were collaborating with the
authorities. The jihadists found some support, probably mostly
grudging: The jihadists' "*zakat*" (formally, alms; but in this case, taxes)
could be lower than state taxes, and jihadist justice was sometimes seen
as more impartial than the aforementioned "rackets" practiced by
village elites, gendarmes, and magistrates.[139] Elsewhere, jihadists did

---

[136] Dubois, "Oumar Aldjana."
[137] Rémi Carayol, "Carte: au centre du Mali, une constellation de groupes armés,"
  Jeune Afrique, June 17, 2016, www.jeuneafrique.com/334457/politique/carte-
  centre-mali-constellation-de-groupes-armes/.
[138] Interview with Modibo Galy Cissé.
[139] FIDH/AMDH, "In Central Mali, Civilian Populations Are Caught," 8. The
  issue of zakat also came up in my interview with Amadou Mody Diall. Paying
  zakat is an obligation on every Muslim who is financially able, and in classical

not take formal control but instead came to villages at night "to remind
them that they are not far away," or preach in village mosques on
Fridays and "force all men to attend."[140] As one village chief told a
journalist, "When the government patrols come, the jihadists hide.
When the soldiers leave, the jihadists then come back and suspect us
of collaboration."[141]

Kouffa's men operate with a certain degree of political savvy at the
hyper-local level. One micro-case of how jihadism functions in central
Mali comes from the village of Gondogouro in Koro *cercle*. The
village, one of its Dogon leaders explained to me, comprised a Dogon
quarter and a Peul quarter, each with its own village head and imam.
The school and the dispensary were located on the Dogon side.[142]

Conflicts and tensions began as early as 2012. A document by
Dogon leaders later complained that "the problems started with the
minor banditry practiced by Peul youths who had procured weapons
of war after the debacle of MUJWA in the zone of Douentza … They
were mounting roadblocks for outsiders' trucks on the Koro-Douentza
road. They often stripped them of their goods and collected all the
mobile phones."[143] In 2017, according to the same document, a local
Dogon hunter organized an anti-banditry mission, but was killed that
June in a reprisal attack by the bandits. The hunter's death precipitated
a Dogon–Peul conflict in which, according to Dogon leaders, Peul
leaders from the nearby village of Nawadjé/Nawadji appealed to jihadists for help. The Dogon leaders write,

The village chief of Nawadji, capable of doing nothing by himself, appealed
to the jihadists of the Kèrènè forest to avenge his dead subjects and sign a
deal. To motivate them, he paid money but also, knowing their Salafist
ideology, he told them that he was opposing unbelievers and pagan Dogons

Islamic legal understandings, mujahidin are one eligible category of recipients
for *zakat*. Most mainstream jurists, however, would not understand Kouffa's
group to be waging a legitimate jihad.
[140] FIDH/AMDH, "In Central Mali, Civilian Populations Are Caught," 35. See
also Human Rights Watch, "Mali: Abuses Spread South."
[141] Philip Kleinfeld, "New Violence Eclipses Mali's Plans for Peace," The New
Humanitarian, November 26, 2018, www.thenewhumanitarian.org/news-
feature/2018/11/26/new-violence-eclipses-mali-s-plans-peace.
[142] Interview with Yoby Guindo, Bamako, March 8, 2018.
[143] L'Association des ressortissants de Diankabou, "Requete de l'Association des
ressortissants de Diankabou pour la creation d'un poste militaire à
Gondogourou," unpublished draft dated May 27, 2019, 3.

(a fact refuted by the jihadists themselves when they discovered the reality). The next day, the Peul and their new jihadist allies sacked the entire chain of hamlets [around Gondogouro] (more than 100 families). Nothing was spared in their murderous fury.[144]

The jihadists encircled the village as a threat and, according to a Dogon leader, conducted an extended intimidation campaign against Gondogouro's inhabitants.[145]

Yet the jihadists' role, even in the limited and partisan accounts available about this case, comes across as nuanced. Even according to their enemies, the jihadists soon revised their opinion regarding the Dogon villagers' religious status or regarding the causes of the conflict between Gondogouro and Nawadjé, or both. Moreover, the jihadists did not seize full control of the village. In a letter, the jihadists proposed terms to Gondogouro that represent a midpoint between accommodation and intimidation. I quote the letter in full:

In the Name of God, the Most Merciful, Most Beneficent, God bless Muhammad and grant peace upon him, we seek refuge in God. This letter is from the Commander of the Faithful to the Imam of Gondogouro. I say: peace upon you. We do not want a great deal of speech in this letter. We are taking up the borders after our past war. Do not enter into our place. In other words, if you go out from your town, go to your west, do not go between Gondogouro and Nawadjé, not to cut trees, not for anything, except with permission. But you will pay a portion of it because of your taking one of our men from us in recent days and now, nothing remains between us except for you to withdraw back to our borders. If not, there will be fighting between us. May God bless and grant peace to Muhammad, may God bless him and grant him peace.[146]

By 2018, the jihadists were dominating affairs in the village, effectively shutting down the school but leaving the dispensary open.[147] The case of Gondogouro sheds light on how jihadist implantation works at the hyper-local level, and how Kouffa's men use a combination of intimidation and bargaining to build abiding presences in rural areas.

---

[144] L'Association des ressortisants de Diankabou, "Requete de l'Association des ressortisants de Diankabou pour la creation d'un poste militaire à Gondogourou," 3.

[145] Interview with Yoby Guindo.

[146] Letter from jihadists to the Imam of Gondo-Ogouro, undated. I thank Yoby Guindo for sharing this document with me.

[147] Interview with Yoby Guindo.

The case also tells us something about how escalating localized violence and prewar tensions play into improvisatory coalition-building with and against jihadists; Kouffa's men ended up dominating Gondogouro as they reacted to other actors' deeds.

As of 2020, the situation in central Mali continues to evolve quickly and in a grim direction. By 2019, Malian analysts were telling me that the "zone inondée" was "nearly a Caliphate,"[148] and that Kouffa had been able to impose much of his vision in areas such as rural Tenenkou and Youwarou.[149] In this context, the situation in the center – and the expanding political influence of Kouffa's battalion – has long alarmed many elites in the capital, including the Peul.

Why Did Peul Politicians Not Join Kouffa?

The answer to this question is simple: The Peul elite, particularly politicians, did not join Kouffa for two reasons. First, they rejected him root and branch: Most of the elite looked down on Kouffa as a low-class upstart and completely rejected his vision. Second, even had they felt compelled by the jihadist project, in joining it they would have lost everything and gained nothing.

But these dynamics, obvious as they may seem, are worth discussing at greater length, given the striking contrast between the center and the north – where even sitting parliamentary deputies joined Ansar al-Din in 2012. Additionally, examining the "negative case" of the Peul politicians can further clarify the makeup of Kouffa's coalition.

The Peul have arguably had greater representation within national Malian politics than have the Tuareg and the Arabs. Mali's President Alpha Konaré (in office 1992-2002) had a Peul mother and a Peul wife. One prominent former president of the National Assembly, Ali Nouhoum Diallo, is Peul. Beyond these figures (and Konaré's increasingly prominent son, the activist Dougoukolo Alpha Oumar Ba-Konaré), the ranks of what might be called Peul civil society in Bamako include former diplomats, businesspersons, intellectuals, and more. This is not to say that Peul have never felt a sense of discrimination within national politics; during my fieldwork in Bamako in 2018 and 2019,

---

[148] Interview with Adam Thiam, Bamako, June 19, 2019.
[149] Interview with Ali Tounkara.

Peul interlocutors argued that the military in particular had never welcomed the Peul.

The crisis in Mopti has spurred the Peul elite to alarm and activism. Peul associations – notably Tabital Pulaaku, founded 1992 – have sought to lobby the central government to pursue a softer, dialogue-based approach to ending the violence. Yet the crisis in Mopti, due to its intra-Peul dimension, has also thrown the Peul elite partly on the defensive vis-à-vis Kouffa. The Peul elite face multiple challenges to their influence and legitimacy: one from Kouffa, another from other ethnic blocs, and a third from the wider demonization of all Peul.

Responding to these pressures, the Peul elite have attempted to spearhead a nonviolent resolution in Mopti. In spring 2017, drawing impetus from the Conference of National Understanding and its formal recommendation that the government pursue dialogue with Iyad ag Ghali and Kouffa, Peul elites, particularly Ali Nouhoum Diallo, made indirect and then direct contact with Kouffa; various efforts at dialogue, few of them with formal government backing, have emerged since that time. Yet the exchanges between Diallo and Kouffa turned acrimonious. Each accused the other of serving external masters – Diallo calling Kouffa a creature of Arab jihadists, and Kouffa calling Diallo a French stooge.

In August 2017, Kouffa released a recording that responded to Diallo's overtures for dialogue, but also to Diallo's accusations that Kouffa was a creature of ag Ghali (n.b.: a Tuareg) and various Arab sponsors. The recording circulated in Peul society, and so anyone who spoke Fulfulde was privy to the conversation. In Bamako, the Peul elite gathered to listen to the recording.

After a preliminary formula of praise to God and an expression of commitment to Islam, Kouffa's message began as follows:

In this response message toward the Peul in Bamako and abroad: We have received an envoy whom we know well, one of our own, a believer in whom we have confidence. When he came here this time, we were a little surprised at his attitude. He saw us, even if he was not able to see the one whom he sought to see personally. He delivered the message, of which he was the bearer, to the right place to know whether a dialogue could be established between us, members of the Peul, being all of the same community. A dialogue for putting an end to the war between us. We have responded to this question in the past. We saw this envoy, in whom we had some doubts this time . . .

In any case, whether he was really sent or not, we deliver our response to the question of establishing a dialogue between us, the jihadists, and our parents among the Peul. A dialogue for a smooth arrangement where each one could conduct his religious life as he understands it. This is what we are going to respond to. [The envoy] cited for us eight personalities, leaders of the Peul community. I remember the names Ali Nouhoum Diallo, Idrissa Sankaré, Amadou Mody Diall, Ismail Cissé, Hassana Barry. Those are the names that come back to me among those he cited for us. They are the leaders of the Peul in Bamako who work against the abuses of which the Peul are victims through the combination of the French forces in Mali and the abuses of the national army in their hunt against the jihadists. They work for the protection of the Peul community against the exactions of France, which, in pursuing the jihadists, makes a conflation in thinking that every Peul is a jihadist.

For you, we jihadists are Peul. In your understanding, even if our combat is not for the Peul cause, we are Peul, Peul rebels against France. For us jihadists, all persons who struggle for the cause of the Prophet, for the return of his values, for the triumph of the Book of God, which is the sole truth, are the only targets of France. If France succeeds in separating them from their community, it will liquidate them alone; failing that, France is capable of liquidating the entirety of their community without any distinction, in order that the will of God will not be applied. You leaders of the Peul community, you know. We are from the same community. France cannot make the distinction between us Peul.[150]

With these statements, Kouffa posited a gulf of understanding between himself and the Peul elite in Bamako. The two sides were divided by their different conceptions of Kouffa's role: Kouffa proclaimed himself a jihadist rather than an ethnic rebel, whereas the Peul elite saw him as a co-ethnic.

The ethnic ties, however, were real even in Kouffa's mind, and here his words turned menacing. If France on its own was too ignorant to differentiate between jihadist and non-jihadist Peul, Kouffa said, the Peul elite in Bamako risked becoming tools in the hands of France and the Malian government. France had already, Kouffa continued, found Tuareg allies to help it target and liquidate Tuareg jihadists – France was now trying to do the same with the Peul elite, who in his view would find themselves obliged to help France in order to prevent the

---

[150] Recorded statement by Amadou Kouffa, August 2017. Unpublished translation from Fulfulde to French by Oumar Sow, 1.

slaughter of the entire Peul community. Not only was Kouffa appearing to reject dialogue but he was even starting to reject the idea that the Peul elite, given the competing pressures they faced, could be credible interlocutors. "In our understanding you have been charged to indicate where we are, how many we are, what means we control, how to localize us so that France can fight us on our own, so that not one hair of another Peul will fall to the ground, so that no calabash of milk will be knocked over, so that no Peul's goat will perish."[151]

Kouffa then challenged the premise that the Peul elite could defend the Peul of central Mali against French-led or ethnic-based violence. "We have never seen you with any arms for defending the Peul community." It was his own forces, Kouffa said, who had stopped the massacres against the Peul.

You have created organizations for better organizing and raising consciousness among the Peul, defending the Peul victims of massacres by the Bambara and others. When you receive this message, call and ask the Bambaras whom we have fought from Hairé, Douentza, and Koro. Ask those who massacred Peul by the dozens, with impunity, ask them, why have they stopped targeting the Peul, why have they stopped massacring the Peul? Did France demand a stop to the massacres of Peul? No! Did the government of Mali demand a stop to the massacre of Peul? No! Or even you, the cadres of the Peul community who were seeking to arm the Peul so that they could defend themselves, were you able to stop the massacres of which the Peul were victims? No! What stopped the patrols of France here, is the same thing that made the Bambara stop targeting the Peul community.[152]

Kouffa was attempting to have it both ways: He denied that his movement was based on ethnicity rather than religion, but he also portrayed himself as a defender of the Peul. "We are and will remain Peul. You cannot exclude us. We are Malians and will remain such." Addressing Ali Nouhoum Diallo by name and relaying a report that Diallo had called Kouffa's group "slaves of the Arabs,"[153] Kouffa angrily rejected that framing, commenting, "We are certainly the followers of one Arab, and that Arab is the Prophet Muhammad, peace and blessings upon him ... We follow this Arab, and you, you follow France. Your request to establish a dialogue with us was only dictated by France."[154]

---

[151] Ibid., 2.   [152] Ibid., 3.   [153] Ibid., 3.   [154] Ibid., 4.

Kouffa seemed to unambiguously reject a dialogue, calling into question not only the motives of his interlocutors among the Peul elite but even their personal faith as Muslims:

We practice God's religion as is proper, whether it pleases France or not. We say to you to come no more to see us for some sort of mediation. To come here no more if it is not to join us in the jihad ... Each one of you is welcome in his village without any fear. The only condition is not to associate with those who fight us. Above all, avoid speaking to us of dialogue with France. Dialogue about what? What are we going to haggle over in this dialogue? Is God to be haggled over?[155]

Harsh words. And yet at the end of Kouffa's message, he turned more accommodationist. Kouffa, it turned out, was willing to countenance certain types of interchanges.

Our desire is that you send us Muslim scholars, they are in a better position to understand what we seek. You, your culture and your education make you understand only democracy. I have always denounced Tabital Pulaaku in its heresies ... We are sparing this envoy because we know him to be Muslim and naïve at the same time. We have realized that he has not come here to locate us and inform our enemies ... If you want a dialogue, go talk to our emir, Iyad ag Ghali. He is not an Arab himself, he is our guide. You know him, for he is an intellectual like you, with the same education as you. He has sat down many times with you. He is our guide, but not so that we might adore him. He is Malian, it's undeniable. If you want peace, go talk to him. If not, you will never have peace, neither on earth or in the afterlife. You will never exterminate us. Each fighter killed, another will replace him. I think you, you Peul, have no fear to come and see your families here ... If you send us Muslim scholars, they are welcome, so that we might talk to them: this means the scholars Mahmoud Dicko, Mahi Banikane, Shaykh Oumar Dia and others so that they might see how we live here, we will enjoy it together. But not you [Diallo], who cannot understand me. Your words just confirmed that; even if you have not denied the existence of God, you have denied the Prophet in comparing him to other Arabs who have nothing to do with him.[156]

Despite all of Kouffa's condemnations of the Peul elite, of Tabital Pulaaku, of Diallo, it was these two points that caught the attention of many of the tape's listeners in Bamako: Kouffa's willingness to talk personally with certain Muslim scholars, and his recommendation that

---

[155] Ibid., 7.   [156] Ibid., 8.

the political elite in Bamako pursue dialogue with ag Ghali. Kouffa's respect for a few religious scholars recalls the context for his own emergence, namely a religious field that saw the rising influence of Salafis and other activists, especially starting in the 1980s.

As Kouffa's rhetorical question indicated – "Is God to be haggled over?" – the specter of absolutism hung over any potential dialogue, but his statements about ag Ghali indicated that accommodation might be possible. In a sense, Kouffa acknowledged that a solution was somehow above his political capacity, whereas ag Ghali "has sat down many times with you" and has "the same education as you." Referring the political problem to ag Ghali, however, limited the role that the Peul elite in Bamako could play – talking to ag Ghali was not necessarily their portfolio. After they heard Kouffa's recording, the Peul elite gave a copy of it to the High Islamic Council of Mali and another to the prime minister.[157]

Several of the religious leaders named by Kouffa do not seem willing, from what I can determine, to attempt the role of mediator. Shaykh Oumar Dia, when I asked him about the possibility of meeting with Kouffa, said he had never met Kouffa, had not been to Mopti in a long time, and had no role to play. "What would I say to him?"[158] As one Malian NGO official commented, clerics such as Dia and Banikane have not accepted a mediator role because the state's weakness and disorganization would leave them highly vulnerable to violence; the furthest Banikane had been willing to go was to communicate to Kouffa that in Banikane's view, the jihadists had acted inappropriately by collecting alms/taxes (*zakat*) by force.[159] The role of Imam Mahmoud Dicko (who is not ethnically Peul) in possible negotiations has been more complex. For part of 2017, it appeared that Dicko had a mandate to open a dialogue in central Mali, but Dicko's turbulent relations with the government in Bamako soon took away that mandate. Dicko reportedly traveled to Mopti in early 2018 to meet Kouffa's fighters, but the effort fizzled out amid the rivalry between Dicko and then-Prime Minister Soumeylou Maiga.[160] Other voices stepped in as well to attempt to engage Kouffa and his fighters on their

---

[157] Interview with Oumar Sow, Bamako, March 8, 2018.
[158] Interview with Oumar Dia, Bamako, June 21, 2019.
[159] Interview with Malian NGO official, Bamako, June 2019.
[160] Interview with Mohammed Mahmoud Abu al-Ma'ali, Nouakchott, April 28, 2018.

understanding of Islam. In 2018, the trader and former Qur'an student Ousmane Bocoum began to debate Kouffa's men over WhatsApp, and even offered to debate Kouffa in Mopti – an offer the jihadist leader declined.[161] The businessman Sékou Allaye Bolly has also worked to "extract Peul youth" from jihadism.[162] But as of the time of writing, the Peul elite's efforts to broker a politically fruitful dialogue with Kouffa have not succeeded.[163] And the NGOs who attempt to mediate in central Mali can only achieve so much without state support. These NGOs' habit of paying a per diem for participants at peacebuilding workshops can even create a form of "rent" that propagates dialogues without including the real decision-makers.[164]

Meanwhile, by 2017, foreign security forces were multiplying in northern and central Mali. This development strengthened, rather than weakened, Kouffa's hand. These forces include the United Nations Multi-Dimensional Integrated Stabilization Mission in Mali (MINUSMA), established in 2013; France's Operation Barkhane, a Sahel-wide counterterrorism mission created in 2014; and the G5 Sahel Joint Force, which launched in 2017 as a regional counterterrorism and border security body drawing units from Mauritania, Mali, Burkina Faso, Niger, and Chad.

The jihadist coalition JNIM, of which Kouffa's fighters are a part, targets foreign forces and Malian government or government-aligned forces across the north and center. For example, in January 2017, shortly before JNIM's formation, AQIM perpetrated a massive suicide bombing against mixed government, pro-government, and ex-rebel forces in Gao, seeking to undermine progress under the Algiers Accord. Central Mali has become a considerable theater of violence against foreign forces, particularly since the creation of the G5 joint force. One of JNIM's most successful attacks in the center targeted the G5 command headquarters in Sévaré, Mopti Region, in June 2018; the attack prompted the G5 joint force to relocate its headquarters to Bamako.

---

[161] Le Cam, "Mali: Ousmane Bocoum."
[162] Baba Ahmed, "Mali: Sékou Allaye Bolly, le commerçant peul qui voulait réintégrer les anciens jihadistes," *Jeune Afrique*, March 17, 2019, www .jeuneafrique.com/748486/politique/mali-sekou-allaye-bolly-le-commercant-peul-qui-voulait-reintegrer-les-anciens-jihadistes/.
[163] For an in-depth look at the question of dialogue with Kouffa's forces, see International Crisis Group, "Speaking with the 'Bad Guys'."
[164] Interview with Boubacar Sangaré, Bamako, June 17, 2019.

G5 forces have also been implicated in human rights abuses in Mopti –
for example, a detachment of Malian soldiers under the G5 killed
twelve civilians in Boulekessi, eastern Mopti, in May 2018. Within
Mopti's matrix of violence, foreign forces are fuel thrown on the fire.

For jihadists, killing G5 soldiers served not just as a military campaign but also as a venue for propaganda. One JNIM statement from
March 2019 bragged that Kouffa's forces had executed a "blessed
raid" on G5 soldiers in Dioura, Tenekou *cercle*, killing nearly thirty
G5 soldiers, including the battalion commander.

This raid comes as retaliation (*radd*) for the atrocious crimes committed by
the formal forces of the government in Bamako, accompanied by the militias
supporting it, against our people among the Peul, amid a disgraceful local
and international silence and the collusion of the forces of the French
occupation and their allies among the Crusaders.[165]

French efforts to track down Kouffa have provided additional propaganda opportunities. After the French government announced that it
had killed Kouffa in a November 2018 raid by Operation Barkhane,
JNIM shocked many observers four months later by releasing a
twenty-minute video featuring an extended interview with Kouffa, as
well as scenes of him moving on the Niger River.[166] Kouffa, despising
the Peul elite as well as the French, has fashioned himself into a symbol
of resistance to both Paris and Bamako.

Even Kouffa, however, faces challenges. By 2019, the deteriorating
security situation in the "zone exondée," including the intercommunal
violence between Dogon and Peul, was exacerbating strains within his
coalition. On the one hand, Kouffa had reportedly recruited up to
100 Dogon jihadists who acted as intermediaries between him and
their own communities. On the other hand, young Peul fighters, under
pressure from Dan Na Ambassagou, were calling on Kouffa to allow

[165] Jama'at Nusrat al-Islam wa-l-Muslimin, "Hujum Kasih 'ala Qa'ida li-Quwwat
    G5 fi Jura," Mu'assasat al-Zallaqa, March 22, 2019, https://jihadology.net/wp-
    content/uploads/_pda/2019/03/jamacc84e28099at-nuscca3rat-al-islacc84m-
    wa-l-muslimicc84n-22a-sweeping-attack-on-the-g5-forces-base-in-dioura22
    .pdf.
[166] Mu'assasat al-Zallaqa, "Wa-Ula'ika Hum al-Kadhibun: Liqa' ma'a al-Shaykh
    al-Mujahid Muhammad Kufa Ithr Khabr Maqtalihi," February 2019, available
    at https://jihadology.net/2019/02/28/new-video-message-from-jamaat-nuṣrat-
    al-islam-wa-l-muslimin-they-are-liars-interview-with-shaykh-muḥammad-
    kufa/.

them to undertake generalized violence against Dogon communities. Such demands had the potential to undercut Kouffa's ambition of fostering a multi-ethnic jihadist project whose ethos would be irreducible to ethnic claims and antagonisms. But the young fighters held a potential trump card: the threat of defecting to the Islamic State, which some of them began to do. Facing these pressures, Kouffa began to consider accepting some of the Peul hardliners' demands for revenge and reprisals against the Dogon.[167] Yet he also issued a tentative proposal for a ceasefire with Dan Na Ambassagou.[168] The ethnicization of violence that had boosted Kouffa's coalition building was now posing problems for his political vision, necessitating continued experimentation on his part.

Conclusion

The point of departure for this chapter was the difference in how jihadist coalitions are structured in northern versus central Mali. If the north's "jihadism from above" is a destabilizing force, it is nevertheless far less violent than the center's "jihadism from below." In the center, jihadism has contributed to an ethnicization of conflict with its own internal momentum. The conflict is now partly propelled by its own endogenous dynamics.

Another question is to what extent Kouffa's model of a jihadist coalition is spreading into Mali's borderlands with Burkina Faso and Niger. In Burkina Faso, the Peul preacher Ibrahim Dicko created "Ansaroul Islam" (Ansar al-Islam, Defenders of Islam) in 2016, provoking reactions somewhat similar to those in central Mali – counter-reactions from the state and "self-defense militias," which in turn fuel conflict by conducting ethnic profiling of the Peul. On the Mali–Niger border, the jihadist entrepreneur 'Adnan Abu al-Walid al-Sahrawi, ex-MUJWA and current Islamic State, has found some success recruiting among Peul herders, and has built something of a shadow state in the sparsely populated Eastern Region of Burkina Faso.

---

[167] Interview with a Malian NGO official, Bamako, June 2019.
[168] "Mali: Amadou Koufa pose des conditions pour négocier avec une milice dogon," RFI, October 5, 2019, www.rfi.fr/afrique/20191005-mali-amadou-koufa-milice-peul-dogon-autodefense-jihadiste-negociation.

5 | The Mali–Niger–Burkina Faso Borderlands

Incorporation and Accommodation at the Peripheries

Map 4 The Mali-Niger-Burkina Faso Borderlands

Many analysts point to "fragile states" and "porous borders" as factors in jihadism's spread. But how does jihadism cross borders in a political sense – what conditions, what relationships, are necessary? As Olivier Walther and William Miles argue, borders are not merely geographical objects but also social spaces, including in Africa. Gesturing toward the importance of prewar networks in coalition-building, they write, "Rebels and violent extremist organizations have been operating along pre-existing social and financial networks across the region, particularly when they extend their activities across borders, due to the uncertainty of operating in a foreign environment."[1] This chapter argues that even where borders are weakly defended, successful jihadist cross-border expansion or relocation requires political savvy.

The chapter examines the borderlands of Mali, Niger, and Burkina Faso. In this subregion, two jihadist movements arose in 2015–2016. They are the Islamic State in the Greater Sahara (ISGS) and Ansaroul Islam (or Ansar al-Islam, "Supporters of Islam"). Both had connections to al-Qa'ida in the Islamic Maghreb (AQIM) and to AQIM's allies in Mali, although ISGS (obviously) defected to the Islamic State.

The chapter also explores relations between Sahelian capitals and their own border regions. As a point of departure, we can observe that jihadist mobilization is hard to achieve, and harder to sustain, in urban centers. By 2016, no Sahelian capital had been spared jihadist attacks – Nouakchott saw terrorist violence as early as 2008, Niamey witnessed a kidnapping in 2011, N'Djamena suffered a suicide bombing in 2015, and both Bamako and Ouagadougou have been hit with attacks on hotels and other expatriate destinations since 2015 and 2016, respectively. Yet no Sahelian capital has seen a durable, active jihadist presence; Chapter 7 will highlight how AQIM sponsored cells in Nouakchott, but ultimately failed to generate high-quality urban networks. In North Africa as well, capitals and major economic hubs have suffered attacks, from Casablanca to Algiers to Tunis to Tripoli, but even in the case of Algeria, security forces eventually pushed jihadists into the mountains and the deserts. Even in conflict-torn Libya, urban centers have only been hospitable to jihadists on a fleeting basis.

Where jihadism has set down deep roots in northwest Africa, it has been far from capitals, in places where jihadists can outcompete the state and evade national or foreign security deployments. Jean-Hervé Jezequel and Vincent Foucher write, "Unlike the region's governments, which are not well disposed toward nomadic communities and struggle to integrate them, radical groups are often ready to consolidate their networks and acquire intelligence by recruiting local people." Violence

---

[1] Olivier Walther and William Miles, "Introduction: States, Borders and Political Violence in Africa" in *African Border Disorders: Addressing Transnational Extremist Organizations*, edited by Olivier Walther and William Miles, 1–13 (London and New York: Routledge, 2018), 5.

at the peripheries can even create a self-reinforcing dynamic, where national governments pull inward and begin to prioritize stability in capitals. External backers can reinforce this dynamic: "Increased international support has had the side effect of reinforcing Sahelian countries' tendency to focus on the political centre, where governing elites and the bulk of voters live."[2]

The view from the capitals is shaped both by authorities' keen perception of their own limited resources and by politicians' relative complacency, even in the face of escalating violence. Some Sahelian peripheries are literally inaccessible during portions of the rainy season, cutting some villages off from security forces and placing them at the mercy of bandits, militias, and jihadists.[3] Ironically, if borders are easy to cross administratively, communities in the borderlands nevertheless often feel that they suffer from "enclavement" – enclosure; their remoteness from the center limits their access to protection, development, and investment.[4]

Politically, Sahelian states have long relied on local brokers to manage the peripheries. Decades of "decentralization" efforts in the Sahel have, if one is feeling cynical, provided cover for center–periphery deal-making rather than democratic empowerment. As one group of researchers notes, "The question one could pose is to know whether the State in Niger and the bordering countries, since gaining independence, has been sufficiently anchored to think, today, about its decentralization ... The weakness of this state, in terms of resources, cannot be replaced by the emergence of regions."[5] Even amid insurgencies, states often seek new brokers or cede regions to insecurity, rather than attempting to reassert a control they never really had. As Matt Herbert comments, in the Sahel and North Africa, "Political and social dissidents were, and often still are, viewed as the preoccupying threats, while smuggling and cross-border criminality were not as long

[2] Jean-Hervé Jezequel and Vincent Foucher, "Forced out of Towns in the Sahel, Africa's Jihadists Go Rural," International Crisis Group, January 11, 2017, www.crisisgroup.org/africa/west-africa/mali/forced-out-towns-sahel-africas-jihadists-go-rural.

[3] Herrick Mouafo Djontu and Karine Gatelier, "Nord-Tillabéri: analyse du conflit lié à l'accès aux ressources naturelles," Haute Autorité à la Consolidation de la Paix, August 2017, 64–65, http://base.irenees.net/docs/publication_hacp_modop.pdf.

[4] Ibid., 67–68.   [5] Ibid., 17.

as they did not intersect with political actors (such as dissidents, insurgents, or terrorists)."[6]

Even jihadist violence does not necessarily represent an existential threat in the imaginations of the Sahel's central authorities. This sense that the center is partly immune to the peripheries' problems helps explain why, in confronting Sahelian jihadism, heads of state have repeatedly defaulted to simplistic strategies: allowing security forces to pursue collective punishment against rural populations, empowering local ethnic militias, and shifting blame amid crisis by reshuffling their cabinets. Damaging but sporadic terrorism in capital cities does not necessarily change this calculus.

Western governments (perhaps not always sincerely), along with human rights organizations, pressure African governments to avoid human rights abuses and to prioritize holistic strategies for bringing "good governance" to rural and border regions. But Sahelian politicians and military officers seem more cognizant than their Western counterparts of just how limited the resources, the troop numbers, and the reach of the state are. Catriona Craven-Matthews and Pierre Englebert even argue that Mali "never quite met the prerequisites for functional statehood" – and so, following the 2012 rebellion, there was not exactly a state to reconstruct. These authors add, "The Malian government and donors [merely] enact reconstruction, contributing to Mali's fictional dimensions more than to empirical foundations of statehood, and ... the combination of crisis and reconstruction represents an acceptable equilibrium for both sets of actors."[7]

Despite state weakness, there is variation in how Sahelian policymakers have approached rural jihadism and insecurity. This chapter highlights differences between the approaches pursued by governments in Mali, Niger, and Burkina Faso. As of 2019, Nigerien policies had inhibited jihadist coalition-building by limiting the use of collective punishment against particular ethnic groups, and by de-emphasizing the use of community-based militias as supposed counterweights to

---

[6] Matt Herbert, "States and Smugglers: The Ties That Bind and the Ties That Fray" in "Transnational Organized Crime and Political Actors in the Maghreb and Sahel," Konrad Adenauer Stiftung Mediterranean Dialogue Series Number 17 (January 2019): 5–7, 5, www.kas.de/documents/282499/282548/MDS+17+Transnational+Organized+Crime+and+Political+Actors+in+the+Maghreb+and+Sahel.pdf/9e2145e6-4935-3278-174b-746c91fd18c8?version=1.1&t=1548758044198.

[7] Catriona Craven-Matthews and Pierre Englebert, "A Potemkin State in the Sahel? The Empirical and the Fictional in Malian State Reconstruction," *African Security* 11:1 (2018): 1–31, 2.

jihadists. The previous chapter highlighted the disastrous effects of those strategies in central Mali; here the emphasis is on the contrast between Niger and Burkina Faso, although that contrast began to blur in 2020. At the same time, the chapter also highlights both jihadist agency and the unintended consequences of other actors' decisions. ISGS, in particular, reacted adroitly to both its opportunities and its setbacks.

Theoretical Implications of the Case

The case of ISGS highlights three important theoretical takeaways. One concerns the interaction between *incorporation* and *marginalization*. It is easy to understand how an organization with military and political momentum can be an attractive partner for tribes, businesspersons, local politicians, clerics, and others. And it is often taken for granted that even when jihadist organizations are marginalized, they nevertheless find it easy to recruit in geographically, politically, and socioeconomically marginalized areas. Yet even at the peripheries, there can be substantial competition for the loyalties of ordinary civilians and of important networks within the civilian population. Competitors include states, local power brokers and elites (political, religious, etc.), criminals (smugglers, traffickers, bandits, etc.), ethnic groups, and communities.

With jihadist recruitment in the peripheries, there are more precise mechanics at work than just the fact that both jihadists and their potential recruits are marginalized. Successful incorporation at the peripheries requires jihadists to demonstrate their strength to specific constituencies, blocs, and networks, and even to make pacts (explicit or implicit) with these groups on a case-by-case basis. Such pacts, as this book has repeatedly stressed, may involve compromise, for example when ideologically committed jihadists and financially motivated criminals find mutual but not identical interests. Even in the borderlands, a group that cannot compromise (at a minimum, to the extent of being willing to help criminals "re-brand" as pious jihadists) is unlikely to get far in coalition-building.

The second takeaway is the fluidity of politics in border regions and peripheries during wartime. Fluidity arises not just because there are multiple important actors but also because the relationships among them shift rapidly as fortunes rise and fall during wartime; state weakness can actually accentuate some actors' tendencies toward

bet-hedging, double-crossing, and opportunism. The presence of jihadists in a war-torn borderland can further complicate local politics and
accelerate political change, given the force (military and political) that
foreign governments sometimes bring to bear as well as the often-
draconian responses that central states attempt to mount against jihadist forces (or conventional rebellions) on their peripheries. When
states target civilian communities for collective punishment, when
external forces (in this case, France) mount counterterrorism operations and/or partner with local ethnic and tribal militias, when jihadists assassinate and intimidate local elites – all of these dynamics
contribute to rapid and destabilizing fluctuations in politics. Jihadists
must navigate these fluctuations, and they have no guarantee of success
in doing so. Sometimes, as this chapter demonstrates, jihadists even
choose relocation because of the turbulence in a particular area's
politics.

The third theoretical takeaway is the possibility of intra-jihadist
accommodation and the advantages that such a situation can offer to
two theoretically opposed jihadist groups, in other words factions
with declared affiliations to either the Islamic State or al-Qaʻida.
Intra-jihadist accommodation can permit any or all of the following
outcomes: a division of territory, military cooperation, political
cooperation, and merger or rapprochement. Within intra-jihadist
accommodation, there may be a parallel to the benefits that mainstream politicians and businessmen derive from the anathematization
of their jihadist partners and allies. When two supposedly rival jihadist organizations accommodate each other but do not merge, their
relationship can create a climate of ambiguity and plausible deniability. This climate can help the different jihadist parties keep their (real)
enemies confused about the nature of jihadist politics and control in a
particular zone.

ISGS, Part One: The Group's Origins in the Fragmentation of MUJWA

Several of the previous chapters mentioned the Movement for Unity
and Jihad in West Africa (MUJWA). We have seen how MUJWA
formed as an offshoot of AQIM, led by Mauritanian and Malian
Arabs, some of whom were close to the AQIM Saharan field commander Mokhtar Belmokhtar. During the jihadist takeover of

northern Mali in 2012, MUJWA and Belmokhtar dominated the northeastern Malian city of Gao.

The French intervention of 2013, Operation Serval, provoked realignments within MUJWA. The core jihadists in the organization joined Belmokhtar, who broke away from AQIM and established his Veiled Men Battalion as a distinct formation notionally affiliated to al-Qaʻida central rather than to AQIM. In August 2013, the Veiled Men and MUJWA merged to form al-Murabitun (The Sentinels), named for a medieval Saharan empire.

More Mali-centric elements of MUJWA dispersed along essentially ethnic lines, part of a "tribalization of armed groups" that affected jihadist and non-jihadist militias across northern Mali.[8] Chapter 4 discussed how some ethnic Peul fighters from central Mali joined MUJWA in 2012, seeking training and protection, and then returned home and/or moved to other formations, jihadist and non-jihadist, after Operation Serval. A similar process occurred with Peul in Mali's northeastern Ménaka Region and across the border in Niger. Some Nigerien Peul "joined [MUJWA] to seek redress for a long history of Tuareg cross-border banditry and cattle theft, to protect themselves from 'exactions', and to advance their social position."[9]

Malian Tilemsi Arabs also flowed into and out of MUJWA. After Serval began, some Arabs joined the Mouvement Arabe de l'Azawad (Arab Movement of Azawad, MAA).[10] As seen in Chapter 3 in the case of Tuareg nobles and Ansar al-Din, in the immediate post-Serval political environment both Malian and French authorities largely tolerated such efforts at political rehabilitation by the circumstantial jihadists in Ansar al-Din and MUJWA. One MAA figure, Yero Ould Daha, later told a journalist how he came to join MUJWA:

[8] Adam Sandor, "Insecurity, the Breakdown of Social Trust, and Armed Actor Governance in Central and Northern Mali," Centre FrancoPaix, August 2017, 20, https://dandurand.uqam.ca/wp-content/uploads/2017/10/Sandor-english-Report.pdf.

[9] Ibid., 11.

[10] On these dynamics see Andrew Lebovich, "Reconstructing Local Orders in Mali: Historical Perspectives and Future Challenges," Brookings Institution, July 2017, 18, fn. 62, www.brookings.edu/wp-content/uploads/2017/08/lebovich_mali.pdf.

At the time, either you relied on the army, but it had fled, or you entered into the MNLA [the National Movement for the Liberation of Azawad, the main Tuareg separatist rebel group in 2012], or you were with the jihadists. Their leader, Ahmed Tilemsi [a Malian Arab], had been wounded. They brought him to my house to treat him and hide him. After that, they recruited me. Then, the MNLA created its form of government of Azawad. We Arabs, we are for Mali, so we fought against the MNLA. MUJWA protected us from the exactions of that group. It was two or three months later that the movement [began to] speak of shari'a. Then, there was no more MNLA, no more Mali. Did we have another choice? 80% of MUJWA is made up of traffickers, merchants, people looking for money.[11]

Such depictions of MUJWA are common, with ex-MUJWA members downplaying whatever affinities they may have had for the group's ideology and instead emphasizing ethnic or economic motivations. Whatever different individuals' motivations for joining originally were, the ethnic fragmentation of MUJWA into Arab and Peul components was one key dynamic that began to shape jihadist politics in eastern Mali and across the border in Niger.

Matters were further complicated when one of al-Murabitun's leading figures, Adnan Abu al-Walid al-Sahrawi, rebelled against Belmokhtar's authority. Reconstructing al-Sahrawi's biography is difficult. He hails from the Western Sahara, which would make him one of the few prominent Western Saharan jihadist field commanders; some sources even suggest that he was the grandson of a prominent politician from the Rgaybat,[12] a major tribe in the Western Sahara and Mauritania. Some outlets have asserted that al-Sahrawi was a fighter or even a field commander for the Sahrawi Polisario Front,[13] but these assertions come in an atmosphere where the Moroccan government has labored to brand the entire Polisario as crypto-jihadists; it is thus hard to separate journalism from propaganda in some cases. What is known of al-Sahrawi's biography becomes more solid when it comes to

---

[11] Dorothée Thienot, "Mali – Yero Ould Daha: 'Le Mujao nous protégeait du MNLA'," *Jeune Afrique*, August 11, 2014, www.jeuneafrique.com/47201/politique/mali-yero-ould-daha-le-mujao-nous-prot-geait-du-mnla/.

[12] "Qui est Walid Abou Adnan Sahraoui, le porte-parole du MUJAO?" Diaspora Saharaui, March 26, 2013, http://diasporasaharaui.blogspot.fr/2013/03/qui-est-walid-abou-adnan-sahraoui-le.html.

[13] See, for example, 'Amru al-Naqib, "Abu al-Walid al-Sahrawi ... Min al-Bulisariyu ila 'Katibat al-Murabitun' al-Da'ishiyya," 24, February 6, 2018, https://24.ae/article/418304/.

his career in MUJWA: He was head of the Shura Council and a key spokesman between approximately 2011 and 2013, and then became deputy leader of al-Murabitun after that coalition's formation.[14] More than any other figure in this book, interlocutors in Mali described al-Sahrawi as a criminal, a "trafficker," and a "bandit."[15]

In May 2015, following the deaths of several al-Murabitun leaders,[16] al-Sahrawi pledged allegiance to the Islamic State in the name of the entire organization.[17] The move reflected a competition for leadership dating back to the group's founding.[18] Additionally, al-Sahrawi may have been frustrated and/or emboldened by Belmokhtar's increasing interest in Libya. Al-Sahrawi may also have been positioning himself as the focal point for whatever support the Islamic State was then attracting amongst Sahelian jihadists.[19]

As noted in other instances throughout this book, pursuing schism is a recurring technique for ambitious jihadists who find their paths blocked. Perhaps al-Sahrawi saw propitious timing in the fact that his men were holding a Romanian national who had been kidnapped in Burkina Faso the previous month.[20] Al-Sahrawi may have hoped

[14] "'Al-Murabitun' tu'lin amiran jadidan wa-tubayi' al-Baghdadi," *Al-Akhbar*, May 13, 2015, http://alakhbar.info/news/9799-2015-05-13-20-45-48.html. See also "Islamists Issue Ultimatum on Kidnapped Diplomats," *The Telegraph*, May 9, 2012, www.telegraph.co.uk/news/worldnews/africaandindianocean/algeria/9253625/Islamists-issue-ultimatum-on-kidnapped-diplomats.html.

[15] Interview with Ahmada ag Bibi, Bamako, June 20, 2019.

[16] Rida Lyammouri, "Key Events That Led to Tensions between Mokhtar Belmokhtar and Adnan Abu Walid al-Sahrawi before Splitting," Maghreb and Sahel, December 7, 2015, https://maghrebandsahel.wordpress.com/2015/12/07/key-events-that-led-to-tensions-between-mokhtar-belmokhtar-and-adnan-abu-walid-al-sahrawi-before-splitting/.

[17] Adnan Abu al-Walid al-Sahrawi, "Announcing a New Amir and Giving Bay'ah to al-Baghdadi," May 13, 2015, https://jihadology.net/2015/05/13/new-audio-message-from-al-murabituns-adnan-abu-walid-al-ṣaḥrawi-announcing-a-new-amir-and-giving-bayah-to-al-baghdadi/.

[18] Muhammad Mahmud Abu al-Ma'ali, "Al-Tanafus Bayn 'al-Dawla al-Islamiyya' wa-'Al-Qa'ida' Yush'il al-Sahra' al-Kubra," Al Jazeera Center for Studies, July 1, 2015, http://studies.aljazeera.net/ar/reports/2015/07/20157191155358221.html.

[19] Interview with a journalist, 2019.

[20] See Adnan Abu al-Walid al-Sahrawi, "Claiming the Kidnapping of the Romanian Hostages in Burkina Faso," May 19, 2015, https://jihadology.net/2015/05/19/new-audio-message-from-jamaat-at-tawhid-wa-l-jihad-fi-gharb-ifriqiyyas-adnan-abu-walid-al-ṣaḥrawi-claiming-the-kidnapping-of-the-romanian-hostages-in-burki/; and "Islamist Group Says Holding Romanian Hostage Seized in Burkina," Reuters, May 19, 2015, www.reuters.com/article/

that the hostage would give his nascent organization credibility and a funding base, just as MUJWA's first major action in 2011 – when it split from AQIM – had been a kidnapping.

Belmokhtar, as head of al-Murabitun's Shura Council, swiftly weighed in to disavow al-Sahrawi's pledge to the Islamic State. Much of al-Murabitun remained under Belmokhtar's leadership while some fighters (likely fewer than two hundred) decamped with al-Sahrawi. Naming his faction the Islamic State in the Greater Sahara (ISGS), al-Sahrawi struggled to earn recognition from the Islamic State's central leadership until October 2016. At the time of writing, ISGS remains part of the Islamic State's Nigeria-centric "West Africa Province" rather than constituting a "province" of its own.[21] At the local level, however, al-Sahrawi had an opportunity to get organized and grow his forces during 2015–2016, during a period when the Mali–Niger borderlands were something of a military–political vacuum.[22]

ISGS, Part Two: ISGS in the Conflict Matrix of the Mali–Niger–Burkina Faso Borderlands

Al-Sahrawi, hailing from outside the Sahel, had little chance to recruit from among his own geographic or tribal constituency. Rather, his recruitment efforts centered on his adopted home, eastern Mali and adjacent zones in Niger and Burkina Faso. There, he sought to absorb former MUJWA elements while conducting quasi-ethnic outreach.

By 2016, ISGS was positioning itself as the defender of ethnic Peul herders in the Mali–Niger borderlands. This positioning involved tapping into historical intercommunal tensions (discussed later) as well as present-day militia relationships. In the Ménaka region, the primary local antagonists of ISGS became two ethnic-based, pro-government militias: the Groupe autodéfense touareg Imghad et alliés (Self-Defense Group for Imghad Tuareg and Allies, GATIA), and the Mouvement pour le salut de l'Azawad (Movement for the Salvation of Azawad, MSA).

us-sahara-militants/islamist-group-says-holding-romanian-hostage-seized-in-burkina-idUSKBN0O41GF20150519.
[21] Jason Warner, "Sub-Saharan Africa's Three 'New' Islamic State Affiliates," *Combating Terrorism Center Sentinel* 10:1 (January 2017), https://ctc.usma.edu/sub-saharan-africas-three-new-islamic-state-affiliates/.
[22] Interview with Fahad ag Mohamed, Bamako, June 21, 2019.

By 2018, both militias were embroiled in intercommunal conflicts with the Peul, which inadvertently benefited ISGS.

GATIA was formed in August 2014 by El Hajj ag Gamou, whose pro-government militia activities in northern Mali date back to the 1990s. Ag Gamou has a long-term rivalry with Iyad ag Ghali. Successive Malian governments have sought to use ag Gamou as a counterweight to Tuareg rebels and ex-rebels, and GATIA is the latest in a line of militias headed by ag Gamou. As its name indicates, GATIA foregrounds Imghad Tuareg. The Imghad are a "non-noble" community whose political identity has sharpened in recent decades, posing an increasing political challenge to the Ifoghas ("noble") Tuareg in Kidal and beyond (see Chapter 3). After GATIA's formation, the group became a major military and political faction in northern Mali. The 2015 Algiers Accord, meant to end the northern Malian conflict, was signed by three parties: the Malian government; the ex-rebel Coordination of Azawad Movements (French acronym CMA), which included the MNLA and the ex-jihadists and other politicians in the High Council for the Unity of Azawad; and the "Plateforme," a coalition of pro-government, largely ethnic-based "self-defense" militias. The leading member of the Plateforme is GATIA. As the CMA established military dominance in Kidal in the mid-2010s, GATIA laid increasing claim to the Ménaka region; for Gamou's detractors in the CMA, the GATIA leader is simply interested in making money and setting himself up as an Imghad chief.[23] Whatever ag Gamou's motivations, it is interesting to observe how jihadists' decisions to relocate (see later) can be shaped by other actors' patterns of relocation – GATIA's turn from Kidal to Ménaka helped to provoke ISGS' growing investments in eastern Burkina Faso.

The MSA, which became GATIA's ally, was created in September 2016 as a dissident faction of the MNLA. The MSA's founder, Moussa ag Acharatoumane, had been a key MNLA spokesperson and intellectual, but he grew dissatisfied with the MNLA's direction after Serval. Ag Acharatoumane also had to adjust to GATIA's dominance in Ménaka starting in 2015.[24] The constituency for the MSA was ag

---

[23] Interview with Ahmada ag Bibi.
[24] Héni Nsaibia, "From the Mali-Niger Borderlands to Rural Gao – Tactical and Geographical Shifts of Violence," ACLED, June 6, 2018, www.acleddata.com/2018/06/06/from-the-mali-niger-borderlands-to-rural-gao-tactical-and-geographical-shifts-of-violence/.

Acharatoumane's Daoussahak/Idaksahak people, a Tuareg-adjacent pastoralist ethnic group centered in Ménaka. When leaving the MNLA (and the umbrella group the MNLA belongs to, the CMA), Ag Acharatoumane criticized the CMA as being unrepresentative of all of northern Mali, and of failing to protect northerners: "We have witnessed an increase in insecurity and the resurgence of fratricidal conflicts, yet the CMA is incapable of putting them to an end."[25] Less glamorously, as journalists noted, "The Daoussahak had little weight against the noble Ifoghas families who dominated the debates" within the CMA. Clashes between Ifoghas and Imghad Tuareg in Kidal in summer 2016 made ag Acharatoumane fear becoming a mere pawn of the Ifoghas.[26] Leaving the CMA, ag Acharatoumane and the MSA soon entered into an alliance with GATIA, whose leader, ag Gamou, was seeking to progressively chip away at the CMA's coalition by courting dissatisfied blocs.[27]

Daoussahak self-assertion through the MSA tapped into deeper tensions in Ménaka, reflecting prior Daoussahak conflicts with other ethnic groups in the region. As United Nations experts explained in a 2018 report, "Conflicts between the Daoussak and the Tuaregs, the Daoussak and the Iboguilitane [another ethnic/tribal group], and the Daoussak/Tuareg tribes and the Fulani [Peul] have been frequent in the Ménaka region for the past 30 years."[28] As discussed in Chapter 4, the 1990 Tuareg rebellion elevated intercommunal conflicts in various regions of Mali, including Ménaka. The spread of arms fostered cycles of violence.

Even as the MSA sought to become the vehicle for Daoussahak representation in Mali's militia politics, the Daoussahak were internally divided along clan/fraction lines. Ag Acharatoumane is "neither the son of traditional authority nor a fighter reputed for his feats of

---

[25] Rémi Carayol, "Mali – Moussa Ag Acharatoumane: 'Nous avons créé le MSA pour représenter tous les Azawadiens'," *Jeune Afrique*, September 8, 2016, www.jeuneafrique.com/355863/politique/mali-moussa-ag-acharatoumane-avons-cree-msa-representer-azawadiens/.

[26] Pierre Alonso and Célian Macé, "'Moussa', l'arme de Paris au Sahel," *Libération*, April 13, 2018, www.liberation.fr/planete/2018/04/13/moussa-l-arme-de-paris-au-sahel_1643338.

[27] Sandor, "Insecurity, the Breakdown of Social Trust, and Armed Actor Governance," 23–24.

[28] United Nations Panel of Experts on Mali, Final Report (August 2018), 17, https://reliefweb.int/sites/reliefweb.int/files/resources/N1823298.DOC.pdf.

arms, which in itself is a novelty in the world of Tuareg leaders."[29] Intellectual force, youthfulness, and cosmopolitanism made him a compelling spokesman for the MNLA, but these traits did not allow ag Acharatoumane to safeguard the unity of the MSA, an essentially ethnic and clan-based organization. In October 2017, the MSA experienced a mass resignation, with various Daoussahak clan leaders defecting to the High Council for the Unity of Azawad (HCUA), which is part of the ex-rebel CMA coalition.[30]

This dynamic also benefited ISGS, broadening its coalition from primarily Arabs and Peul to include Daoussahak. The same UN experts commented that "many Daoussaks are also known to be holding key military positions within [ISGS] leadership, such as its deputy leader, Al Mahmoud Ag Baye, also known as Ikaray; [and] Mohamed Ag Almouner, also known as Tinka."[31] Some Daoussahak clans may have begun to strategically place their members within ISGS as part of the wider field of militia politics in northern Mali. For example, ag Almouner belonged to the Idoguiritane clan within the Daoussahak,[32] as does Siguidi ag Madit, one of the most important leaders to defect from the MSA to the HCUA in October 2017.[33] In January 2018, ag Madit's son Mohamed was arrested on suspicions of collaborating with ISGS to attack GATIA.[34] Perhaps these were merely individual choices, but perhaps there was intra-clan coordination within the Idoguiritane in order to undermine the MSA and GATIA.

Daoussahak clan leaders did not all share ag Acharatoumane's assessment that ISGS was their enemy. Ag Madit, in a 2017 interview, had complained that ag Acharatoumane's strategy was going to destroy the Daoussahak.

We learned that he had engaged us, the Daoussahak, in a war against the Peul to help fight MUJWA [i.e., ISGS], while MUJWA was in a war against

[29] Alonso and Macé, "'Moussa', l'arme de Paris au Sahel."
[30] "Moussa Ag Acharatoumane: The Resignations Have 'No Impact on the MSA'."
[31] United Nations Panel of Experts on Mali, Final Report (August 2018), 17.
[32] MENASTREAM, "Mali: French Forces Killed ISGS Commander Involved in Tongo Tongo Ambush," August 27, 2018, http://menastream.com/mali-barkhane-isgs-menaka/.
[33] Acherif Ag Ismaguel, "Ménaka: Le MSA se désagrège," *Journal du Mali*, October 19, 2017, www.journaldumali.com/2017/10/19/menaka-msa-se-desagrege/.
[34] United Nations Panel of Experts on Mali, Final Report (August 2018), 19–20.

the foreign forces. If we put ourselves in MUJWA's path, they will chase us out of our land. MSA cannot do anything more against those people, it can no longer protect us.[35]

ISGS was both a cause and a beneficiary of the MSA's fragmentation – although, to make matters still more complicated, the MSA's remnants may have absorbed some of al-Sahrawi's former allies as this hyper-local series of realignments occurred.[36] The takeaway is that ISGS made itself a viable political–military vehicle for key actors within multiple ethnic groups in Ménaka. ISGS may have even, as one GATIA leader alleged, used figures such as ag Madit as "intermediaries" with more mainstream political factions.[37]

By 2017–2018, ISGS had at least three major ethnic components in addition to, and overlaying, its roots within MUJWA. There were elements of the Daoussahak. There were also Arabs, and in 2017 al-Sahrawi scored a major coup in absorbing the prominent Arab jihadist Sultan Ould Badi, a former MUJWA leader, and his Salaheddine Battalion. Ould Badi and al-Sahrawi found common cause in fighting GATIA and the MSA,[38] at least for a time. Then, in August 2018, Ould Badi surrendered to Algerian authorities in a context that remains opaque.[39] Meanwhile, ISGS' war with GATIA and the MSA was helping ISGS attract Peul support, a dynamic that I will revisit later.

GATIA and MSA had initially angered ISGS by helping French soldiers pursue and kill ISGS fighters after jihadists' cross-border attack into Niger in June 2017;[40] the previous month, GATIA's ag Gamou and MSA's ag Acharatoumane met with representatives of

---

[35] Ag Ismaguel, "Ménaka: Le MSA se désagrège."

[36] Sandor, "Insecurity, the Breakdown of Social Trust, and Armed Actor Governance," 19.

[37] Interview with Fahad ag Mohamed.

[38] MENASTREAM, "Video: Another Video Released by Katiba Salaheddine (ISGS) – 'Response to Aggression by MSA and GATIA'," June 30, 2018, http://menastream.com/katiba-salaheddine-response-to-aggression/.

[39] "Algérie: reddition du chef terroriste malien Sultan Ould Badi à Tamanrasset," RFI, August 13, 2018, www.rfi.fr/afrique/20180813-algerie-reddition-chef-terroriste-malien-sultan-ould-badi-tamanrasset.

[40] "Attaque meurtrière contre l'armée nigérienne près de la frontière malienne," RFI, June 1, 2017, www.rfi.fr/afrique/20170601-attaque-meurtriere-contre-armee-nigerienne-pres-frontiere-malienne; see also "Le chef jihadiste Al-Sahraoui accuse et menace deux communautés du Mali," RFI, June 27, 2017, www.rfi.fr/afrique/20170627-chef-jihadiste-al-sahraoui-accuse-menace-communautes-mali-imghad-idaksahak.

France's Operation Barkhane in Paris to discuss coordination against jihadists in Ménaka.[41] The ensuing months brought escalation. In October 2017, ISGS fighters ambushed a joint American-Nigerien patrol in the far western Nigerien village of Tongo-Tongo. The incident took the lives of four Nigerien soldiers, a Nigerien interpreter, and four American soldiers.[42] ISGS did not claim the attack until several months later,[43] but the incident had far-reaching effects. One was an intensification of French counterterrorism efforts in the subregion as Operation Barkhane tracked the perpetrators of the ambush.

To enhance its military and intelligence capabilities in Ménaka, Operation Barkhane turned to GATIA and the MSA. Between February and April 2018, the MSA and GATIA hunted ISGS, repeatedly declaring that they had killed ISGS fighters and destroyed ISGS camps.[44] Barkhane, according to a GATIA spokesman, "associated itself" with this operation. The campaign, the spokesman continued, achieved results that had eluded Barkhane for three years: "the Satanic State [a play on ISGS' name] was totally destroyed," with its remnants pushed into Mali's Gourma region, Niger, and elsewhere.[45] As the analyst Héni Nsaibia comments, "These operations ... resulted in the killings and arrests of a significant

---

[41] Jules Crétois, "Nord du Mali: Ag Gamou et Ag Acharatoumane en visite de travail à Paris," *Jeune Afrique*, May 24, 2017, www.jeuneafrique.com/441394/politique/nord-mali-ag-gamou-ag-acharatoumane-visite-de-travail-a-paris/.

[42] Rukmini Callimachi, Helene Cooper, Eric Schmitt, Alan Blinder, and Thomas Gibbons-Neff, "'An Endless War': Why 4 U.S. Soldiers Died in a Remote African Desert," *New York Times*, February 20, 2018, www.nytimes.com/interactive/2018/02/17/world/africa/niger-ambush-american-soldiers.html?mtrref=www.google.com.

[43] "'Tanzim al-Dawla' Yu'lin Mas'uliyyatahu 'an Hajamat Istahdafat Quwwat Amrikiyya wa-Faransiyya fi al-Nijar wa-Mali," Agence Nouakchott d'Information, January 12, 2018, http://ani.mr/?q=node/7245.

[44] See GATIA/MSA, "Communiqué Conjoint GATIA-MSA suite aux affrontements du 22 février 2018," February 22, 2018, www.msa-azawad.com/actualites/63-communiqu%C3%A9-conjoint-gatia-msa-suite-aux-affrontements-du-22-f%C3%A9vrier-2019.html; and "Mali: le récit exclusif de la traque de Abou Walid al-Sahraoui," *Jeune Afrique*, March 5, 2018, www.jeuneafrique.com/mag/538970/politique/mali-le-recit-exclusif-de-la-traque-de-abou-walid-al-sahraoui/?utm_source=Twitter&utm_medium=Articles&utm_term=Twitter&utm_content=Twitter&utm_campaign=Tweet.

[45] Interview with Fahad ag Mohamed.

number of militants, and seizures of arms, ammunition, vehicles, motorbikes, and other military equipment."[46]

The campaign prompted ISGS to recolate some of its forces into eastern Burkina Faso. As the Burkinabè analyst Mahamadou Savadogo wrote in April 2019, the collapse of security in eastern Burkina Faso correlated with ISGS' losses to Barkhane, GATIA, and MSA in Mali. Starting in early 2018, Savadogo wrote, ISGS had become "well established in the north[ern portion] of the East Region, straddling Niger and Burkina. It controls almost all the gold [mining] sites in the locality."[47]

ISGS' implantation in eastern Burkina Faso was not automatic or inevitable. Rather, the group reached accommodations with various members and levels of society in the region. These constituencies ranged from communities that felt marginalized on an ethnic basis; to artisanal gold miners frustrated over their exclusion and displacement by multinational corporations working hand-in-glove with Burkinabè authorities; to "the bearers of power," a segment of the customary chiefly establishment, particularly individuals frustrated at their inability to win power struggles within their own families.[48]

In eastern Burkina Faso, ISGS built a remarkably politically diverse coalition within a relatively short period, combining the bottom-up mobilization styles used effectively by Katibat Macina in central Mali (see Chapter 4) with a dose of the top-down incorporation of elites practiced by AQIM and then JNIM in northern Mali (see Chapter 3). As Ruth MacLean has commented, "The armed groups are painted as 'terrorists', and it is true they are backed by extremist groups. But in the east, where conflict is rising fastest, the groups are made up of ordinary Burkinabés taking up arms against a 'predatory' government seen as taking land and mineral wealth while offering nothing in return." Jihadists wielded both carrots and sticks against the population, offering "maize, medicine and money" but also cracking down on

---

[46] Héni Nsaibia, "Targeting of the Islamic State in the Greater Sahara (ISGS)," ACLED, March 21, 2018, www.acleddata.com/2018/03/21/targeting-of-the-islamic-state-in-the-greater-sahara-isgs/.

[47] Mahamadou Savadogo, "Note d'analyse sur la situation sécuritaire au Burkina Faso," unpublished analysis, April 2019, 2.

[48] Interview with Luc Damiba, Ouagadougou, June 15, 2019.

smoking, prostitution, alcohol, and music.[49] ISGS fueled a regional war economy: Locals reclaimed access to gold mining sites; alternative services, such as solar panels, flourished in the absence of state services; and ISGS paid new recruits while maintaining the salaries of compliant local functionaries who kept doing their jobs.[50] The jihadists also benefited from the wider economic devastation that they and other armed actors caused. As schools closed, tourism evaporated, transport worsened, and curfews slammed down,[51] the resulting slowdown in mainstream economic sectors positioned jihadists as an economic magnet in the emerging war economy.

Meanwhile, ISGS had not abandoned Ménaka, and the Barkhane/GATIA/MSA campaign there was hurting civilians, particularly the Peul. At an April 2018 press conference, a United Nations spokeswoman pointed to the "particular gravity" of allegations about human rights violations in Ménaka. The spokeswoman referenced "summary executions of at least ninety-five persons who were accused of terrorism and banditry and who were killed during operations conducted by a coalition of armed groups." She further mentioned "orders for forced displacements given to entire villages in view of relocating them and submitting them to the effective control of certain armed movements."[52] ISGS saw opportunity. By April 2018, ISGS was retaliating indirectly against MSA and GATIA. ISGS killed Daoussahak civilians in order "to target communities associated with the militias, to deter the militias, reduce their support, and demonstrate that the militias are unable to protect their communities."[53] Civilians, once again, were victims of both jihadist and anti-jihadist forces.[54]

---

[49] Ruth Maclean, "Kalashnikovs and No-Go Zones: East Burkina Faso Falls to Militants," *The Guardian*, April 22, 2019, www.theguardian.com/global-development/2019/apr/22/kalashnikovs-and-no-go-zones-east-burkina-faso-falls-to-militants.

[50] Ibid.

[51] Alassane Neya, "Attaques terroristes à l'Est du Burkina: À la rencontre d'une population courageuse," Sidwaya, March 25, 2019, www.sidwaya.info/carrefour/2019/03/25/attaques-terroristes-a-lest-du-burkina-a-la-rencontre-dune-population-courageuse/.

[52] Multi-Dimensional Integrated Stabilization Mission in Mali, "Point de presse de la MINUSMA du 12 Avril 2018," April 12, 2018, https://minusma.unmissions.org/point-de-presse-de-la-minusma-du-12-avril-2018.

[53] Nsaibia, "From the Mali-Niger Borderlands to Rural Gao."

[54] See Ibrahim Yahaya Ibrahim and Mollie Zapata, "Regions at Risk: Preventing Mass Atrocities in Mali," United States Holocaust Memorial Museum, April

These dynamics reinforced ISGS recruitment among Peul in the borderlands. Here, deeper histories involving the border came into play. In the 1970s, Nigerien Peul herders crossed to Mali "in search of greener pastures," but in the 1990s the Tuareg-led rebellions on both sides of the border led to repeated Tuareg attacks on Peul communities. After one 1997 massacre, "some Fulani herders escaped back to Niger and created the North Tillabéri Self-Defence Militia, sparking a cycle of retaliation" that lasted until the militia disbanded in 2011.[55]

The 2012 Tuareg-led rebellion in northern Mali reawakened Tuareg–Peul tensions in the borderlands. With the Peul feeling themselves on the defensive, ISGS' al-Sahrawi (then a part of MUJWA) had recruited some young fighters into his ranks, giving him a foothold among Peul communities in both Ménaka and Tillabéri. One prominent militant was Doundou Chefou, who participated in the ambush of the Nigerien and American soldiers at Tongo-Tongo.[56] Another was Aboubacar "Petit" Chapori, who became a key ISGS recruiter in Niger.[57] According to one interlocutor, ISGS recruited in these pastoralist communities by offering families protection so long as they would offer one of their sons as a recruit; ISGS did not present itself as the "Islamic State," a name that might have meant little to locals.[58] Offering firepower, mobility, and the strategic benefits found in operating from the shadows, ISGS cultivated a kind of political credibility among some communities in the borderlands.

Conflict dynamics in the borderlands reflect the nature of Niger's Tillabéri Region, Mali's Ménaka Region, and Burkina Faso's Sahel and East Regions as a "cross-border space." Ethnic communities extend over the borders of these three countries and "share the same

2018, 21–26, www.ushmm.org/m/pdfs/Mali_Report_English_FINAL_April_2018.pdf.

[55] Giacomo Zandonini and Francesco Bellina, "Niger, Part 3: Guns Won't Win the War," *The New Humanitarian*, April 15, 2019, www.thenewhumanitarian.org/special-report/2019/04/15/niger-part-3-guns-conflict-militancy.

[56] Tim Cocks and David Lewis, "Why Niger and Mali's Cattle Herders Turned to Jihad," Reuters, November 12, 2017, www.reuters.com/article/us-niger-mali-security-insight/why-niger-and-malis-cattle-herders-turned-to-jihad-idUSKBN1DC06A.

[57] Ruth Maclean, "Niger Islamic State Hostage: 'They Want to Kill Foreign Soldiers'," *The Guardian*, June 5, 2018, www.theguardian.com/world/2018/jun/05/hostage-niger-islamic-state-group-they-want-to-kill-foreign-soldiers.

[58] Interview with a journalist, 2019.

socio-economic, cultural, and religious practices."[59] Cooperation and conflict are unevenly distributed in these borderlands; one 2018 conflict map showed that hotspots in Tillabéri were often very near to hotspots in Ménaka and vice versa.[60] As ISGS recruited locally, it developed a growing ability to read these hyper-local variations in cross-border dynamics, enhancing its ability to cross the border in not just a physical but also a political sense.

These borderlands also suffer from endemic poverty. Tillabéri is a vulnerable and food insecure region – the northern part of the region, as one 2014 report by the Famine Early Warning Systems Network noted, is part of an "agropastoral belt" characterized by "frequent below average rainfall, imbalanced agropastoralism, [and] heavy dependency on assistance."[61] The same report noted that in Niger, "the highest levels of poverty [are] located in some of the most agriculturally productive regions of the country (Dosso, Maradi, Tillaberi), where decreasing land holdings from overcrowding, high variation in seasonal rainfall, and market sensitivity pose additional vulnerability."[62] Tillabéri had the highest incidence of poverty (68.9 percent) in Niger.[63]

As in other conflict zones studied in this book, Tillabéri has seen the provocative dynamic where pastoralists seek to extend their grazing zones southward even as farmers seek to extend their zones of cultivation northward.[64] The resulting conflicts, several experts insist, are not merely farmer–herder violence but rather a multi-faceted competition between actors seeking access to water and land while at the same time diversifying their economic activities into new commercial spheres and thereby engendering new forms of competition.[65] Meanwhile, some Tuareg and Peul pastoralists feel that the state discriminates against them on an ethnic, cultural, and economic basis, and that carrying

---

[59] Djontu and Gatelier, "Nord-Tillabéri," 24.

[60] Cluster Protection Niger, "NIGER: Localités affectées par le conflict inter-communautaire dans la région de Tillabéri," May 19, 2018, https://reliefweb.int/sites/reliefweb.int/files/resources/ner_tillaberi_conflit_communautaire_19_mai_2018.pdf.

[61] Famine Early Warning Systems Network, "Niger Food Security Brief," May 2014, 14, http://fews.net/sites/default/files/documents/reports/Niger_Food_Security_Brief_Final.pdf.

[62] Ibid., 29.   [63] Ibid., 30.   [64] Djontu and Gatelier, "Nord-Tillabéri," 48.

[65] Ibid., 43.

weapons is the only way to elicit respect.[66] These factors indirectly facilitated ISGS' recruitment in the borderlands.

ISGS, Part Three: Finding a Niche in a Competitive Environment

Intercommunal conflicts in the borderlands provided ISGS with opportunities to recruit. Yet the group also faced constraints. One was something of a saturation of jihadism in the area. ISGS did not have the military strength – or the political strength – of AQIM or of AQIM's Mali-centric coalition structure, Jama'at Nusrat al-Islam wa-l-Muslimin (The Group for Supporting Islam and Muslims, JNIM). One reason ISGS may have ended up so far east within Mali was not just its roots in MUJWA's period of control over Gao but also the fact that more powerful jihadist actors lay to the west.[67] As of late 2017, some analysts estimated that ISGS had only around eighty fighters.[68]

The thick presence of proximate jihadist organizations helped make ISGS prone to cooperate, for a time, with its ostensible rivals. The global competition between the Islamic State and al-Qa'ida became muted at the hyper-local level in the central Sahel. Already by 2017, ISGS and JNIM may have had a formal liaison.[69] By early 2019, ISGS and JNIM appeared to be coordinating to fight GATIA and MSA in Ménaka: "JNIM and ISGS are increasingly melting together in order to consolidate ranks, sharing objectives and adversaries."[70] As discussed in Chapter 2, AQIM has consistently left a door open for breakaway factions to reintegrate. For ISGS, cooperating with AQIM and JNIM brought additional firepower to bear against key enemies, while avoiding a scenario – at least for a time – where ISGS would have to fight JNIM itself.

In Mali and Niger, ISGS thus specialized in the hit-and-run operations that are common to other small jihadist and terrorist organizations,

---

[66] Ibid., 66.

[67] A 2019 map of the jihadist presence in the Sahel, designed by Andrew Lebovich, helps to make this point visually. See "Mapping Armed Groups in Mali and the Sahel," European Council on Foreign Relations, May 2019, www.ecfr.eu/mena/sahel_mapping.

[68] Cocks and Lewis, "Why Niger and Mali's Cattle Herders Turned to Jihad."

[69] United Nations Panel of Experts on Mali, Final Report (August 2018), 20–21.

[70] MENASTREAM, "Mali: Complex Attack against French Forces in Menaka," March 11, 2019, http://menastream.com/mali-complex-attack-against-french-forces-in-menaka/.

rather than attempting to control territory. Some of ISGS' most prominent attacks, in addition to the 2017 ambush at Tongo-Tongo, include the October 2016 kidnapping of American missionary Jeffrey Woodke in Abalak (Tahoua Region, Niger), as well as a second ambush at Tongo-Tongo in May 2019 that killed upwards of thirty Nigerien soldiers. In the classical sense of terrorism as an effort by weak parties to have an outsized impact on politics, such attacks drew disproportionate national and international attention to ISGS, providing invaluable propaganda opportunities. In 2019, the Islamic State's central leadership took increasing notice of ISGS, highlighting their activities in its weekly *al-Naba'* newsletter.[71] But within Mali, ISGS had nothing like the political sway that JNIM sometimes reached in regional capitals such as Kidal and Timbuktu; ISGS was at the periphery of the periphery.

Ironically, it was not just the crowded jihadist field but also the crowding in of foreign forces that benefited ISGS. In Niger's Tillabéri and Tahoua regions, ISGS attacks evoked a growing security presence. This presence added to the pressure ISGS was under but also gave ISGS new opportunities to work with civilians; the escalating presence of both jihadists and security forces in Tillabéri made civilian life there extremely complicated. Consider the behavior of Tongo-Tongo's chief, Mounkaila Alassane, before, during, and after the ISGS attack on the Nigerien-American patrol in October 2017. During their time in the village, the patrol became suspicious that Alassane was deliberately seeking to delay their departure from Tongo-Tongo. The mayor reportedly asked the patrol for medicine for the village's children, and he insisted that the soldiers stay to eat a slaughtered sheep.[72]

Yet after the battle between ISGS and the Nigerien-American patrol began, Alassane reportedly began "calling everyone he could think of for help: the governor, the local prefect, and the commander of the military base in Ouallam, about an hour's drive away. He also called his local member of parliament, Karimou Yacouba, whose home

---

[71] See Islamic State, "Ba'd al-Hujum 'ala Ashadd al-Sujun Harasa fi al-Nijar," *Al-Naba'* 182 (May 16, 2019): 9, https://jihadology.net/wp-content/uploads/_pda/2019/05/The-Islamic-State-al-Nabā'-Newsletter-182.pdf.

[72] Callimachi et al., "An Endless War."

village is about 7km from Tongo Tongo. Yacouba said the first call came just after the attack began at about 10am."[73]

Following the attack, Alassane was arrested on charges of deliberately stalling the patrol's departure from the village in order to give ISGS time to organize its attack; phone numbers of ISGS contacts were found in his telephone.[74] After authorities found no other evidence of complicity, they released him. Afterwards, he spoke frankly to the *Washington Post* about his interactions with jihadists:

The government can't protect us. That's why we collaborate with the jihadists … This is a very dangerous place. When we need protection, we call on the jihadists. This is how we survive here … They threatened me. If I don't cooperate with them, they will kill me and my family. I have no choice – I have to cooperate with them.[75]

For civilians, counterterrorism campaigns are not the black and white struggles that Washington and Paris make them out to be. As both jihadists and foreign militaries push civilians to choose a side, civilians may respond by courting multiple sides simultaneously, or by playing the sides against each other.

For one perspective, let us return to the rebel-turned-politician Mohamed Anacko. In a 2015 interview, Anacko was asked about Operation Barkhane. He replied:

First of all, I should say that if Barkhane had not been there, the last Nigerien lock would have been forced open during the war in Mali. The national army would not have been able to prevent the terrorists from coming to set up shop in the north. But it is true that from the start, Barkhane suffered from a lack of communication. When you send helicopters and planes into the desert, without having created an information mechanism, you should expect that the populations will see a new form of colonialism in it … The inhabitants do not understand that Barkhane only takes action against certain armed groups. There are gangs, coming from Chad or Sudan for

---

[73] Ruth Maclean, "A Swarm of Motorbikes, Then Heavy Fire: Witnesses Shed New Light on Niger Attack," *The Guardian*, November 15, 2017, www .theguardian.com/world/2017/nov/15/niger-us-troops-military-ambush-attack.

[74] Callimachi et al., "'An Endless War'."

[75] Sudarsan Raghavan, "In the Area Where U.S. Soldiers Died in Niger, Islamist Extremists Have Deep Roots," *The Washington Post*, November 20, 2017, www.washingtonpost.com/world/africa/in-the-area-where-us-soldiers-died-in-niger-islamist-extremists-have-deep-roots/2017/11/20/6a892130-c66f-11e7-9922-4151f5ca6168_story.html?utm_term=.ba534f5fb9c4.

example, that practice looting, particularly since gold panning became important. But Barkhane, because that is not its mission, does not take an interest in them. Neither do the Nigerien security forces, moreover. However, these are the persons who create conditions propitious for the installation of terrorism. The risk is that the population will create militias to defend itself. What's more, the struggle against terrorism, it's first of all about intelligence. There must be collaboration with the inhabitants, who know the region. If not, Barkhane will have to content itself with doing tourism in the desert.[76]

Here we see the intersection of key questions in Niger's borderlands: Who is a threat? Who is a terrorist? Who is a bandit? What are the priorities of each actor in the zone, where do their priorities diverge, and what misunderstandings result? Western counterterrorism operators, pursuing those defined as "terrorists," ignore the most pressing security threats from the vantage of the civilian population. Civilians, with their security concerns unaddressed, question the stated intentions of the foreigners. National governments, attempting to leverage their Western donors' concerns in order to enhance their own prospects for survival and success, de-prioritize civilians' quotidian security concerns. And so the very counterterrorism measures that are meant to improve security and heighten the national government's legitimacy can end up sowing suspicions and mistrust, setting the stage for further insecurity.

In this atmosphere, the border remained a strategic resource for ISGS. Their enemies made increasing efforts to promote border security and cross-border military cooperation in the Sahel, especially through the G5 Sahel Joint Force. Yet ISGS could take advantage of its ability to cross borders in ways that Sahelian and Western forces could not do quite as easily. One cause of the first Tongo-Tongo ambush was that American forces became overextended by trying to track ISGS out of Niger and into Mali, and then the American-Nigerien patrol was fatigued and exposed as they moved back into Niger.

Cross-border displacement caused further chaos for civilians, which could also benefit ISGS. In July 2018, a report on the humanitarian

---

[76] Mathieu Olivier, "Mohamed Anacko, (PCR d'Agadez): 'Le Mali va au devant d'un danger qu'il n'a jamais connu auparavant'," *Jeune Afrique*, September 22, 2015, www.jeuneafrique.com/258645/politique/mohamed-anacko-gouverneur-dagadez-le-mali-va-au-devant-dun-danger-quil-na-jamais-connu-auparavant/.

situation in Tillabéri commented, "The Nigeriens coming from Mali following the ongoing conflict are indexed as being complicit with the armed elements, the former fighters, which renders their integration into the community difficult."[77] The same report suggested that ISGS had relative freedom of movement across the border and on either side of it, and that various armed groups could simply adjust to whatever new patrols and operations the militaries of Mali, Niger, and Burkina Faso introduced:

Joint cross-border military operations conducted by military special forces from the Nigerien and Malian armies between Mali and Niger led to the withdrawal of elements of armed groups toward certain localities in the north of Tillabéri ... According to the community, the current rainy reason could favor the reorganization and installation of new bases for armed groups in the localities that are not habited and are little covered by the military patrols ... Certain routes are very insecure for the populations because many movements of armed men are observed (raids, livestock thefts, threats against the population, stocking of fuel).[78]

Sahelian militaries, with their limited capacity, could only achieve so much at the peripheries. Competing with jihadists for control, they sometimes unwittingly aided jihadist recruitment and momentum. And across the border in Burkina Faso, the problems were even worse.

Burkina Faso: Ansaroul Islam and Escalating Insecurity at the Peripheries

Burkina Faso was a target of AQIM long before homegrown jihadists emerged. It was AQIM and JNIM that perpetrated the major terrorist attacks in Burkina Faso's capital Ouagadougou, such as the January 2016 murders at the Splendid Hotel and a nearby café, and the March 2018 assault on the Burkinabè military headquarters and the French embassy. AQIM and JNIM depicted these events as part of the larger war in the Sahel. The January 2016 attacks were meant, AQIM explained, to disrupt the global "war on Islam."[79] And the March

---

[77] Cluster Protection Niger, "Rapport d'analyse mensuelle des données du monitoring de protection," July 2018, 14, https://reliefweb.int/sites/reliefweb .int/files/resources/rapport_monitoring_protection_tillaberi_juillet_2018.pdf.

[78] Ibid., 2.

[79] Al-Qa'ida in the Islamic Maghreb, "Bayan Hawla 'Ghazwat Burkina Fasu'," January 17, 2016, 1, available at https://jihadology.net/wp-content/uploads/_pda/

2018 attacks, a JNIM statement said, came as revenge for a French raid in Mali that had killed prominent jihadists, as well as to "deter the Burkinabè regime and the regimes of the countries that rushed to join the G5 operation."[80]

But Burkina Faso soon became more than just an extension of the AQIM/JNIM regional war. In December 2016, a group called Ansaroul Islam emerged. Ansaroul Islam was led by a Peul Salafi preacher, Ibrahim Dicko. From the vicinity of Soboulé, in the Soum Province of northern Burkina Faso, Dicko began preaching around 2009. He founded an Islamic charitable and preaching association, Al Irchad (Al-Irshad, "Guidance"), which received government recognition in 2012. Dicko found a platform on local radio, delivering strident preaching. Dicko and Al Irchad, however, also encountered resistance from traditionalist clerics, Sufi orders, and hereditary ruling families in Soum, who objected to the content of Dicko's preaching and to Al Irchad's efforts to build a network of mosques.[81] According to some observers, Dicko's public speeches were much more political than religious in the beginning: He focused on telling people in Soum that the central state had forgotten and abandoned them.[82] Dicko also benefited from the social changes wrought by several decades of non-violent Salafi organizing in northern Burkina Faso, which had attracted youth not just with religious messages but also with the "possibility of freeing oneself" through participation in Salafi commercial networks, reduced costs of marriages, and the internal solidarities that Salafi communities fostered.[83] Only a fraction of the region's Salafis joined Ansaroul Islam, but Dicko was able to tap into existing infrastructures and networks.

2016/01/al-qacc84_idah-in-the-islamic-maghrib-22about-the-raid-of-burkina-faso-when-it-avenges-african-muslim-victims22.pdf.

[80] Jama'at Nusrat al-Islam wa-l-Muslimin, "Bayan Tabannin li-l-Ghazwa al-Mubaraka 'ala al-Sifara al-Faransiyya wa-Mabna Hay'at al-Arkan al-Burkini," March 3, 2017 [sic], 2, available https://jihadology.net/wp-content/uploads/_pda/2018/03/jamacc84_at-nuscca3rat-al-islacc84m-wa-l-muslimicc84n-22adopting-the-blessed-raid-upon-the-french-embassy-and-chief-of-staff-headquarters-of-burkina-fasos-armed-forces22.pdf.

[81] International Crisis Group, "The Social Roots of Jihadist Violence in Burkina Faso's North," October 12, 2017, 3, https://d2071andvip0wj.cloudfront.net/254-the-social-roots-of-jihadist-violence-in-burkina-faso-s-north.pdf.

[82] Interview with Abdoulaye Diallo, Ouagadougou, June 14, 2019.

[83] Interview with Koudbi Kaboré, Ouagadougou, June 11, 2019.

Meanwhile, Dicko was developing ties to Iyad ag Ghali and Amadou Kouffa. In late 2013, French forces reportedly arrested Dicko near Tessalit in the far northern Malian Sahara. Released in 2015, Dicko returned to Soum.[84] He still enjoyed some mainstream credibility – he was married to a daughter of the grand imam of Djibo, one of Soum's larger towns – but in early 2016 both the imam and Djibo's emir "disowned him." Dicko and his hardcore followers then headed to Mali for training,[85] and divisions grew within Al Irchad over the future of the network.[86]

The rise of Kouffa's forces across the border, in central Mali, provided crucial opportunities for Dicko when his own group turned to violence. Soum borders the Malian administrative *cercle* of Douentza. As discussed in Chapter 4, that *cercle* had been affected by the northern Malian rebellion of 2012 and had been partly controlled by MUJWA. Kouffa's absorption of some former Peul fighters from MUJWA created "links with the Peul communities of Niger and Burkina Faso."[87] After Kouffa's jihad began in 2015, jihadist violence spread into Douentza once again. The possibility of crossing back and forth across the border, and into relatively friendly territory, contributed to Ansaroul Islam's initial rise. In December 2016, the first attack by Dicko's Ansaroul Islam targeted a military post in Nassoumbou, Soum Province, killing twelve soldiers. Nassoumbou is roughly thirty kilometers from the border with Mali. Dicko's "followers regularly move from one side to the other of the border between Burkina and Mali, where the assailants on the Nassoumbou camp withdrew after their attack."[88] Dicko may have had help from other jihadist elements in the vicinity, including ex-MUJWA as well as the southern battalions of ag

---

[84] Benjamin Roger, "Qui est l'imam Ibrahim Dicko, la nouvelle terreur du nord du Burkina?" *Jeune Afrique*, January 9, 2017, www.jeuneafrique.com/390558/ politique/limam-ibrahim-dicko-nouvelle-terreur-nord-burkina/.

[85] International Crisis Group, "Social Roots of Jihadist Violence," 4.

[86] Morgane Le Cam, "Comment est né Ansaroul Islam, premier groupe djihadiste de l'Histoire du Burkina Faso," *Le Monde*, April 11, 2017, www.lemonde.fr/ afrique/article/2017/04/11/comment-est-ne-ansaroul-islam-premier-groupe-djihadiste-de-l-histoire-du-burkina-faso_5109520_3212.html. Le Cam has a somewhat different chronology of events than do other sources – she writes that Dicko was arrested in Mali in September 2015 and held there until mid-2016.

[87] Adam Thiam, "Centre du Mali: Enjeux et dangers d'une crise négligée," Humanitarian Dialogue, March 2017, 45, www.hdcentre.org/wp-content/ uploads/2017/03/Centre-du-Mali-Enjeux-et-dangers-dune-crise-négligée.pdf.

[88] Roger, "Qui est l'imam Ibrahim Dicko."

Ghali's Ansar al-Din.[89] Ansaroul Islam's initial success partly reflected its embeddedness in ethnic, social, and jihadist networks on both sides of the Mali-Burkina Faso border.

Ansaroul Islam was not merely an extension of Kouffa's project. Much of the violence that began in late 2016 was hyper-local. Ansaroul Islam settled scores, assassinating rival imams and former Al Irchad members, accusing them of collaboration with the security services.[90] In 2017, Ansaroul Islam began "punishing teachers who had received benefits from Al-Irchad but refused to support the group's evolution into an armed insurgency."[91] Ansaroul Islam's field of vision was primarily local – and as the violence escalated, dynamics discussed in previous chapters set in, with Ansaroul Islam targeting local village authorities, whom the jihadists denounced as collaborators of the authorities. Many of the victims were known personally to their assailants.[92]

Ansaroul Islam's social base reflected resentment against what International Crisis Group has called "an ossified and unequal social order" in northern Burkina Faso. Directing his ire at hereditary religious leaders and chiefs, Dicko denounced what he saw as financial corruption among local office-holders, who in his view used imam-ships and chieftancies to extort money from ordinary people.[93] Dicko, although a member of the "nobility" himself,[94] called for equality between different social categories in Peul and northern society, decrying the subordinate position of Rimaybé or former slaves.[95] Dicko exploited multiple cleavages within Soum – Salafis versus Sufis, newly empowered artisanal and former slave constituencies contesting the power of the traditional ethnic elites, and so forth.

---

[89] MENASTREAM, "Burkina Faso: The Jihadist Threat Continuously Rising in the Far North – A New Ansar Dine Branch in Gestation, Ansaroul Islam?" January 3, 2017, http://menastream.com/burkina-faso-jihadist-threat-north/.

[90] International Crisis Group, "Social Roots of Jihadist Violence," 4; MENASTREAM, "Burkina Faso: The Jihadist Threat"; Human Rights Watch, "'By Day We Fear the Army, By Night the Jihadists': Abuses by Armed Islamists and Security Forces in Burkina Faso," May 2018, 14–15, www.hrw.org/sites/default/files/report_pdf/burkinafaso0518_web2.pdf.

[91] Human Rights Watch, "'By Day We Fear the Army'," 23.   [92] Ibid., 13–20.

[93] International Crisis Group, "Social Roots of Jihadist Violence," 4–5.

[94] Interview with Koudbi Kaboré.

[95] Le Cam, "Comment est né Ansaroul Islam."

Other factors came into play as well. Amid widespread immerisation, jihadists were distinguished by their ability to pay their recruits. Even this is not the end of the story – "even so," as one Burkinabè historian told me, "Malam Dicko was not miserable" himself. Beyond the financial appeal of Ansaroul Islam, Dicko also tapped into a widespread "feeling of frustration, humiliation, and hatred of the West" – a sense that the West had coopted Burkina Faso's leaders while imposing its culture to the detriment of local values.[96]

What is known of Dicko's coalition, and of JNIM's presence in northern Burkina Faso, indicates that the jihadist presence had several primary components. There is the aforementioned, partially socioethnic and partially economic mobilization of segments of Peul communities. Sometimes, jihadist attacks in the north seem to target non-Peul zones on a partly ethnic basis. For example, there have been repeated attacks in the zone around the town of Arbinda, inhabited by the Gouroumba ethnic group who are seen by jihadists as collaborators of the state and as "an ethnic category that resists Islam."[97] Then there appears to be a component consisting of bandits and traffickers, groups that "were controlling the grey economy in the Sahel [Region of Burkina] well before the arrival of JNIM. Developing on the same terrain, JNIM and these small groups, which were subsequently radicalized, have seen an interest in collaborating. Thus, these groups can peacefully continue their traffic and criminal activities under JNIM's protection and above all with its logistical and technical support."[98]

In spring 2017, Ibrahim Dicko was reported killed. Leadership of Ansaroul Islam passed to his brother Jafar. Meanwhile, hints of cooperation between Ansaroul Islam and al-Sahrawi's ISGS appeared. Even during Ibrahim Dicko's lifetime, there were rumors that he planned to pledge allegiance to the Islamic State; more important than the question of global affiliations, however, was the ability of different jihadist factions to cooperate locally. As discussed previously, the small but ambitious ISGS had incentives to maintain friendly relations with nearby jihadists, and JNIM did not seem to discourage cooperation between Ansaroul Islam and ISGS. In eastern Burkina Faso, ISGS seems to have developed a working relationship with Ansaroul Islam

---

[96] Interview with a Burkinabè historian, Ouagadougou, June 13, 2019.
[97] Interview with Koudbi Kaboré.   [98] Savadogo, "Note d'analyse," 1.

as it carved out a zone of operations and sway.[99] In April 2019, *The Guardian*'s Ruth Maclean reported, "Much of the east has been carved up under several local leaders, allied with Ansarul Islam, [ISGS], and [JNIM]. There appears to be no conflict between the factions."[100]

Cooperation was not the only factor in this success, of course. There was also the absence of the state. But this absence was not simply due to the inertia of state weakness but also due to conscious strategies and avoidances that Sahelian states choose. Ansaroul Islam, ISGS, and other jihadists thrived in Burkina Faso partly because authorities made a strategic decision to cede the peripheries to them and to various community-based militias.

State Policies toward Jihadism in Niger and Burkina Faso

In the 2010s, the political trajectories of Niger and Burkina Faso have had both contrasts and parallels. In Niger, the decade opened with a military coup against civilian President Mamadou Tandja, who had taken office in 1999. Tandja's ouster came after he engineered a referendum that allowed him to stay in the presidency beyond his constitutionally mandated two-term limit. The military stepped in, as it had amid Niger's earlier round of democratic experimentation in the 1990s. After fourteen months in power, the junta stepped aside in April 2011 in favor of newly elected civilian President Mahamadou Issoufou, who won reelection in 2016 and remains in office at the time of writing.

Burkina Faso witnessed a dramatic October 2014 revolution that overthrew the dictator Blaise Compaoré, who had taken office in a 1987 coup. As in Niger, the issue at stake in the ousting of Compaoré was term limits; having manipulated the quasi-democratic opening and the largely uncompetitive elections of the 1990s and early 2000s to his advantage, Compaoré faced unprecedented resistance when his supporters attempted to lift term limits in advance of the 2015 elections. The protesters in 2014 evoked memories and grievances that dated back to the murder of Compaoré's predecessor, the leftist revolutionary Thomas Sankara, as well as the disappearance of the investigative

[99] Héni Nsaibia, "The Fledgling Insurgency in Burkina's East," ACLED, September 20, 2018, www.acleddata.com/2018/09/20/the-fledgling-insurgency-in-burkinas-east/.
[100] Maclean, "Kalashnikovs and No-Go Zones."

journalist Norbert Zongo in 1998; the protesters also built on waves of demonstrations and mutinies that had occurred in 2008 and 2011. In the charged atmosphere of October 2014, protesters' destruction of the National Assembly building prevented a vote on term limits and prompted a segment of the military to declare an end to Compaoré's reign. A transitional civilian government soon took over, followed by elections in November 2015 and the inauguration of civilian President Roch Kaboré.[101]

If Niger has a longer democratic pedigree than does Burkina Faso, the political classes of the two countries nevertheless share marked similarities – similarities common to politicians across the Sahel. In Niger, Burkina Faso, and beyond, the leading opposition figures are often the incumbents of yesteryear; both Issoufou and Kaboré served as prime ministers, from 1993–1994 and 1994–1996, respectively; Kaboré did not leave Compaoré's ruling party until early 2014. The relative staleness of the Sahelian political class may contribute, indirectly, to the rise of jihadism, banditry, and intercommunal violence in the region. As Dan Eizenga has commented, the continued dominance of the same politicians "has led to political systems which are unable to effectively address the socio-political grievances of Sahelian citizens and allows for the perpetuation of the violence in the region and a growing disillusionment that typifies much of Sahelian politics today."[102]

Political turbulence alone, however, does not predict how jihadists will fare in particular countries, nor does it predict how states will respond to jihadists. Despite Niger's earlier turmoil, since 2011–2012 the country has enjoyed a reputation – exaggerated, but consequential – as an "island of stability" in a difficult neighborhood, a foil to the chaos in its neighbors Mali, Nigeria, and Libya.[103] Yet the problems of those countries affect Niger and give it a unique position in the region,

---

[101] For a masterful history of the revolution see Ernest Harsch, *Burkina Faso: A History of Power, Protest, and Revolution* (London: Zed Books, 2017).

[102] Dan Eizenga, "The Deteriorating Security Situation in Burkina Faso," *Bulletin FrancoPaix* 4:3 (March 2019): 1–5, 1, https://dandurand.uqam.ca/wp-content/uploads/2019/04/Bulletin-FrancoPaix-vol-4_no-3_EN.pdf.

[103] For an analysis of how Nigerien officials self-consciously deploy the phrase "island of stability," see Ibrahim Yahaya Ibrahim, "Niger in the Face of the Sahelo-Saharan Islamic Insurgency: Precarious Stability in a Troubled Neighborhood," Sahel Research Group Working Paper 4 (August 2014), 2, fn. 1, https://sites.clas.ufl.edu/sahelresearch/files/Yahya_NigerStakes_Final.pdf.

as a conduit for the ambitions of all sides in the region's multifaceted conflicts. AQIM and its offshoots have periodically targeted Niger, most brutally in the May 2013 attacks in Arlit and Agadez. Niger has faced even more deadly assaults from the Nigeria-born jihadist movement Boko Haram, which has conducted over 200 attacks on Niger's southeastern Diffa region since early 2015.[104] Yet Niger has not been the site of any attempted jihadist emirate-building project, as have Mali, Nigeria, and Libya. Jihadists have often looked to western Niger not as a site of operations, but as a passageway or a zone for intermittent spectacular attacks.

The American and French militaries have also given Niger a central place in their Sahelian security architecture. In contrast to France's major combat operations in Mali and in contrast to the French and American airstrikes and raids in Libya, Niger has not been treated as an ongoing combat zone or a recipient of frequent "kinetic" actions. Rather, the United States and France use Niger as a platform from which to mount surveillance and make the country a node in several regional counterterrorism projects.

In terms of state policies toward jihadism, a strain of pragmatism and even cynicism runs through both Niamey and Ouagadougou. This cynicism is shaped by senior politicians' long experience. Particularly in Niger, many politicians have seen multiple rebellions come and go. Like Mali, Niger has witnessed its own cycle of uprisings in the north, including rebellions led by Tuareg. Two major Nigerien Tuareg-led rebellions ran roughly concurrently with their Malian equivalents: the uprising of 1990–1995 and that of 2007–2009.

In the latter rebellion, the Mouvement des Nigériens pour la justice (Movement of Nigeriens for Justice, MNJ) presented deeply political demands: "There is no work, no schools, not even drinking water in all Niger. It's terrible, it's a genocide, and the government is corrupt, taking money from people and leaving them to live in poverty," a spokesman said in 2007.[105] In its manifesto, the MNJ excoriated

[104] United Nations Office for the Coordination of Humanitarian Affairs, "Niger – Diffa: Access, Insecurity and Population Movement," August 2017, https://reliefweb.int/sites/reliefweb.int/files/resources/NER_ENG_Diffa_Access_Insecurity_Displacements_%20300817.pdf.

[105] "New Touareg Rebel Group Speaks Out," The New Humanitarian, May 17, 2007, www.irinnews.org/report/72223/niger-new-touareg-rebel-group-speaks-out.

Niger's political and economic status quo, denouncing political parties for their schemes to "share the cake" while leaving Niger's population impoverished and desperate.[106]

Yet the government tended to dismiss rebels as mere bandits. For example, Nigerien Colonel Lawel Chekou Koré published a book in 2010 on the MNJ's rebellion. While acknowledging that the rebellion had multiple causes, Koré spotlighted what he saw as the rent-seeking, personal ambition, and outright banditry of rebels.

One observes that for the leaders of fronts of armed resistance, the fight loses its ideological character and becomes a way to satisfy personal ambitions. The fighters, as for them, conduct themselves with the population as armed bandits – all matters that have a tendency to transform this fratricidal war into [a source of] funds for commerce.[107]

The MNJ and the Nigerien government not only questioned each other's sincerity but they also accused each other of involvement in narcotrafficking. Koré wrote, "According to the Nigerien government, there is the insertion of the rebellion into mafia circuits of the traffic in arms and drugs across the Sahara. The objective of the rebellion is to control the north of the country, and to leave the field open to narco-traffickers."[108] In this telling, the MNJ's call for "justice" was mere rhetoric, as were the group's calls for a broader sharing of uranium revenues – behind the scenes, Koré contended, the real economic spoils were those of the illicit economy. The MNJ did not hesitate to throw these charges back in the face of the Nigerien government. In 2007, an MNJ spokesman averred, "There are traffickers and they work with the government and the presidency. The Sahara is being turned into a transit route by them, we don't have the means to do it."[109] Even before the rise of jihadism in Niger's peripheries, the state and its enemies were both suggesting that illicit economies, patterns of collusion, and political ambiguity were constituent features of the conflict landscape. The rise of jihadism and narcotrafficking has only

---

[106] Mouvement des Nigériens pour la Justice, "Programme des revendications du Mouvement des Nigériens pour la Justice (M.N.J)," undated, 4, www.ipacc.org .za/en/2007/14-mnj-niger-manifesto/file.html.

[107] Lawel Chekou Koré, *La rébellion touareg au Niger: Raisons de persistance et tentatives de solution* (Paris: L'Harmattan, 2010), 25.

[108] Ibid., 31.   [109] "New Touareg Rebel Group Speaks Out."

made Nigerien politics more tangled. After the events of 2012 in northern Mali, telling who was who became even harder.

By the time ISGS appeared in the Mali–Niger borderlands, official statements sometimes frankly acknowledged that Nigerien authorities could not identify the perpetrators of some violence. There is a corresponding frankness regarding the difficulty of categorizing such perpetrators. After an October 2016 attack by unknown gunmen on a refugee camp in Tazalit, a western border area, Niger's Defense Minister Hassoumi Massaoudou said:

> This attack was perpetrated by narco-terrorists coming from northern Mali, probably from the zone of Kidal and Tin Zaouaten, who attacked isolated groups of our defense and security forces. Clearly these are heavy losses, but we will take the necessary measures so that this costs them dearly ... The armed groups of northern Mali are a continuum between terrorist groups, the armed groups who sometimes participate in the Algiers [peace] process, and the groups of traffickers, narco-traffickers. So, there is not a distinction between these different groups: Ansar Dine, AQIM, HCUA, and narco-traffickers. In reality, they go from one status to the other. We have pursued them, [but] they entered Malian territory. We are going to make sure that it will cost them more and more dearly to carry out this kind of attack against our country, against our soldiers.[110]

In Massaoudou's view, Malian malefactors exploited not just the permeable physical border between Mali and Niger but also the permeable political borders between local jihadism (Ansar al-Din), regional/transnational jihadism (AQIM), political actors accorded legitimacy by the Malian government and the West (the HCUA), and drug dealers. There is some merit to Massaoudou's assessment: A feature of northern Malian politics since the 1990s, and with accelerating force since 2011, has been the propensity of actors to shift affiliations and in the process shift identities. Nigerien President Mahamadou Issoufou has characterized the situation in vaguer but essentially similar terms, saying in an August 2019 interview, "Kidal is a sanctuary for the terrorists, and those who attack us often withdraw

---

[110] "Niger: l'attaque de Tazalit menée par des 'groupes de narcoterroristes'," RFI, October 7, 2016, www.rfi.fr/afrique/20161007-niger-attaque-tazalit-perpetree-groupes-narcoterrorites-nord-mali.

there. Kidal is a threat for Niger and it is absolutely necessary that the Malian state reclaim its rights."[111]

Partly because of their view that jihadists were sometimes little different than rebels, bandits, or narcotraffickers, Nigerien authorities were initially willing to explore a truce with ISGS. In 2018, then-Interior Minister Mohamed Bazoum bluntly told *The Guardian*'s Maclean that he had tried to negotiate with al-Sahrawi:

When Bazoum took the interior minister job [in 2016], he sent emissaries to ask what they wanted.

"I said 'listen, if you have political claims, or problems with the justice, the administration, the state, then tell me … We are ready to discuss your problem with you and resolve it. Declare that you're a rebel front with specific claims on the Nigerien state'."

In contrast to Western governments' anathemization of jihadists, Bazoum wanted ISGS to accommodate itself to older patterns of government–rebel interaction. Maclean's account continues:

He said he received a handwritten letter from Sahraoui himself, which said: "No, we have no problem with you; we are waging jihad against Mali."

According to Bazoum, the letter contained a list of Sahraoui's comrades in Nigerien jails, whom he wanted released. If they were freed, ISGS promised to shield Niger from attack.

"I freed some of them to show my good will, but I couldn't free all of them because some were on trial," Bazoum said.

After that, the communication channel broke down and attacks escalated. Some believe the group's militants could still be offered an olive branch to demobilise and be reintegrated into Nigerien society. But Bazoum is not among them.[112]

Issoufou, too, has publicly rejected dialogue: In the aforementioned 2019 interview, he said that dialogue with jihadists "was not conceivable. We do not negotiate with terrorists and they, moreover, do not seek to do so."[113]

[111] François Soudan, "Mahamadou Issoufou: 'Ma décision de respecter la Constitution et de ne pas me représenter est irrévocable'," *Jeune Afrique*, August 14, 2019, www.jeuneafrique.com/mag/814617/politique/mahamadou-issoufou-ma-decision-de-respecter-la-constitution-et-de-ne-pas-me-representer-est-irrevocable/.
[112] Ruth Maclean, "Niger Islamic State Hostage."
[113] Soudan, "Mahamadou Issoufou: 'Ma décision de respecter la Constitution'."

One potential strategy for managing violence at the periphery had faltered, but other strategies were available as Nigerien authorities sought a balance between coercion and accommodation. In 2017, Nigerien authorities declared a state of emergency in parts of Tillabéri and Tahoua Regions, but continued to tread relatively lightly with ISGS. Through 2019, Nigerien authorities seem to have consciously avoided the strategies of collective punishment that have thrown fuel on the fires of jihadist insurgency in central Mali and northern Burkina Faso. There have been reports of collaboration between the Nigerien government and pro-government militias in Mali,[114] but Nigerien authorities seem to have avoided any "militia-fication" of the conflict on their side of the border. Reports of Nigerien security forces committing abuses, however, surfaced increasingly over the years, especially in 2020.

As ISGS provided a vehicle for former criminals and ethnic militia members, that dynamic reinforced Nigerien authorities' cynicism about jihadists' identities and motivations. Speaking of Chefou, one Nigerien official told Reuters, "He is a terrorist, a bandit, someone who intends to harm to Niger."[115] Yet that same dynamic led some civil society voices to push the government to reconsider dialogue. In early 2019, one Peul activist told journalists, "Fighters with jihadist groups are ready to give up their arms if incursions by Tuareg militias stop, emergency state measures are retired, and some of their colleagues are released from prison."[116] Perhaps Bazoum had given up too quickly on the idea of a truce – or perhaps, as ISGS' coalition expanded, different coalition elements had different attitudes toward the possibility of political settlements.

In Burkina Faso, a strain of pragmatism also influenced the thinking of the Compaoré regime, starting in the late 2000s and extending well

---

[114] In late 2017, the MSA denied that it had struck a deal with Niger. See "Moussa Ag Acharatoumane: The Resignations Have 'No Impact on the MSA'," Sahelien, October 20, 2017, https://sahelien.com/en/moussa-ag-acharatoumane-the-resignations-have-no-impact-on-the-msa/. But in May 2018, the MSA claimed that it and GATIA had participated in joint operations with the armed forces of Mali, Niger, and France against ISGS. See Amara Ag Hamdouna and Mohamed Ag Albachar, "Communiqué Conjoint GATIA-MSA suite au massacre de Tindibawen le 01 Mai 2018," Mouvement pour le Salut de l'Azawad, May 1, 2018, www.msa-azawad.com/actualites/74-communiqué-conjoint-gatia-msa-suite-au-massacre-de-tindibawen-le-01-mai-2018.html.

[115] Cocks and Lewis, "Why Niger and Mali's Cattle Herders Turned to Jihad."

[116] Zandonini and Bellina, "Niger, Part 3."

into the 2010s. Burkinabè authorities were frank, at least in private, about their own lack of capacity to monitor AQIM's incipient presence in their country. In a December 2009 meeting, then-Minister of Defense Yero Boly confided to the Americans that certain northern Burkinabè cities had been "infiltrated" and "Islamicized." Boly said that the government had identified individuals who might be acting as liaisons for AQIM but, according to the Americans' paraphrase, the authorities did not "know how to move forward and properly exploit that information. Boly noted that small cells of the type AQIM are know[n] to dispatch currently have a relatively high chance of circulating undetected by Burkinabe security forces."[117]

Meanwhile, Compaoré established himself as a regional mediator in AQIM's kidnapping economy after the kidnapping of two Canadian diplomats in Niger in 2008. One of Compaoré's advisors, the Mauritanian dissident Moustapha Ould Limam Chafi, negotiated directly with Belmokhtar to ransom the Canadians as well as, later, two Spanish hostages.[118] Ould Chafi and other connections positioned Compaoré and his then-Foreign Minister Djibril Bassolé to act as mediators when northern Mali's rebellion broke out in 2012; as discussed in Chapter 3, Compaoré hosted leaders of Ansar al-Din for several rounds of talks in Ouagadougou, and Bassolé met face-to-face with Iyad ag Ghali in Mali in August 2012. Even amid the early rebellion, Compaoré's team negotiated ransom payments with AQIM and Ansar al-Din; in April 2012, General Gilbert Diendéré flew to Timbuktu to receive a Swiss woman from Ansar al-Din's hands; footage of Diendéré meeting with Ansar al-Din's spokesman Sanda Ould Bouamama was aired on Burkinabè national television.[119]

Compaoré's team presented these interventions as peacemaking, problem-solving initiatives. Yet since Compaoré's fall from power in

---

[117] U.S. Embassy Ouagadougou, "Burkina Faso: MOD Discusses Wide Range of Regional Security Issues with CDA," leaked cable 09OUAGADOUGOU1136, December 8, 2009, https://search.wikileaks.org/plusd/cables/09OUAGADOUGOU1136_a.html.

[118] Vincent Hugeux, "Sahel: les secrets d'un sauveur des otages," *L'Express*, March 10, 2013, www.lexpress.fr/actualite/monde/afrique/sahel-moustapha-limam-chafi-les-secrets-d-un-sauveur-d-otages_1227809.html; and "Moustapha Chafi: l'homme qui murmurait à l'oreille des terroristes," *Jeune Afrique*, September 23, 2010, www.jeuneafrique.com/194989/politique/moustapha-chafi-l-homme-qui-murmurait-l-oreille-des-terroristes/.

[119] Radiodiffusion Télévision du Burkina, "Le Burkina libère Béatrice STOCKLY des mains du mouvement islamiste Ansar Dine," April 25, 2012, www.youtube.com/watch?v=ronsAfJoBZM.

2014, critics inside and outside Burkina Faso have charged that darker motives were at work.[120] As the journalist Joe Penney has written, Compaoré's willingness to host Ansar al-Din for peace talks eventually "[gave] way to rumors that Compaoré had a tacit agreement to allow their presence in exchange for no attacks."[121] This is essentially the view of Roch Kaboré, Compaoré's successor, who told *Le Monde* in November 2017, "Ex-president Blaise Compaoré played a role in mediation in Mali, which meant that, in a constant fashion, we had his collusions with the jihadist forces in Mali."[122]

Even more darkly, some observers speculate that Compaoré's Presidential Security Regiment (French acronym RSP) began to covertly sponsor jihadist attacks after their patron's fall. The 2014 revolution split the RSP. The organization's second-in-command, Isaac Zida, played a decisive role in Compaoré's ouster; after the president resigned, Zida challenged and sidelined the president's hand-picked successor, General Honoré Traoré. When a transitional civilian regime was installed, Zida returned as prime minister. In September 2015, however, the transitional authorities recommended that the RSP be disbanded, which prompted a coup by dissident elements of the RSP. The coup-makers named Compaoré's longtime associate, RSP head General Diendéré, as military head of state. This RSP coup was quickly reversed, and the planned dismantling of the RSP was carried out, but these events set in motion longlasting contestation around the fate of the RSP and Diendéré. The trial for Diendéré and Bassolé, also accused of involvement in the coup, became one of the central, running dramas of post-revolution Burkinabè politics; both men were convicted in 2019. Amid these events, some Burkinabè citizens began to allege that embittered RSP elements and Compaoré loyalists were abetting jihadist violence. As one civil society member said to Penney, "There is a

---

[120] Multiple interlocutors made this argument to me during fieldwork in Burkina Faso in 2019. See my "Escalating Conflicts in Burkina Faso," Rosa Luxemburg Foundation, September 2019, available at http://rosalux.sn/en/escalating-conflicts-in-burkina-faso-by-alex-thurston/.

[121] Joe Penney, "Blowback in Africa: How America's Counterterror Strategy Helped Destabilize Burkina Faso," The Intercept, November 22, 2018, https://theintercept.com/2018/11/22/burkina-faso-us-relations/.

[122] Christophe Ayad, "Le président burkinabé met en cause les 'collusions' de son prédécesseur avec les djihadistes," *Le Monde*, November 6, 2017, www.lemonde.fr/afrique/article/2017/11/06/le-president-burkinabe-met-en-cause-les-collusions-de-son-predecesseur-avec-les-djihadistes_5210917_3212.html.

common interest between the terrorist groups that operate in West Africa and the Burkinabè political camp that is no longer in power."[123]

Such theories are hard to substantiate. One former senior Ansar al-Din leader, in a 2019 interview with me, cast doubt on the idea that Compaoré and AQIM ever had an accord – in his view, circa 2012, AQIM had little interest in Burkina Faso and Compaoré's role was limited to mediating hostage releases.[124] Yet something fundamentally changed in the transition from Compaoré to Kaboré, whether in terms of an end to collusion, a diminishing of the security and intelligence capabilities of the state, or the arrival of new forms of clandestine collaboration.

With a weaker hand than Compaoré had, Burkina Faso's new authorities defaulted to policies of collective punishment and militia empowerment. As in central Mali, collective punishment targeted the Peul, who were tarred as sympathizers of Ansaroul Islam. As one mayor from northern Burkina Faso told Human Rights Watch in 2018, "The army acts like all Peuhls are jihadists, yet it is the very Peuhl who are victimized by the jihadists – we have been killed, decapitated, kidnapped and threatened." That report's authors added, "Those interviewed consistently described being caught between Islamists' threats to execute those who collaborated with the state, and the security forces, who expected them to provide intelligence about the presence of armed groups and meted out collective punishment, including mistreatment and arbitrary detention, when they didn't."[125] One Burkinabè human rights activist told me bluntly, "the counterattack strategy" is summary, extrajudicial executions of suspected jihadists.[126]

As in central Mali, ethnic profiling fueled the rapid degradation of the situation. In May 2019, the researcher José Luengo-Cabrera pointed out that the fatality figures in Burkina Faso for 2019 were, up to that time, sixteen times what they had been in 2018. For Burkina

---

[123] Penney, "Blowback in Africa." See also Abdoul Karim Saidou, "Burkina Faso: où en est la réforme de l'armée, deux ans après l'insurrection populaire?" GRIP, January 12, 2017, 12, www.grip.org/sites/grip.org/files/NOTES_ANALYSE/2017/NA_2017-01-12_FR_AK-SAIDOU.pdf.
[124] Interview with Ahmada ag Bibi.
[125] Human Rights Watch, "'By Day We Fear the Army'," 4, www.hrw.org/sites/default/files/report_pdf/burkinafaso0518_web2.pdf.
[126] Interview with Chrysogone Zougmoré, Ouagadougou, June 11, 2019.

Faso, Mali, and Niger collectively, "less than halfway through 2019, total fatalities from violence attributed to jihadist groups & communal militia have surpassed the toll in all (full) years since 2012."[127] In the period January 2018–March 2019, Burkina Faso's security forces had killed a reported 337 civilians, mostly in the northern regions of Sahel and Nord, whereas jihadists had killed a reported 111 civilians.[128] The center was lashing out, mostly blindly, at the periphery.

The center's willingness to use or tolerate collective punishment also sent signals to communal "self-defense" militias. Burkina Faso's majority ethnic group, the Mossi (an estimated 52 percent of the population, in contrast to the estimated 8.4 percent that the Peul represent),[129] have provided the demographic base for the Koglweogo ("Guardians of the Brush"), loosely organized community-based militias. The Koglweogo began to appear around 2013 as crime and banditry reached intolerable levels in much of the eastern half of Burkina Faso; the group received considerable rhetorical and political support from parts of the Mossi chiefly hierarchy.[130] The Koglweogo inflicted harsh punishments on alleged criminals and were accused of human rights abuses. They developed an ambivalent relationship with the state: "Even though these groups are violent and take over some of the State's prerogatives, they continuously play an important role in the political and social landscape in Burkina Faso."[131] The Koglweogo criticized the state but also benefited from sponsorship by hereditary authorities, businesspersons, and even current or former officials, creating patterns of political interdependence.[132]

In this atmosphere of state toleration for militias and implicit state sanction of collective punishment against the Peul, severe intercommunal clashes began to occur in northern Burkina Faso. The

[127] José Luengo-Cabrera, Twitter, May 28, 2019, https://twitter.com/J_LuengoCabrera/status/1133407887223607296.
[128] José Luengo-Cabrera, Twitter, March 22, 2019, https://twitter.com/J_LuengoCabrera/status/1109137675775287296.
[129] Central Intelligence Agency World Factbook, "Burkina Faso," accessed May 2019, www.cia.gov/library/publications/the-world-factbook/geos/uv.html.
[130] Interview with Samir Abdulkarim, Ouagadougou, June 14, 2019.
[131] Romane Da Cunha Dupuy and Tanguy Quidelleur, "Self-Defence Movements in Burkina Faso: Diffusion and Structuration of Koglweogo Groups," NORLA, November 2018, 5, www.noria-research.com/app/uploads/2018/11/NORIA__publi_nov_2018_EN-1.pdf.
[132] Ibid., 7.

first half of 2019 witnessed two major incidents: the killing of at least forty-nine civilians around Yirgou, Centre-Nord Region, in January; and the deaths of some sixty civilians around Arbinda, Sahel Region, over several days in March and April. In both cases, presumed jihadists attacked and killed prominent individuals – a village chief in Yirgou, and a religious leader in Arbinda – and then reprisal attacks followed, targeting Peul villagers.[133] The Koglweogo were widely blamed for the reprisals against the Peul, especially around Yirgou, but militia spokesmen denied the charges.[134]

Peul leaders felt deeply aggrieved by both the state and the militias. A spokesman for the Collective against Impunity and the Stigmatization of Communities, a Peul civil society organization, told *Le Monde*:

The State has lost its sovereign role of guarantor of security and justice in certain parts of its territory. The failure of the authorities has favored the proliferation of self-defense groups, notably the Koglweogo, principally Mossi. Faced with the rise of insecurity and impunity, the rural militias were created to track and punish criminals. In Yirgou and Arbinda, they conducted veritable "manhunts" against the Peul. In the sub-region, this community is more and more stigmatized, often accused of complicity with jihadists. Sometimes we hear: "If we wipe out the Peul, there will be no more terrorism."[135]

A triple pressure on the Peul had set in: security forces from one side, militias from another, and the jihadists from a third side. This unbearable situation reinforced the very conflict dynamics that the security forces and militias were attempting to end.

This comparison of state policies toward jihadism in Niger and Burkina Faso shows how limited Sahelian states' options really are. If tacit agreements, truces, or collusive arrangements are not possible or

---

[133] See United Nations Office for the Coordination of Humanitarian Affairs, "Burkina Faso: Armed Attacks in Arbinda, Flash Update," April 5, 2019, https://reliefweb.int/sites/reliefweb.int/files/resources/BFA%20-%20Flash%20update%20Arbinda%20-%204avril19_EN.pdf.

[134] Philip Kleinfeld, "Burkina Faso, Part 2: Communities Buckle as Conflict Ripples through the Sahel," The New Humanitarian, April 18, 2019, www.thenewhumanitarian.org/special-report/2019/04/18/burkina-faso-part-2-communities-buckle-conflict-ripples-through-sahel.

[135] Quoted in Sophie Douce, "Au Burkina Faso, 'les Peuls sont victimes d'un délit de faciès'," *Le Monde*, April 17, 2019, www.lemonde.fr/afrique/article/2019/04/17/au-burkina-faso-les-peuls-sont-victimes-d-un-delit-de-facies_5451716_3212.html.

viable, then the remaining options tend to fall somewhere on a spectrum between lashing out and outsourcing security. This is not to excuse what are often grotesquely unfair policies, but it is to point out that what Washington idolizes as "population-centric counterinsurgency" is even harder to pursue in the Sahel than in the Middle East and South Asia (where, one might add, it has failed even with the United States' vast resources to back it up).

Conclusion

There is much to be said for the cliché that jihadists benefit from porous borders. Yet, as the borderlands of Mali, Niger, and Burkina Faso demonstrate, there is more to the equation than just the lack of security deployments along borders. Jihadists benefit from the sociological and political aspects of borderlands as neglected peripheries, zones where state power is often outsourced to hereditary authorities, militias, and even smugglers. Jihadists find purchase in the borderland zones where they can establish local roots among, or emerge out of, communities who find the outsourced management strategies at the peripheries unbearable – that is, communities that resent either the hereditary rulers, militias, or other figures whom states have empowered. Jihadists who thrive in the borderlands also find a way to present their mobility, their protection services, and their roles in war economies as strategic assets to local partners.

This chapter has also examined the unintended consequences of aggressive border management strategies. It is all too natural a choice for weak central Sahelian authorities to turn to militias to tamp down insurgencies in their borderlands. Yet such militias often exacerbate conflict, particularly intercommunal conflict. When state security forces appear, moreover, they often become vehicles for collective punishment and/or objects of profound suspicion, trapping civilians between multiple essentially hostile armed actors, state and nonstate. The resulting dynamics leave Sahelian states (and their foreign backers) trapped in cycles of escalation, yet simultaneously reluctant to walk away from the few tools they do possess for managing restive peripheries.

6 | *Libya*
Fratricide in Derna

Jihadism has had a wide but patchy presence in Libya. Al-Qa'ida in the Islamic Maghreb (AQIM) has had footholds from the southwestern desert up through the coastal northeast – although as one journalist shrewdly observed after a visit to the southern town of Ubari, "The problem was that everyone called everyone else Al Qaeda."[1] The AQIM field commander Mokhtar Belmokhtar cultivated Libyan jihadist ventures and would eventually be reported dead in Libya, following a 2016 airstrike by France. Other AQIM leaders have regularly commented on and tried to shape events in Libya. For its part, the Islamic State carved out temporary enclaves in Derna (2014–2015), Sirte (2015–2016), and to a lesser extent in Sabratha; the Islamic State also staged attacks in Libya's capital Tripoli and elsewhere.[2]

This chapter focuses on Derna, a case that offers important lessons about the mechanisms and limits of jihadist coalition-building. In Derna, the more accommodationist, loosely al-Qa'ida-aligned faction, led by relatively older men, found itself caught in a dilemma: There were political exigencies to partner with non-jihadists, yet such partnerships incurred costs. Namely, accommodationism alienated younger, more hardline jihadists, who eventually affiliated to the Islamic State. The differences between the Islamic State and its rivals reflected not just theological–ideological splits but also political divisions shaped by generational identities and cohorts' divergent experiences of politics and war. Different jihadists adapted their theological–legal pronouncements to rapidly changing circumstances, with accommodationists attempting to use Islamic law as a unifying force but with the Islamic State weaponizing jurisprudence against their elders. The accommodationists

---

[1] Sarah Topol, "Guns and Poses," *Harper's Magazine* (December 2014), https://harpers.org/archive/2014/12/guns-and-poses/?single=1.

[2] For an overview and analysis of the Islamic State's career in Libya, see Frederic Wehrey, *The Burning Shores: Inside the Battle for the New Libya* (New York: Farrar, Straus and Giroux, 2018), ch. 12.

eventually won, driving the Islamic State mostly out of Derna, but in doing so they lost leaders and fighters. They also lost crucial time as their larger, non-jihadist enemies gathered strength.

Theoretical Implications of the Case

Derna's jihadists offer the clearest example in this book of a jihadist schism that then resulted in horizontally directed violence or fratricide. We are not talking here about vertically directed purges by the senior leadership against "internal enemies"; rather, we will examine a series of battles, standoffs, and competitions between two factions capable of inflicting significant damage on each other.

The case is valuable not just for refining what is meant by fratricide, but more importantly for helping to explain fratricidal violence. It may seem inevitable that violence would follow a schism, but recall that the GSPC did not engage in full-blown warfare with the GIA after their schism in Algeria (see Chapter 1). The AQIM-related cases discussed in Chapters 2 through 5 also showed, in different ways, that jihadist schisms often result in a fair amount of accommodation; AQIM refrained from trying to kill dissidents and schismatics.

Yet accommodation requires the consent of both sides. In contrast to the intra-jihadist accommodation discussed in Chapters 2 through 5, the present chapter deals with the breakdown of a tenuous pattern of accommodation amid repeated and violent provocations from one faction against the other. Fratricide is thus not a natural or inevitable outcome of schism but rather the result of essentially political choices. These choices are political rather than blindly doctrinal because they do not map neatly onto the supposed binary of a more accommodating al-Qa'ida and a less accommodating Islamic State; in the Mali–Niger borderlands there was, for a time, a case of accommodation between an al-Qa'ida affiliate and an Islamic State affiliate, whereas in Libya one finds fratricide. Fratricide thus seems to require a political motive for rejecting accommodation. The question of political motive takes us back to the question of "prewar politicized social networks,"[3] and how it is not just doctrinal outlooks but also the composition of networks that can affect blocs' choices.

[3] Paul Staniland, *Networks of Rebellion: Explaining Insurgent Cohesion and Collapse* (Ithaca, NY: Cornell University Press, 2014), 9.

The Derna case also allows for an examination of how fratricide affects coalition-building. Violence propels realignments among blocs, prompting some blocs to pursue mergers and causing local players to seek more intensive forms of external support. As I have stressed periodically in this book, these choices are more complex than local players acting as "front groups" for al-Qaʻida or the Islamic State. Local actors display considerable agency and often leverage external resources to reinforce decisions already taken at the local level, or decisions taken as a result of a dialogue between locals and outsiders.

Meanwhile, the fratricidal environment affects civilians in complex ways, as civilians adjust and readjust to changing power balances, sometimes in ways that then affect those power balances. In the context of fratricide, jihadists' externally facing (i.e., civilian-facing) political postures can have dramatic and unintended consequences. Among these consequences is the potential for strategies of intimidation to backfire and drive civilians into the rival jihadists' arms.

Finally, the case of Derna illustrates the political risks, for jihadists, of *dilution*.[4] The dilemma is this: Jihadists and particularly their leaders may calculate that a large degree of accommodation is necessary for either coalition-building or simple survival, yet that very same accommodation can antagonize hardliners and even lead to infighting. We caught a glimpse of these dilemmas with AQIM's approach to governance in northern Mali in 2012, where the overall and mostly remote emir, Droukdel, pushed for substantial accommodation; field commanders responded by essentially ignoring his advice, only to slowly take some of it on board in the years that followed. Yet the disagreements Droukdel had with his subordinates were mild compared to the violent disagreements in Derna between the accommodationists and the absolutists. On a purely intellectual level, it must be admitted, the absolutist argument has some force – there is a point at which accommodationist jihadism would no longer be jihadism, but rather something else. These disputes thus exemplify even more dramatically the question I posed at the end of Chapter 2: Is jihadist politics fundamentally a dead end, caught as it is between (a) the impossibility of building a state immune to Western military might,

---

[4] I borrow this term from Cole Bunzel. See "Diluting Jihad: Tahrir al-Sham and the Concerns of Abu Muhammad al-Maqdisi," *Jihadica*, March 29, 2017, www .jihadica.com/diluting-jihad/.

(b) the implication that accommodationist coalition-building will
dilute jihadism down into something else, and (c) the futility of
terrorist violence uncoupled from any concrete state-building effort?
As with Mali, the Libyan case seems to underline this futility – a
futility that has become much more explicitly acknowledged by
"post-jihadists" in Mauritania, the final case study and the topic of
Chapter 7.

The Roots of Jihadism in Derna

Derna sits on the Libyan coast approximately 250 kilometers east of
Benghazi. Derna is an old city, built on the site of an ancient Greek
colony, but it remained relatively small into the twentieth century:
Italian colonizers, at the beginning of their colonial occupation in
1911, estimated its population at 9,500.[5] Through brutal repression
and mass detention, Italian authorities temporarily halted the region's
population growth in the 1920s and 1930s.[6]

Libya's independence, and the beginning of oil exports in 1961,
sparked rapid growth and development in Tripoli and Benghazi, but
most other towns were left behind. One oil industry expert wrote in
1963 that Tripoli and Benghazi were "the only two towns with
modern urban amenities ... the small ports of Derna, Ras el Hilal,
Susa (Apollonia), and Tolmeta are all in need of repair."[7] Eastern
Libya, or Cyrenaica, enjoyed political prominence under Libya's first
postcolonial ruler, King Idris. Yet Benghazi, rather than Derna, was
Cyrenaica's political center.

After Colonel Muammar al-Qadhafi overthrew the king in 1969,
the east suffered neglect and repression. Whether or not Qadhafi
believed in his own revolutionary and anti-tribalist rhetoric, in practice he ruled through a personalist, heavily tribal network that
favored his own Qadhadhfa, as well as the Warfalla and the
Magharba. None of these three tribes is primarily eastern. The

[5] E. E. Evans-Pritchard, *The Sanusi of Cyrenaica* (Oxford: Oxford University Press, 1949), 42.
[6] Chia-Lin Pan, "The Population of Libya," *Population Studies* 3:1 (June 1949): 100–125; 105.
[7] John I. Clarke, "Oil in Libya: Some Implications," *Economic Geography* 39:1 (January 1963): 40–59; 53.

eastern tribes were largely sidelined due to their association with the deposed king and due to conflicts between the Qadhadhfa and the eastern Sa'adi confederation.[8]

Amid Qadhafi's antipathy toward the east, Derna suffered. A "verdant oasis,"[9] Derna was a rich and tempting target for expropriation, and its culture of activism provoked repression. The historical record of Qadhafi's Libya remains somewhat opaque, but one account says that after an anti-Qadhafi protest in Derna in 1970 – one of the earliest expressions of discontent following Qadhafi's coup – the city attracted the colonel's wrath.[10] One Libyan study, published during the Qadhafi era, suggests that the post-1969 period did bring some development to Derna: factories for clothing, food, water, cement, and sponges, as well as new schools and colleges.[11] The city's population growth, however, outpaced development. From an estimated 21,432 inhabitants in 1964, Derna grew to 97,122 in 1995.[12] The city's "marginalization," one Arab newspaper later said, continued until "the city became empty of any economic activity that could contain the energies of its youth, and with the years its infrastructure fell apart."[13]

In the mid-1990s, Derna was a hub for the Libyan Islamic Fighting Group (LIFG).[14] The LIFG formed around 1989. Its founders, Libyans who had fought the Soviets in Afghanistan, were angered by the

---

[8] Alison Pargeter, "Localism and Radicalization in North Africa: Local Factors and the Development of Political Islam in Morocco, Tunisia and Libya," *International Affairs* 85:5 (September 2009): 1031–1044; 1035.

[9] Muhammad Muhammad al-Mufti, *Sahari Darna: Al-Tarikh al-Ijtima'i li-l-Madina* (Benghazi: Dar al-Kutub al-Wataniyya, 2007), 34.

[10] Daniel Howden, "The Rebel City Gaddafi Says Is Full of Recruits for al-Qa'ida," *The Independent*, May 8, 2011, www.independent.co.uk/news/world/africa/the-rebel-city-gaddafi-says-is-full-of-recruits-for-al-qaida-2281170.html.

[11] Salima al-Mansuri, "Madinat Darna: Dirasa fi Jughrafiyat al-Mudun," M. A. thesis, Garyounis University (University of Benghazi), 1996, quoted in Amraji' Muhammad al-Khajkhaj, *Madinat Darna: Dirasa Hadariyya* (Benghazi: Dar al-Saqiya li-l-Nashr, 2008), 29.

[12] Ibid., 76.

[13] "Darna al-Libiyya…Madina 'ala Hafat al-Sira'at wa-l-Ightiyalat," *Al-Araby al-Jadid*, November 16, 2014, www.alaraby.co.uk/politics/2014/11/16/
درنة-الليبية-مدينة-على-حافة-الصراعات-والاغتيالات.

[14] For background on the LIFG, see Camille Tawil, *Brothers in Arms: The Story of al-Qa'ida and the Arab Jihadists* (London: Saqi Books, 2011), ch. 3.

Qadhafi regime's repression of domestic Islamists.[15] The LIFG sought
to overthrow Qadhafi, considering him an illegitimate, infidel ruler – a
conclusion that other returnees from Afghanistan had reached about
their own rulers, including in neighboring Algeria (see Chapter 1). The
most intensive years of the LIFG's insurrection were 1995–1996, when
the LIFG waged a guerrilla campaign in the east and sought to assassinate Qadhafi.[16]

The LIFG's rebellion brought more repression to Derna. In March
1996, after a prison break near Benghazi, the regime cut the electricity
and water in Derna. Security forces "sealed off" Derna and nearby
al-Bayda.[17] Hundreds of local men were imprisoned, including in the
Abu Salim facility in Tripoli. There, in June 1996, authorities committed a massacre with lasting repercussions for the jihadist scene in
Libya, and for Libyan politics overall. At that time, an estimated
1,700 men were held in the "political wing" of the prison: dissidents,
jihadists, as well as many people who had simply been very unlucky.
Three jihadists, veterans of Afghanistan, attempted to escape. They
broke hundreds of prisoners out of their cells. In response, senior
regime officials rounded up and shot over 1,200 inmates.[18] Later, in
Derna, the "Abu Salim Martyrs' Brigade" – named after those events –
was a major player in the events described later.

After the LIFG's defeat, some jihadists fled back to Afghanistan or
elsewhere. They included the LIFG's leader 'Abd al-Hakim Belhadj,
who was captured in 2004 in Thailand and turned over to Libyan
authorities.[19] In the years that followed, LIFG leaders took divergent
paths. Jihadists in Libya began negotiating a reconciliation with the
Qadhafi regime, as part of tentative reform efforts spearheaded by
Qadhafi's son Sayf al-Islam. While still in captivity at Abu Salim

[15] "Bilhajj al-Jihadi..al-Mu'tadil," *Al-Sharq al-Awsat*, September 30, 2011, http://
archive.aawsat.com/details.asp?section=45&article=642686&issueno=11994#
.WfiXH2JSxz9.

[16] Omar Ashour, "Ex-Jihadists in the New Libya," Brookings Institution, August
29, 2011, www.brookings.edu/articles/ex-jihadists-in-the-new-libya/; "Bilhajj
al-Jihadi..al-Mu'tadil."

[17] Associated Press/*New York Times*, March 28, 1996, A4.

[18] Human Rights Watch, "Libya: Abu Salim Prison Massacre Remembered," June
27, 2012, www.hrw.org/news/2012/06/27/libya-abu-salim-prison-massacre-
remembered; and Evan Hill, "Libya Survivor Describes 1996 Prison Massacre,"
Al Jazeera, October 21, 2011, www.aljazeera.com/indepth/features/2011/09/
20119223521462487.html.

[19] "Bilhajj al-Jihadi..al-Mu'tadil."

Prison, Belhadj and other LIFG luminaries publicly recanted most of their beliefs. LIFG members were released in several waves between 2008 and 2010.

In Afghanistan and Pakistan, some exiled LIFG members joined al-Qaʻida. One of them, Abu Layth al-Libi, announced in November 2007 that the LIFG had merged with al-Qaʻida. But LIFG leaders inside Libya publicly rejected the merger.[20] The announcement may have represented al-Libi's effort to "snatch the leadership of the LIFG for himself and to try to scupper the continuation of negotiations between the true LIFG leadership and the regime." Al-Libi's death in a US drone strike in Pakistan in January 2008 may have accelerated the negotiations back in Libya.[21] In any case, the al-Qaʻida-aligned LIFG members did not control the group's trajectory back home.

The LIFG faced other challenges. As the LIFG's leaders were reconciling with Qadhafi, a younger jihadist wave was appearing, especially in Derna. In the mid-2000s, Derna became a hub for recruits heading to Iraq to join al-Qaʻida's franchise there. The US Combating Terrorism Center, analyzing records about foreign fighters captured in a raid at Sinjar, Iraq, found that Libya was the second-highest country of origin for foreign fighters. Out of 595 records that included individuals' nationalities, Libya accounted for 112 (behind Saudi Arabia, at 244).[22] Nearly half of the Libyan fighters (52) came from Derna, surpassing any other individual city in the collection both in absolute terms (Saudi Arabia's Riyadh was next, at 51) and on a per capita basis (as the report's authors noted, Riyadh's population of approximately 4.3 million vastly outnumbered Derna's population of around 80,000 in their estimate, or perhaps 100,000 if one takes a higher estimate). Benghazi, meanwhile, was home to only twenty-one fighters.[23]

---

[20] Barak Mendelsohn, *The Al-Qaeda Franchise: The Expansion of Al-Qaeda and Its Consequences* (Oxford: Oxford University Press, 2015), 155–159.

[21] Alison Pargeter, "The LIFG's Current Role in the Global Jihad," Countering Terrorism Center *Sentinel* 1:5 (April 2008), https://ctc.usma.edu/v2/wp-content/uploads/2010/06/Vol1Iss5-Art2.pdf.

[22] Joseph Felter and Brian Fishman, "Al-Qaʻida's Foreign Fighters in Iraq: A First Look at the Sinjar Records," Combating Terrorism Center, January 2, 2007, 7, https://ctc.usma.edu/v2/wp-content/uploads/2010/06/aqs-foreign-fighters-in-iraq.pdf.

[23] Felter and Fishman "Al-Qaʻida's Foreign Fighters," 10–11, https://ctc.usma.edu/v2/wp-content/uploads/2010/06/aqs-foreign-fighters-in-iraq.pdf.

What motivated these young jihadists? A *Newsweek* reporter, visiting Derna in 2008, concluded that the recruits were "young men with bleak lives in search of redemption," but who simultaneously had "an almost obsessive devotion to their town's place in history." This devotion centered on Umar al-Mukhtar (d. 1931), an anticolonial fighter and Sufi shaykh.[24] Another factor may have been residents' anger at the intense surveillance they faced from Qadhafi's security services – after the reporter left, "some residents were closely questioned by security officials."[25]

A decade later, Derna again supplied numerous fighters to the Islamic State. One 2016 report found that per capita, Derna was the region, worldwide, that contributed the most volunteers: 21.5 per 100,000 persons.[26] Compared to other Islamic State recruits, Derna's fighters were better-versed in Islamic education and jihadist ideology, but also younger. Their average birth year was 1991–1992.[27]

The wave that left Derna and Benghazi in the mid-2000s foreshadowed the generational break between the LIFG-era jihadists and the younger fighters who would eventually fill the ranks of the Islamic State in Libya. As Alison Pargeter has written, the LIFG and AQIM were probably not the main recruiters for eastern Libyans headed to Iraq. Rather, "it is more likely that such volunteers went through loose networks tied into a number of preachers or mosques." Pargeter raises the possibility that the Qadhafi regime tolerated or even encouraged such recruitment.[28] The regime may have calculated that Iraq offered a release valve for domestic pressures, particularly the simmering discontent in the eastern coastal cities. At the same time, eastern Libya's numerous small mosques were exceptionally difficult for the regime to control. "Coded phrases" allowed Friday speakers to promote jihad in Iraq while maintaining plausible deniability.[29]

---

[24] Kevin Peraino, "The Jihadist Riddle," *Newsweek*, April 19, 2008, www.newsweek.com/cover-jihadist-riddle-85605.

[25] U.S. Embassy Tripoli, "Die Hard in Derna," leaked cable 08TRIPOLI430, June 2, 2008, https://wikileaks.org/plusd/cables/08TRIPOLI430_a.html.

[26] Nate Rosenblatt, "All Jihad Is Local: What ISIS' Files Tell Us about Its Fighters," New America Foundation, July 2016, 13, https://na-production.s3.amazonaws.com/documents/ISIS-Files.pdf.

[27] Ibid., 16.   [28] Pargeter, "LIFG's Current Role."

[29] U.S. Embassy Tripoli, "Extremism in Eastern Libya," leaked cable 08TRIPOLI120, February 15, 2008, https://wikileaks.org/plusd/cables/08TRIPOLI120_a.html.

An American diplomat, visiting Derna in May 2008, also suspected that mosques were recruitment hubs: "Unbidden, [a local resident] pointed out a number of small, discrete [sic] mosques tucked away in side alleys, noting that the profusion of 'popular mosques' complicated effective monitoring by security forces."[30] The American official, like *Newsweek*'s reporter, felt that Derna's unusually high rates of jihadist recruitment reflected not only a lack of opportunities for youth, but also local memories of the anticolonial jihad. The diplomat further noted the role of media, including satellite television that broadcast rousing images of Muslims' suffering in Iraq and Palestine.

The diplomat heard that in the 1980s and after, Derna had been the site not just of jihadist mobilization but also of sustained efforts to promote hardline understandings. For context, Qadhafi's attitude toward Islam was both idiosyncratic and authoritarian: As part of the so-called rule by the masses (*jamahiriyya*) that Qadhafi claimed to be building, Qadhafi challenged the authority of various Muslim currents. These included not just the Muslim Brotherhood, which Qadhafi suppressed, but also the classical *'ulama'*.[31] In 1978, after a public debate, Qadhafi placed the country's grand mufti under house arrest; in 1980, security forces arrested and likely killed the imam of Tripoli.[32]

With these maneuvers, the regime inadvertently helped to open up the religious field to efforts to promote hardline understandings of Islam – particularly in marginalized locales such as Derna. In the 1980s and 1990s, fighters returning from Afghanistan conducted what one Derna resident later called a "deliberate, coordinated campaign to propagate more conservative iterations of Islam."

According to [the resident], these returned former fighters deliberately targeted towns and areas known to be less heavily surveilled and controlled by government security officials. Many of those were located in eastern Libya, where authorities have since Ottoman times experienced difficulty extending the writ of the central government. [He] mentioned a small group of Libyans who had reportedly fought in Afghanistan, subsequently

---

[30] U.S. Embassy Tripoli, "Die Hard in Derna."
[31] Dirk Vandewalle, "Qadhafi's 'Perestroika': Economic and Political Liberalization in Libya," *Middle East Journal* 45:2 (Spring 1991): 216–231, especially 220–221.
[32] Alison Pargeter, *Libya: The Rise and Fall of Qaddafi* (New Haven, CT, and London: Yale University Press, 2012), 116–117.

undergone religious training in northern Syria and Lebanon, and then returned to Derna in the late 1980's as having been particularly instrumental in steering the community in a more conservative direction. Stressing their conservatism, he said they had spearheaded campaigns against many aspects of daily life, such as smoking cigarettes, which they deemed "un-Islamic." He pointed out the large number of religiously-themed audio cassettes and DVDs on offer in Derna's markets.[33]

By the eve of the revolution, the stage was set for Derna's jihadists to play a significant role in the anti-Qadhafi uprising. Yet conditions were also ripe for conflict among jihadists. In 2008–2010, as older, veteran figures were reconciling with the regime and exploring roles for themselves within mainstream politics, many younger figures were moving away from the LIFG and into smaller, less hierarchical, and more militant networks.

Eastern Libya and the 2011 Revolution: Competing Interests and Identities

Libya's revolution broke out in February 2011, shortly after popular protests toppled Tunisia's President Zine El Abidine Ben Ali on January 14 and Egypt's President Hosni Mubarak on February 11. Libya's first demonstrations occurred in Benghazi, the most populous city in the east and the country's second most populous city overall. The situation in Benghazi soon escalated into confrontations between authorities and demonstrators. These events led to a full-scale rebellion, with NATO intervening on behalf of the rebels.

The Benghazi demonstrations were not just an echo of the "Arab Spring" – they also tapped into local histories. The February 17 demonstrations commemorated protests held in Benghazi in 2006, when activists had attacked the Italian consulate in response to the Danish cartoon controversy. When authorities dispersed the protesters, at least eleven people were killed.[34] In 2011, other histories also came into play. One trigger for unrest in Benghazi was authorities' arrest of Fathi

---

[33] U.S. Embassy Trioli, "Die Hard in Derna."
[34] Human Rights Watch, "Libya: Men Face Possible Death for Planning Peaceful Demonstration," August 13, 2007, www.hrw.org/news/2007/08/13/libya-men-face-possible-death-planning-peaceful-demonstration.

Terbil on February 15. A lawyer, Terbil represented families of prisoners massacred at Abu Salim prison in 1996.

As the revolution gained momentum, divisions emerged – not just within Libya, but within the east as well. The revolution was diverse, open to people ranging from longtime dissidents to last-minute regime defectors. The National Transitional Council (NTC), which received international recognition, projected itself as the face of the revolution. Yet the NTC's suit-wearing, university-educated technocrats did not represent the full spectrum contained within the revolutionary ranks. By July 2011, when the regime defector Major General 'Abd al-Fattah Yunis was killed by unknown assailants, possibly hardline Islamists, divisions among the revolutionaries were coming to light.

One key division was between politicos and hardliners. By politicos, I mean all those willing to profess a commitment to constitutional multi-party democracy and recognize the NTC. The politicos included prominent former jihadists and senior leaders of the defunct LIFG. For example, former LIFG leader 'Abd al-Hakim Belhadj rallied quickly to the revolution. Belhadj rose to command the Tripoli Military Council. According to some accounts, he personally led the assault on Qadhafi's Bab al-Aziziya compound in Tripoli in August 2011.[35] These ex-jihadists remained willing to participate in mainstream politics after Qadhafi's overthrow. In 2012, as Libya prepared for national elections, Belhadj formed a minor political party (Al-Watan, or Homeland), as did another former LIFG leader, Sami al-Saadi. Other LIFG members entered postrevolutionary governments.[36]

The hardliners joined the revolution but did not embrace the vision of a liberal, multi-party Libya. One key jihadist in Derna was Abu Sufyan bin Qumu (b. 1959 in Derna). A former soldier, Bin Qumu was imprisoned in the 1980s, but he escaped in 1993. He fled to Egypt and later to Afghanistan, where he joined al-Qa'ida. In the mid-1990s, when Bin Laden was living in Sudan, Bin Qumu worked as a truck driver for one of Bin Laden's firms. In 1997, Bin Qumu left for South

[35] Sudarsan Raghavan, "These Libyans Were Once Linked to al-Qaeda. Now They Are Politicians and Businessmen," *Washington Post*, September 28, 2017, www.washingtonpost.com/world/middle_east/these-libyan-ex-militiamen-were-once-linked-to-al-qaeda-now-they-wield-power-in-a-new-order/2017/09/27/8356abf8-97dd-11e7-af6a-6555caaeb8dc_story.html?utm_term=.f8e703596a67.

[36] Ibid.

Asia to fight alongside the Taliban. Detained by Pakistani security forces, he was handed over to the Americans. He was held at Guantanamo Bay from 2002–2007, when he was transferred back to Libya.[37] In September 2010, as part of the reconciliation between the Qadhafi regime and the LIFG, Bin Qumu was released.[38]

When the revolution began, Bin Qumu emerged as a leading militia commander in Derna.[39] One account suggests that Bin Qumu, given his personal history, was initially poised to act as a focal point for jihadist-leaning youth in Derna. At a public meeting early in the revolution, however, Bin Qumu's vague intervention reportedly disappointed some audience members. Others drifted away from him later, complaining that he lacked a clear vision.[40] In any case, Bin Qumu soon gravitated toward open jihadism.

In 2012, groups calling themselves Ansar al-Shari'a (Supporters of Islamic Law) emerged in Tunisia, Libya, and Yemen. In Libya, Benghazi and Derna were the hubs for these jihadist-leaning militias. A former Abu Salim inmate, Muhammad al-Zahawi, led the Benghazi branch, while Bin Qumu headed Ansar al-Shari'a in Derna. Across the countries where they appeared, Ansar al-Shari'a movements benefited from strategic ambiguity surrounding their identities and intensions. Depending on local circumstances, they presented themselves as vigilantes, charities, or jihadists. Many Ansar al-Shari'a leaders ended up committing to full-blown jihadism, including the Tunisian Sayf Allah Ben Hassine, but in my view it is a mistake to depict all of Ansar al-Shari'a, root and branch, as a mere front group for al-Qa'ida. Developments in Derna would highlight this complexity.

Derna's jihadists occupied points along the spectrum between politicos and hardliners. In 2011–2012, the Abu Salim Martyrs' Brigade's

---

[37] "Abu Sufian Ibrahim Ahmed Hamuda Bin Qumu," The *New York Times* Guantanamo Docket, undated, www.nytimes.com/interactive/projects/ guantanamo/detainees/557-abu-sufian-ibrahim-ahmed-hamuda-bin-qumu.

[38] Ahmad Shilbi and Safa' Salih, "Sufyan bin Qumu..Sa'iq bin Ladin Tahawwala ila 'Amir'," Al-Masry Al-Youm, October 14, 2014, www.almasryalyoum.com/ news/details/544178.

[39] Rod Nordland and Scott Shane, "Libyan, Once a Detainee, Is Now a U.S. Ally of Sorts," *New York Times*, April 24, 2011, www.nytimes.com/2011/04/25/world/ guantanamo-files-libyan-detainee-now-us-ally-of-sorts.html.

[40] "Sira' 'Da'ish' wa-'Al-Qa'ida' Yantaqil ila Libiya," Al-Araby, March 12, 2015, www.alaraby.co.uk/investigations/2015/3/11/صراع-داعش-و-القاعدة-ينتقل-إلى-ليبيا.

(ASMB's) leaders figured among the revolution's politicos – or, at least, they were pragmatic jihadists, rather than uncompromising hardliners. One founder of the ASMB was 'Abd al-Hakim al-Hasadi, who was in Afghanistan and Pakistan for much of the 1990s and early 2000s. After spending the mid-2000s in prison in Libya,[41] he found a niche for himself in Derna amid the revolution. In March 2011, he said, "the youth rallied around me and I started coordinating their activities for the advancement and success of the revolution." His militia sought to control key infrastructure in Derna, starting with the port.[42] Al-Hasadi's background made him credible to some young men in Derna, especially those seeking new leaders in a moment of chaos and fluidity.

The prominence of jihadists and former jihadists among the revolutionaries, and particularly in Derna, provided Qadhafi with a rhetorical tool. He accused the revolutionaries of being dupes or agents for al-Qa'ida. Figures such as al-Hasadi rejected such allegations; without denying that he had been in Afghanistan or that he had been involved with al-Qa'ida, al-Hasadi publicly denied any plans to establish an Islamic emirate in Derna.[43] He would later disavow any ongoing al-Qa'ida ties, sometimes disingenuously.[44] Similar allegations of al-Qaida ties resurfaced in 2012, after the death of US Ambassador Chris Stevens and three other Americans in Benghazi. Even the leader of Ansar al-Shari'a in Benghazi, Muhammad al-Zahawi, took pains to deny involvement in the attack and to deny any organizational linkages to al-Qa'ida, even though he expressed admiration for the group.[45] In eastern Libya, the more flexible

---

[41] Roberto Bongiorni, "Reportage. 'Noi ribelli, islamici e tolleranti'," Il Sole 24 Ore, March 22, 2011, www.ilsole24ore.com/art/notizie/2011-03-21/reportage-ribelli-islamici-tolleranti-231527_PRN.shtml; and Ayman al-Sisi, "Al-Qiyadi al-Islami 'Abd al-Hakim al-Hasadi fi Darna: Lasna 'Umala' li-l-Afghan wa-la Nas'a li-Taqsim Libiya," Al-Ahram, March 5, 2011, www.masress.com/ahram/65773.

[42] Al-Sisi, "Al-Qiyadi al-Islami 'Abd al-Hakim al-Hasadi."

[43] "Nafy 'Abd al-Hakim al-Hasadi Hadith al-Qadhdhafi," Al Jazeera, February 24, 2011, www.youtube.com/watch?v=m6OIUcnqUAE.

[44] "Al-Qa'id al-Maydani 'Abd al-Hakim al-Hasadi Yukadhdhib Taqarir al-Akhbariyya Hawla Tawajud al-Milishiyat al-Islamiyya al-Musallaha fi Madinat Darna," The Libya New, May 18, 2012, https://ruclip.com/video/pf5i-UO5kcA/درنة.html.

[45] Ahmed Maher, "Meeting Mohammed Ali al-Zahawi of Libyan Ansar al-Sharia," BBC, September 18, 2012, www.bbc.com/news/world-africa-19638582.

jihadists tried to localize their image and keep channels of communication open with other revolutionary forces.

Al-Hasadi and another major jihadist in Derna, Salim Darbi, were comfortable working within the revolution. The uprising gave them opportunities to achieve their short-term objective: greater political and religious control in Derna and in eastern Libya more broadly. According to one account, during the revolution, al-Hasadi and Darbi led jihadist-leaning youth from Derna in the fight against Qadhafi's forces in Benghazi, Ajdabiya, and the oil crescent.[46] Al-Hasadi sometimes partnered with the NTC; although he declined any official roles, he and his young followers worked to "capture a number of black mercenaries and turn them over to the transitional government through Mustafa 'Abd al-Jalil in al-Bayda."[47]

'Abd al-Jalil (b. 1952) is a lawyer by training. A native of the east, he worked as a judge in Benghazi, Derna, and Bayda.[48] He served as Qadhafi's Minister of Justice from 2007 until the revolution. When the protests broke out, the regime dispatched him to Benghazi to negotiate with the rebels, but he defected to their side – becoming the first member of Qadhafi's cabinet to do so. He became chairman of the National Transitional Council (NTC), the political coordinating body for the rebels.[49] He served as interim head of state through August 2012, when the General National Congress took over following national elections. Often described as a conservative, 'Abd al-Jalil extolled what he called "moderate Islam" in Libya: "Ninety percent of Libyans want a moderate Islam. There are five percent who are liberals, and five percent who are extremists."[50]

In July 2011, 'Abd al-Jalil visited Derna.[51] The ASMB provided security for the visit. Long after 'Abd al-Jalil came and went, jihadists

[46] "Sira' 'Da'ish' wa-'Al-Qa'ida' Yantaqil ila Libiya."
[47] Al-Sisi, "Al-Qiyadi al-Islami 'Abd al-Hakim al-Hasadi."
[48] 'Adil al-Tarifi, "Al-Mustashar Mustafa 'Abd al-Jalil: Lam Akun Yawman Damn Manzumat al-Qadhdhafi...wa-Kunna Musta'iddin li-Qubul al-Musalaha," Al-Sharq al-Awsat, October 21, 2013, https://aawsat.com/home/article/6796.
[49] "Libya Crisis: Profile of NTC Chair Mustafa Abdul Jalil," BBC, August 22, 2011, www.bbc.com/news/world-africa-14613679.
[50] "Mustafa 'Abd al-Jalil," Al Jazeera, March 24, 2011, www.aljazeera.net/encyclopedia/icons/2011/3/24/مصطفى-عبد-الجليل.
[51] Frederic Wehrey and Ala' Alrababa'h, "Rising out of Chaos: The Islamic State in Libya," Carnegie Endowment *Diwan*, March 5, 2015, http://carnegie-mec.org/diwan/59268?lang=en.

debated each other over whether protecting him had been justified. For the ASMB, protecting him had been an act of political improvisation. Later, it became a point of contention. So did the ASMB's decision to enter (for a time) the revolutionary state's Supreme Security Committee.[52] Hardliners and accommodationists were divided over the question of how revolutionary militias should relate to the state. In 2012, some jihadist-leaning groups, such as Ansar al-Shari'a, said they would not subordinate themselves to state authority unless they received guarantees that Libya would have an Islamic constitution; failing this, many jihadists refused to join state structures.[53] Hardline jihadist muftis, meanwhile, condemned not just the NTC[54] but also the decision to protect 'Abd al-Jalil.[55] Nevertheless, the ASMB weathered the first round of tensions over these controversies in 2011–2012.

By 2012, the ASMB was administering parts of Derna. Although the BBC estimated its size at just 200 fighters, the BBC also noted that the ASMB's Facebook page brimmed with requests from school and hospital administrators for the Brigade's protection – and with posts from other local leaders offering thanks for services already rendered. The BBC's profile stated further that the ASMB was "the only force that was applying law and order there."[56] Initially, the ASMB thrived amid Libya's chaos. But Derna's divisions would soon complicate life for the Brigade.

Divisions in Libya, Divisions in Derna

The years 2012 and 2013 seemed promising for Libya. The country held parliamentary elections in July 2012 to select members of the new General National Congress. The European Union praised the conduct of the elections,[57] but observers also noted some problems. One

[52] "Sira' 'Da'ish' wa-'Al-Qa'ida' Yantaqil ila Libiya."

[53] Personal communication, Frederic Wehrey, February 2018.

[54] Abu Muslim al-Jaza'iri, fatwa in response to "Kayfa Tarawna al-Majlis al-Watani al-Intiqali fi Libiya?" undated (likely April 2011), www.ilmway.com/site/maqdis/FAQ/MS_3694.html.

[55] Abu Muslim al-Jaza'iri, fatwa in response to "Hirasat Mustafa 'Abd al-Jalil 'Allamat Istifham fi Libiya," undated (likely August 2014), https://web.archive.org/web/20140805113856/http://tawhed.ws/FAQ/display_question?qid=5050.

[56] "Nabdha 'an al-Majmu'at al-Musallaha fi Sharq Libiya," BBC, September 26, 2012, www.bbc.com/arabic/middleeast/2012/09/120926_libyaeast.shtml.

problem was that "the electoral environment in some areas of eastern Libya diverged significantly from the rest of the country. Security challenges in Benghazi, Ajdabiya, and Kufra both immediately preceding the polls and on election day significantly marred polling in these areas."[58] The east was still turbulent.

Meanwhile, the revolution's militias did not go away. In many places, militias were incorporated into the fabric of life and politics, whether officially or unofficially. In October 2011, the NTC created the Supreme Security Committee, under the authority of the Ministry of the Interior, with a mandate to subsume armed revolutionaries and militia members. Another security structure, the Libya Shield units, followed in March 2012 and was placed under the Chief of Staff.[59] These formations sought in part to sideline jihadists, but organizations such as the ASMB maintained a presence in the east. In March 2011, the ASMB's al-Hasadi had said that "when things settle down in the country I will return to my house and my school and turn in my weapons."[60] A year later, a *Time* reporter called him "Darnah's most powerful man in the post-Gaddafi era."[61]

In Derna and Benghazi, there was a "wave of political assassinations."[62] Two of those targeted were al-Hasadi[63] and Bin Qumu,[64] although both survived. Their assassins may have come from among the various small jihadist groups in the city, groups too hardline for

---

[57] European Union Election Assessment Team, "Libya – Final Report: General National Congress Election," July 7, 2012, www.eods.eu/library/FR%20LIBYA %2021.10.2012_en.pdf.

[58] The Carter Center, "General National Congress Elections in Libya – Final Report," July 7, 2012, 6, www.cartercenter.org/resources/pdfs/news/peace_ publications/election_reports/libya-070712-final-rpt.pdf.

[59] Fiona Mangan and Christina Murtaugh, "Security and Justice in Postrevolution Libya: Where to Turn?" United States Institute of Peace, 2014, www.usip.org/ sites/default/files/PW100-Security-and-Justice-in-Post-Revolution-Libya.pdf.

[60] Al-Sisi, "Al-Qiyadi al-Islami 'Abd al-Hakim al-Hasadi."

[61] Abigail Hauslohner, "With Libya's Ascendant Islamists: 'Don't Get the Wrong Idea'," *Time*, March 30, 2012, http://content.time.com/time/world/article/ 0,8599,2110520,00.html.

[62] Human Rights Watch, "Libya: Wave of Political Assassinations," August 8, 2013, www.hrw.org/news/2013/08/08/libya-wave-political-assassinations.

[63] David Kirkpatrick, "Libya Democracy Clashes with Fervor for Jihad," *New York Times*, June 23, 2012, www.nytimes.com/2012/06/24/world/africa/libya- jihadis-offer-2-paths-democracy-or-militancy.html?_r=0.

[64] "Najat Sufyan bin Qumu Ra'is Katibat Ansar al-Shari'a fi Darna min Hujum fi Libiya," *Al-Quds al-Arabi*, April 15, 2013, www.alquds.co.uk/?p=34291.

ASMB and even for Ansar al-Shari'a to absorb or control. The small groups targeted "security agents, judges, journalists, activists, and human rights workers."[65]

2014 was a pivotal year for both Libya and Derna. New parliamentary elections were held in June, but this time some major actors rejected the outcome. Turnout fell from 60% in 2012 to less than 20% in 2014. Official results gave a sweeping victory to liberal forces while reducing Islamists' seats. The victors established the new House of Representatives, based in the eastern city of Tobruk. But the Islamist-leaning General National Congress (GNC) refused to dissolve and instead constituted a rival parliament. This political and geographical conflict quickly became a military one as well. Each side aligned with a coalition of militias as it prepared to confront the other. In the west, the militia coalition called itself "Operation Dawn," while in the east the coalition was "Operation Dignity."

The latter force, a so-called Libyan National Army (LNA), was led by Khalifa Haftar. In the 1980s, as a senior military officer, Haftar had led Qadhafi's incursions in northern Chad. He was captured and disavowed by Qadhafi in 1987. He then spent years exiled in the United States. Haftar returned to Libya in 2011. He soon became the most controversial figure in the country: to his supporters, a beacon of hope; to his detractors, a vehicle for the reimposition of Qadhafi-style tyranny. As Operation Dignity began, Haftar indicated that he saw little difference between the Muslim Brotherhood and other "terrorists." He sought to consolidate power in northeastern Libya, especially Benghazi, by neutralizing jihadists, controlling resources, and either breaking other militias or bending them to his rule. For the jihadists watching in Derna, Haftar loomed as their greatest external threat.

At the same time, the global intra-jihadist competition reached Derna. On April 4, 2014, local jihadists created the Consultative Council of the Youth of Islam (Majlis Shura Shabab al-Islam, MSSI). MSSI propaganda made its sympathies for the Islamic State clear.[66] The MSSI presented itself as an initiative that promoted Muslim unity. In its founding statement, the group quoted one of the Qur'an verses

---

[65] "Sira' 'Da'ish' wa-'Al-Qa'ida' Yantaqil ila Libiya."

[66] Aaron Zelin, "The Islamic State's First Colony in Libya," Washington Institute for Near East Policy, October 10, 2014, www.washingtoninstitute.org/policy-analysis/view/the-islamic-states-first-colony-in-libya.

most favored by the Islamic State: "Hold firmly to the rope of Allah, together, and do not become divided" (3:103). Its first task, the MSSI said, would be "forming a legal committee to break up disputes and reconcile people through the law of God." The MSSI made plain that such unity would be on its own terms. The group called on all those associated with "the laws of unbelief, the customs of un-Islamic ignorance, and the institutions that oppose the law of God" to repent – to give a public display of deference to the MSSI. The group further stated, "We extend a helping hand to all the people of righteousness (*ahl al-salah*) among the youth and the discerning people (*al-'uqala'*) who want the law of God."[67]

This reference to "the youth and the discerning people" was telling, especially in terms of the MSSI's attitudes toward older Libyan jihadists. The MSSI had a different demographic base than the ASMB, reflecting the different prewar networks out of which each faction emerged. The Islamic State's presence in Derna revolved around a foreign leadership contingent and a base of youthful Libyan fighters; the city's veteran jihadists largely rejected the group. The Libyan youth who joined initially came from the ranks of returning fighters from Syria and from the many small, extremely hardline jihadist groups in Derna – such groups craved "unity in the ranks," but not under ASMB or Ansar al-Shari'a.[68]

The foreign leaders included Iraqi national Wisam al-Zubaydi (also known as Abu Nabil al-Anbari and Abu al-Mughira al-Qahtani), who was killed outside Derna in November 2015 by a US airstrike.[69] Another foreigner was Saudi Arabian national Abu 'Ammar al-Jazrawi (d. 2017), who served as a judge for the group. Al-Jazrawi later served as one of the group's emirs in Sirte.[70] The Saudi Arabian national Abu Hubayb al-Jazrawi (perhaps the same individual as Abu 'Ammar) was another key leader, and the person who officially accepted the pledge

---

[67] "Fi Darna 'Majlis Shura Shabab al-Islam'," Assakina, April 14, 2014, https://web.archive.org/web/20140417023052/https://www.assakina.com/center/parties/42346.html.

[68] "Sira' 'Da'ish' wa-'Al-Qa'ida' Yantaqil ila Libiya."

[69] See Ibn al-Sadiqa, "Kalimat fi Ritha' al-Nabil/Abi al-Mughira al-Qahtani," January 5, 2016, https://justpaste.it/q793.

[70] Muhammad al-'Arabi, "Qiyadi Da'ishi Yakshif Tafasil Jadida 'an Wujud al-Tanzim fi Sirt," Al Arabiya, August 25, 2017, www.alarabiya.net/ar/north-africa/2017/08/25/قيادي-داعشي-يكشف-تفاصيل-جديدة-عن-وجود-التنظيم-في-سرت.html.

of allegiance from Derna militants.[71] The Islamic State's "scholar-in-arms,"[72] Bahraini national Turki al-Bin'ali (1984–2017), also traveled to Libya. According to one Libyan source, al-Bin'ali first arrived in Libya in October 2013. He toured Sirte, Benghazi, and Derna, seeking allies for the Islamic State even before the group's declaration of a caliphate in June 2014. In Derna, al-Bin'ali reportedly met the ASMB's Salim Darbi and Bin Qumu, eliciting a rejection from Darbi and acceptance from Bin Qumu.[73] If this assertion about Bin Qumu is true, it would make him one of the only prominent older local Derna jihadists to join the Islamic State. Other sources, however, list Bin Qumu as one of the anti-Islamic State leaders there. Overall, the generational split was far-reaching among Derna's jihadists.

Initially, the MSSI made progress in imposing its control over Derna, but the group quickly antagonized both ordinary residents and veteran jihadists. During the summer and autumn of 2014, the group implemented its version of shari'a. Through its court and its *hisba* (force for the enforcement of virtue and the punishment of vice and sin), MSSI flogged and executed accused criminals and deviants.[74] Meanwhile, disagreements between Islamic State supporters and the ASMB turned violent. In May 2014, unknown gunmen killed an ASMB commander, Muhammad Abu Bilal.[75] On July 18, gunmen assassinated the ASMB's Maziq 'Abd al-Qadir al-Qabisi.[76] Approximately six months after its formation, the MSSI pledged allegiance to the Islamic State,

---

[71] Munira al-Hadib, "Sa'udi Yatallaqa 'al-Bay'a' li-'Khalifat Da'ish' al-Baghdadi min al-Libiyyin," Al Hayat, November 2, 2014, www.alhayat.com/Articles/ 5450419. See also "Haqa'iq Asasiyya 'an Tanzim al-Dawla al-Islamiyya fi Libiya," Reuters, December 9, 2016, https://ara.reuters.com/article/ME_ TOPNEWS_MORE/idARAKBN13Y1N4.

[72] Cole Bunzel, "The Caliphate's Scholar-in-Arms," Jihadica, July 9, 2014, www .jihadica.com/the-caliphate%E2%80%99s-scholar-in-arms/.

[73] Al-'Arabi, "Qiyadi Da'ishi Yakshif Tafasil Jadida"; and "Al-Bin'ali Yadghat li-Tawsi' Nufudh 'Da'ish' fi Libiya Raghm Tazayud al-'Araqil 'ala al-'Ard," Al-Sharq al-Awsat, May 11, 2015, https://aawsat.com/home/article/357561/ البنعلي-يضغط-لتوسيع-نفوذ-»داعش«-في-ليبيا-رغم-تزايد-العراقيل-على-الأرض.

[74] Human Rights Watch, "Libya: Extremists Terrorizing Derna Residents," November 27, 2014, www.hrw.org/news/2014/11/27/libya-extremists-terrorizing-derna-residents.

[75] Salim al-'Ubaydi, "Ightiyal Amir Katibat Shuhada' Bu Salim fi Darna," Al-Wasat, May 30, 2014, http://alwasat.ly/ar/news/libya/20403/.

[76] Salim al-'Ubaydi, "Ightiyal Qiyadi bi-Katibat Shuhada' Bu Salim Darna," Al-Wasat, July 19, 2014, http://alwasat.ly/ar/news/libya/27767/.

becoming Wilayat Barqa (Eastern Libya Province). The pledge paralleled announcements that came simultaneously from Saudi Arabia, Yemen, Algeria, and Sinai.

The Libyan pledge accelerated the intra-jihadist conflict in Derna. The Islamic State's rivals closed ranks, highlighting how incipient fratricide could prompt mergers and realignments: In December 2014, ASMB and the Derna wing of Ansar al-Shari'a formed the Consultative Council of the Mujahidin of Derna (Majlis Shura Mujahidi Darna, usually abbreviated DMSC in English). The council's formation instantiated a broader trend in eastern Libya. Similar councils formed in Benghazi and Ajdabiya, also with broadly anti-Islamic State outlooks. The DMSC was led by an older generation of jihadists who opposed the Islamic State: These leaders included Salim Darbi, Bin Qumu (representing Ansar al-Shari'a), and Nasir al-'Akar of the ASMB.[77] Ironically, the Islamic State's divisive posture actually prompted a fair amount of intra-jihadist consolidation among other groups.

Many Islamic State fighters looked down on those older jihadists and rejected the approach followed by the ASMB and even by Ansar al-Shari'a. Yet the Islamic State in Derna could not ignore those other actors – the Islamic State's initial instincts were not accommodationist, but neither did the Islamic State immediately default to fratricide. As in Syria, the Islamic State's most promising recruitment strategy was to attract defectors from local jihadist groups and from al-Qa'ida's members, allies, and sympathizers. In Derna, this effort meant attracting leaders and members of Ansar al-Shari'a.[78]

Those the Islamic State could not coopt, it would try to discredit – including by saying that the ASMB had absorbed the taint of unbelief (*kufr*) by protecting a *taghut* (idolatrous tyrant), namely Mustafa 'Abd al-Jalil. Although the ASMB had not gone as far as the ex-LIFG leader Belhadj and others in accepting multi-party elections, the Islamic State

[77] Frederic Wehrey and Ala' Alrababa'h, "Splitting the Islamists: The Islamic State's Creeping Advance in Libya," Carnegie Endowment *Diwan*, June 19, 2015, http://carnegie-mec.org/diwan/60447?lang=en. On Aqar's membership in ASMB see Khalid Mahmud, "Libiya...Harb Mufaja'a bayn al-Jama'at al-Mutatarrifa fi Darna wa-Maqtal al-'Asharat," Al-Sharq al-Awsat, June 11, 2015, https://aawsat.com/home/article/381056/ليبيا-حرب-مفاجئة-بين-الجماعات-المتطرفة-في-درنة-ومقتل-العشرات.

[78] "Sira' 'Da'ish' wa-'Al-Qa'ida' Yantaqil ila Libiya."

still charged ASMB with de facto apostasy as a result of the ASMB's improvisations during the revolution.

The Debate over Protecting Mustapha 'Abd al-Jalil

Had the ASMB acted wrongly, un-Islamically, by protecting the NTC's Mustapha 'Abd al-Jalil when he visited Derna in 2011? Had the ASMB acted wrongly, un-Islamically, by enrolling as a militia with the Ministry of the Interior? For the hardliners, the ASMB had sold out, and the Islamic State used memories of the controversy as a rhetorical lever in their effort to peel supporters away from ASMB/DMSC and to delegitimize those groups. For the young radicals, the question of 'Abd al-Jalil's protection was an Islamic legal issue, one that touched on fundamental issues of identity and legitimacy. In the radicals' eyes, 'Abd al-Jalil was an infidel and a *"taghut."* By extension, anyone who had helped him had been tainted by his unbelief.

The ASMB understood the protection of 'Abd al-Jalil as an act of realpolitik. That act, they later explained, had been necessary to advance the revolution against Qadhafi, on both a practical and a rhetorical level. One *fatwa*-seeker from the ASMB wrote, "When he came to visit the city of Derna, it was after one of Qadhafi's spokesmen had warned him not to enter Derna, saying to him if you enter Derna, the extremists (*al-mutatarrifin*) will kill you!" Protecting 'Abd al-Jalil had offered Derna's jihadists a chance to refute Qadhafi's portrayal of the revolution and to challenge stereotypes of local jihadists as "extremists" – although it was exactly this type of accommodationism that the Islamic State was now denouncing.

The same ASMB *fatwa*-seeker implied another pragmatic reason for protecting 'Abd al-Jalil: his popularity among the revolutionaries. The fatwa-seeker said that in 2011, 'Abd al-Jalil "had unanimous support from 99% of the Libyan people because he was among the first defectors from Qadhafi and he was known among the people for his religiosity (if the expression is correct) – and in the Qadhafi regime he was working as minister of justice!"[79] Political engagement in 2011, the ASMB argued, had demanded some acknowledgment of

---

[79] Abu Muhammad al-Maqdisi, "Hukm Hirasat al-Mustashar Mustafa 'Abd al-Jalil wa-Ma Jara bi-Sabab Dhalik min Ikhtilaf wa-Fitan fi Libiya," Minbar al-Tawhid wa-l-Jihad, March 16, 2016, www.ilmway.com/site/maqdis/FAQ/MS_3927.html.

'Abd al-Jalil's status. Perhaps the ASMB had even felt itself caught up in the wave of admiration for his defection and prior reputation. In 2011, Derna's jihadists had been swimming with the current of the revolution. In 2014, Derna's jihadists were competing for legitimacy against each other in Libya where there was no longer just one enemy, but many.

In late 2014, the Islamic State asked the ASMB to submit to formal legal proceedings concerning the issue of protecting 'Abd al-Jalil. The Islamic State had already decided that the LIFG had apostatized: "Its kufr is clear due to its participation in the Tarābulus [Tripoli] government and the democratic process under the leadership of Abdelhakim Belhadj." But the ASMB's case was slightly more complicated, hence the need for a trial. As one Islamic State leader explained,

As for the "Abū Salīm Martyrs Brigade," then it was a brigade that was once Salafi. Most of the soldiers of the Islamic State in Darnah were from the brigade's founders. They abandoned the brigade after it fell into a number of nullifiers of Islam, most infamous of which was its operating as part of the interior ministry in what was known as the "security committee." This is in addition to their security for the tāghūt Mustafa Abdul Jalil, Chairman of the National Transitional Council, when he visited Darnah and called to democracy. Since then, the people of proper methodology abandoned the brigade. They even killed leaders of the brigade who led it to the depths of kufr. All this was before the official expansion of the Islamic State to Libya. After Allah blessed it with expansion to Libya and most of the groups in Darnah pledged bay'ah to it, the Abū Salīm brigade requested its opponents from the other groups refer to the court of the Islamic State for a resolution. After studying the condition of the brigade and what it fell into, the court of the Islamic State ruled that the brigade had committed apostasy and called its individuals to repentance. A number of its followers and leaders repented whereas the remaining gathered together with the "Libyan Islamic Fighting Group" to form what they called "Majlis Shūrā Darnah."[80]

Through a formal legal process, the Islamic State's authorities claimed, they had determined the ASMB's guilt and unbelief. If the ASMB would not repent, then it and the DMSC should be exterminated. Underlying the symbolism of the trial, meanwhile, was a nakedly

[80] Islamic State, "Interview with Abul-Mughirah al-Qahtani," *Dabiq* 11 (August/ September 2015): 60–63, 61, http://clarionproject.org/wp-content/uploads/Issue %2011%20-%20From%20the%20battle%20of%20Al-Ahzab%20to%20the %20war%20of%20coalitions.pdf.

political demand from the Islamic State to the ASMB/DMSC: submit to our authority.

The ASMB had a far different understanding of the trial. Shortly after its conclusion, an anonymous questioner from the ASMB wrote to the global jihadist ideologue Abu Muhammad al-Maqdisi. The questioner signed his name merely as "enemy of the apostates (*'aduww al-murtaddin*)" – a monikor meant to highlight the ASMB's own jihadist credentials, but perhaps also a veiled suggestion that the Islamic State's followers were falling into apostasy. The ASMB's petitioner reviewed the trial that the Islamic State had conducted, and explained:

Some of those [Islamic State fighters] set about making a fool of some of the brothers in charge on our side, using cunning and honeyed words (*bi-daha' wa-kalam ma'sul*) on the part of a Saudi judge whom they brought, together with a committee allied to them, from another city. They said to the brothers, "You, for us, are Muslims, and we see you as our brothers. We only ask you to sit for the law of God to have another look at the above-mentioned issues that divide us, in order to prevent bloodshed among the brothers. We should say, 'We hear and obey the ruling of God' when we are called to it, and [overall Islamic State leader Abu Bakr] al-Baghdadi sends his greetings to you and says that he does not pronounce *takfir* on you, and blah blah blah (*wa-wa-wa*)." So the brothers, who wanted to preserve peace within the city – in order to devote themselves to [fighting] Haftar and his henchmen among the *tawaghit* who were taking up positions in most of the nearby cities and villages, accompanied by secularists – looked into the matter.[81]

Just as protecting 'Abd al-Jalil had been an improvised response to various constraints, so too was the decision to submit to the Islamic State's judgment: According to this account, the ASMB hoped first to avoid further fighting and second to avoid appearing squeamish about submitting to Islamic law: An accommodationist gesture but also an act of symbolic self-defense. The ASMB was also watching Khalifa Haftar and his Libyan National Army warily; the veteran jihadists were trying not to get distracted by other concerns as they prepared for a fight for survival against Haftar. But, the anonymous petitioner complained, "It became clear when he [i.e., the Saudi judge] issued his

---

[81] 'Aduww al-Murtaddin (pseudonymous questioner), "Hawla Hukm Radd al-Natija al-Sadira min al-Tahkim alladhi Radiya bihi al-Tarafan Idha Khalafa Shar' Allah," October 11, 2014, https://justpaste.it/hj3i.

ruling that he had extremism in *takfir* (*'indahu ghuluww fi al-takfir*)."
Moreover, the judge's ruling had come only after the ASMB had
categorically refused to pledge allegiance to the Islamic State: The
ruling, according to the ASMB, was an act of political revenge by the
Islamic State rather than a purely legal decision.

Nevertheless, some of the ASMB's fighters worried about the optics
and the permissibility of contravening an official ruling from a judge
whom both sides had initially deemed qualified. Issues of both belief
and symbolic positioning were at play, and in my view are impossible
for the analyst to disentangle. The questioner appealed to al-Maqdisi:

Is it permissible to reject this arbitration when it becomes plain that the
ruling judge contradicts the legal texts in his judgments, or when it becomes
clear that he harbors extremism in the issue that the ruling concerns? . . .
And do you have any general advice for the brothers in Libya, whether
from the youth who have pledged allegiance to the [Islamic] State organization or the others?[82]

Al-Maqdisi responded as the questioner hoped, releasing the ASMB
from obedience to the Islamic State's court: "The ruling is not a ruling
of the law, but rather the ruling of the ignorant extremists (*al-ghulat al-
jahala*) who, out of their ignorance and extremism, declare Muslims
unbelievers, without precepts or bases . . . [and the brothers] should not
empower the ignorant extremists to control them or control the brothers."[83] The trial did not settle the dispute; rather, different visions of
politicized Islamic jurisprudence competed for jihadists' sympathies.

As conflict between the Islamic State and the DMSC continued into
2015, the Islamic State continued to raise the issue of 'Abd al-Jalil as a
means of aggravating the DMSC and attracting defectors. In April
2015, a clearly frustrated ASMB issued a statement entitled "Clearing
the Doubts about the Abu Salim Martyrs' Brigade (*Kashf al-Shubuhat
'an Katibat Shuhada' Abi Salim*)." The ASMB said, "We, the Abu
Salim Martyrs' Brigade, are free of guilt toward God (*nabra' ila
Allah*) of protecting the *tawaghit* and the apostates to aid their religion, and of helping them to spread their unbelief." As for protecting
'Abd al-Jalil, the ASMB said, "We see it as an Islamic legal duty and
we do not disavow it before God (*wa-la nabra' ila Allah minha*). It

[82] Ibid.
[83] Abu Muhammad al-Maqdisi (respondent), "Hawla Hukm Radd al-Natija
al-Sadira."

was done by some members of the Brigade out of hope that he would [truly] accept Islam and to ward off, for the city, [the consequences of] the heinous act of killing him (*wa-dar'an li-mafsadat qatlihi 'an al-madina*)." The doctrine of "warding off evil" is a core principle in Islamic jurisprudence, and so the ASMB's argumentation was not haphazard but rather was done through scholarly conventions. The ASMB cited classical Islamic authorities in support of their position. In their concluding points, they dissociated themselves from anyone who protected "*tawaghit*" in order to spread unbelief, but they warned others not to pronounce *takfir* against ASMB.[84] The ASMB's/DMSC's accommodation of the Islamic State was coming to an end.

The controversy did not die there. April 2015 became a turning point in the overall conflict between the Islamic State and the DMSC. On the one hand, the Islamic State was gaining some ground. The group attracted the defection of a major judge, Abu 'Abd Allah al-Libi, from Ansar al-Shari'a. In April 2015, he published *Legal and Practical Justifications for Pledging Allegiance to the Islamic State* (*Al-Mubarrirat al-Shar'iyya wa-l-Waqi'iyya li-Bay'at al-Dawla al-Islamiyya*).

On the other hand, the Islamic State's overreach antagonized swaths of Derna's population, giving a valuable insight into how jihadist intimidation of civilians can backfire. On April 20–21, 2015, the Islamic State killed several members of a prominent local clan, the Harir. After one member of the clan killed another, the slain man's family asked the Islamic State for help, and they intervened. But the accused murderer's family refused the Islamic State entry into their house. The situation devolved into an hours-long gunfight that killed, according to one account, six members of the accused's family (including two women) and as many as ten Islamic State fighters.[85] The DSMC positioned itself as the Harir clan's protector. Months later, the DSMC was still killing Islamic State fighters in revenge for the

---

[84] Katibat Shuhada' Abi Salim, "Kashf al-Shubuhat 'an Katibat Shuhada' Abi Salim," Facebook, April 2, 2015, www.facebook.com/686604671438538/photos/a.687176638048008.1073741828.686604671438538/746912422074429/?type=3.

[85] Abu Azuhayr al-Azdi, "Sal al-Husam li-Muwajahat Ahl al-Baghy wa-l-Ijram," May 4, 2015, https://justpaste.it/kvl7.

family's losses.[86] The Islamic State's intimidation inadvertently opened opportunities for the DMSC to broaden its coalition.

Further Islamic State provocations followed. On a Friday in late April 2015, the Islamic State attempted to impose one of its preachers at Fatimat al-Zahra' mosque on the Derna coast. According to one critic's account, the Islamic State preacher was largely spurned by the neighborhood's residents, who put forth another man to preach. When the Islamic State preacher spoke after the prayer, the residents refused to listen to him and left the mosque. The next Friday, the Islamic State returned with many gunmen and succeeded (after tense discussions with an armed group of neighborhood mosque-goers) in imposing their preacher. Again, however, most of the local men refused to pray behind him and instead conducted their own prayer in the mosque's courtyard.[87] These incidents provoked polemicists to publish arguments against the Islamic State's behavior.[88] They also angered many Derna residents, giving the DMSC more recruits.

The Islamic State's actions can be seen as short-sighted and counter-productive, or as blindly doctrinal. Yet they also had an internal political logic, reflecting the dilemmas confronting the Islamic State. If the DMSC's problems reflected the costs of accommodationism, the Islamic State now seemed to be locking itself into a vicious cycle: Attempts at intimidation produced backlashes, prompting further intimidation.

The Islamic State's sermon on May 1, delivered despite the refusal of most mosque-goers at Fatimat al-Zahra' to listen to it, was inflammatory toward the DMSC. In response, the DMSC issued a "The Final Warning to the Extremists of Takfir (*Al-Tahdhir al-Akhir li-Ghulat al-Takfir*)." The DMSC complained that "one of the young idiots climbed the pulpit of the Fatimat al-Zahra mosque last Friday and began barking at the mujahidin who are undertaking, by the grace of God, the guarding of the ports. He claimed – may God rebuke him

---

[86] Majlis Shura Mujahidi Darna, "Al-Qasas Hayah," July 6, 2015, available at https://jihadology.net/wp-content/uploads/_pda/2015/07/majlis-shc5abrc481-al-mujc481hidc4abn-darnah-22implementation-of-the-retribution-upon-some-of-the-members-of-the-state-involved-in-shedding-blood-of-majlis-shc5abrc481-al-mujc481.pdf.

[87] Abu Azuhayr al-Azdi, "Taslit al-Adwa' 'ala Ma Fa'alahu Tanzim al-Dawla bi-Masjid Fatimat al-Zahra'," May 5, 2015.

[88] Al-Azdi, "Sal al-Husam"; Al-Azdi, "Taslit al-Adwa'."

(*qabbahahu Allah*) – that they [i.e., the Islamic State] alone preserve the limits of God and that groups other than them only exist to protect the *tawaghit*." The DMSC now mounted its own effort at intimidation: "We showed his words to their leader (*kabirihim*) and he dissociated himself from his words and said that he [i.e., the preacher] does not represent them … And had it not been for this leader of theirs dissociating himself from the words of their little one, it would have been another affair altogether for us and for them."[89]

The DMSC now rejected the Islamic State's symbolic authority. In its "Final Warning," the DMSC now suggested that it was the Islamic State that had grossly distorted Islam. "Where is the judgment of God on your preacher who gave a sermon in your alleged caliphate (*khila-fatikum al-maz'uma*) and spoke about the Messenger of God, peace and blessings upon him, with frank, clear unbelief, and claimed that if he were alive he would have followed your imam?" Regarding Derna politics, the DMSC asked, "Why is it that your shaykhs have only screeched about *takfir* of the mujahidin who have opposed them, and about *takfir* of those who made a legal judgment call to whom it became clear that it was permissible to safeguard a man in hope that he would accept Islam and out of fear for the Muslims should he be killed (*man ijtahadu wa-tabayyana lahum jawaz ta'min rajul raja'a islamihi wa-khawfan 'ala al-muslimin min qatlihi*)?"[90] These were doctrinal arguments, but they were also highly political ones – not just "cheap talk," since they were backed up by a willingness to fight and die, but political in the sense that they responded to events and represented an evolution in the DMSC's rhetorical posture.

The DMSC also highlighted the bitter generational splits underlying the conflict. The Islamic State in Libya, the DMSC suggested, was a mix of youngsters and foreigners who had claimed credit for the accomplishments of more seasoned jihadists. "The rule of God – you idiot, fugitive, turncoat (*safih abiq mariq*) – we had already begun to establish, by the grace of God, for we removed the rule of the *taghut* [i.e., Qadhafi], we secured the fearful, we fed the hungry, and we barricaded the ports. And had it not been for God's grace upon us and His help for us in that, there would have been no foothold

---

[89] Majlis Shura Mujahidi Darna wa-Dawahiha, "Al-Tahdhir al-Akhir li-Ghulat al-Takfir," May 6, 2015, 1, www.facebook.com/1416578635237918/photos/pcb .1645407012355078/1645406909021755/?type=3&theater.

[90] Ibid., 1.

(*mawti' qadam*) for you in the city." The Islamic State should know
better, the DMSC said, than to pronounce *takfir* against "your over-
lords among the mujahidin, on whose jihad you have piggybacked
(*asyadikum min al-mujahidin, alladhina tataffaltum 'ala jihadihim*)."[91]
A sense of resentment comes through, directed against the youth who
had rhetorically outflanked their elders. The statement closed by
warning the young preacher and his associates to repent.

The conflict between the DMSC and the Islamic State escalated in
June 2015. On June 9, two DMSC leaders were assassinated: al-'Akar,
the DMSC's deputy leader, and Faraj al-Huti.[92] In the ensuing clashes,
the major jihadist leader Darbi was killed, evoking widespread anger
and mourning not just among jihadists, but among a wide spectrum of
Libyan Islamists.[93] Darbi's death prompted a full-scale war in central
Derna's streets; the Libyan Air Force reportedly bombed Islamic State
sites, including the Hisbah headquarters, during the clashes.[94] The
DMSC reportedly attracted significant support from local civilians,[95]
demonstrating how Islamic State intimidation efforts had benefited the
DMSC and expanded its ranks. Clashes continued through the
summer,[96] ending in a decisive victory for the DSMC. The Islamic
State presence was reduced to a few positions in the city's 400 neigh-
borhood and the southern suburb of al-Fatayeh; by April 2016, the
Islamic State had been driven from these areas as well.[97]

Who benefited? The DMSC scored the eventual military victory. But
the chaos of intra-jihadist fighting cost both sides dearly, not just in

[91] Ibid., 2.
[92] Usama al-Jarid, "Tafasil Maqtal Qiyadiyayn bi-Majlis Shura Mujahidi Darna,"
  Al-Wasat, June 9, 2015, http://alwasat.ly/ar/news/libiya/78149/; and Mahmud,
  "Libiya..Harb Mufaja'a."
[93] Wehrey and Alrababa'h, "Splitting the Islamists."
[94] Mahmud, "Libiya...Harb Mufaja'a."
[95] Ulf Laessing and Ayman al-Warfalli, "Expulsion from Derna Bastion May Show
  Limits for Islamic State in Libya," Reuters, July 24, 2015, www.reuters.com/
  article/us-libya-security/expulsion-from-derna-bastion-may-show-limits-for-
  islamic-state-in-libya-idUSKCN0PY1A620150724.
[96] "Maqtal Qiyadi min Katibat Bu Salim Darna wa-Ithnayn min Rifaqihi fi Hujum
  li-'Da'ish'," Akhbar Libya 24, August 19, 2015, https://akhbarlibya24.net/
  archives/58556/; and "Tanzim Da'ish Yaqsif Masjid Fatimat al-Zahra' fi
  Madinat Darna," Qanat Libiya, August 26, 2015, https://libyaschannel.com/
  ‏2015/08/26/م-في-هراء-الزـفاطمة-مسجد-يقصف-داعش-تنظيم/.
[97] Ayman al-Warfalli, "Islamic State in Retreat around East Libyan City:
  Military," Reuters, April 20, 2016, www.reuters.com/article/us-libya-security/
  islamic-state-in-retreat-around-east-libyan-city-military-idUSKCN0XH27H.

terms of the dead (who, even for the winning side, included some of the most prominent and skilled commanders) but also in terms of time. As jihadists clashed in Derna, Khalifa Haftar consolidated his hold on Benghazi and prepared to move out along the coast and deep into southern Libya. In 2018, Haftar took Derna.

Analysts widely assume that jihadists are masters of chaos. It is true that revolutions and civil wars can boost jihadists' prospects for building support, taking territory, and making money. This scenario occurred in Libya.[98] Yet chaos can also thwart jihadists' ambitions. As Geoff Porter wrote in 2016, "Libya's open spaces and its intensely contested landscape leave little room for the Islamic State."[99]

Conclusion

When pushed, veteran jihadists inside Derna and in the orbit of al-Qaʿida cited notions of realpolitik to defend their actions against theological–legal challenges from young hardliners. At stake was the question of accommodationism, and who had the power to define the sphere of jihadist political action.

The lessons of Derna are important to consider when assessing claims that al-Qaʿida and its allies behaved skillfully in the conflict zones that opened up during and after the Arab Spring. Starting in 2012, various commentators began to argue that jihadists were major beneficiaries of the popular protests against Arab autocrats.[100] It is true that starting in 2011, jihadist movements broadened their followings and asserted themselves in public life in Tunisia, eastern Libya, Egypt's Sinai, southern Yemen, and parts of Syria and Iraq.

Yet there are reasons to be cautious about such analysis. First, as I have argued elsewhere, defining "who counts as al-Qaʿida" is not easy, particularly when ties between fighters on the ground and the

---

[98] See Wehrey and Alrababaʿh, "Rising out of Chaos," for a succinct treatment of how Libya's chaos enabled the Islamic State's initial emergence there.

[99] Geoff Porter, "How Realistic Is Libya as an Islamic State 'Fallback'?" *Combating Terrorism Center Sentinel* 9:3 (March 2016), https://ctc.usma.edu/how-realistic-is-libya-as-an-islamic-state-fallback/.

[100] See Robert F. Worth, "Jihadists' Surge in North Africa Reveals Grim Side of Arab Spring," *New York Times*, January 19, 2013, www.nytimes.com/2013/01/20/world/africa/in-chaos-in-north-africa-a-grim-side-of-arab-spring.html.

formal al-Qa'ida organization are indirect.[101] The veteran jihadists in Derna were not merely an extension of al-Qa'ida; they also had local identities and local stakes; and there was considerable variation in the strength of individual leaders' ties to global jihadism.

Second, one should not forget that the primary "winners" of the Arab Spring turned out to be the Arab autocrats themselves. At the time of writing, more than eight years after the protests of 2011, one finds more continuity than change in terms who really rules in the Middle East. In Egypt, the military reasserted its rule; in Syria, Bashar al-Assad clung to power; in Tunisia, the president from 2014 to 2019 was an octogenarian veteran of the ancien regime. Even in territories gripped by civil war, the main political players are not jihadists but rather factions with complex alliances and broad-based support, such as the Houthis in Yemen or the military commander Khalifa Haftar in Libya.

Where jihadists thrived in the shadow of the Arab Spring, it was either in zones where the bigger players were temporarily too busy fighting amongst themselves to worry about pockets of jihadist control (as in Libya and Yemen), or in the special case of eastern Syria and western Iraq, where the Islamic State achieved an unprecedented degree of jihadist territorial consolidation. Even there, however, it was central authorities' venality and embrace of "sectarianization"[102] that abetted jihadist ambitions. And some authorities were crafty – as a famous cartoon by Mana Neyestani suggested, Assad likely allowed jihadists to flourish after 2011 in order to present the international community with a binary choice: him or the mujahidin.[103] Jihadist control during and after the Arab Spring did not arise solely due to jihadists' strategic brilliance.

Moreover, one should not forget that even if some jihadist groups grew emboldened during the Arab Spring and afterwards, this period also saw waves of death among jihadist leaders. By sticking their necks

---

[101] Alex Thurston, "Who Counts As Al-Qaeda: Lessons from Libya," Lawfare, May 7, 2017, www.lawfareblog.com/who-counts-al-qaeda-lessons-libya.

[102] Nader Hashemi and Danny Postel, "Introduction: The Sectarianization Thesis" in *Sectarianization: Mapping the New Politics of the Middle East*, edited by Nader Hashemi and Danny Postel, 1–22 (New York: Oxford University Press, 2017).

[103] Zack Beauchamp, "One Cartoon That Captures the Horrible Truth about Assad and ISIS," Vox, August 22, 2014, www.vox.com/2014/8/22/6057055/ syria-cartoon.

out in a more public fashion, many jihadists with decades-long careers died at the hands of the United States or at the hands of other jihadists. Scores of other local leaders and fighters met their ends during this period as well, including in Derna.

Jihadists also have internal divisions when it comes to questions of strategy, and these strategic differences came to the fore during the Arab Spring. The popular revolutions of 2011 immediately evoked profound debates: Hotheads clamored for action, and more reflective voices urged caution. In early 2011, the leader of al-Qa'ida's franchise in Yemen, Nasir al-Wuhayshi, wrote to Usama bin Laden. "If you wanted San'a' some day," al-Wuhayshi enthused, "today is the day!"[104] Bin Laden discouraged any premature moves: "The greater enemy . . . still possesses the capabilities that allow him to topple any state we establish."[105] Bin Laden expressed skepticism about the desirability of revolution at all: "We are still in the preparation stage, and it is not in our interest to rush in working to bring down the regime."[106] Today, Bin Laden's words seem more prescient than al-Wuhayshi's – but in any case, both men are dead, and it is the non-jihadist Houthis who rule in San'a'. In Derna, many of the jihadists on both sides of the ASMB–Islamic State battle are dead as well, and it is Khalifa Haftar whose forces rule in eastern Libya.

---

[104] "Letter from Basir to the Brother in Command," document recovered at Usama bin Laden's compound in Abbottabad, Pakistan, translated and declassified by the Office of the Director of National Intelligence, declassified March 1, 2016, 1, www.dni.gov/files/documents/ubl2016/arabic/Arabic%20Letter%20from%20Basir%20to%20the%20Brother%20in%20Command.pdf.

[105] "Letter to Abu Basir," document recovered at Usama bin Laden's compound in Abbottabad, Pakistan, translated and declassified by the Office of the Director of National Intelligence, declassified March 1, 2016, 1–2, www.dni.gov/files/documents/ubl2016/arabic/Arabic%20Letter%20to%20Abu%20Basir.pdf. See also Nelly Lahoud et al., "Letters from Abbottabad: Bin Laden Sidelined?" Combating Terrorism Center Harmony Project, May 3, 2012, 29–35, http://nsarchive.gwu.edu/NSAEBB/NSAEBB410/docs/UBLDocument16.pdf.

[106] "Letter to Abu Basir," 3.

7 | Mauritania
Post-Jihadism?

From 2005 to 2011, Mauritania was in the crosshairs of the Salafi Group for Preaching and Combat (French acronym GSPC) and the GSPC's successor, al-Qaʻida in the Islamic Maghreb (AQIM). After 2011, AQIM attacks on Mauritania largely ceased. Patterns of jihadist recruitment there also shifted. In the mid-2000s, the GSPC/AQIM had some incipient success at building local Mauritanian cells, especially in the capital Nouakchott. But by the 2010s, Mauritanians interested in jihadism were leaving the country for the greater opportunities available in neighboring Mali and elsewhere in the Sahel.

Mauritania contrasts with the preceding cases, all of which dealt with relatively successful jihadist coalition-building exercises. All of those coalitions sooner or later ran into internal political challenges and external political obstacles, but they all temporarily succeeded in mobilizing numerous fighters and developing complex internal structures. Mauritania's domestic militants never grew beyond small cells; Mauritania is a negative case of jihadist coalition-building.

Why did jihadist mobilization hit a ceiling in Mauritania? I start from the assumption that macro explanations such as demography, the economy, or the relative strength of the state do not have sufficient explanatory power: For example, jihadism blossomed in Algeria in the 1990s despite the Algerian state and the Algerian economy being stronger than their Mauritanian equivalents. Rather, this chapter argues that three crucial political factors came into play and interacted.

First, the quality of most jihadist recruits in Mauritania was low, reflecting political decisions made by the GSPC/AQIM field commanders: One decision was that high-quality Mauritanian recruits were siphoned off to fight elsewhere in northwest Africa. The young, amateurish networks that remained in Mauritania lacked effective leadership, making them prone to attempt half-baked plots. Based primarily in Nouakchott, they were highly vulnerable to disruption by the security services, who repeatedly identified militant safe houses. When more hardened GSPC/AQIM units did attack Mauritanian territory, their aggression sometimes alienated ordinary Mauritanians. Between the sloppiness of the local recruits and the harshness of the core AQIM cadres, jihadism had difficulty finding a solid base of support in the country.

Second were state policies: Violent jihadism appeared in the country at a period when Mauritanian authorities were toning down earlier policies of repression against a range of Muslim activists, and state responses to jihadism likely included a conscious decision to decrease repression against nonviolent activists. In this climate, Mauritanian authorities broke up in-country jihadist networks without resorting to the kind of collective punishment that Algerian authorities used in the early 1990s or that Malian authorities used in the 2010s. Mauritanian authorities then offered jihadists and would-be jihadists viable offramps back into mainstream society, a choice that denied the diehards the opportunity to build a broad-based coalition. Notably, the state's maltreatment of prominent Muslim scholars became a rallying cry for the jihadist mobilization in the mid-2000s. When the state eased up on imprisoning and torturing symbolic figures, authorities weakened one driver of recruitment. And by allowing some hardline preachers a degree of freedom, authorities drew some preachers and followers from jihadism back into more mainstream life, and also likely prevented other preachers from crossing into jihadist recruitment and coalition-building. Mauritanian authorities avoided producing the professionally frustrated "clerics of jihad" that Richard Nielsen has identified in the context of the wider Middle East.[1] As Frederic Wehrey has written, "Jihadi violence in Mauritania is thus circumscribed by firm state control and conventional military counterterrorism, leavened with tactical permissiveness toward jihadi media and 'soft' measures such as clerical intercession with imprisoned jihadists."[2]

Third, as mentioned earlier, Mali represented a pressure release valve for Mauritanian jihadism. Particularly in northern Mali and in the company of the AQIM field commander Mokhtar Belmokhtar,

---

[1] Richard Nielsen, *Deadly Clerics: Blocked Ambition and the Paths to Jihad* (Cambridge: Cambridge University Press, 2017).
[2] Frederic Wehrey, "Control and Contain: Mauritania's Clerics and the Strategy against Violent Extremism," Carnegie Endowment for International Peace, March 29, 2019, https://carnegieendowment.org/2019/03/29/control-and-contain-mauritania-s-clerics-and-strategy-against-violent-extremism-pub-78729.

skilled Mauritanian jihadists found opportunities to take on prominent roles and to pursue jihadist action on a scale that had proven infeasible in their own country. There may have been a geographical sifting of talent even before state policies of accommodation really took off in Mauritania; AQIM, and particularly Belmokhtar, kept the most talented Mauritanian recruits near his side while sending enthusiastic but less competent recruits back to Mauritania. Advancement opportunities for Mauritanians appeared to an even greater degree in the AQIM offshoot the Movement for Unity and Jihad in West Africa (MUJWA), which was headed by the Mauritanian national Hamada Ould Mohamed Kheirou from 2011 to 2013. Mauritanian authorities seem to have tacitly accepted the benefits that the Malian release valve offered them – in 2013, Mauritania was a notable exception among Sahelian countries when its government declined to send soldiers to Mali amid France's counter-jihadist Operation Serval.

As a counter-factual, one could have imagined a Mauritanian jihadist coalition that counted relatively prominent clerics. Those clerics could in turn have mobilized networks of students. Alternatively, a coalition based on racial, ethnic, or tribal identities could have emerged, with or without clerical support. These outcomes were avoided because of the political decisions (and in some cases, mistakes) made by local jihadist networks, fence-sitting clerics, the Mauritanian state, and the GSPC/AQIM.

Theoretical Implications of the Case

The Mauritanian counter-case invites a rethinking of what *accommodation* can mean in the context of jihadist politics. In the other cases discussed in this book, accommodation has involved jihadists' adaptation to the demands and preferences of constituencies and actors around them. It has also involved the the willingness of non-jihadists to tolerate some jihadist activity – in other words, situations where states, local politicians, tribal or ethnic constituencies, or businesspersons accommodate (or collude with) jihadists in their respective territories. In all of these cases, accommodation may dilute but not fundamentally derail the jihadist project.

In contrast, the Mauritanian counter-case highlights a form of accommodation where the state tolerated individuals with some jihadist-esque views. Such individuals regard certain foreign states as illegitimate, and they believed jihadist action was viable under certain theoretical conditions – but they renounced or denied the idea that jihadist violence inside Mauritania was feasible and desirable. The Mauritanian model of accommodation extended to former imprisoned and accused jihadists willing to renounce violence; in murkier ways, this accommodation may also entail political arrangements along the Mauritanian–Malian border that are closer to the types of accommodation seen earlier in this book – that is, state toleration of economic and even military activities by jihadists engaged in violence, just not violence within Mauritania's borders. In combination with other factors, the Mauritanian model has proved relatively successful at keeping the country essentially free of jihadist violence since 2011. It represents a situation where the state tacitly encourages dilution of the jihadist project to the point that jihadism transforms into something else.

This chapter chronicles two major themes: First, it examines the jihadist cells in Mauritania, the challenges they faced in trying to assemble a wider coalition, and the shifting state policies that initially contributed to jihadism's emergence in Mauritania but that eventually constrained jihadism there. Second, the chapter turns to what might be called "post-jihadist" Mauritania – a society where proto-jihadist messages still circulate, including among relatively prominent preachers, but where active jihadist mobilization is minimal. Here it is worth recalling Asef Bayat's theorization of "post-Islamism" as a condition that arises where "the appeal, energy, and sources of legitimacy of Islamism are exhausted even among its once-ardent supporters." When "Islamists become aware of their discourse's anomalies and inadequacies," they embrace pragmatism, discard "certain . . . underlying principles," and push the movement to "reinvent itself."[3] Certain trends in Mauritania exemplify "post-jihadism": a more pragmatic, stripped-down understanding of the political implications of Salafi-jihadist theology.[4] In twenty-first-century Mauritania, new

---

[3] Asef Bayat, "Post-Islamism at Large" in *Post-Islamism: The Changing Faces of Political Islam*, edited by Asef Bayat, 3–32 (Oxford: Oxford University Press, 2013), 8.

[4] Omar Ashour uses the term "post-jihadism" to refer to certain Libyan jihadists' (seeming?) renunciation of violence circa 2010. See his "Post-Jihadism: Libya and the Global Transformations of Armed Islamist Movements," *Terrorism and Political Violence* 23:3 (2011): 377–397. Here my usage is similar, although some

iterations of jihadist thought are emerging, partly through creative tension with the exigencies of living under an authoritarian regime that wants to keep its face as friendly as possible. The chapter closes by asking how long Mauritania's "post-jihadist" settlement can last, and how likely renewed jihadist mobilization is in the future.

The Mauritania case also allows for analysis of jihadist agency in pursuing *relocation*. The tendency of the best Mauritanian recruits to leave the country points back to the importance of not just local and national but also regional contexts for understanding jihadist politics. Mauritanian patterns of relocation suggest that jihadists do not move passively within regional theaters, as though they are unthinking particles flowing by osmosis into the least resistant subregional political environments. Instead, jihadists are conscious decision-making political actors who experiment with different types of political postures in different environments and then adapt to the results. The remarkable range of activities that AQIM, and particularly Belmokhtar, pursued in Mauritania within a brief six-year window undermines the widespread but flawed metaphor of jihadists as a kind of epidemic, and points instead to an understanding of jihadists as political agents. Crucially, relocation can occur even before a military and political defeat, exhibiting the ways that jihadists allocate limited manpower resources for both strategic and experimental ends.

The GSPC's Arrival in Mauritania: Political Context

In June 2005, the GSPC conducted its first major raid outside of Algeria's borders. A unit led by Belmokhtar attacked a Mauritanian military outpost at Lemgheitty, in the northeastern desert. As many as 150 GSPC fighters participated, and some fifteen Mauritanian soldiers were killed.[5] The GSPC portrayed the attack as revenge for Mauritanian arrests of Islamist activists. Referring to Mauritania's then-president as

---

Mauritanian post-jihadists appear to engage not in full renunciation but rather in accommodation to political and military realities.

[5] "Algerian Islamist Group Claims Mauritania Attack," Agence France-Presse, June 8, 2005, available at www.dailystar.com.lb/ArticlePrint.aspx?id=67086& mode=print. See also "Mauritania Has Proof Algerian Group Led Attack," Agence France-Presse, June 11, 2005, available at www.dailystar.com.lb/News/ Middle-East/2005/Jun-11/67111-mauritania-has-proof-algerian-group-led- attack.ashx.

"the Karzai of Mauritania and the agent of the Jews,"[6] the GSPC
excoriated the Mauritanian regime's participation in training exercises
associated with the US-led "War on Terror." Long before the GSPC/
AQIM proclaimed sweeping political ambitions in Mali, the group
singled out Mauritania for political condemnation. The advantage of
this rhetoric was that it could harness anger at the pronounced aggression that both the United States and its allies displayed in Afghanistan
and Iraq during the early War on Terror; the disadvantage was that it
also focused on particular Mauritanian state policies that the state ended
up being able to adjust within a period of just a few years.

Belmokhtar also explained the Lemgheitty attack as a response to
Mauritanian state policies and the wider regional context of northwest
Africa as a theater in the War on Terror. Belmokhtar cited what he
called "the thickening presence of activity by American forces in the
Sahel region and the Algerian Sahara." According to Belmokhtar, such
activity had increased in response to the GSPC and its growing contact
with al-Qaʻida.[7] The countries of the Sahel, he continued, were increasingly subservient to the United States and Israel. Here he singled out
Mauritania, which had established diplomatic relations with Israel in
1999 as part of Mauritanian authorities' efforts to rehabilitate their
regime following diplomatic and economic isolation for much of the
1990s. In Belmokhtar's telling,

The Mauritanian regime had shown complete deference to the Americans,
and the Israelis before that. This was represented especially in the recurring
attacks on the sons of the Islamic movement, and especially after the visit of
the Israeli Foreign Minister Silvan Shalom to Mauritania and the preparation
for joint military maneuvers with American forces. And the base for the
maneuvers in open country – for the occasion – was the Lemgheitty region.
The same region had witnessed joint maneuvers approximately two years
earlier. After that, we decided to attack that military site as a pre-emptive
strike (*darba istibaqiyya*), so that these regimes in this region would know
that we will not stay with our hands tied in view of what is happening.[8]

---

[6] US diplomats translated the statement in the aftermath of the attack. See U.S.
Embassy Nouakchott, "GSPC Communique Extols Attack in Mauritania, Links
It to Flintlock Exercise," leaked cable 05ALGIERS1163, June 7, 2005, https://
search.wikileaks.org/plusd/cables/05ALGIERS1163_a.html.

[7] "Hiwar maʻa al-Qaʼid Khalid Abi al-ʻAbbas – Amir al-Mintaqa al-Sahrawiyya li-
l-Jamaʻa al-Salafiyya li-l-Daʻwa wa-l-Qital," Minbar al-Tawhid wa-l-Jihad, May
25, 2006, www.ilmway.com/site/maqdis/MS_37048.html.

[8] Ibid.

The GSPC/AQIM was making sweeping critiques of the regime. For its part, the regime proved to be brittle on the surface but, at a deeper level, highly durable.

In power at the time of the Lemgheitty attack was Colonel Maaouya Ould Sid'Ahmed Taya (b. 1941), who had taken power in a 1984 coup. Originally from the northern Mauritanian town of Atar, the career soldier succeeded a series of three relatively short-lived military governments. Ould Taya's reign brought continuity to Mauritanian politics but also involved repression against multiple targets. His government cracked down brutally on dissent from Afro-Mauritanian military officers and elites, the Afro-Mauritanians being one of three broad, socially constructed racial categories in the country (the other two being the *bidan* or "whites" and the *haratin* or Arabic-speaking "blacks"). Afro-Mauritanian elites' 1986 "Manifesto of the Oppressed Black Mauritanian" and Afro-Mauritanian officers' alleged coup-plotting efforts in 1987 threatened a political system and social order based on the supremacy of *bidan*, Arabic-speaking tribes. In the late 1980s, the regime's crackdowns widened into collective punishment of Afro-Mauritanians in the Senegal River valley, leading to inter-communal clashes, disputes with Senegal, and lingering tensions on both sides of the border.[9]

Tensions also surfaced regarding the social position of the *haratin*. Despite a 1981 law banning slavery in Mauritania, *haratin* activists decried what they called a widespread system of underground enslavement and coerced labor. Ironically, most of the central figures in Mauritania's jihadist cells two decades later would be *bidan*; racial tensions in Mauritania did not lead to widespread jihadist recruitment among either *haratin* or Afro-Mauritanians, although several suicide bombers were *haratin*.[10] Ould Taya's regime was seen by jihadists, however, as favoring northern Mauritania: one prominent Mauritanian jihadist alleged in 2006 that Mauritanian authorities, when dealing with imprisoned jihadists and Islamists, discriminated against

---

[9] For background on these events, see Human Rights Watch, "Mauritania's Campaign of Terror: State-Sponsored Repression of Black Africans," April 1994, www.hrw.org/sites/default/files/reports/MAURITAN944.PDF.

[10] Cédric Jourde, "Sifting through the Layers of Insecurity in the Sahel: The Case of Mauritania," Africa Center for Strategic Studies, September 30, 2011, https://africacenter.org/publication/sifting-through-the-layers-of-insecurity-in-the-sahel-the-case-of-mauritania/.

prisoners from the south: "I challenge anyone to bring one person, not from the region of the south, upon whom torture was practiced."[11] Yet the story of jihadism in Mauritania is partly the tale of jihadists' repeated failures to take advantage of the country's history of racial tensions generally, as well as more specific resentments against the networked tribes (Ould Taya's Smassid, his successor Mohamed Ould Abdel Aziz's Awlad/Oulad Bou Sbaa, or current President Mohamed Ould Ghazouani's Ideiboussat) that have dominated the presidency and its clientelist networks.[12]

In other sectors, there were consequences of Ould Taya's penchant for internal repression. In the 1990s, the regime experienced international isolation due to its domestic human rights record and its decision to side with Saddam Hussein during the Gulf War. The regime policies that Belmokhtar decried in 2005 – Mauritania's recognition of Israel and its willingness to conduct counterterrorism training with American forces – reflected Ould Taya's effort to rebuild his government's relationship with the United States. Recognizing Israel in 1999 was a relatively drastic (albeit also relatively successful) maneuver by Ould Taya; at a time when nearly every other Arab state condemned Israel, Ould Taya's diplomatic opening helped him to rebuild relations with the United States.

The arrival of the War on Terror just two years later was a stroke of good fortune for Ould Taya, at least initially.[13] As with other authoritarian regimes, participating in the War on Terror allowed Ould Taya

---

[11] "Al-Khadim Wuld al-Siman: Al-Haraka al-Salafiyya al-Muritaniyya," Al Jazeera, July 15, 2006, www.aljazeera.net/programs/today-interview/2006/7/15/الخديم-ولد-السمان-الحركة-السلفية-الموريتانية. Many of the Mauritanian jihadists were indeed from the south. See "Alak Kum Tanshur al-Sira al-Dhatiyya li-l-Sajin al-Rahil Wuld al-Hayba," Alegcom, May 2014, http://alegcom.blogspot.com/2014/05/blog-post_8346.html; and "Al-Siraj Tanshur al-Qissa al-Kamila 'li-Tanzim Ansar Allah al-Murabitin' fi Muritaniya," Essirage, October 18, 2010, http://webcache.googleusercontent.com/search?q=cache:H2S67UieqggJ:essirage.net/archive/index.php/news-and-reports/447-2010-10-18-22-11-44.html+&cd=18&hl=en&ct=clnk&gl=us&client=safari. Many others in the network were born in Nouakchott.

[12] As Cédric Jourde comments, "Alliances across tribes are a necessity." See "Mauritania: The New Strongman in Nouakchott," Italian Institute for International Political Studies, September 9, 2019, www.ispionline.it/en/pubblicazione/mauritania-new-strongman-nouakchott-23850.

[13] See Cédric Jourde, "Constructing Representations of the 'Global War on Terror' in the Islamic Republic of Mauritania," *Journal of Contemporary African Studies* 25:1 (2007): 77–100.

to increase Mauritania's visibility and utility to Washington while sidestepping questions about democratization and human rights. Between 2001 and 2004, Mauritania detained at least three alleged terrorists and handed them over to the Central Intelligence Agency's renditions program, making Mauritania one of at least fifty-four governments to participate.[14] Mauritania also joined US counterterrorism programs for the Sahel and northwest Africa.[15] Despite Mauritania's participation in the War on Terror, however, some security personnel felt that in the early 2000s the Mauritanian military was weak and corrupt, whereas the GSPC had the benefit of surprise, as well as the financial resources that came from its 2003 mass kidnapping in southern Algeria and the ensuing hostage payment (see Chapter 2).[16]

The early War on Terror arrived in a context where the Ould Taya regime had already gone far in repressing nonviolent forms of Islamist activism. From the 1970s on, Mauritania saw an uptick in Islamism as well as other forms of nontraditionalist religious activism. Such activism was concentrated in the rapidly growing capital, where "public religiosity" was an increasing feature of Muslims' lives.[17] The activists represented diverse tendencies, especially Muslim Brotherhood-style political Islamism, the missionary ethos of Jama'at al-Tabligh (see Chapter 3), and the theological literalism of Salafism. These activist currents had hybrid roots, reflecting the influence of Mauritanian students returning home from Gulf countries and beyond but also reflecting the rise of reformist, locally trained scholars such as Buddah Ould al-Busayri (1920–2009).[18]

The Islamists, who had the most overtly political program of these three currents, were interested in a deeper "Islamization" of the Mauritanian state, including through the application of their understanding of shari'a. These Islamists were not jihadists; they envisioned working through the Mauritanian political arena rather than overthrowing the

---

[14] Open Society Justice Initiative, "Globalizing Torture: CIA Secret Detention and Extraordinary Rendition," 2013, 96, www.opensocietyfoundations.org/sites/default/files/globalizing-torture-20120205.pdf.

[15] These are the Pan-Sahel Initiative (which ran 2002–2004) and the Trans-Saharan Counter-Terrorism Partnership (2005–present).

[16] Interview with Colonel (ret.) El Boukhary Mohamed Mouemel, Nouakchott, April 30, 2018.

[17] Elemine Moustapha, "Negotiating Islamic Revival: Public Religiosity in Nouakchott City," *Islamic Africa* 5:1 (Spring 2014): 45–82.

[18] Interview with Jamil Mansour, Nouakchott, September 27, 2017.

state. Through a series of organizations and political parties, the Islamists sought to pressure the state, reshape society, and compete in elections.[19] They professed (and in my view, largely demonstrated) a commitment to democracy, viewing themselves as peers to Islamist parties in Morocco and Turkey.[20]

There were, by the 1990s, some hardliners. In his youth, one of the key clerics discussed in this chapter, Mahfouz Ould al-Walid or Abu Hafs al-Muritani, wrote a postgraduate thesis entitled "Al-Sahwa al-Islamiyya fi Muritaniya (The Islamic Awakening in Mauritania)." In one passage, al-Muritani wrote, "After independence, Muslims' hopes hung on the modern Islamic republic ... but the modern state disappointed those hopes and broke its promises. For instead of ruling by the Law of God, it ruled by man-made laws."[21] Al-Muritani saw the military ruler Mohamed Khouna Ould Haidallah's decision to declare the implementation of shari'a in the early 1980s as a "bright spot" in an otherwise dark period. Al-Muritani called Ould Haidallah "an ignorant military man" who was nevertheless seemingly "sincere." Still, al-Muritani added, none of the traditionalist scholars, the Islamists, or the government had been prepared to implement a full shari'a system. Then had come Ould Taya, whom al-Muritani said "pleased the Westerners on one side and pleased the Arab nationalists and Communists on the other side."[22] Al-Muritani had an overall positive view of the Islamic movement in Mauritania, including its Muslim Brotherhood component, but he appended to the thesis a short overview of Salafi and proto-jihadi condemnations of democracy, secularism, and "man-made laws," implying his own rejection of the political process that Mauritania's Islamists were pursuing.

Meanwhile, Islamist parties were denied official recognition. There were periods of relative openness, where Islamist candidates could

---

[19] For broader discussions of Islamism in Mauritania, see Zekeria Ould Ahmed Salem, *Prêcher dans le désert: Islam politique et changement social en Mauritanie* (Paris: Karthala, 2013); and Francesco Cavatorta and Raquel Garcia, "Islamism in Mauritania and the Narrative of Political Moderation," *Journal of Modern African Studies* 55:2 (June 2017): 301–325.

[20] Interview with Jamil Mansour. Incidentally, I do not claim that Turkey's Islamists are democrats.

[21] Mahfuz Wuld al-Walid (Mahfouz Ould al-Walid/Abu Hafs al-Muritani), "Al-Sahwa al-Islamiyya fi Muritaniya," unpublished *maitrise* thesis at Al-Ma'had al-'Ali li-l-Dirasat wa-l-Buhuth al-Islamiyya, 1992, 38.

[22] Ould al-Walid, "Al-Sahwa al-Islamiyya fi Muritaniya," 42.

compete in elections as independents or run on the ticket of opposition parties. For example, the Islamist leader Jamil Mansour was elected mayor of the Arafat district of Nouakchott, serving from 2001–2003. Yet openings for Islamists alternated with regime crackdowns, especially in 1994 and 2003. The latter crackdown in particular reflected the rising instability Mauritania faced in the early 2000s, amid repeated attempted and rumored coups. Ould Taya reacted to the threats from within his own military by jailing Islamist leaders, accusing them of plotting against him; he also branded dissident soldiers as Islamist sympathizers.

The Islamist movement gained impetus from the repression. As discussed later, the torture of detainees and particularly of Muslim scholars under Ould Taya and his successors became a major grievance for young Mauritanian jihadists. The Islamist movement drew additional popularity by positioning itself as the foremost critic of Ould Taya's outreach to Israel.

The GSPC's 2005 attack on Lemgheitty was one of the triggers for the coup effort that finally unseated Ould Taya. After the attack, Ould Taya sent the country's elite red berets chasing fruitlessly after the GSPC in the desert, feeding discontent in the ranks and leaving him more vulnerable.[23] The increasingly isolated and erratic Ould Taya alarmed other leading members of his regime, particularly three senior officers: Mohamed Ould Abdel Aziz, Mohamed Ould Ghazouani, and Ely Ould Mohamed Vall. After helping Ould Taya repel a coup attempt in 2003, these officers staged their own successful coup against Ould Taya in August 2005.

After Ould Taya fell, the GSPC could hope to profit from uncertainty in the country; one could imagine a counter-factual where the 2005 coup might have marked the start of a political implosion that might have afforded the GSPC new coalition-building opportunities. Yet the new junta of Ould Abdel Aziz, Ould Ghazouani, and Vall were seasoned professionals who were interested above all in stability. They organized a much-lauded (but also partly stage-managed) transition to civilian democracy. In the March 2007 presidential election, economist and former cabinet minister Sidi Ould Cheikh Abdallahi won, becoming the first civilian head of state in a generation. Yet after a brief

---

[23] Noel Foster, *Mauritania: The Struggle for Democracy* (Boulder, CO: Lynne Rienner, 2011), ch. 3.

tenure marred by conflict with his prime minister and with the senior officers, Abdallahi was overthrown by Ould Abdel Aziz and Ould Ghazouani in August 2008; part of the stated justification for the coup was senior officers' contention that civilians were flailing in their response to jihadist attacks. Ould Abdel Aziz became military head of state, and then shed his uniform to run as a civilian – and win – in the July 2009 presidential elections. The net effect of the 2003–2009 period was the preservation of Ould Taya's system, just without Ould Taya.[24] Democratization had proved relatively fleeting.

Meanwhile, religious authority was undergoing a generational change in Mauritania. In 2009, two senior scholars died: Buddah Ould al-Busayri and Mohamed Salem Ould 'Addoud (1929–2009). As US diplomats commented at the time, "Mauritanians have been deeply affected by these losses and many make a connection between the deaths and the climate of division in the country. They think something must be really wrong in Mauritania if the country has been deprived of these saintly mens' [sic] presence at almost the same time."[25] Al-Busayri, the long-serving imam of Nouackhott, had been a "godfather" of sorts to the Islamists, Tablighis, and Salafis. His passing marked a fragmentation in the religious landscape – none of his successors could replicate his unifying role. One of his prominent young students, Mohamed Salim al-Majlisi (b. 1976), gravitated toward aspects of the jihadist project even as al-Busayri's more established successors adopted relatively loyalist or quietist postures. In this more fragmented landscape, Islamists and jihadist-leaning clerics found a wider audience. Ultimately, however, these clerics (including al-Majlisi) would either abandon or never fully endorse and thus reduce jihadists' chances for building a major coalition.

The Early GSPC/AQIM Cells in Mauritania

It is unclear how many Mauritanians actually participated in the Lemgheitty attack; according to the GSPC, the five casualties it took

---

[24] Foster (see ibid.) makes this argument at length.

[25] U.S. Embassy Nouakchott, "Ambassador's Luncheon with Anti-Coup Political Parties," leaked cable 09NOUAKCHOTT323, May 11, 2009, https://wikileaks .org/plusd/cables/09NOUAKCHOTT323_a.html.

there were all Algerians.[26] Yet in the second half of the 2000s, the GSPC/AQIM made some headway in recruiting Mauritanians. In a 2008 interview with the *New York Times*, AQIM's emir 'Abd al-Malik Droukdel bragged, "The Maghreb region is witnessing an awakening blessed jihad in Mauritania, Morocco, Libya, Nigeria, after the nation and its youths discovered the size of employment for the crusaders and the treason committed by this government against its people."[27]

Some Mauritanians gravitated toward AQIM units that fought elsewhere in the Sahel-Sahara. Other Mauritanians, at the suggestion of Belmokhtar, remained inside Mauritania to build up small cells. In terms of the criteria Belmokhtar used when allocating personnel, it appears highly likely that talent played a role; the Mauritanians sent home were not particularly professional as jihadists, indicating that Belmokhtar may have given them relatively wide rein but relatively little confidence. Another feature of Belmokhtar's decision-making was that even with the greenest Mauritanian recruits, he preferred to keep them in northwest Africa rather than funneling them – as some of them initially wished – to Iraq or other remote conflict theaters. Even as Belmokhtar allocated manpower resources in different ways, the scope of his thinking was regional rather than global.

One of the most important Mauritanian jihadists was Khadim Ould Semane (b. 1974 or 1976), who became the face of a small and ultra-hardline Mauritanian jihadist constituency. Ould Semane, born in Senegal to middle-class Mauritanian parents, grew up as a Sufi by background and, allegedly, a "bon vivant." He gravitated toward jihadism in the early 2000s, anguished over the US-led wars in Afghanistan and Iraq as well as the travails of Muslims in Palestine, Chechnya, and elsewhere. Initially hoping to fight Americans in Iraq, Ould Semane began organizing a cell in Senegal and Mauritania at Belmokhtar's direction.[28] Another young Mauritanian who followed a

---

[26] U.S. Embassy Nouakchott, "GSPC Announces 'Names' of Five Members Killed in Attack on Mauritania," leaked cable 05ALGIERS1525, July 19, 2005, https://search.wikileaks.org/plusd/cables/05ALGIERS1525_a.html.

[27] "An Interview with Abdelmalek Droukdal," *New York Times*, July 1, 2008, www.nytimes.com/2008/07/01/world/africa/01transcript-droukdal.html.

[28] Lemine Ould M. Salem, *Le Ben Laden du Sahara: Sur les traces du jihadiste Mokhtar Belmokhtar* (Paris: Éditions de la Martinière, 2014), 85–87. See also "Al-Khadim Wuld al-Siman," where Ould Semane describes how the unity of the Muslim world mandates action in the face of any individual Muslim's suffering.

similar trajectory was Sidi Ould Sidna, who grew up as a delinquent in Mauritania's capital Nouakchott. Like Ould Semane, he was angered by geopolitical events of the early 2000s and sought to reach Iraq. The GSPC sent him, too, back to Mauritania.[29] What is known of their biographies echoes the widespread caricature of the delinquent-turned-jihadist; such recruits, in my view, tend to be of lower quality and reliability than others with more formidable backgrounds.

By joining GSPC/AQIM, Ould Semane and others of his generation were reacting not just to events in far-off Iraq and Afghanistan but also to regime policies in Mauritania. In a 2006 interview with Al Jazeera, Ould Semane said:

When the Israeli, or Jewish, Embassy came to Mauritania, or to the land of Shinqit, the Islamist-secularist conflict really began. Those who assist the Jews and those who assist – in the regime, of course – those who assist the West and assist the Jews began to bare their fangs (*yukashshiruna 'an anyabihim*). They have the authority, the capabilities, and the powers, and they began harassing the Muslims, throwing the scholars into prisons and torturing them and abasing them, and violating people's honor.[30]

Ould Semane went on to say that the torture inflicted on imprisoned Islamists, Salafis, and jihadis was even worse than the torture the United States practiced at Guantanamo. He added that the Mauritanian state did not even make the pretense of taking prisoners to a torture site outside of constitutional authority – the state, he said, flouted its own constitution by torturing prisoners in the heart of Nouakchott. Of course, Ould Semane considered that constitution illegitimate, but he cited it in order to show what he considered the state's hypocrisy.

Some contemporaneous reporting supports Ould Semane's assertions about the severity of the torture. Amnesty International has alleged that between 2003 and 2008, authorities inflicted electric shocks, cigarette burns, beatings, contorted postures, sleep deprivation, sexual violence, and other torture on prisoners, including

---

[29] Nicholas Schmiddle, "The Saharan Conundrum," *New York Times Magazine*, February 13, 2009, www.nytimes.com/2009/02/15/magazine/15Africa-t.html.
[30] "Al-Khadim Wuld al-Siman."

suspected jihadists.[31] The 2005 wave of arrests targeting Islamists and suspected jihadists became part of GSPC/AQIM's stated justifications for attacks, including the attack at Lemgheitty in 2005.[32] Again, the fact that jihadists' grievances were predicated on state policies implicitly meant that the state had an opportunity to undercut jihadist recruitment by changing its policies.

After Lemgheitty, the GSPC/AQIM struck Mauritania at least a dozen times. These attacks fell into three broad categories:

1. military operations, or attacks in which large numbers of AQIM fighters participated;
2. supervised terrorist operations, where AQIM field commanders directly organized attacks; and
3. seemingly unsupervised terrorist incidents, where local recruits may have acted on their own initiative.

Among the military operations were the Lemgheitty attack (led by Belmokhtar), the December 2007 attack on a garrison at al-Ghalawiyya (led by the AQIM field commander Yahya Abu al-Hammam),[33] and the September 2008 ambush of a military patrol at Tourine, near Zouérate (led by the AQIM field commander 'Abd al-Hamid Abu Zayd and his then-subordinate Abu al-Hammam).[34]

AQIM's Saharan field commanders were also organizing and supervising small terrorist attacks in Mauritania, especially in Nouakchott. It is sometimes difficult to determine which AQIM unit perpetrated which attacks, but all of the three major Saharan field commanders at this time – Belmokhtar, Abu Zayd, and Abu al-Hammam – were

---

[31] Amnesty International, "Mauritania: Torture at the Heart of the State," December 3, 2008, 11–12. Available for download at: www.amnesty.org/download/Documents/52000/afr380092008en.pdf.

[32] "Algerian Islamist Group Claims Mauritania Attack."

[33] Foster, *Mauritania*, 154; "Mauritania's Goals in Its Struggle against al-Qaeda," Al Jazeera Center for Studies, July 25, 2011, 4, http://studies.aljazeera.net/mritems/Documents/2011/7/26/201172612214818734Mauritanias%20goals%20in%20its%20struggle%20against%20al-Qaeda.pdf.

[34] "4 peines capitales prononcées contre des combattants d'Aqmi," Tahalil, March 21, 2011, www.journaltahalil.com/detail.php?id=4884; "Al-Qaida nomme un nouvel émir au Sahara," October 8, 2012, Magharebia/Algérie 360, www.algerie360.com/al-qaida-nomme-un-nouvel-emir-au-sahara/; Benjamin Roger, "Visuel interactif: le nouvel organigramme d'Aqmi," *Jeune Afrique*, October 25, 2013, www.jeuneafrique.com/167651/politique/visuel-interactif-le-nouvel-organigramme-d-aqmi/.

interested in targeting Mauritania. Abu al-Hammam reportedly directed, from afar, the cell that attempted to kidnap an American teacher in June 2009, fatally shooting him when he resisted. Abu al-Hammam also reportedly organized the August 2009 suicide bombing at the French embassy in Nouakchott and the December 2009 kidnapping of an Italian couple near Kobenni, close to the Mauritanian–Malian border,[35] although this kidnapping has also been attributed to Belmokhtar's unit.[36] Meanwhile, Belmokhtar's men seem to have carried out the kidnapping of three Spanish aid workers near the Mauritanian coast in November 2009,[37] although that attack has also been attributed to Abu al-Hammam.[38]

During this time, AQIM still hoped to mobilize wide support within Mauritania. Just days after the August 2008 coup that brought Ould 'Abd al-Aziz to power, AQIM's Droukdel called the new junta a stooge of France, Israel, and the United States.[39] Yet even at the peak of its attacks in Mauritania, AQIM was attracting relatively small numbers of Mauritanians in comparison to the larger numbers of Malians it would later recruit.[40] And there emerged no Mauritanian equivalent to Mali's Iyad ag Ghali or even to Amadou Kouffa – AQIM found no

---

[35] Roger, "Visuel interactif." Ultimately, one Mauritanian and one Malian national received prison sentences in connection with the kidnapping. See "Mauritanian Men Sentenced for Kidnapping Italians," Associated Press, March 22, 2011, available at www.foxnews.com/world/mauritanian-men-sentenced-for-kidnapping-italians.

[36] "Mufawadat li-l-Ifraj 'an Thalathat Isban wa-Faransi Liqa' Fidya Maliyya," Al-Hayat, December 29, 2009, www.alhayat.com/article/1414077.

[37] Laurent Prieur and Jason Webb, "Three Spanish Aid Workers Kidnapped in Mauritania," Reuters, November 29, 2009, www.reuters.com/article/us-mauritania-tourists/three-spanish-aid-workers-kidnapped-in-mauritania-idUSTRE5AS23W20091129; "Spanish Hostages Freed by al Qaeda Return Home," France24, August 24, 2010, www.france24.com/en/20100824-spanish-hostages-freed-al-qaeda-return-home-mali-mauritania-aqmi.

[38] "Hal Yaqif 'Abu al-Hammam' wara' Ikhtitaf al-Raha'in al-Isban?" CNN Arabic, December 30, 2009, http://edition.cnn.com/arabic/2009/middle_east/12/1/mauritania.spain/index.html.

[39] "Mauritanie: attaque attribuée à Al-Qaïda, 12 morts ou disparus," *Le Parisien*, September 16, 2008, www.leparisien.fr/flash-actualite-monde/mauritanie-attaque-attribuee-a-al-qaida-12-morts-ou-disparus-16-09-2008-228355.php.

[40] Some of the kidnappers involved in seizing the Italian couple and the Spanish aid workers, meanwhile, were Malians. See "Mauritanian Men Sentenced for Kidnapping Italians"; and "I'tiqal Mali Mushtabah bi-Dulu'ihi fi Khatf Italiyyin," Al-Hayat, December 24, 2009, www.alhayat.com/article/1413502.

Mauritanian allies who could bring large blocs of fighters into a jihadist coalition there.

The actual Mauritanian-led cells within the country were relatively unprofessional and sloppy, which made them prone to arrests. In May 2005, Khadim Ould Semane was swept up in the broader regime crackdown on Islamists. He escaped in 2006 alongside fellow Mauritanian militant Hamada Ould Mohamed Kheirou, the eventual leader of MUJWA.[41] Fleeing into the Sahara, Ould Semane trained with Belmokhtar and then one of them proposed to the other (accounts vary) the idea of creating a local Mauritanian AQIM cell, which took the name Ansar Allah al-Murabitun fi Bilad Shinqit (God's Supporters, the Sentinels, in the Land of Mauritania). Returning to Mauritania, Ould Semane created the group in 2007; according to one Mauritanian journalistic investigation he recruited "tens of youth," but this may be an exaggeration. The group staged a robbery at the port of Nouakchott that furnished some money for the outfit (and they set aside a portion for Belmokhtar), but the robbery brought twin repercussions in the form of heightened vigilance by Mauritanian authorities and a rebuke from Belmokhtar, who directed them to focus on recruitment rather than attacks.[42] Ultimately, Ould Semane's group seems to have staged just one real attack, firing at the Israeli Embassy in Nouakchott and at a nearby nightclub in February 2008. Ould Semane's cell also planned to kidnap a German diplomat in Nouakchott,[43] but the plot failed. According to one account, Belmokhtar's hand-picked men, sent to assist, barely escaped.[44] Ould Semane was rearrested in April 2008,[45] having already been convicted in absentia of setting up an AQIM-linked cell.[46]

The delinquent-turned-jihadist Ould Sidna, meanwhile, participated in murdering four French tourists near Aleg in December 2007. He and his companions, Ma'ruf Ould al-Hayba and Muhammad Ould

[41] Ould M. Salem, *Ben Laden du Sahara*, 87–88.
[42] "Al-Siraj Tanshur al-Qissa al-Kamila." This source gives micro-biographies of fourteen Mauritanians involved in Ould Semane's network. See also "Fi Buyut al-Qa'ida..Rihla Khalf al-Israr," *Majallat Al-Akhbar* (June 2008), 27–35.
[43] "Hal Yaqif 'Abu al-Hammam' wara' Ikhtitaf al-Raha'in al-Isban?"
[44] "Al-Siraj Tanshur al-Qissa al-Kamila."
[45] Ould M. Salem, *Ben Laden du Sahara*, 91.
[46] Vincent Ferty, "Mauritania Captures Eight al Qaeda Suspects," Reuters, April 30, 2008, www.reuters.com/article/us-qaeda-mauritania/mauritania-captures-eight-al-qaeda-suspects-idUSL3013347720080430.

Charbanou, may have been acting on their own, "to improve their image with the Group after some of them were accused of being agents for Mauritanian security [services]."[47] Even Ould Semane later denied any involvement in the incident, stating that Ould Sidna and his companions had acted on their own initiative.[48] Ould Sidna was soon arrested (in Guinea-Bissau, where he had fled) and then, after escaping dramatically from Mauritanian custody, he was rearrested together with Ould Semane in April 2008.[49] Ould al-Hayba, after the Aleg murders, found refuge in an AQIM camp for a few months, but he too was arrested when authorities dismantled Ould Semane's cell in the aftermath of the failed plot to seize the German diplomat.[50] The Aleg attack was self-destructive; politically, it advanced nothing.

Ould Semane, Ould Sidna, and their circles were not true "lone wolves," but their relative lack of success suggests that support from the more hardened AQIM field commanders was either limited or not decisive. The Mauritanian cells may also have slipped through the cracks of the rivalry between Abu Zayd and Belmokhtar, which was widening at just the moment when Ould Semane's network was being dismantled. Notably, one Mauritanian security source claims that both Abu Zayd's and Belmokhtar's fighters participated in the Lemgheitty attack of 2005;[51] if true, that attack may have marked a high point in these two field commanders' cooperation, given what we know of their bitter feuds just a few years later (see Chapters 2 and 3). Their rivalry may also have been one factor in Belmokhtar's eagerness to absorb capable Mauritanians into his own forces, so as to counterbalance Abu Zayd.

Another factor in the local Mauritanian hardliners' failure was the urban context of Nouakchott. As opposed to the opportunities for mobility offered by the desert, safe houses in Nouakchott were particularly vulnerable to detections and raids by the authorities. Jihadists

---

[47] "Al-Siraj Tanshur al-Qissa al-Kamila." See also "Alak Kum Tanshur al-Sira al-Dhatiyya." This is also the view of the analyst Mohammed Mahmoud Abu al-Ma'ali. Interview, Nouakchott, April 28, 2018.

[48] "Al-Siraj Tanshur al-Qissa al-Kamila."

[49] Schmiddle, "Saharan Conundrum"; and Ferty, "Mauritania Captures Eight al Qaeda Suspects."

[50] "Alak Kum Tanshur al-Sira al-Dhatiyya."

[51] Institut Mauritanien d'Etudes Strategiques, "La lute contre le terrorismse: Le Colonel Abdallahi Ould Ahmed Aicha," June 16, 2016, www.youtube.com/watch?v=zOAvk3uom0Y.

appear not have won the confidence of a critical mass of passive supporters who might have helped them escape detection. As leaders were rounded up, recruitment was possibily still accelerating, but cells' ability to absorb and guide recruits was collapsing. In November 2008, worried US diplomats wrote that "Some reports indicate over 100 Mauritanians have been recruited in recent months – driven by a supply/demand combination of AQIM's increased 'credibility' and AQIM's need to rebuild its disabled internal networks." Yet the intelligence services continued to arrest suspected AQIM members – sometimes perhaps scooping up "wannabes" or local troublemakers rather than actual members,[52] but also chilling overall recruitment. AQIM's local outfit remained a smattering of individuals rather than a coherent coalition.

Finally, some of AQIM's actions horrified Mauritanians and evoked a backlash; fighting the Mauritanian military and targeting foreign embassies was one thing, but killing foreign civilians was another. At least in the view of American diplomats, the killing of the American citizen in Nouakchott in 2009 was a turning point: "In the wake of the [Christopher] Leggett murder, the Mauritanian population as well as authorities have demonstrated a willingness to cooperate and security services have proven to be the US's best partners in the region."[53] AQIM's harsh treatment of captured Mauritanian soldiers (particularly one incident where twelve soldiers were decapitated in 2008) probably also alienated ordinary Mauritanians.[54] Neither the indisciplined local recruits nor the Mali-based AQIM field commanders could find a real political foothold in the country.

---

[52] U.S. Embassy Nouakchott, "The Post-Coup Al Qaeda Threat in Mauritania," leaked cable 08NOUAKCHOTT666, November 13, 2008, https://search .wikileaks.org/plusd/cables/08NOUAKCHOTT666_a.html. See also U.S. Embassy Nouakchott, "The Mayor of Tidjikja," leaked cable 08NOUAKCHOTT629, October 27, 2008, https://search.wikileaks.org/plusd/ cables/08NOUAKCHOTT629_a.html.

[53] U.S. Embassy Nouakchott, "Mauritania: Layered Security Strategy," leaked cable 09NOUAKCHOTT575, September 9, 2009, https://search.wikileaks.org/ plusd/cables/09NOUAKCHOTT575_a.html.

[54] Interview with Sidi Mohamed Ould Maham, Nouakchott, May 3, 2018. On the beheadings, see "Mauritania Says 12 Held by al Qaeda Were Decapitated," Reuters, September 20, 2008, www.reuters.com/article/us-mauritania-attack-bodies/mauritania-says-12-held-by-al-qaeda-were-decapitated-idUSLK23028720080920.

Other political and religious developments – the Arab Spring's echoes in Mauritania, the increasing visibility of anti-slavery organizations, etc. – might have blunted AQIM's appeal or at least focused young people's attention elsewhere. Jihadist recruitment of youth within Mauritania seemingly peaked in the early to mid-2000s, when the emotional impact of the American invasions of Afghanistan and Iraq collided with Mauritania's domestic repression of a wide spectrum of religious activists. By 2011, generations younger than that of Ould Semane and Ould Sidna seemingly began losing interest in jihadism.

The last major Nouakchott-centric plot reveals additional amateurishness among Mauritanian AQIM fighters. In February 2011, a three-car AQIM convoy entered Mauritania from Mali with the apparent goal of assassinating Ould Abdel Aziz. Authorities detained two of the cars, and the other exploded approximately twelve kilometers south of Nouakchott after soldiers fired on it. A few days later, local residents near the Senegalese borders tipped off authorities to the presence of two militants who had fled from the convoy; one blew himself up while the other was captured.[55] The captured jihadist, Mauritanian national Cheikh Ould Saleck (b. 1984), reportedly had several years' experience with AQIM in northern Mali,[56] and may have participated along with Ould Sidna in killing the French tourists at Aleg in 2007.[57] Other members of the attack party also belonged to Ould Semane's old network, such as Al-Tayyib Ould Sidi ʿAli, who had reportedly participated in the Nouakchott port robbery.[58] The assassination plot was claimed by AQIM, but its primary authors were the same local networks that had repeatedly faltered over approximately five years. These networks were now almost completely broken.

[55] "Mauritania: 'Al-Qaeda Men Die' As Troops Fire on Car," BBC News, February 2, 2011, www.bbc.com/news/world-africa-12344931; and "Al Qaeda Suspect Blows Self Up in Mauritania Clash," Reuters, February 5, 2011, https://af.reuters.com/article/maliNews/idAFLDE7140G720110205.

[56] Benjamin Roger, "Cheikh Ould Saleck, le jihadiste mauritanien en cavale, pourrait-il se trouver au Sénégal?" *Jeune Afrique*, January 6, 2016, www.jeuneafrique.com/291474/politique/cheikh-ould-saleck-jihadiste-mauritanien-cavale-pourrait-se-trouver-senegal/.

[57] U.S. Department of State, "State Department Terrorist Designation of AQIM Operative Saleck Ould Cheikh Mohamedou," December 21, 2016, https://2009-2017.state.gov/r/pa/prs/ps/2016/12/265897.htm.

[58] "Al-Aman al-Muritani Yukaththif Istiʿdadat al-Tasaddi li-Tahdid Muftarad min Intihari Tabiʿ li-l-Qaʿida," Sahara Medias, October 13, 2011, www.saharamedias.net/الأمن-الموريتاني-يكثف-استعدادات-التص/.

Clashes between the Mauritanian military and AQIM continued into the summer of 2011, including in a series of battles around Bassiknou in July 2011.[59] Threats continued into the fall of 2011.[60] Nevertheless, the failed assassination plot marked the beginning of the end of AQIM's efforts to target Mauritania.

Mauritanian Authorities' Responses to AQIM

When Mauritania was under regular attack, the Mauritanian state, and particularly the regime of Ould Abdel Aziz, adopted a multi-pronged strategy for dealing with AQIM. The initial response was domestically focused and coercive, with an emphasis on rooting out cells in Nouakchott. As noted previously, the authorities had substantial success in tracking down the young, homegrown Mauritanian jihadists who were killing foreigners. Authorities often fumbled, especially in allowing imprisoned suspected jihadists to escape (with a frequency that could hint at collusion among prison guards). Yet even in these embarrassing instances the security forces could usually mobilize quickly and recapture the escapees.[61] On the whole, Mauritania raised the costs for AQIM of operating on its territory to a level where AQIM seemingly found Mauritania more useful as a rear base than as a combat zone and terrorist target.

Responding to the military assaults by AQIM in eastern Mauritania took more time and effort than it took to break up the cells in Nouakchott. Some Mauritanian security personnel argue that the military's thinking and capabilities evolved rapidly during this time, as authorities elaborated more sophisticated strategies and as units developed greater mobility and firepower.[62] By 2010, Mauritanian authorities had concluded that they needed to take the fight into Mali: otherwise, they thought, they could not reverse the trend where highly mobile AQIM units repeatedly crossed the border and ambushed

---

[59] "Mauritanian Military Attacks al Qaeda Group," CNN, July 6, 2011, www.cnn .com/2011/WORLD/africa/07/05/mauritania.al.qaeda/index.html.

[60] "Al-Aman al-Muritani Yukaththif Isti'dadat."

[61] For a snapshot of one mobilization, see "Nuwakshut Takhud Thani Akbar Tahaddi mundhu Muwajahat 2008," Zahrat Shinqit, undated, www.zahraa.mr/ node/5149.

[62] Interview with Col. (ret.) El Boukhary Mohamed Mouemel; interview with Sidi Mohamed Ould Maham.

Mauritania's soldiers. The years 2010 and 2011 brought Mauritanian military offensives against AQIM along the border and across it. In July 2010, with French support, Mauritanian forces staged a raid with the hopes of recapturing a French hostage (the raid failed, and AQIM executed the hostage shortly thereafter).[63] In September 2010, the Mauritanian military and AQIM clashed around the Malian town of Raz-el-Ma (Ra's al-Ma').[64] In November of that year, Mauritania and Mali launched joint patrols in the Timbuktu region.[65] In June 2011, Mauritanian troops claimed to have destroyed an AQIM camp in Mali's Wagadou Forest.[66] A series of battles ensued, with reprisals and counter-reprisals inside Mauritanian territory.[67] A Mauritanian air raid on Wagadou Forest followed in November 2011.[68]

Over time, the governments of Mauritania and Algeria grew increasingly frustrated with the administration of Malian President Amadou Toumani Touré, especially as Mali became the epicenter of the Saharan kidnapping economy. In September 2009, Mauritanian President Ould Abdel Aziz "voiced doubts about Malian commitment to the fight noting Bamako had previously been 'at peace' with AQIM to avoid attacks on its territory."[69] In February 2010, Mauritania and Algeria withdrew their ambassadors from Mali to protest the Malian government's release of four AQIM members,[70] one of whom was the

[63] "French-Backed Troops Fail to Free Hostage from Al-Qaeda-Linked Group," RFI, July 23, 2010, http://en.rfi.fr/africa/20100723-mauritanian-troops-fail-free-french-hostage-al-qaeda-linked-group.
[64] "Mauritania Strikes at Militants on Mali Border," BBC News, September 18, 2010, www.bbc.com/news/world-africa-11354029.
[65] "Mali Joins Mauritania to Fight AQIM," News24, November 7, 2010, www.news24.com/africa/news/mali-joins-mauritania-to-fight-aqim-20101107.
[66] Laurent Prieur, "Mauritania Says 17 Died in al Qaeda Operation," Reuters, June 26, 2011, www.reuters.com/article/us-mauritania-alqaeda/mauritania-says-17-died-in-al-qaeda-operation-idUSTRE75P21E20110626.
[67] "Mauritanian Military Attacks al Qaeda Group."
[68] "Mauritanian Forces Hit AQIM Leadership," News24, October 22, 2011, www.news24.com/Africa/News/Mauritanian-forces-hit-AQIM-leadership-20111022.
[69] U.S. Embassy Nouakchott, "Mauritania: President Aziz on Terrorism and Extremism," leaked cable 09NOUAKCHOTT593, September 15, 2009, https://search.wikileaks.org/plusd/cables/09NOUAKCHOTT593_a.html.
[70] Lamine Chikhi, "Algeria Recalls Envoy from Mali over Qaeda Row," Reuters, February 23, 2010, https://af.reuters.com/article/topNews/idAFJOE61M0LJ20100223.

Mauritanian national and future MUJWA leader Ould Kheirou.[71] By 2010–2011, Mauritania's hopes for a united "regional approach" were eroding.

Even as Mauritanian authorities moved away from military actions in Mali, however, northeastern Mauritania remained highly securitized and restricted, even for its own residents. One of the most inscrutable aspects of the situation in the Mauritania–Mali borderlands is the role of smuggling and illicit economies in AQIM's career in Mauritania. Cédric Jourde has written, "Some high-ranking military officers, as well as members of their families and tribes, play key roles in this illicit economy and are involved in numerous local power struggles. The result is a seemingly irreconcilable tension: the state as an abstract entity is threatened by this illicit business, yet simultaneously many state agents are deeply involved in these activities."[72] Whether Mauritania's post-2011 peace with AQIM reflected a disruption of local patterns of collusion in the northeast or a growing toleration of them is difficult to determine.

Mauritanian authorities' responses to AQIM in 2008–2011 were also shaped by politics, namely Ould Abdel Aziz's need to legitimate his 2008 coup and continued tenure. Just as Ould Taya had leveraged the early War on Terror to improve relations with the United States in the early 2000s, Ould Abdel Aziz used the problem of AQIM to justify his takeover; the new junta argued that the previous civilian administration's weakness had allowed the attacks at Aleg and elsewhere to happen.[73] Foreign powers were tacitly receptive to this argument. Just a few months after the 2008 coup, calls for the restoration of ousted civilian President Sidi Ould Cheikh Abdallahi began fading; in April 2009, a senior French official told US diplomats that she favored a scenario where Ould Abdel Aziz held a credible election that would allow the country to turn the page and concentrate on its security challenges.[74] That election, in July 2009, sealed Ould Abdel Aziz's

[71] "Was French Hostage Swapped for Detained Jihadists," France24, December 10, 2014, www.france24.com/en/20141210-france-mali-dangerous-trade-offs-hostage-qaeda-jihadists.

[72] Jourde, "Sifting through the Layers of Insecurity in the Sahel."   [73] Ibid.

[74] U.S. Embassy Paris, "Mauritania/France: Worries over AQIM Trump Search for a Perfect Democracy," leaked cable 09PARIS483, April 2, 2009, https://search.wikileaks.org/plusd/cables/09PARIS483_a.html.

claim to power. By pursuing counterterrorism cooperation with France and the United States, he established himself as one of the West's foremost allies in the Sahel – and deflected Western concerns about his democratic bonafides.

The state's response to AQIM was not just coercive, however. Even before the coup, civilian authorities drafted a "National Strategy for Combating Terrorism" that involved a "soft approach." Civilians identified social injustice, poverty, precarity, lack of education, unemployment, and urban in-migration as drivers of extremism; they proposed various measures, from sensitization campaigns to employment programs, to undercut AQIM recruitment.[75] Ould Abdel Aziz's team continued thinking along similar lines.

In January 2010, the Mauritanian government promulgated a new counter-terrorism law. Almost immediately, authorities brought in major Islamic scholars to conduct dialogues with imprisoned jihadists, suspected jihadists, and hardline Salafis. The scholars had floated the idea of dialogue under Ould al-Taya, who had rejected the notion;[76] Ould Abdel Aziz gave the green light. The dialogues aimed at convincing the prisoners to renounce violence. Ould Abdel Aziz told journalists, "We understand the situation of these youths. They are lost, and have embarked on fights that do not concern them."[77] Privately, one leading judge criticized the dialogue effort as a veiled move to "appease AQIM."[78] Here, then, was an emerging state experiment with accommodation, mostly on its own terms but designed with an eye to mitigating grievances and creating off-ramps.

The dialogue caused – or revealed – a schism between the prisoners. A group of forty-seven detainees led by 'Abd Allah Ould Sidiya welcomed the dialogue. Another group, under Ould Semane, also participated in the dialogue – as an opportunity to air jihadist

---

[75] U.S. Embassy Nouakchott, "Emerging Mauritanian 'Soft' Counterterrorism Strategy," leaked cable 08NOUAKCHOTT365, July 13, 2008, https://search .wikileaks.org/plusd/cables/08NOUAKCHOTT365_a.html.

[76] Interview with Ahmedou Ould Lemrabott, Nouakchott, April 28, 2018.

[77] "Mohamed Ould Abdelaziz: 'Je dois tout contrôler moi-même'," *Jeune Afrique*, September 2, 2010, www.jeuneafrique.com/195361/politique/mohamed-ould-abdelaziz-je-dois-tout-contr-ler-moi-m-me/.

[78] U.S. Embassy Nouakchott, "Meeting with New Counter-Terrorism Judge," leaked cable 10NOUAKCHOTT54, January 21, 2010, https://search.wikileaks .org/plusd/cables/10NOUAKCHOTT54_a.html.

views.[79] In one video from the proceedings, Ould Semane can be seen saying,

> We know that we are correct (*na'rif bi-annana 'indana al-haqq*) ... We are correct in fighting the unbelievers in all the Muslims' land until they leave the Muslims' land (*'indana al-haqq fi muqara'at al-kuffar fi jami' ard al-muslimin hatta yakhruju min ard al-muslimin*) ... We do not call Muslims unbelievers, and the Muslim peoples are Muslim peoples, all the peoples are Muslim peoples ... But ... the rulers, the rulers are apostates from the religion of God, may He be glorified and exalted (*nahnu la nukaffir al-muslimin, wa-l-shu'ub al-muslima*).[80]

Ould Semane also held up a plaque that said "Al-Qa'ida" during the first session.[81] Ultra-hardliners likely knew that they had no chance at parole – as one journalist has commented, "The state made it clear that convicted jihadists involved in episodes like the killing of four French tourists in Aleg in 2007 would not be released."[82]

Despite the presence of irreconcilables, by February 2010 the government-aligned scholars were saying that the dialogue "had succeeded at a rate of 90%."[83] In September 2010, the young cleric Mohamed Salem al-Majlisi and thirty-two others benefited from a presidential amnesty and obtained their release. Since that time, clerics across the ideological spectrum – from the quietist imam of Nouakchott, Ahmedou Ould Lemrabott, to the ex-al-Qa'ida cleric Abu Hafs al-Muritani – have praised the dialogues and considered them successful.[84]

---

[79] "Ula Jalasat al-Hiwar ma'a al-Salafiyyin Tantaliq Wasat Sira' 'ala Za'amat al-Masajin," Anba', January 18, 2010, www.anbaa.info/?p=4068.

[80] "Al-Hiwar ma'a al-Salafiyyin fi Muritaniya," Al-Akhbar, January 18, 2010, www.youtube.com/watch?v=KZhPRiusnM4. Ould Semane made similar statements about takfir in his 2006 interview with Al Jazeera. See "Al-Khadim Wuld al-Siman."

[81] "'Ulama' Muritaniya Yuhawirun Sujana' 'al-Salafiyya al-Jihadiyya'," Al-Arabiya, February 4, 2010, https://web.archive.org/web/20100208182609/https://www.alarabiya.net/articles/2010/02/04/99315.html.

[82] Chris Simpson, "Debunking Mauritania's Islamist Militancy Mythology," IRIN/The New Humanitarian, August 23, 2016, www.thenewhumanitarian.org/analysis/2016/08/23/debunking-mauritania-s-islamist-militancy-mythology.

[83] "'Ulama' Muritaniya Yuhawirun Sujana' 'al-Salafiyya al-Jihadiyya'."

[84] Interview with Ahmedou Ould Lemrabott; interview with Abu Hafs al-Muritani, Nouakchott, April 30, 2018.

Alongside the dialogues, there were prosecutions, which accelerated in early 2010. A criminal court handed down several sentences in May 2010, including a six-year prison term for Ould Sidiya, a three-year sentence for al-Majlisi, and death sentences for Sidi Ould Sidna and his alleged accomplices Maʿruf Ould al-Hayba and Muhammad Ould Charbanou.[85] Reacting to the decision, one Mauritanian journalist observed that if this was a message to the "moderate wing" of the prisoners, "then what will be the [court's] message to the extremist wing?"[86]

The dialogues and the sentencing represented carrots and sticks that the regime offered to the prisoners. Those who accepted the dialogues reaped rewards – despite their sentences, Ould Sidiya and al-Majlisi were among those released in September 2010.[87] The beneficiaries of the dialogues then reportedly convinced many of their own friends not to become jihadists,[88] undercutting whatever jihadist coalition-building efforts were still ongoing. Those who rejected dialogue remained in prison, with death sentences hanging over them. Ould Semane, Ould Sidna, and Ould Hayba were all sentenced (or, in the latter two cases, re-sentenced) to death in October 2010,[89] although at the time of writing the sentences have not been carried out.

State authorities were also making wider changes that helped to remove some of the grievances that had initially propelled local recruitment and violence. Additionally, Mali was beginning to offer a markedly more favorable arena for jihadism than Mauritania was. Before discussing this confluence of trends, however, it is worth

---

[85] "Al-Iʿdam li-l-Irhabiyyin al-Muttahamin bi-Qatl al-Suyyah al-Faransiyyin fi Muritaniya," Al-Nahar, May 26, 2010, www.ennaharonline.com/-الإعدام السلا-بقتل-المتهمين-الإرهابيين/.

[86] "Muritaniya Tabdaʾ Muhakamat Sujanaʾ al-Qaʿida," DW, May 18, 2010, www .dw.com/ar/موريتانيا-تبدأ-محاكمة-سجناء-القاعدة/a-5585873.

[87] "'Anbaʾ Tanshur Laʾihat al-Salafiyyin al-Mufraj ʿanhum," Anbaʾ, September 9, 2010, www.anbaa.info/?p=5062.

[88] Interview with Mohammed Mahmoud Abu al-Maʿali.

[89] "Mauritania Sentences Qaeda-Linked Militant to Die," Reuters, October 21, 2010, www.defenceweb.co.za/index.php?option=com_content&view=article& id=10133:mauritania-sentences-qaeda-linked-militant-to-die&catid=49: National%20Security&Itemid=115. Other death sentences have also been handed down, though not yet carried out. See "Muritaniya: Hukm bi-Iʿdam Aʿdaʾ bi-l-Qaʿida," Al Jazeera, March 21, 2011, www.aljazeera.net/news/arabic/ 2011/3/21/موريتانيا-حكم-بإعدام-أعضاء-بالقاعدة.

probing the vexed question of whether Mauritanian authorities made a deal with AQIM.

Was There a Deal between Mauritania and al-Qaʿida?

Among the documents discovered at Usama bin Laden's compound in Pakistan, after the raid that killed him in May 2011, was a document that discussed a possible negotiated settlement between al-Qaʿida, represented by AQIM, and the government of Mauritania. The document, dated March 2010, envisioned an initial one-year agreement that would require the Mauritanian state to release all imprisoned AQIM members, refrain from arresting other militants and students, and pay 10–20 million euros per year as a guarantee against the safety of tourists. In exchange, "the Mujahidin are committed to not carry out any military activity in Mauritania." The document was a draft rather than a memorandum of an already concluded agreement; the drafters acknowledged that al-Qaʿida would first have to propose this arrangement to AQIM's Droukdel and also "correspond with the Mauritanian brothers to convince them."[90] Washington declassified the document in 2016. If nothing else, the document captures a striking willingness on the part of al-Qaʿida core to consider accommodation and even collusion with a supposedly detested regime – an indication, as I have stressed throughout this book, that jihadists are political animals rather than slaves to inflexible doctrine.

Despite some willingness from the al-Qaʿida side, it is doubtful that any formal deal was ever implemented, even in part. For starters, no deal could have been finalized before late 2011, when Mauritanian raids against AQIM were still ongoing. Nor was the entire deal, as originally described by al-Qaʿida, ever implemented – after all, many prisoners were never released. The state still periodically arrests militants and preachers. Mauritanian participation in regional military efforts to combat AQIM and allied groups, such as the G-5 Sahel Joint Force that was considerably expanded starting in 2017, also points to

---

[90] Mukhtar Abu al-Zubayr, "Letter about the Matter of the Islamic Maghreb," March 5, 2010, 1, available through the Office of the Director of National Intelligence (ODNI), www.dni.gov/files/documents/ubl2016/english/Letter%20about%20matter%20of%20the%20Islamic%20Maghreb.pdf. Here I quote from the English translation. The Arabic version as posted by ODNI does not correspond to this English document.

the lack of a deal. Both Mauritanian and American authorities deny the conclusion of any formal deal.[91]

Then there is the view of Abu Hafs al-Muritani, ex-al-Qa'ida cleric, speaking in 2016:

The documents that the United States of America released are genuine, but they do not contain anything proving that the Mauritanian government concluded any agreement with the al-Qa'ida organization ... In my view it is likely that the Mauritanian government did not conclude any agreement of that kind. I find it very far-fetched that the Mauritanian authorities would have paid any money to the al-Qa'ida organization, or even have negotiated with it. But they saw that it was in their security interest (*min maslahatiha al-amaniyya*) to confine their military operations against al-Qa'ida within their borders so long as al-Qa'ida or other armed groups were not interfering with the security of the country.[92]

In an interview with me, al-Muritani expanded on this idea, arguing that Mauritania's refusal to participate in the "War on Terror" in Mali conveyed to AQIM that Mauritania was not going to target them outside its own borders – but this does not mean there is an explicit deal.[93]

Al-Muritani's comments raise the possibility of a tacit understanding between AQIM and the Mauritanian state. One unanswered question is whether a more limited version of the proposed arrangement – perhaps a straightforward payment of protection money to AQIM in order to allow the revival of tourism – was brokered. As early as 2010, US diplomats reported that AQIM was seeking a communications channel with Mauritanian authorities to discuss prisoner exchanges.[94] At least one prisoner exchange may have occurred in early 2012; according to AQIM, Mauritanian authorities traded a jihadist, Malian national 'Abd al-Rahman Ould Middu (or Imdu), for a Mauritanian

---

[91] Mark Hosenball, "Al Qaeda Leaders Made Plans for Peace Deal with Mauritania: Documents," Reuters, March 1, 2016, www.reuters.com/article/us-usa-binladen-mauritania/al-qaeda-leaders-made-plans-for-peace-deal-with-mauritania-documents-idUSKCN0W356G.

[92] "Mufti al-Qa'ida al-Sabiq li-Shabakatina: La Nihaya li-l-'Unf Ma Damat al-Quwa al-Kubra Tastahdif al-Muslimin," CNN Arabic, April 20, 2016, https://arabic.cnn.com/world/2016/04/20/interview-ex-mufti-al-qaeda.

[93] Interview with Abu Hafs al-Muritani.

[94] U.S. Embassy Bamako, "AQIM Seeking Intermediary in Mauritania via Malian Government," leaked cable 10BAMAKO17, January 12, 2010, https://search.wikileaks.org/plusd/cables/10BAMAKO17_a.html.

gendarme who had been kidnapped in late 2011.[95] Mauritanian authorities seemingly came around to some of the policies they had condemned when Mali's government adopted them just a few years before (perhaps because, ironically, the Mauritanian authorities had despaired of their Malian counterparts' ability to contribute to regional security). Another question, then, is whether Mauritanian authorities' view of Mali shifted around 2010, as they pulled back from raiding AQIM and instead took advantage of Mali's potential as a pressure release valve.

The Malian Pressure Release Valve

Even in the mid-2000s, Mauritanian would-be jihadists seeking training from AQIM tended to head outside the country, especially to northern Mali. At an early point in this process, AQIM field commanders seem to have identified certain Mauritanians as particularly promising aides and fighters. Field commanders kept these Mauritanians in their own units rather than sending them home. One such figure was Hacen Ould Khalil (better known as "Joulaybib," 1981–2013), who became a key deputy to Belmokhtar.[96] MUJWA's future leader Hamada Ould Mohamed Kheirou had been imprisoned in 2005 for causing a violent disturbance in a Nouakchott mosque. Escaping a few months later, he fled to Mali and henceforth based himself outside Mauritania.[97] Mali was in many ways a more permissive environment for jihadist activity than was Mauritania or any other

---

[95] "Sahara Midiya Tuhawir 'Unsuran min al-Qa'ida Hurrira fi 'Amaliyat Tabadul ma'a al-Jaysh al-Muritani," Sahara Medias, August 5, 2012, www .saharamedias.net/صحراء-ميديا-تحاور-عنصرا-من-القاعدة-حرر; "Al-Ifraj 'an Daraki Muritani Ikhtatafathu al-Qa'ida," Al Jazeera, March 10, 2012, www.aljazeera .net/news/arabic/2012/3/10/الإفراج-عن-دركي-موريتاني-اختطفته-القاعدة; and "Tasjil Musawwar li-l-Daraki al-Muritani al-Mukhtataf lada al-Qa'ida," Al Akhbar, January 14, 2012, www.youtube.com/watch?v=SfZGHIHfchU.

[96] Ould M. Salem, *Ben Laden du Sahara*, 111. See also "French Forces Kill Islamist Chief Belmokhtar's No. 2," France24, November 21, 2013, www.france24 .com/en/20131121-french-forces-kill-islamist-commander-belmokhtar-deputy-hacene-khalil-mali.

[97] Laurent Touchard, Baba Ahmed, and Cherif Ouazani, "Mali: Hamada Ould Mohamed Kheirou, le cerveau du Mujao," Jeune Afrique, October 3, 2012, www.jeuneafrique.com/139880/politique/mali-hamada-ould-mohamed-kheirou-le-cerveau-du-mujao/.

Sahelian country, due to the issues of collusion, accommodation, and alliance-building that were discussed in Chapter 3.

A turning point came with the jihadist takeover of northern Mali in 2012 and the ensuing French-led military intervention in 2013. After their earlier interventions in Mali in 2010 and 2011, Mauritanian authorities decided to refrain from military action in Mali in 2012 and 2013. Moreover, one Mauritanian journalist told me that Mauritanian authorities had meant to keep their cross-border raids into Mali in 2010–2011 quiet, and that it was the French who had decided to make those events public; Mauritania had never intended to make a habit of external interventions against AQIM.[98]

Perhaps, in Mali's crisis, Ould Abdel Aziz saw an opportunity to step away from the AQIM problem and leave it to Mali, France, Chad, Niger, the United States, and others. Perhaps Ould Abdel Aziz's administration also concluded that the time had come for Mauritania to look after itself. Notably, Mauritania is *not* a member of the Economic Community of West African States (ECOWAS), the organization that became France's primary regional partner in responding to the Malian crisis of 2012–2013 (Mauritania left ECOWAS in 2000).

Mauritanian authorities may have also calculated that if they stayed out of Mali amid the 2012 crisis, AQIM would leave Mauritania alone. One well-informed observer told me that Iyad ag Ghali asked AQIM to leave Mauritania alone because of the large presence of northern Malian refugees there amid the 2012 conflict.[99] For their part, AQIM leaders declared that their conflict in Mali would only involve France and those African governments that were directly involved. In a December 2012 message, AQIM's Droukdel said:

The al-Qaʻida organization does not, and will not, constitute a danger to Mali, nor to the neighboring countries, nor to Africans, as France lies and claims. The goal of the *mujahidin* is clear, and it is to defend their religion and the interests of their umma by targeting the Zionist-Crusader alliance until it stops occupying Muslims' lands and intervening in their affairs. As for the neighboring countries and the African countries, they are not among our targets unless it is in terms of defending ourselves. Therefore the leaders

---

[98] Interview with Ahmad al-Wadiʻa, Nouakchott, May 3, 2018.
[99] Interview with Mohammed Mahmoud Abu al-Maʻali.

of these countries should not be pulled into a war that is not their war (*li-dha
'ala qadat hadhihi al-duwal an la yanjarru ila harb laysat hiya harbahum*).[100]

AQIM's Yahya Abu al-Hammam was even more explicit about
Mauritania's status in AQIM's eyes. In a 2012 interview with Mauritania's Agence Nouakchott d'Information, he repeated earlier AQIM
rhetoric in describing the Mauritanian state as an infidel regime and an
American puppet. He complained about what he called the self-
contradictory discourse of the Mauritanian authorities when it came
to northern Mali. He added, however, that "if the Mauritanian government wants to remain outside the circle of our targeting, it knows
better than others what it must do."[101]

Alongside jihadists' threats, there was domestic pressure for
Mauritania to stay out of the conflict. In late 2012, the popular young
cleric Mohamed Salim al-Majlisi and several dozen others signed a
fatwa condemning plans for a military intervention against the jihadist forces in northern Mali.[102] After France's Operation Serval
began in 2013, the Islamist luminary and Salafi-leaning cleric
Muhammad al-Hasan Ould al-Dedew, one of the most popular
shaykhs in the country, delivered a sermon denouncing the intervention. Al-Dedew encapsulated his view on Twitter as well, writing in
January 2013, "Helping France against the Muslims in Mali and
supporting it in the war occurring there is an abominable crime and
a matter legally forbidden [by Islam] (*jarima munkara wa-amr
muharram shar'an*)."[103]

---

[100] Abu Mus'ab 'Abd al-Wadud/'Abd al-Malik Droukdel, Ghazw Mali: Harb
       Faransiyya bi-l-Wikala, December 2012, 7, available at https://jihadology.net/
       wp-content/uploads/_pda/2012/12/abc5ab-mue1b9a3ab-abd-al-wadc5abd-
       abd-al-malik-drc5abkdc4abl-22the-mali-invasion-frances-proxy-war22-ar.pdf.
[101] Muhammad Mahmud Abu al-Ma'ali, "Abu al-Hammam: Muritaniya
       Ta'rif Kayfa Tatajannab Muwajahatina ... wa-Harb Huland Tawqi'
       'ala al-I'dam," Agence Nouakchott d'Information, October 13, 2012,
       available at https://web.archive.org/web/20180416092414/http://www
       .tawassoul.net/fr/الرئيسية/الأرشيف/item/6636--أبو-الهمام
       موريتانيا-تعرف-كيف-تتجنب-مواجهتنا-وحرب-هولاند-توقيع-على-الإعدام.html.
[102] "Fatwa 'Ulama' Shinqit Hawla Mali," November 10, 2012, available at www
       .eltwhed.com/vb/showthread.php?51062-%DD%CA%E6%EC-%DA%
       E1%E3%C7%C1-%D4%E4%DE%ED%D8-%CD%E6%E1-%E3%C7%
       E1%ED.
[103] Muhammad al-Hasan Ould al-Dedew, Twitter, January 20, 2013, https://
       twitter.com/shaikhdadow/status/293065853832925184.

There are strong cultural, religious, economic, and familial linkages between Mauritania and much of Mali, particularly northern Mali. And many Mauritanians, like many northern Malians, have a fundamentally different view of the conflict in Mali than do Western officials who view the fight from Washington or Paris and think in terms of terrorism and stability. Abu Hafs al-Muritani perhaps spoke for many Mauritanians when he told me that he did not consider it "extremism" when a people that is 100 percent Muslim asked for the implementation of shari'a. Neither does he consider it "extremism" when Mali's Muslims complain that their leaders are corrupt agents of Western governments.[104] AQIM, meanwhile, was "calling the Mauritanian Muslim people to stand alongside their brother Muslims in Azawad [northern Mali] against this Crusader campaign."[105] Facing such pressures, Mauritanian authorities may have decided that staying out of the conflict was the best way to avoid blowback.

AQIM's view of Mauritania's place in the Sahelian jihadist project may have also evolved. With Ould Semane's network dismantled, the remaining Mauritanians in AQIM helped keep AQIM connected to Mauritania, but not always in a combat sense. As Geoff Porter has pointed out, post-2011 Mauritania could be a considered "a locus of passive jihadi activity." For example, AQIM's Mauritanian spokesmen, along with its Algerian field commanders, routinely turn to the Mauritanian media to give statements and interviews, trusting that their words will not be censored and will find both Francophone and Arabophone audiences.[106] Meanwhile, alongside figures such as Joulaybib and Ould Kheirou who took prominent leadership positions, a number of Mauritanians continued to fight in the rank-and-file of AQIM and other jihadist units in the Sahel[107] – just not, after 2011, in Mauritania itself.

---

[104] Interview with Abu Hafs al-Muritani.

[105] Abu al-Ma'ali, "Abu al-Hammam: Muritaniya Ta'rif Kayfa Tatajannab Muwajahatina."

[106] Geoff Porter, "The Renewed Jihadi Terror Threat to Mauritania," Combating Terrorism Center *Sentinel* 11:7 (August 2018), https://ctc.usma.edu/renewed-jihadi-terror-threat-mauritania/.

[107] One local Mauritanian media outlet lists eight Mauritanians who were killed in northern Mali in 2013, presumably during Operation Serval. "Ashhar Qatla al-Muritaniyyin min Tanzim al-Qa'ida fi Bilad al-Maghrib al-Islami," Kifa li-l-Anba'/Kiffa Info, April 18, 2014, www.kiffainfo.net/article6431.html.

Post-Jihadist Mauritania?

By the early 2010s, Mauritanian authorities were modifying their approach to the domestic religious and political arena. Beyond offering dialogues to hardliners and using more restraint in torture, authorities were also rethinking their postures regarding religio-political activism. After 2005, Salafis and Islamists found greater political and social space in which to organize, as well as more permissive (though sometimes still unstated and variable) rules governing their activities. One aspect of this process was the legalization of Tewassoul, a mainstream Islamist political party, in 2007. Thenceforth, Tewassoul could compete in elections; Tewassoul's presidential candidate placed fourth in 2009, and the party received the second-highest scores in the parliamentary elections of 2018.

Leaving mainstream Islamism aside, the chapter now turns to the question of what space exists in Mauritania for the airing of views that are not quite jihadist, but very close to jihadist thought. To reiterate, part of the argument of this chapter is that a new social contract has allowed jihadist-leaning clerics to speak out on controversial issues, provided they remain within certain red lines dictated by the regime. The following sections discuss two notable Mauritanian clerics, both of whom have been briefly mentioned already in the chapter. The first is Mahfouz Ould al-Walid (better known as Abu Hafs al-Muritani, b. 1967), former religious advisor to Usama bin Laden and the Taliban's Mullah Omar. The second is Muhammad Salim al-Majlisi (b. 1976), a Salafi preacher who has strongly criticized democracy and constitutionalism.

These figures have complex relationships with jihadism. Since 2012, al-Muritani has publicly rejected al-Qa'ida's transnational terrorist efforts. He has also publicly dismissed, as impractical, various jihadist projects that aim at overthrowing regimes in Muslim-majority societies. For his part, al-Majlisi's relationship with global jihadism is less clear. Al-Majlisi has been accused of ties to AQIM and the Islamic State, and his writings have been lauded and shared by jihadist outlets, including the now-defunct but tremendously influential Minbar al-Tawhid wa-l-Jihad (Pulpit of Monotheism and Jihad). Al-Majlisi has disavowed any organizational connection to armed jihadists – and if one believes that he once possessed such connections, he appeared not to possess any connections by the mid-2010s. Al-Majlisi regards national-level jihadism as legitimate in many contexts but he rules out this option in Mauritania and other countries where strident preaching is permitted. He describes his own role as that of preacher, rather than jihadist organizer. Since approximately 2010–2012, these two scholars and other like-minded thinkers and activists have navigated a tenuous physical and rhetorical freedom within Mauritania.

Abu Hafs al-Muritani

Abu Hafs al-Muritani, born Mahfouz Ould al-Walid in Mauritania's Trarza region,[108] is now widely known as the "former mufti" of Usama bin Laden. Al-Muritani joined al-Qa'ida around 1991.[109] Al-Muritani is a cousin of the longtime Guantanamo Bay detainee Mohamedou Salahi (b. 1970), who was released in 2016 and who appears to have been innocent of involvement in 9/11.[110]

Bin Laden's deputy and successor, Ayman al-Zawahiri, gives the following brief account of al-Muritani's early career:

He participated in the Afghan jihad against the Communists, and then emigrated to the Islamic Emirate in Afghanistan. He established a center for teaching the Arabic language in Kandahar, and supervised the publication of the Arabic journal "The Student (al-Talib)" that spoke in the name of the Islamic Emirate in Afghanistan. He was among those close to Shaykh Usama bin Laden and was among the people he consulted (*min ahl mashuratihi*, i.e. his Shura Council). Shaykh Usama had a special interest in his poems, which he delivered at occasions and meetings. In addition to organizational and administrative burdens, the shaykh [al-Muritani] supervised Islamic legal enlightenment programs (*baramij al-taw'iya al-shar'iyya*) in the military camps.[111]

Al-Muritani taught al-Zawahiri and other jihadists in Afghanistan in fields such as grammar, theology, and Qur'anic recitation. Al-Muritani

---

[108] "Mufti al-Qa'ida al-Sabiq li-Shabakatina."
[109] "Abu Hafs al-Muritani..Hajamat 11 Sibtimbir J1," Al Jazeera, October 20, 2012, www.aljazeera.net/programs/today-interview/2012/10/20/ أبو-حفص-الموريتاني-هجمات-11-سبتمبر-ج1.
[110] See Ben Taub, "Guantanamo's Darkest Secret," *The New Yorker*, April 15, 2019, www.newyorker.com/magazine/2019/04/22/guantanamos-darkest-secret.
[111] Ayman al-Zawahiri, *Al-Tabri'a* (self-published, 2008), 53–54, available at http://ia801408.us.archive.org/17/items/el-tabre2ah/kitab-v_1.pdf.

became so close to Bin Laden that the latter even named him in his will as the intended recipient of part of his fortune in Sudan.[112]

At some point prior to June 2001, al-Muritani authored a treatise entitled *Al-'Amal al-Islami bayn Dawa'i al-Ijtima' wa-Du'at al-Niza'* (The Islamic Project Between the Grounds for Uniting and the Callers to Strife). The treatise called for unity among Muslim activists. Bin Laden authored the foreword, writing, "The treatise furnishes the most important evidences from the Book and the Sunna and the words of the Muslim community's scholars concerning the obligation for unity and coming together, and for rejecting disunion and strife, explaining the effects and harms of division."[113] Al-Muritani, according to al-Zawahiri, "has major credit for encouraging me and my brothers to carry out the unification of Islamic Jihad and al-Qa'ida."[114]

Al-Muritani remained part of al-Qa'ida during its many transform-ations in the 1990s. After Bin Laden moved to Sudan, al-Muritani went there as well. In his telling,

> In that stage, most of al-Qa'ida's activities were investment activities, charit-able activities, preaching activities within narrow limits, activities [involving] communication with some of the Islamic groups and movements in the Islamic world. [There were] political activities in that stage. Shaykh Usama, may God have mercy on him, had founded the advice and reform group (*hay'at al-nasiha wa-l-islah*), which was an opponent of the Saudi regime at that time. The activity of this group was one of the reasons for the pressure the Saudi government put on the Sudanese government to expel al-Qa'ida from Sudan.[115]

In Sudan and later, back in Afghanistan, al-Muritani headed the group's shari'a committee (*al-lajna al-shar'iyya*). When Bin Laden and al-Qa'ida left Sudan for Afghanistan in 1996, al-Muritani remained in Sudan for a time "to pursue my higher studies, and my situation was a legal, normal situation."[116]

---

[112] Usama bin Ladin, "In Regard to the Money That Is in Sudan," declassified by the Office of the Director of National Intelligence, available at www.dni.gov/files/documents/ubl2016/arabic/Arabic%20in%20regard%20to%20the%20money%20that%20is%20in%20Sudan.pdf.

[113] Usama bin Ladin, "Taqdim" in Abu Hafs al-Muritani, *Al-'Amal al-Islami bayn Dawa'i al-Ijtima' wa-Du'at al-Niza'* (self-published, undated), available at www.ilmway.com/site/maqdis/MS_12964.html.

[114] Al-Zawahiri, *Al-Tabri'a*, 54.

[115] "Abu Hafs al-Muritani..Hajamat 11 Sibtimbir J1."   [116] Ibid.

The 9/11 Commission later stated that al-Muritani was involved in planning attacks against American interests around 1998–1999,[117] whereas al-Muritani says that he had no involvement in al-Qaʿida's 1998 bombings of the US embassies in Kenya and Tanzania, nor in al-Qaʿida's attack on the USS Cole destroyer in Yemen in 2000. Even if he did not have any role in these attacks, al-Muritani's continued association with Al-Qaʿida in the 1990s could be taken as evidence of his tacit acceptance of bin Laden's statements against the United States, especially bin Laden's 1996 "Declaration of War against the Americans Occupying the Land of the Two Holy Places" (which al-Muritani may have helped to draft) and bin Laden's 1998 statement on behalf of the "World Islamic Front for Jihad against Jews and Crusaders." But according to al-Muritani, these decisions were not his own. Al-Muritani only participated, he said, in the meetings concerning the 9/11 plot. "I was at the head of those who opposed that action." Al-Muritani said he objected to the plot on multiple grounds from an Islamic jurisprudential perspective. "Our opposition originated in Islamic legal points of departure (*muʿaradatuna kanat intilaqan min muntalaqat sharʿiyya*)." It was objectionable, he felt, to target civilians, and it was also objectionable to break the trust that accepting a government's visa implied.[118]

Several weeks before 9/11, al-Muritani has said, he resigned from al-Qaʿida despite bin Laden's protestations. Al-Muritani decided not to announce his resignation publicly, he told bin Laden, "so as not to negatively affect your position." After the attacks and the ensuing American invasion, the Taliban asked him and others to leave Afghanistan.[119] Heading to Iran with a group of militants, their families, and orphans, al-Muritani helped negotiate passage for some of these individuals. He remained in Iran under various forms of compulsion, ranging from house arrest to what he described as "hospitality with some restrictions (*al-diyafa fiha baʿd al-quyud*)."[120]

Eventually, Mauritanian authorities extradited him and his family. Handed over to Mauritanian authorities in 2012, he was allowed to go

---

[117] *The 9/11 Commission Report* (Washington, 2004), 130 and 141, available at http://govinfo.library.unt.edu/911/report/911Report_Ch4.pdf.

[118] "Abu Hafs al-Muritani ... Hajamat 11 Sibtimbir J1."   [119] Ibid.

[120] "Abu Hafs al-Muritani ... Hajamat 11 Sibtimbir J2," Al Jazeera, 23, October 2012, www.aljazeera.net/programs/today-interview/2012/10/23/ أبو-حفص-الموريتاني-هجمات-11-سبتمبر-ج2.

free after interrogations.[121] In Nouakchott, he has become a media figure, appearing on Arabic television stations to comment on developments in the global jihadist scene – for example, dismissing and denouncing the Islamic State's proclamation of a Caliphate in 2014.

One of al-Muritani's first media appearances came in October 2012, when he recorded an interview with Al Jazeera giving his account of al-Qaʻida's internal debates before the 9/11 attacks. Al-Muritani explained his perspective on why jihadists targeted America, or even why Muslims generally, in his view, hated America. He rejected the explanations that the Bush administration had offered – explanations having to do with jihadists' supposed hatred of Americans' political and social freedoms. He also rejected the idea that the issue was necessarily about hating unbelievers. He pointed to China as an example of a major, primarily non-Muslim power that had not attracted the same anger. Instead, he said, the central issue was Palestine. In his discussions with Americans prior to his release from Iran, he recounted, they had discussed Palestine.

I said to them, "Getting out of this [issue] is simple." They said, "What do you advise us?" I said to them, "I, as a Muslim, advise you to be Muslims, to be in Islam, but if you do not enter Islam, the Muslims will not cross the oceans to you to force you into Islam and to fight you so that you enter Islam ... " I said to them that the past policies, which I mentioned to you and which are the reason for this enmity – change them and get out of Muslims' countries that have been occupied. Stop plundering the wealth and treasure of Muslims, stop supporting the corrupt regimes you support in the region, stop supporting Israel. We do not want you to help us in resisting the occupation in Israel and in Palestine, or in regaining Palestine, but it would be enough for us if you would stop supporting this usurper and adhere to the international laws that you believe in.[122]

Al-Muritani was not disavowing jihad in Muslim-majority lands, but he was saying that the United States had within its grasp political solutions that could eliminate its conflicts with jihadists.

Asked by the interviewer if this stance represented a "revision (*muraja'a*)" of his older stances, al-Muritani said no, adding that he had

---

[121] Jemal Oumar, "Retour de l'ancien leader d'al-Qaida en Mauritanie," *Magharebia*, April 12, 2012, available at http://cridem.org/imprimable.php?article=628222.

[122] "Abu Hafs al-Muritani ... Hajamat 11 Sibtimbir J1."

always opposed *takfir* and had long opposed efforts to overthrow local regimes.

I am one of the most intense opponents of the tyrannical regimes that rule the Islamic world. I am among those most cognizant of the bad role that these regimes undertake in plotting with the forces of global unbelief (*quwa al-kufr al-'alami*) in conspiring against this Muslim community, and against its peoples, and against its religion, and against everything in it. But despite that, at the same time I was one of the most intense opponents of undertaking armed action against these regimes and seeking to overthrow them, for a simple reason: history has taught us that a group, small in number and small in count, will not be able to defeat a regime equipped with the fiercest weapons and the largest armies, with global unbelief helping it from all sides.[123]

Later in the interview, al-Muritani added another note of caution about jihadist projects, saying, "The most important [conclusion] I reached through a scrutinizing, evaluating look at the performance of jihadist groups is that success is not written for jihad unless the [entire] Muslim community adopts it and the peoples embrace it."[124] Such stances recall Asef Bayat's argument that exhaustion and internal contradiction are key factors in propelling post-Islamism, or in this case post-jihadism.

At the end of the interview, the questions turned to the subject of democracy. Al-Muritani said,

The best part of democracy is that it gives people the right to choose their leaders, hold them accountable, question them, and remove them if the situation demands it. That is found in Islam, and we do not need to import it. The worst part of democracy is that it wrests away sovereignty (*al-hakimiyya*, a key idiom in jihadist thought) from God, the Glorified and Exalted, and gives it to the people. Here the worst part of democracy clashes with the best part of Islam. Really, this is an obstacle that is not easy to overcome, but it is possible.[125]

If democracy could be adapted to Islamic contexts such that it would not be possible for the people to make what was *haram* into something *halal*, he said, then it might be possible for Islam to take some of the better aspects of democracy for itself.

[123] Ibid.   [124] "Abu Hafs al-Muritani ... Hajamat 11 Sibtimbir J2."
[125] Ibid.

After the 2012 Al Jazeera interview, al-Muritani continued to appear on Arabic-language television stations. His appearances came at key moments, as when he condemned the Islamic State in November 2014, roughly five months after the group declared its caliphate.[126] His freedom extends to the social media arena as well, where he maintains a Twitter account,[127] Facebook page,[128] and Telegram channel.[129]

Why did the Mauritanian government permit al-Muritani to air his views to international audiences? Clearly, the state has the power to detain and silence him. His television appearances, then, remained within the red lines tacitly laid down by Mauritania's rulers. Among the opinions al-Muritani expressed were some potentially controversial views – open admiration for bin Laden, skepticism over details in the United States government's account of bin Laden's death,[130] unapologetic discussion of al-Qaʻida's career in the 1990s, extended and sympathetic explanations of jihadists' grievances against the United States and Arab regimes, and also explicit condemnation of democracy as practiced over much of the world. Yet, in al-Muritani's interviews, there are also silences that seem strategic. He offers almost no discussions of Mauritanian politics or even affairs in northwest Africa as a whole. When asked by the Al Jazeera interviewer in 2012 about jihadism in Mali and about the impact of the Arab Spring, al-Muritani spoke in abstract and general terms, disavowing detailed knowledge of al-Qaʻida's affiliates in Africa or elsewhere.

If you said to me that I am an expert in the affairs of al-Qaʻida central (*al-Qaʻida al-umm*), I would say you have not missed the truth by much, but ... I do not have sufficient expertise on the branches of al-Qaʻida (*furu' al-Qaʻida*) ... But my explanation for them is that they are part of the state of Islamist rejection of the Western policy in the Islamic world and of the regimes linked to this Western policy.[131]

[126] ʻAli al-Balwi, "Mufti al-Qaʻida al-Sabiq Mahfuz Wuld al-Walid al-Maʻruf bi-'Abu Hafs al-Muritani'," Al-Yawm, November 28, 2014, www.alyaum.com/article/4030335.

[127] Available at https://twitter.com/abuhafsmuritani?lang=en; accessed May 23, 2019.

[128] Available at www.facebook.com/AbuHafsMuritani/; accessed May 23, 2019.

[129] Available at http://t.me/AbuHafsMuritani; accessed May 23, 2019.

[130] "Mufti al-Qaʻida al-Sabiq li-Shabakatina."

[131] "Abu Hafs al-Muritani ... Hajamat 11 Sibtimbir J1."

Having given this caveat, al-Muritani then criticized AQIM's approach in Mali:

Really, in principle I do not agree with the style that the Islamic groups in northern Mali have taken. Of course I do not know the motives they have but I do not think that this is a salutary style (*uslub nafi‘*) in establishing an Islamic state. I think that jihad is only a jihad if it prevails among the people of competence and expertise and those who stand for it … Any jihad that does not lead to that result is not really a legal, desirable jihad (*jihad shar‘i matlub*).[132]

Al-Muritani rhetorically undercut the jihadists who might once again threaten Mauritania.

He has also made clear that he is neutral or even pro-government within Mauritanian politics. In an interview with CNN Arabic, he was asked whether he had helped arrange a visit by Ould Abdel Aziz to al-Muritani's hometown, Arkiz (R'Kiz). Al-Muritani responded:

I do not engage in politics in its narrowly ordered conception, which limits it to partisanship and entrenchment (*al-tahazzub wa-l-takhandaqa*), either with loyalty, or with opposition … Yes, Mr. President of the Republic visited us in our village … It was the legal duty, and the polite thing to do to do well in welcoming him, and I do not consider that to be engaging in local political affairs in the negative sense that I mentioned before.[133]

Al-Muritani has political utility for the Mauritanian government. His extradition, release, and media freedom are not gestures of state benevolence but rather indications of a strategic calculation by the authorities. Like other analysts and journalists who have met al-Muritani in recent years,[134] when interviewing him I was struck by the comfort of his accommodations and by the relative ease I had in meeting him; as of 2018 he was undoubtedly under surveillance, but he also had considerable freedom.

Unlike in Libya, where the Qadhafi regime's late-game efforts to rehabilitate jihadists ended up releasing men who then joined the revolution against the regime, al-Muritani has not publicly challenged the Mauritanian state. Moreover, he is positioned to wield significant credibility with Mauritanian youth who feel curiosity or sympathy for jihadism. He has helped to tamp down tensions at sensitive moments,

---

[132] Ibid.   [133] "Mufti al-Qa‘ida al-Sabiq li-Shabakatina."
[134] See, for example, Taub, "Guantanamo's Darkest Secret."

for example when Mauritanian authorities closed a prominent Islamist school in September 2018. Al-Muritani can claim both to have known and loved bin Laden personally, as well as to have rejected individual jihadist plots and broader jihadist strategies on both pragmatic and Islamic legal grounds. To benefit from al-Muritani's message, Mauritanian authorities would not need any explicit "deal" with him – they would simply let him understand that his freedom may be conditional.

Mohamed Salim al-Majlisi

Mohamed Salim Ould Mohamed Lemine al-Majlisi has been called the foremost ideological exponent of AQIM inside Mauritania, a claim he rejects. Al-Majlisi refers to himself as a scholar and a "*da'iya,*" or one who calls people to deeper engagement with Islam. When asked about his relationship with Salafi-jihadism in a 2015 interview, al-Majlisi gave a complicated answer. Undertaking armed jihad was legitimate in places experiencing armed conflict, he said, giving the examples of Palestine, Iraq, and Syria. Yet he rejected the tactic of killing women and children, and he also rejected the extension of armed jihad to peaceful countries.

When we hear that it is necessary for a spark or sparks from that war to move to our country or other countries that are not really theaters of fighting, then here the disagreement occurs. Because the safe countries, where there is a living Islamic call (*da'wa hayya*), where there are certain doors open, even if not all the doors are open, there is no doubt that [launching war] is a gross error.[135]

One might categorize al-Majlisi as a limited supporter of jihadism outside Mauritania, someone reluctant to criticize jihadist movements elsewhere but equally reluctant to advocate the violent overthrow of the Mauritanian state.

Relatively little is known about al-Majlisi's early life. In terms of his intellectual formation, al-Majlisi was one of the last generations of students to study under Buddah al-Busayri, the previously mentioned long-serving imam of Nouakchott and one of the pioneers of Salafism in contemporary Mauritania. Yet whereas al-Busayri, a towering figure

---

[135] BellewarMedia, "Barnamij Liqa' al-Sahil ma'a al-Da'iya al-Salafi Muhammad Salim al-Majlisi," December 10, 2015, www.youtube.com/watch?v=oIyGzZgmvZA.

of twentieth-century Mauritanian Islam, criticized but did not fundamentally reject the political authorities, al-Majlisi has been more confrontational vis-à-vis the political order. The context is very different: al-Busayri spent much of his career carving out an independent voice for himself under one-party regimes (civilian and military), while al-Majlisi has come to political maturity in a more fluid context where unprecedented levels of public political debate have occurred.

Mauritanian authorities have detained al-Majlisi several times. He spent nearly three years in prison after the murders of the French tourists at Aleg, accused of belonging to AQIM and of having issued a fatwa authorizing the murders.[136] At least three members of Khadim Ould Semane's network were allegedly students of al-Majlisi.[137] In September 2010, he and thirty-two other prisoners were released under a presidential amnesty,[138] following the prison dialogues. After his release, al-Majlisi told Mauritanian media that the security services closely monitored all of his lectures and lessons, and that they continued to hold his identity papers, which heavily restricted his ability to move freely in Nouakchott or elsewhere.[139]

During his detention from 2008 to 2010, al-Majlisi published several essays outlining his political and religious thought. These essays were uploaded to Abu Muhammad al-Maqdisi's Minbar al-Tawhid wa-l-Jihad (The Pulpit of Monotheism and Jihad), and circulated on other jihadist and Salafi platforms. After his release, other writings also appeared in jihadist publications. For example, his June 2011 "So the Scholars Stop Participating in the Creation of Tyranny" was picked up on jihadist-leaning blogs and was even mentioned in *Inspire*, the English-language magazine of al-Qaʿida in the Arabian Peninsula.[140] If one wants to give al-Majlisi the benefit of the doubt, one could say

---

[136] "Muritaniya Tuqif Daʿiya Yuʾayyid 'Daʿish'," Al Arabiya, August 29, 2015, www.alarabiya.net/ar/north-africa/mauritania/2015/08/29/ موريتانيا-توقف-داعية-يؤيد-داعش.html.

[137] "Al-Siraj Tanshur al-Qissa al-Kamila."

[138] "'Anba' Tanshur Laʾihat al-Salafiyyin." See also "Itlaq Sirah al-Salafiyyin fi Muritaniya," Al Jazeera, September 8, 2010, www.youtube.com/watch?v=3wAceaHPMsA.

[139] "Al-Salafi al-Majlisi: Tamma Iʿtiqali Marratayn baʿd Khuruji min al-Sijn Kullama Marartu bi-Qurb Thakna ʿAskariyya," Sahara Medias, December 11, 2010, www.saharamedias.net/السلفي-المجلسي-تم-اعتقالي-مرتين-بعد-خر/.

[140] Al-Qaʿida in the Arabian Peninsula, *Inspire* 8 (May 2015), 10, available at https://jihadology.net/2012/05/03/al-qaidah-in-the-arabian-peninsulas-al-malahim-media-releases-inspire-magazine-issue-8-and-9/.

that he is not responsible if jihadist outlets republish his writing. Yet some jihadists, at the very least, have perceived him as a fellow jihadist.

Much of al-Majlisi's writing and preaching has concerned democracy. Similarly to thinkers such as Sayyid Qutb (1906–1966), al-Majlisi sees human-led majority rule as contradicting not only details of God's revelation but also some of the political principles inherent in the idea of revelation itself. Al-Majlisi's attitudes toward democracy differ substantially from those of mainstream Islamists. In his 2009 essay "Democratic Islam Is an American Substitute (*Al-Islam al-Dimuqrati Badil Amriki*)," al-Majlisi denounced mainstream Islamist movements as puppets of the West. Referring to Islamist parties in Turkey, Egypt, and Palestine, he wrote,

Here we ask ourselves about what has been accomplished through this [electoral] success. Have they implemented the shari'a or established the *hudud* (corporal punishments mentioned in the Qur'an) or liberated the countries or driven back the scheme of the enemy[?] Rather, nothing has happened except the dilution of the religion (*tamyi' al-din*).[141]

Al-Majlisi has clarified that he is not interested in discussing theoretical conceptions of democracy, but rather in condemning democracy as practiced. In one 2014 lecture, he responded to the world's most famous Islamist scholar today, Yusuf al-Qaradawi. Referencing al-Qaradawi's *Min Fiqh al-Dawla fi al-Islam* (On the Jurisprudence of the State in Islam), al-Majlisi said, "He imagines a democracy in his mind in order to say that democracy in general does not contradict Islam. He talks about something that he himself imagines. He does not talk about something that has a relationship with reality."[142]

In August 2015, al-Majlisi and a small group were briefly detained again, accused of providing support to the Islamic State.[143] Following his release, he appeared on the satellite station Sahel TV for an interview. Asked about his arrest, he responded that in a climate of fear and declining morals, slander was common, and that the state had received false reports about him concerning the Islamic State. Once the state

---

[141] Muhammad Salim al-Majlisi, "Al-Islam al-Dimuqrati Badil Amriki," Minbar al-Tawhid wa-l-Jihad, April 2, 2009, www.ilmway.com/site/maqdis/MS_16887.html.

[142] Muhammad Salim al-Majlisi, "Muhammad Salim al-Majlisi Yarudd 'ala al-Qaradawi wa-l-Dadaw," published on YouTube November 4, 2014, www.youtube.com/watch?v=xDo_5l-VLms.

[143] "Muritaniya Tuqif Da'iya Yu'ayyid 'Da'ish'."

conducted its investigation and found nothing, he said, the authorities released him. He added that he was not under surveillance, and that prison conditions had improved in comparison with years past – when he fell ill with a cough and a fever, authorities took him to a doctor, treatment he would not have received during previous spells in prison.[144] I quote another section of the interview:

Interviewer:　What is the reason for your repeated arrests?

Al-Majlisi:　I would say that there is an issue that has become known as terrorism. And this issue has become globalized in our time. The issue is no longer an issue for the country on its own, but rather it is a general issue. So I put my past arrests in the column of what is known as the globalization of the War on Terror and I consider myself a victim of this globalization. For we, in this time, in reality when you talk about divine unity, about the unity of God the Blessed and Exalted, and about the necessity of keeping away from polytheism, unbelief, and atheism, you get accused of calling the whole society unbelievers, and of throwing everyone into [the category] of polytheism and unbelief. And when you call people to what the Prophet, God's blessings and peace upon him, called people to, and following in his footsteps, you get accused of rebelling against the Imams of the major legal schools, and of insulting them and attacking them. Likewise when you say that in imposed constitutions and in man-made laws (*al-dasatir al-mutabbaqa wa-l-qawanin al-wad'iyya*) there are things that contradict the shari'a of Islam, it is also said that you are saying the rhetoric of the groups that take up weapons against societies and regimes.[145]

Regardless of whether he was or was not a religious authority for AQIM in the past, it is interesting to note how in recent years he has framed his career as one of speaking the truth and sometimes being punished for it. What al-Majlisi implicitly asks for is not the right to declare a jihad but rather the space to criticize fundamental aspects of Mauritanian state and society. The authorities, to a large degree, have

---

[144] BellewarMedia, "Barnamij Liqa' al-Sahil ma'a al-Da'iya al-Salafi Muhammad Salim al-Majlisi."
[145] Ibid.

granted him that space: As of 2019, he was at liberty to teach in some of Nouakchott's mosques.

Conclusion

To conclude this chapter, it is worth returning to Khadim Ould Semane's 2006 interview with Al Jazeera. Asked about the Lemgheitty attack – the incident that touched off six years of armed conflict between the GSPC/AQIM and the Mauritanian state – Ould Semane offered a justification for the GSPC's actions.[146]

They [i.e., the Mauritanian state] are the ones who started the war against this Group [i.e., the GSPC]. Fundamentally, it is well known that the Group does not undertake anything outside of Algeria ... The situation in Mauritania had been under control, but when the first shot is fired we cannot keep anything under control after that ... Pressure generates explosion ... It would be best for these [members] of the clan that rules Mauritania – a weak, soft clan with no power and strength, that has nothing – it would be better for it to leave things calm. For the youth cannot continue watching scholars get imprisoned, scholars getting tortured, getting shocked with electricity, having their reputations slandered, having their honor violated, being thrown into prison and separated from their small children, their wives, their parents, and so forth. [The youth cannot] sit and watch. A reaction might take place, and when the reaction occurs, we cannot, in that way, keep the situation under control.[147]

Even in 2006, the GSPC's own recruits were spelling out a formula whereby the Mauritanian state could reduce tensions within the country and make itself less of a target for jihadist attacks. Part of this formula involved the regime's treatment of Muslim scholars. As the Mauritanian journalist Ahmad al-Wadi'a suggested to me, perhaps what is exceptional is not the lack of attacks since 2011, but rather the period of heavy-handed repression and attacks from 2003 to 2011; arguably, the default perspective of Mauritanian authorities is to avoid confrontation with jihadists and hardliners, rather than to court it.[148]

Prevailing wisdom suggests that strident preaching drives recruitment to jihadism. The particular case of Mauritania hints at the opposite

---

[146] Ould Semane also briefly speculated – unconvincingly – that the attack might have been staged by Ould Taya's agents.

[147] "Al-Khadim Wuld al-Siman."   [148] Interview with Ahmad al-Wadi'a.

possibility – that allowing strident preaching may blunt recruitment and deny jihadists the ability to build formidable coalitions. Mauritania's jihadist cells initially responded, in part, to state maltreatment of scholars, but jihadists could not make those very same scholars into durable allies and partners. In Mauritania's experiment with giving figures such as al-Majlisi and al-Muritani latitude to preach and speak, the outcome will depend in part on what intentions such figures have over the long term. The state, however, seems to convey that freedom is contingent; the state will closely monitor both the content of scholars' speech and their activities behind closed doors.

Whatever success Mauritania has achieved is unlikely to last forever. Over the years, serious and well-informed analysts – as well as various alarmists – have suggested that Mauritania was on the verge of finding itself, once again, in AQIM's crosshairs. When I spoke with an official at the G5 Sahel's counter-radicalization unit CELLRAD in September 2017, he mentioned concerns about youth radicalization and discontent in the Nouakchott suburbs.[149] In May 2018, an AQIM communiqué mentioned Mauritania and drew a new round of commentary. Experts such as Geoff Porter have plausibly argued that Mauritania's increasing participation in counterterrorism in Mali, as well as the then-approaching 2019 elections, could change AQIM's calculus about attacking Mauritania.[150] No attacks materialized, however, in 2018 or 2019. Meanwhile, the French government and others were declaring more and more of Mauritania to be relatively safe for tourists – though not, crucially, the border regions with Mali.

Other sources of strain exist. From an early point in the prison dialogues and releases, some of those amnestied have complained that they were not receiving the support they were promised;[151] on the other hand, one highly placed politician told me that recidivism rates have been only around 3 percent.[152] Alongside complaints from older, amnestied ex-jihadists, the passage of time may elicit new waves of young hardliners. As Wehrey has written, "The government's triumphalist narrative is ultimately built on a shaky foundation, especially

---

[149] Interview with Amadou Sall, Nouakchott, September 26, 2017.
[150] Porter, "Renewed Jihadi Threat."
[151] Amin Muhammad, "Shakawa min But' Damj al-Salafiyyin bi-Muritaniya," Al Jazeera, July 19, 2011, www.aljazeera.net/news/reportsandinterviews/2011/7/19/شكاوى-من-بطء-دمج-السلفيين-بموريتانيا.
[152] Interview with Sidi Mohamed Ould Maham.

given Mauritania's bleak socioeconomic picture, ongoing corruption, and existing societal tensions – afflictions that violent extremists have exploited in the past."[153] Finally, there were signs in 2018 that the authorities were once again losing patience with critical clerics – in September, authorities closed the Islamist mega-cleric Mohamed al-Hasan Ould al-Dedew's school in Nouakchott, Markaz Takwin al-'Ulama' (The Center for Training Islamic Scholars). Authorities may have been attempting to show al-Dedew where the red lines were – but aggressive actions against clerics could anger some of their supporters.

Cracks in the model aside, does Mauritania represent a broader model that could bring greater peace between national states and jihadist-inclined youth? The answer is likely no, at least to the extent that Mauritania's particular political settlement draws heavily on the structure of its society and the arc of its history. Moreover, on many other fronts Mauritania lacks a political settlement, particularly when it comes to the issue of race. In another way, though, the Mauritanian case does suggest a wider lesson: When dealing with jihadist movements, states have to generate their own, locally specific political settlements that constrain violence without generating grievance.

[153] Wehrey, "Control and Contain."

Conclusion
Northwest Africa and the War on Terror

In Western policymakers' thinking, North Africa and the Sahel are theaters, albeit secondary ones, in the "War on Terror." The Sahel has repeatedly been portrayed as a sort of echo of Afghanistan, or the assumed experience of Afghanistan. The suffix "-stan" has been regularly appended to the Sahel, or to Mali, just as various Saharan field commanders have been nicknamed the next "Bin Laden." In this analogical thinking, the drivers of jihadism are generic: "fragile states," "bad governance," "civil wars," and "extremism" are seen as one-size-fits-all explanations of jihadism, and northwest Africa is seen as a paradigmatic case where these forces intersect. To conclude this book, I want to argue that if northwest Africa is a microcosm of the War on Terror, it is even more so a microcosm of the War on Terror's flawed assumptions.

Nearly two decades after 9/11, forecasts about the future of the global jihadist movement run toward the pessimistic. In Washington, an entire industry is dedicated to peddling alarmism about jihadism. Often, such alarmism presents itself as running counter to conventional wisdom even when the alarmists are pleading for a retrenchment of the policy status quo. Amid global fears about the Islamic State, alarmists cautioned policymakers not to forget al-Qaʻida; and once the Islamic State appeared largely defeated, those same alarmists began predicting that it was only a matter of time before ISIS reemerged. It is a simple but effective game, where you win column inches or lucrative gigs simply by arguing that there is always someone, somewhere, who is raising the black flag and plotting to hurt Americans. On a long enough timeline and with vague enough forecasts, the alarmists can always count on seeming to be proven right.

Some of the think tankers and policymakers who are most hawkish about confronting jihadism are also the least sanguine about the possibility of defeating jihadism. Such analysts envision, and embrace, only the possibility of a "long war." For example, a 2018 report from the

Center for Strategic and International Studies (CSIS) peddled alarmist figures about the supposed size of the Salafi-jihadi movement (CSIS' high estimate ran to 230,000 fighters). The report concluded that the policy status quo was the only viable option: "A significant withdrawal of US special operations forces, intelligence operatives, intelligence resources, and development and diplomatic experts for counterterrorism in key areas of Africa, the Middle East, and South Asia would be unnecessarily risky."[1]

Even ostensible peacemakers seem to perceive no way out of the tunnel except by making refinements to the War on Terror. After I served on an expert working group under the auspices of the United States Institute of Peace (USIP) in 2016, I was disheartened to see the final report close by asserting, "The reality is that jihadis may always be one step ahead."[2] Three years later, a USIP "Task Force on Extremism in Fragile States" rehashed the same ideas about jihadism, arguing, "After each supposed defeat, extremist groups return having grown increasingly ambitious, innovative, and deadly."[3] Under the guise of innovation, the Task Force presented various recommendations about new modes of funding and new emphasis on interagency coordination within the United States government. But the underlying message was to continue existing policy. Washington's apparent consensus is that if the War on Terror has any fundamental flaws, they are managerial rather than conceptual; we can tinker with the long war, the logic runs, but ending it is inconceivable.

And yet the War on Terror has failed. The West's strongest armies have proven incapable of eliminating insurgencies at the peripheries of the capitalist world. The United States, occupying Afghanistan since 2001, is at the time of writing grudgingly negotiating with the Taliban,

---

[1] Seth Jones et al., "The Evolution of the Salafi-Jihadist Threat: Current and Future Challenges from the Islamic State, Al-Qaeda, and Other Groups," Center for Strategic and International Studies, November 2018, 51, https://csis-prod.s3 .amazonaws.com/s3fs-public/publication/Jones_EvolvingTerroristThreat_FULL_ WEB.pdf.

[2] Robin Wright et al., "The Jihadi Threat: ISIS, Al Qaeda, and beyond," United States Institute of Peace, December 2016, 39, www.usip.org/sites/default/files/ The-Jihadi-Threat-ISIS-Al-Qaeda-and-Beyond.pdf.

[3] Task Force on Extremism in Fragile States, "Preventing Extremism in Fragile States: A New Approach," United States Institute of Peace, February 2019, 6, www.usip.org/sites/default/files/2019-02/preventing-extremism-in-fragile-states- a-new-approach.pdf.

having failed to defeat them. France, whose intervention in Mali in 2013 was initially hailed as an exemplar of modern warfare,[4] is bogged down in Mali while insecurity grips Burkina Faso and deepens in Niger. Here, the Sahel is representative, though not in the way that policymakers might like: Various efforts aimed at preventing the spread of jihadism, from the launch of the United States Department of State's Pan-Sahel Initiative in 2002 up through the time of writing, have had almost no net positive effects.

There are conceptual problems that the War on Terror's architects and executors should confront. This book has argued for looking at jihadism as an inherently political mode of mobilizing violence, treating politics not as the grand visions of Usama bin Laden but as the day-to-day work of building and maintaining coalitions. This depiction of jihadist politics emphasizes that jihadists are not rootless ideological predators who pounce on unsuspecting civilians in fragile states and civil wars; oftentimes, jihadists are local to the areas where they operate and are intimately familiar with the micro-politics that surround them.

Yet when policymakers and analysts consider politics at all, they treat politics as part of the environment surrounding jihadism, and not as part of jihadism itself. The CSIS report urges, "Policymakers need to better understand the specific political and other factors that allowed groups like the Islamic State and al-Qaeda to establish a foothold and to focus U.S. diplomatic and development efforts on better addressing them." But what the authors mean by "political" is "disenfranchisement," "local grievances," and "governance."[5] In this view, politics constitutes the environment in which jihadists operate but excludes the jihadists themselves. This view of politics mutes the agency of all actors except governments. The implication is that jihadists are some kind of disease, and the only independent variable in how far they spread is the health of the "host" societies. Any acknowledgment of politics as a competition for power, where jihadists not only compete but also become strategic assets for other actors in the arena, is missing.

Any alternative understanding and policy framework will have to grapple with the following six themes, three of which relate

---

[4] Christopher Chivvis, *The French War on Al-Qa'ida in Africa* (Cambridge: Cambridge University Press, 2015).
[5] Jones et al., "Evolution of the Salafi-Jihadist Threat," 1.

directly to jihadist political agency and three of which relate to environmental factors:

First, both Western and national governments may have to learn to live with a residual jihadist presence at the peripheries of the capitalist world; in a sense, they already do. Since 9/11, the assumption has been that any jihadist enclave is a potential "safe haven" and therefore a latent national security threat to the United States. But consider that the Sahara's "most wanted man," Mokhtar Belmokhtar, in more than twenty years of fighting in Algeria, Mauritania, Mali, Niger, and Libya, never seems to have targeted American or European soil. As I have argued throughout the book, I suspect that many jihadists are indeed deeply ideological and religious – yet I think many of them, especially in the Sahara, are (also) essentially parochial figures and jumped-up bandits. How many millions of dollars is it worth expending to hunt and kill these men? How far should Western governments go in distorting regional politics in order to make sure that AQIM is crushed?[6] Will drawn-out, costly ventures in Mali prevent the kind of terrorist attacks that have befallen Paris in recent years – none of which were plotted in Mali?

Second, both Western and national governments should confront the realities of the collusive arrangements that seem to exist between jihadists and various actors, even some states. Part of why jihadism thrives politically in some areas, this book has emphasized, is not because jihadists prey on a prone population but because jihadists find partners who see political advantage in working with them. Sometimes, such collusion proves profoundly destabilizing; at other times, tacit agreements and nonaggression pacts seem to spare some countries from jihadist violence. Mauritania's "post-jihadism" may not be a Western policymaker's dream, but it is better than Mali's chaos. In other contexts, it makes little sense to "partner" with a government to "fight terrorism" if that government is simultaneously abetting jihadism.

Third, giving jihadists viable offramps other than full capitulation can help to fragment jihadist coalitions and take advantage of existing internal tensions and splits. Algerian authorities undercut both the

---

[6] See Nathaniel Powell, "A Flawed Strategy in the Sahel: How French Intervention Contributes to Instability," *Foreign Affairs*, February 1, 2016, www .foreignaffairs.com/articles/west-africa/2016-02-01/flawed-strategy-sahel.

Armed Islamic Group (GIA) and the Salafi Group for Preaching and Combat (GSPC) through amnesties at group and individual levels. In northern Mali, most of the Ansar al-Din coalition was allowed (by Malian, French, and regional authorities) to reenter mainstream politics in 2013. That decision may have empowered the jihadists in the shadows to some extent, but it likely spared the north what could have been even more bloodshed. Mauritania's prison dialogues allowed some hardliners back into society, with what seems to be a low rate of recidivism and a damper on overall recruitment.

One question hanging over Mali's conflict has been whether it would be possible to have a fruitful, peace-oriented dialogue with the Mali-born jihadist leaders Iyad ag Ghali and Amadou Kouffa; as Chapter 4 noted, Kouffa has demonstrated some willingness to talk. Excluding jihadists from peace talks can have unintended consequences, empowering jihadists as spoilers and encouraging clandestine collaboration between "mainstream" forces and jihadist politicians. In February 2020, Mali's president announced that his government was pursuing a dialogue with some jihadists.

Fourth, a foreign presence can often have the opposite of the intended effect. Of the case studies in this book where governments achieved anything approaching a resolution of their domestic jihadist challenges (Algeria and Mauritania), they did so without a heavy presence of foreign combat troops. Meanwhile, Mali has sunk ever deeper into conflict despite – and I would argue because of – the lasting French combat presence there. Foreign forces, not just in Mali but also in Afghanistan, Iraq, Somalia, and elsewhere, become targets for jihadist violence and rallying cries for jihadist mobilization. It is easy for Western governments to box themselves into the assumption that if they withdraw their forces, insurgencies will grow and their own countries will become more vulnerable to attack; this is the thinking that has kept the United States imprisoned in Afghanistan, and that increasingly traps France in Mali. But when insurgencies feed off the foreign presence, it is time to begin winding that presence down.

Fifth, collective punishment is a central feature of the War on Terror, not an unfortunate byproduct of it. The West's instinct after 9/11 was to treat terrorism as political violence rather than criminal acts. Mahmoud Mamdani has spelled out why the implications of that choice often involve collective punishment: "Unlike crime, political acts make sense only when linked to collective grievances ... If there is a logic

316 Conclusion

behind the practice of collective punishment, it is the acknowledgment
that collective punishment can only be a response to political acts, not
criminal deeds."[7] Lashing out against populations, including Muslim
populations and particular ethnic groups, has been a recurring
response to jihadist violence. Western governments have engaged in
their own forms of collective punishment, notably through the US-led
wars in Iraq and Afghanistan and through Washington's drone
assassination programs. There has also been wide-ranging Western
complicity in enabling governments and government-aligned militias
to perpetrate collective punishment against their own citizens or the
citizens of nearby countries. Western policymakers' feeble objections
to other governments' human rights violations notwithstanding, it is
clear that from the wars in the Sahel to the Saudi-Emirati venture in
Yemen, Western governments largely and in some cases actively abet
collective punishment. But it is collective punishment – the profiling
and targeting of particular ethnic groups, the demonization of Islam as
a religion, the labeling of all men in certain areas as combatants, the
rejection of legitimate protesters as "terrorists," and so forth – that
provides jihadists with the greatest opportunities to move from the
political and geographical margins into more central roles.[8] Both the
War on Terror framework and the practice of collective punishment
need to be discarded to make progress against jihadism.

Sixth, the role of religion in jihadism is not as a set of disembodied
interpretations of the Qur'an or a generic "Islamic extremism," but
rather as a set of fluid and politicized discourses that adapt to conflict
realities. It makes little sense for Western development agencies and
NGOs, their local contractors, or Sahelian governments to think that
they can prevent or contain the spread of jihadism through "Countering Violent Extremism," in other words by talking people out of
particular religious viewpoints. Is the "radical preacher" more dangerous if he can speak his mind from the pulpit or if, in detention, he
becomes a symbol of government repression against Muslims and
authorities' subordination to Western dictates? The preachers who
have risen to lead jihadist organizations – Amadou Kouffa or, to range
beyond the cases in this book, Boko Haram's Muhammad Yusuf –

---

[7] Mahmood Mamdani, *Good Muslim, Bad Muslim: America, the Cold War, and
the Roots of Terror* (New York: Three Leaves Press, 2004), 217.
[8] See Mohammed Hafez, *Why Muslims Rebel: Repression and Resistance in the
Islamic World* (Boulder, CO: Lynne Rienner Publishers, 2003), 21–22.

have done so for specific reasons that reflect the environments that surrounded them, rather than due to the inherent lure of their messages. It took the profound crisis of 2012 in northern Mali, and the ensuing heavy-handed reinsertion of a security presence into central Mali, to elevate Kouffa, just as it took, first, elite collusion and then collective punishment in northeastern Nigeria to elevate Yusuf. Religious extremism is not an automatic gateway to jihadism. Religious hardliners only become security threats when they take up arms; to think otherwise is to commit to a foolhardy and counterproductive project of social engineering in contexts that Washington and Paris, and many northwest African states themselves, do not really understand.

But what, if anything, is likely to change in the policy approaches of Paris, Washington, Bamako, Ouagadougou, or elsewhere? In the decades to come, will policymakers be able to think beyond the framework of securitization? Or are policies going to remain heavy-handed even as other problems, particularly climate change and its effects, render life more and more difficult for ordinary people in northwest Africa?

Forecasts for the future of the region are grim. If I find fears of a permanent conflict with jihadists overblown, it is harder to refute what the pessimists say about northwest Africa more broadly, especially concerning the Sahel: The regimes are brittle and oppressive, even when run by civilians who win credible elections;[9] the populations are growing while the economies sputter; and climate change is exacerbating the pressures that demography places on lands and resources. In February 2019, following French airstrikes against (non-jihadist) rebels in northern Chad, *The New Yorker*'s Ben Taub took an appropriately cynical look at the way the French government and Chadian President Idriss Déby colluded to shut down Chadians' grievances, all in an atmosphere stamped by the politics of the endless War on Terror. "Jihadi groups thrive in the margins of broken states," Taub wrote, "and, where there are no terrorists, Déby has seen it as politically advantageous to fabricate them." Taub concluded on an apocalyptic note:

---

[9] Take the case of Niger under Mahamadou Issoufou. See Sebastian Elischer and Lisa Mueller, "Niger Falls Back Off Track," *African Affairs* 118:471 (April 2019): 392–406.

Catastrophic trends are converging in unfathomably dangerous ways and will soon collide with the rudderless geopolitics of our era. Absent radical changes in local Sahelian governance and priorities, no humanitarian crisis in Africa's recent history will compare to the hell to come. What is likely doesn't have to be inevitable. The question for Western governments is whether they will be complicit in its acceleration.[10]

Where USIP's experts see "fragile states" as the weak links in the War on Terror, Taub rightly pointed out that the War on Terror distorts the politics of those same states.

The most likely disaster for the Sahel is not one where jihadists overrun territories from Nouakchott to N'Djamena. Rather, as Taub says, the grimmest likely future is an authoritarian hellscape where a poor, repressed, and hungry population has little say over how their rulers allocate the meagre available resources. And as Taub suggests, the obsession with hunting jihadists (or with labeling more and more rebels "terrorists") accelerates that future. But other futures are possible. What would it look like to take a more expansive view of some of the core vocabularies used to talk about jihadism? What would it mean to rethink "human security," "civilian protection," "deradicalization," and "stabilization"?

This book has offered a way of thinking about jihadists as both exceptional and banal, as both anathema within the political systems of their countries and simultaneously interwoven with those systems. Given the interweaving of jihadism and politics in parts of northwest Africa, I strongly doubt that a policy of hunting and exterminating jihadist leaders while "de-radicalizing" the remnants of their fighters will succeed in restoring stability. Rather, to secure a vibrant future, North Africa and the Sahel will need a more imaginative approach, and a more three-dimensional understanding of jihadists as political actors.

[10] Ben Taub, "A Shadow Rebellion in Chad," *The New Yorker*, February 21, 2019, www.newyorker.com/news/news-desk/a-shadow-rebellion-in-chad.

Bibliography

The 9/11 Commission Report. Washington, 2004.

Abu al-Ma'ali, Mohammed Mahmoud. "Al-Qaeda and Its Allies in the Sahel and the Sahara." Al Jazeera Center for Studies, May 1, 2012.

"Al-Tanafus Bayn 'al-Dawla al-Islamiyya' wa-'Al-Qa'ida' Yush'il al-Sahra' al-Kubra." Al Jazeera Center for Studies, July 1, 2015.

Ahmad, Aisha. *Jihad & Co.: Black Markets and Islamist Power*. New York: Oxford University Press, 2017.

Al-Ahnaf, Mustafa, Bernard Botiveau, and Franck Frégosi, eds. *L'Algérie par ses islamistes*. Paris: Karthala, 1991.

Amnesty International. "Mauritania: Torture at the Heart of the State." December 3, 2008.

Anas, 'Abd Allah. *Wiladat al-Afghan al-'Arab: Sirat 'Abd Allah Anas bayn Mas'ud wa-'Abd Allah 'Azzam*. London: Dar al-Saqi, 2017.

Armstrong, Hannah. "Winning the War, Losing the Peace in Mali." *The New Republic*, February 28, 2013.

Ashour, Omar. "Ex-Jihadists in the New Libya." Brookings Institution, August 29, 2011.

"Post-Jihadism: Libya and the Global Transformations of Armed Islamist Movements." *Terrorism and Political Violence* 23:3 (2011): 377–397.

Atran, Scott. "The Devoted Actor: Unconditional Commitment and Intractable Conflict across Cultures." *Current Anthropology* 57:13 (June 2016): S192–S203.

Bâ, Amadou Hampâté and Jacques Daget. *L'Empire Peul du Macina (1818–1853)*. Abidjan: École Pratique des Hautes Études, 1984 [1962].

Ba-Konaré, Dougoukolo Alpha Oumar. "Entre faux djihadistes et faux chasseurs traditionnels, les civils piégés dans le centre du Mali." *The Conversation*, October 22, 2018.

Bacon, Tricia and Daisy Muibu. "The Domestication of Al-Shabaab." *Journal of the Middle East and Africa* 10:3 (July–September 2019): 279–305.

Bano, Masooda. *The Rational Believer: Choices and Decisions in the Madrasas of Pakistan*. Ithaca, NY: Cornell University Press, 2012.

Barriere, Olivier and Catherine Barriere. *Le Foncier-Environment: Pour un egestion viable des ressources naturelles renouvelables au Sahel: Approche interdisciplinaire dans le delta intérieur du Niger (Mali).* Paris: Mission Française de Coopération, 1995.

Bayat, Asef. "Post-Islamism at Large." In *Post-Islamism: The Changing Faces of Political Islam*, edited by Asef Bayat, 3–32. Oxford: Oxford University Press, 2013.

Bencherif, Adib. "From Resilience to Fragmentation: Al Qaeda in the Islamic Maghreb and Jihadist Group Modularity." *Terrorism and Political Violence*, published online August 2017.

Benjaminsen, Tor and Boubacar Ba. "Farmer-Herder Conflicts, Pastoral Marginalisation and Corruption: A Case Study from the Inland Niger Delta of Mali." *Geographical Journal* 175:1 (March 2009): 71–81.

Benthall, Jonathan. "Islamic Aid in a North Malian Enclave." *Anthropology Today* 22:4 (August 2006): 19–21.

Bøås, Morten. "Guns, Money, and Prayers: AQIM's Blueprint for Securing Control of Northern Mali." *Combating Terrorism Center Sentinel* 7:4 (April 2014).

"Northern Mali: Criminality, Coping and Resistance along an Elusive Frontier." In *The Politics of Conflict Economies: Miners, Merchants and Warriors in the African Borderland*, 86–98. New York: Routledge, 2015.

Bøås, Morten and Liv Elin Torheim. "The Trouble in Mali – Corruption, Collusion, Resistance." *Third World Quarterly* 37:4 (2013): 1279–1292.

Boilley, Pierre. *Les Touaregs Kel Adagh. Dépendances et révoltes: du Soudan français au Mali contemporain.* Paris: Karthala, 1999.

Brachet, Julien. "Manufacturing Smugglers: From Irregular to Clandestine Mobility in the Sahara." *The Annals of the American Academy of Political and Social Science*, published online February 21, 2018.

Brenner, Louis. *Controlling Knowledge: Religion, Power, and Schooling in a West African Muslim Society.* Bloomington: Indiana University Press, 2001.

Bunzel, Cole. "The Caliphate's Scholar-in-Arms." *Jihadica*, July 9, 2014.

"Diluting Jihad: Tahrir al-Sham and the Concerns of Abu Muhammad al-Maqdisi." *Jihadica*, March 29, 2017.

Byman, Daniel. "Judging al-Qaeda's Record, Parts I and II." *Lawfare*, June 27 and 28, 2017.

Campana, Aurélie. "Between Destabilization and Local Embeddedness: Jihadist Groups in the Malian Conflict Since 2015." Centre FrancoPaix, August 2018.

The Carter Center. "General National Congress Elections in Libya – Final Report." July 7, 2012.

Cavatorta, Francesco and Raquel Garcia, "Islamism in Mauritania and the Narrative of Political Moderation." *Journal of Modern African Studies* 55:2 (June 2017): 301–325.

Chauzel, Grégory and Thibault van Damme. "The Roots of Mali's Conflict: Moving Beyond the 2012 Crisis." Clingendael, March 2015.

Chelin, Richard. "From the Islamic State of Algeria to the Economic Caliphate of the Sahel: The Transformation of Al Qaeda in the Islamic Maghreb." *Terrorism and Political Violence*, published online June 7, 2018.

Chivvis, Christopher. *The French War on Al-Qa'ida in Africa*. Cambridge: Cambridge University Press, 2015.

Chonka, Peter. "Spies, Stonework, and the *Suuq*: Somali Nationalism and the Narrative Politics of Pro-*Harakat Al Shabaab Al Mujaahidiin* Online Propaganda." *Journal of Eastern African Studies* 10:2 (2016): 247–265.

Christia, Fotini. *Alliance Formation in Civil Wars*. Cambridge: Cambridge University Press, 2012.

Clarke, John I. "Oil in Libya: Some Implications." *Economic Geography* 39:1 (January 1963): 40–59.

Cluster Protection Niger. "NIGER: Localités affectées par le conflict intercommunautaire dans la region de Tillabéri." May 19, 2018.

"Rapport d'analyse mensuelle des données du monitoring de protection." July 2018.

Collier, Paul and Anke Hoeffler. "Greed and Grievance in Civil War." *Oxford Economic Papers* 56 (2004): 563–595.

Cotula, Lorenzo and Salmana Cissé. "A Case Study: Changes in 'Customary' Resource Tenure Systems in the Inner Niger Delta, Mali." In *Changes in 'Customary' Land Tenure Systems in Africa*, edited by Lorenzo Cotula, 81–101. International Institution for Environment and Development, 2007.

Craven-Matthews, Catriona and Pierre Englebert. "A Potemkin State in the Sahel? The Empirical and the Fictional in Malian State Reconstruction." *African Security* 11:1 (2018): 1–31.

Djontu, Herrick Mouafo and Karine Gatelier. "Nord-Tillabéri: analyse du conflit lié à l'accès aux ressources naturelles." Haute Autorité à la Consolidation de la Paix, August 2017.

Dowd, Catriona and Clionadh Raleigh. "The Myth of Global Islamic Terrorism and Local Conflict in Mali and the Sahel." *African Affairs* 112:448 (2013): 498–509.

Dupuy, Romane Da Cunha and Tanguy Quidelleur. "Self-Defence Movements in Burkina Faso: Diffusion and Structuration of Koglweogo Groups." NORLA, November 2018.

Duyvesteyn, Isabelle. "How New Is the New Terrorism?" *Studies in Conflict & Terrorism* 27:5 (2004): 439–454.

Eickelman, Dale and James Piscatori. *Muslim Politics*. Princeton, NJ: Princeton University Press, 1996.

Eizenga, Dan. "The Deteriorating Security Situation in Burkina Faso." *Bulletin FrancoPaix* 4:3 (March 2019): 1–5.

Elischer, Sebastian and Lisa Mueller. "Niger Falls Back Off Track." *African Affairs* 118:471 (April 2019): 392–406.

European Union Election Assessment Team. "Libya – Final Report: General National Congress Election." July 7, 2012.

Evans, Martin and John Philipps. *Algeria: Anger of the Dispossessed*. New Haven, CT, and London: Yale University Press, 2007.

Evans-Pritchard, E. E. *The Sanusi of Cyrenaica*. Oxford: Oxford University Press, 1949.

Famine Early Warning Systems Network. "Fatwa 'Ulama' Shinqit Hawla Mali." November 10, 2012.

"Niger Food Security Brief." May 2014.

Felter, Joseph and Brian Fishman. "Al-Qa'ida's Foreign Fighters in Iraq: A First Look at the Sinjar Records." Combating Terrorism Center, January 2, 2007.

Filiu, Jean-Pierre. "The Local and Global Jihad of al-Qa'ida in the Islamic Maghrib." *Middle East Journal* 63:2 (Spring 2009): 213–226.

Finkel, Evgeny and Scott Straus. "Macro, Meso, and Micro Research on Genocide: Gains, Shortcomings, and Future Areas of Inquiry." *Genocide Studies and Prevention* 7:1 (2012): 56–67.

Fishman, Brian. *The Master Plan: ISIS, al-Qaeda, and the Jihadi Strategy for Final Victory*. New Haven, CT: Yale University Press, 2016.

Foster, Noel. *Mauritania: The Struggle for Democracy*. Boulder, CO: Lynne Rienner, 2011.

Fowler, Robert. *A Season in Hell: My 130 Days in the Sahara with Al Qaeda*. New York: HarperCollins, 2011.

Gartenstein-Ross, Daveed and Nathaniel Barr. "How al-Qaeda Survived the Islamic State Challenge." *Current Trends in Islamist Ideology*, March 1, 2017.

"How Al-Qaeda Works: The Jihadist Group's Evolving Organizational Design," *Current Trends in Islamist Ideology*, June 1, 2018.

"GIA (Groupe islamique armé) (Armed Islamic Group)." In *The Columbia World Dictionary of Islamism*, edited by Antoine Sfeir, 45–47. New York: Columbia University Press, 2007.

"GSPC" (Group Salafite [sic] pour la Predication et le Combat) (Salafi Group for Preaching and Combat)." In *The Columbia World Dictionary of Islamism*, edited by Antoine Sfeir, 47–50. New York: Columbia University Press, 2007.

Guichaoua, Yvan and Héni Nsaibia. "Comment le djihad armé se diffuse au Sahel." The Conversation, February 24, 2019.

Guidère, Mathieu. "The Timbuktu Letters: New Insights about AQIM." *Res Militaris* (2014).

Gutelius, David. "Islam in Northern Mali and the War on Terror." *Journal of Contemporary African Studies* 25:1 (January 2007): 59–76.

Testimony to the Senate Committee on Foreign Relations Subcommittee on African Affairs, November 2009.

Hafez, Mohammed. "Fratricidal Rebels: Ideological Extremity and Warring Factionalism in Civil Wars." *Terrorism and Political Violence*, published online 2017.

Why Muslims Rebel: Repression and Resistance in the Islamic World. Boulder, CO: Lynne Rienner Publishers, 2003.

Hall, Bruce. *A History of Race in Muslim West Africa, 1600–1960.* Cambridge: Cambridge University Press, 2011.

Hamid, Mustafa and Leah Farrell. *The Arabs at War in Afghanistan.* Oxford: Oxford University Press, 2016.

Hansen, Stig Jarle. *Al-Shabaab in Somalia: The History and Ideology of a Militant Islamist Group.* Oxford: Oxford University Press, 2013.

Harmon, Stephen. *Terror and Insurgency in the Sahara-Sahel Region: Corruption, Contraband, Jihad and the Mali War of 2012–2013.* London and New York: Routledge, 2016.

Harmony and Disharmony: Exploiting al-Qa'ida's Organizational Vulnerabilities. West Point, NY: Combating Terrorism Center, 2006.

Harsch, Ernest. *Burkina Faso: A History of Power, Protest, and Revolution.* London: Zed Books, 2017.

Hashemi, Nader and Danny Postel. "Introduction: The Sectarianization Thesis." In *Sectarianization: Mapping the New Politics of the Middle East*, edited by Nader Hashemi and Danny Postel, 1–22. New York: Oxford University Press, 2017.

Hefner, Robert. "Introduction: Shari'a Politics – Law and Society in the Modern Muslim World." In *Shari'a Politics: Islamic Law and Society in the Modern World*, edited by Robert Hefner, 1–54. Bloomington: Indiana University Press, 2011.

Hegghammer, Thomas. "The Ideological Hybridization of Jihadi Groups." *Current Trends in Islamist Ideology*, Volume 9, November 18, 2009.

Jihad in Saudi Arabia: Violence and Pan-Islamism since 1979. New York: Cambridge University Press, 2010.

ed. *Jihadi Culture: The Art and Social Practices of Militant Islamists.* New York: Cambridge University Press, 2017.

Herbert, Matt. "States and Smugglers: The Ties That Bind and the Ties That Fray." In "Transnational Organized Crime and Political Actors in the Maghreb and Sahel," Konrad Adenauer Stiftung Mediterranean Dialogue Series Number 17 (January 2019): 5–7.

HiiL. "Justice Needs and Satisfaction in Mali 2018: Legal Problems in Daily Life." March 2019.

Hill, Evan and Laura Kasinoff. "Playing a Double Game in the Fight against AQAP." *Foreign Policy*, January 21, 2015.

Hoechner, Hannah. *Quranic Schools in Northern Nigeria: Everyday Experiences of Youth, Faith, and Poverty*. Cambridge: Cambridge University Press, 2018.

Hoffman, Bruce. "Al Qaeda's Resurrection." Council on Foreign Relations Expert Brief, March 6, 2018.

Hudson, Valerie and Hilary Matfess. "In Plain Sight: The Neglected Linkage between Brideprice and Violent Conflict." *International Security* 42:1 (Summer 2017): 7–40.

Human Rights Watch. "'By Day We Fear the Army, By Night the Jihadists': Abuses By Armed Islamists and Security Forces in Burkina Faso." May 2018.

"Libya: Abu Salim Prison Massacre Remembered." June 27, 2012.

"Libya: Extremists Terrorizing Derna Residents." November 27, 2014.

"Libya: Men Face Possible Death for Planning Peaceful Demonstration." August 13, 2007.

"Libya: Wave of Political Assassinations." August 8, 2013.

"Mali: Abuses Spread South." February 19, 2016.

"Mauritania's Campaign of Terror: State-Sponsored Repression of Black Africans." April 1994.

"'We Used to Be Brothers': Self-Defense Group Abuses in Central Mali." December 2018.

Hüsken, Thomas and Georg Klute. "Political Orders in the Making: Emerging Forms of Political Organization from Libya to Northern Mali." *African Security* 8 (2015): 320–337.

Ibrahim, Ibrahim Yahaya. "Islamisme dans le Sud, jihadisme dans le Nord: pourquoi l'activisme islamique au Mali s'est-il exprimé différemment?" *Bulletin FrancoPaix* 2:10 (December 2017).

"Niger in the Face of the Sahelo-Saharan Islamic Insurgency: Precarious Stability in a Troubled Neighborhood." Sahel Research Group Working Paper 4 (August 2014).

"The Wave of Jihadist Insurgency in West Africa." OECD West African Papers Number 7 (August 2017).

Ibrahim, Ibrahim Yahaya and Mollie Zapata. "Regions at Risk: Preventing Mass Atrocities in Mali." United States Holocaust Memorial Museum, April 2018.

Ibrahimi, Niamatullah and Shahram Akbarzadeh. "Intra-Jihadist Conflict and Cooperation: Islamic State–Khorasan Province and the Taliban in Afghanistan." *Studies in Conflict & Terrorism*, published online January 7, 2019.

Idrissa, Rahmane. *The Politics of Islam in the Sahel: Between Persuasion and Violence*. New York: Routledge, 2017.

Institut Malien de Recherche Action Pour la Paix *Autoportrait du Mali: Les Obstacles à la Paix*. Bamako: Institut Malien de Recherche Action Pour la Paix, 2015.

International Criminal Court. "Decision on the confirmation of charges against Ahmad Al Faqi Al Mahdi." March 24, 2016.

International Crisis Group. "Central Mali: An Uprising in the Making?" July 6, 2016.

"Islam et politique au Mali: entre réalité et fiction." July 18, 2017.

"Mali: Avoiding Escalation." July 18, 2012.

"The Social Roots of Jihadist Violence in Burkina Faso's North." October 12, 2017.

"'Speaking with the Bad Guys': Toward Dialogue with Central Mali's Jihadists." May 28, 2019.

International Federation for Human Rights/Malian Association for Human Rights (FIDH/AMDH). "In Central Mali, Civilian Populations Are Caught between Terrorism and Counterterrorism." November 2018.

"An Interview with Abdelmalek Droukdal." *The New York Times*, July 1, 2008.

Jenkins, Jack. "The Book That Really Explains ISIS (Hint: It's Not the Qur'an)." Think Progress, September 10, 2014.

Jezequel, Jean-Hervé and Vincent Foucher. "Forced out of Towns in the Sahel, Africa's Jihadists Go Rural." International Crisis Group, January 11, 2017.

Joffé, George. "Trajectories of Radicalisation: Algeria 1989–1999." In *Islamist Radicalisation in North Africa: Politics and Process*, edited by George Joffé, 114–137. London: Routledge, 2012.

Jones, Seth et al. "The Evolution of the Salafi-Jihadist Threat: Current and Future Challenges from the Islamic State, Al-Qaeda, and Other Groups." Center for Strategic and International Studies, November 2018.

Jourde, Cédric. "Constructing Representations of the 'Global War on Terror' in the Islamic Republic of Mauritania." *Journal of Contemporary African Studies* 25:1 (2007): 77–100.

"Mauritania: The New Strongman in Nouakchott." Italian Institute for International Political Studies, September 9, 2019.

"Sifting through the Layers of Insecurity in the Sahel: The Case of Mauritania." Africa Center for Strategic Studies, September 30, 2011.

Kalyvas, Stathis. "Jihadi Rebels in Civil War." *Daedalus* 147:1 (Winter 2018): 36–47.

The Logic of Violence in Civil War. Cambridge: Cambridge University Press, 2006.

Kenney, Jeffrey. *Muslim Rebels: Kharijites and the Politics of Extremism in Egypt*. New York: Oxford University Press, 2006.

Kepel, Gilles. *Jihad: The Trail of Political Islam*, translated by Anthony F. Roberts. Cambridge, MA: Harvard University Press, 2002.

Al-Khajkhaj, Amraji' Muhammad. *Madinat Darna: Dirasa Hadariyya*. Benghazi: Dar al-Saqiya li-l-Nashr, 2008.

Kilcullen, David. *The Accidental Guerrilla: Fighting Small Wars in the Midst of a Big One*. Oxford: Oxford University Press, 2009.

Klute, Georg. "Hostilités et alliances: Archéologie de la dissidence des Touaregs au Mali." *Cahiers d'Études Africaines* 35:137 (1995): 55–71.

Koré, Lawel Chekou. *La rébellion touareg au Niger: Raisons de persistance et tentatives de solution*. Paris: L'Harmattan, 2010.

Lacher, Wolfram. "Challenging the Myth of the Drug-Terror Nexus in the Sahel." West Africa Commission on Drugs, Background Paper Number 4, 2013.

"Organized Crime and Conflict in the Sahel-Sahara Region." Carnegie Endowment for International Peace, September 2012.

Lacher, Wolfram and Guido Steinberg. "Spreading Local Roots: AQIM and Its Offshoots in the Sahara." In *Jihadism in Africa: Local Causes, Regional Expansion, International Alliances*, edited by Guido Steinberg and Annette Weber, 69–84. Berlin: Stiftung Wissenschaft und Politik, 2015.

Lahoud, Nelly et al. "Letters from Abbottabad: Bin Laden Sidelined?" Combating Terrorism Center Harmony Project, May 3, 2012.

Lauzière, Henri. "Bouyali, Moustafa [1940–1987]." In *Encyclopedia of the Modern Middle East and North Africa*, edited by Philip Mattar, Second Edition, Volume 1, 505–506. New York: Macmillan Reference USA, 2004.

Lav, Daniel. *Radical Islam and the Revival of Medieval Theology*. New York: Cambridge University Press, 2012.

Lebovich, Andrew. "AQIM's Formalized Flexibility." In *How al-Qaeda Survived Drone Strikes, Uprisings, and the Islamic State*, edited by Aaron Zelin, 56–66. Washington: Washington Institute for Near East Policy, 2017.

"AQIM Returns in Force in Northern Algeria." Combating Terrorism Center *Sentinel* 4:9 (September 2011).

"The Death of a Jihadist: A Chance to Curb Mali's Conflict." European Council on Foreign Relations, December 13, 2018.

"The Hotel Attacks and Militant Realignment in the Sahara-Sahel Region." Combating Terrorism Center *Sentinel* 9:1 (January 2016).

"The Local Face of Jihadism in Northern Mali." Combating Terrorism Center *Sentinel* 6:6 (June 2013).

"A Look Inside AQIM." *The Wasat*, January 15, 2012.

"Mali's Sleeper Cell." African Arguments, May 30, 2013.

"Reconstructing Local Orders in Mali: Historical Perspectives and Future Challenges." Brookings Institution, July 2017.

"Trying to Understand MUJWA." The Wasat, August 22, 2012.

Lecocq, Baz. "The Bellah Question: Slave Emancipation, Race, and Social Categories in Late Twentieth-Century Northern Mali." *Canadian Journal of African Studies* 39:1 (2005): 42–68.

Disputed Desert: Decolonisation, Competing Nationalisms and Tuareg Rebellions in Northern Mali. Leiden: Brill, 2010.

Lecocq, Baz and Paul Schrijver. "The War on Terror in a Haze of Dust: Potholes and Pitfalls on the Saharan Front." *Journal of Contemporary African Studies* 25:1 (January 2007): 141–166.

Li, Darryl. "A Jihadism Anti-primer." *Middle East Report* 276 (Fall 2015).

Lia, Brynjar. *Architect of Global Jihad: The Life of Al Qaeda Strategist Abu Mus'ab al-Suri*. New York: Columbia University Press, 2009.

"Understanding Jihadi Proto-States." *Perspectives on Terrorism* 9:4 (2015).

Lyammouri, Rida. "Key Events That Led to Tensions between Mokhtar Belmokhtar and Adnan Abu Walid al-Sahrawi before Splitting." Maghreb and Sahel, December 7, 2015.

Maher, Shiraz. *Salafi-Jihadism: The History of an Idea*. Oxford: Oxford University Press, 2016.

Al-Majlisi, Muhammad Salim. "Al-Islam al-Dimuqrati Badil Amriki." Minbar al-Tawhid wa-l-Jihad, April 2, 2009.

Mamdani, Mahmood. *Good Muslim, Bad Muslim: America, the Cold War, and the Roots of Terror*. New York: Three Leaves Press, 2004.

Mangan, Fiona and Christina Murtaugh. "Security and Justice in Postrevolution Libya: Where to Turn?" United States Institute of Peace, 2014.

Marchand, Trevor. "The Djenné Mosque: World Heritage and Social Renewal in a West African Town." In *Religious Architecture: Anthropological Perspectives*, edited by Oskar Verkaaik, 117–148. Amsterdam: University of Amsterdam Press, 2013.

Marks, Monica. "Youth Politics and Tunisian Salafism: Understanding the Jihadi Current." *Mediterranean Politics* 18:1 (2013): 107–114.

Martinez, Luis. *The Algerian Civil War, 1990–1998*. New York: Columbia University Press, 2000.

Maruf, Harun and Dan Joseph. *Inside Al-Shabaab: The Secret History of Al-Qaeda's Most Powerful Ally*. Bloomington: Indiana University Press, 2018.

Matfess, Hilary. *Women and the War on Boko Haram: Wives, Weapons, Witnesses*. London: Zed Books, 2017.

"Mauritania's Goals in Its Struggle against al-Qaeda." Al Jazeera Center for Studies, July 25, 2011.

Mazarr, Michael et al. *Measuring the Health of the Liberal International Order*. Santa Monica, CA: RAND Corporation, 2017.

McCants, William. *The ISIS Apocalypse: The History, Strategy, and Doomsday Vision of the Islamic State*. New York: St. Martin's Press, 2015.

Mendelsohn, Barak. *The Al-Qaeda Franchise: The Expansion of Al-Qaeda and Its Consequences*. New York: Oxford University Press, 2016.

Mercy Corps. "'We Hope and We Fight': Youth, Communities, and Violence in Mali." September 2017.

Michael, Maggie, Trish Wilson, and Lee Keath, "Yemen: U.S. Allies Spin Deals with al-Qaida in War on Rebels." Associated Press, August 6, 2018.

Miller, Judith. *God Has Ninety-Nine Names: Reporting from a Militant Middle East*. New York: Touchstone/Simon and Schuster, 1996.

Mironova, Vera. *From Freedom Fighters to Jihadists: Human Resources of Non State Armed Groups*. New York: Oxford University Press, 2019.

Mokeddem, Mohamed. *Les Afghans Algériens: De la Djamaâ À la Qa'ida*. Algiers: Editions ANEP, 2002.

Morgan, Andy. "Alghabass ag Intalla: Interview with the Head of the MIA." Andy Morgan Writes, January 31, 2013.

"What Do the Touareg Want?" Andy Morgan Writes, February 1, 2013.

Mosinger, Eric. "Balance of Loyalties: Explaining Rebel Factional Struggles in the Nicaraguan Revolution." *Security Studies* 28:5 (2019): 935–975.

Moustapha, Elemine. "Negotiating Islamic Revival: Public Religiosity in Nouakchott City." *Islamic Africa* 5:1 (Spring 2014): 45–82.

Al-Mufti, Muhammad Muhammad. *Sahari Darna: Al-Tarikh al-Ijtima'i li-l-Madina*. Benghazi: Dar al-Kutub al-Wataniyya, 2007.

Mundy, Jacob. *Imaginative Geographies of Algerian Violence: Conflict Science, Conflict Management, Antipolitics.* Stanford, CA: Stanford University Press, 2015.

Naji, Abu Bakr. *Idarat al-Tawahhush: Akhtar Marhala sa-Tamurr biha al-Umma.* Self-published online, 2004.

Neumann, Peter. *Radicalized: New Jihadists and the Threat to the West.* London: I.B. Tauris, 2016.

Nielsen, Richard. *Deadly Clerics: Blocked Ambition and the Paths to Jihad.* Cambridge: Cambridge University Press, 2017.

Notin, Jean-Cristophe. *La Guerre de la France au Mali.* Paris: Tallandier, 2014.

Nsaibia, Héni. "The Fledgling Insurgency in Burkina's East." ACLED, September 20, 2018.

"From the Mali-Niger Borderlands to Rural Gao – Tactical and Geographical Shifts of Violence." ACLED, June 6, 2018.

"Targeting of the Islamic State in the Greater Sahara (ISGS)." ACLED, March 21, 2018.

Open Society Justice Initiative. "Globalizing Torture: CIA Secret Detention and Extraordinary Rendition." 2013.

Ould Ahmed Salem, Zekeria. *Prêcher dans le désert: Islam politique et changement social en Mauritanie.* Paris: Karthala, 2013.

Ould M. Salem, Lemine. *Le Ben Laden du Sahara: Sur les traces du jihadiste Mokhtar Belmokhtar.* Paris: Éditions de la Martinière, 2014.

Ould Mohamedou, Mohammed-Mahmoud. *A Theory of ISIS: Political Violence and the Transformation of the Global Order.* London: Pluto Press, 2018.

Ould al-Walid, Mahfouz (Mahfuz Wuld al-Walid/Abu Hafs al-Muritani). "Al-Sahwa al-Islamiyya fi Muritaniya." Unpublished *maitrise* thesis at Al-Ma'had al-'Ali li-l-Dirasat wa-l-Buhuth al-Islamiyya, 1992.

Pahlavi, Pierre and Jérôme Lacroix Leclair. "L'institutionnalisation d'AQMI dans la nébuleuse Al-Qaida." *Les Champs de Mars* 24:2 (2012): 9–28.

Pan, Chia-Lin. "The Population of Libya." *Population Studies* 3:1 (June 1949): 100–125.

Pargeter, Alison. "The LIFG's Current Role in the Global Jihad." Countering Terrorism Center *Sentinel* 1:5 (April 2008).

"Localism and Radicalization in North Africa: Local Factors and the Development of Political Islam in Morocco, Tunisia and Libya." *International Affairs* 85:5 (September 2009): 1031–1044.

Libya: The Rise and Fall of Qaddafi. New Haven, CT, and London: Yale University Press, 2012.

Pelckmans, Lotte. "Stereotypes of Past-Slavery and 'Stereo-styles' in Post-Slavery: A Multidimensional, Interactionist Perspective on Contemporary

Hierarchies." *International Journal of African Historical Studies* 48:2 (2015): 281–301.

Pellerin, Mathieu. "Les trajectoires de radicalisation religieuse au Sahel." IFRI, February 2017.

Pigné, Jérôme. "Sahel: Quelle recomposition après l'élimination d'Hamadou Kouffa dans le centre du Mali?" Institut Thomas Moore, November 27, 2018.

Porter, Geoff. "How Realistic Is Libya as an Islamic State 'Fallback'?" Combating Terrorism Center *Sentinel* 9:3 (March 2016).

"The Renewed Jihadi Terror Threat to Mauritania." Combating Terrorism Center *Sentinel* 11:7 (August 2018).

Powell, Nathaniel. "A Flawed Strategy in the Sahel: How French Intervention Contributes to Instability." *Foreign Affairs*, February 1, 2016.

Qajali, Amina. *Al-I'lam wa-l-'Unf al-Siyasi.* Amman: Markaz al-Kitab al-Akadimi, 2015.

Raineri, Luca and Francesco Strazzari. "State, Secession, and Jihad: The Micropolitical Economy of Conflict in Northern Mali." *African Security* 8 (2015): 249–271.

Rasmussen, Susan. "Re-Formations of the Sacred, the Secular, and Modernity: Nuances of Religious Experience among the Tuareg (Kel Tamajaq)." *Ethnology* 46:3 (Summer 2007): 185–203.

Roberts, Hugh. *The Battlefield: Algeria 1988–2002: Studies in a Broken Polity.* New York: Verso, 2003.

"From Radical Mission to Equivocal Ambition: The Expansion and Manipulation of Algerian Islamism, 1979–1992." In *Accounting for Fundamentalisms: The Dynamic Character of Movements*, edited by Martin Marty and R. Scott Appleby, 428–489. Chicago: University of Chicago Press, 1994.

Rosenblatt, Nate. "All Jihad Is Local: What ISIS' Files Tell Us About Its Fighters." New America Foundation, July 2016.

Roy, Olivier. *The Failure of Political Islam.* Translated by Carol Volk. Cambridge, MA: Harvard University Press, 1994.

"Introduction." In *Tribes and Global Jihadism*, edited by Virginie Collombier and Olivier Roy, 1–13. Oxford: Oxford University Press, 2018.

Rupesinghe, Natasja and Yida Diall. "Women and the Katiba Macina in Central Mali." Norwegian Institute of International Affairs, September 3, 2019.

Ryan, Michael W. S. *Decoding Al-Qaeda's Strategy: The Deep Battle against America.* New York: Columbia University Press, 2016.

Sageman, Marc. *Understanding Terror Networks.* Philadelphia: University of Pennsylvania Press, 2004.

Sanankoua, Diarah Bintou. "Les écoles 'Coraniques' au Mali: problèmes actuels." *Canadian Journal of African Studies* 19:2 (1985): 359–367.

Sandor, Adam. "Insecurity, the Breakdown of Social Trust, and Armed Actor Governance in Central and Northern Mali." Centre FrancoPaix, August 2017.

Sangaré, Boukary. "Le Centre du Mali: épicentre du djihadisme." GRIP, May 20, 2016.

Sauvain-Dugerdil, Claudine. "Youth Mobility in an Isolated Sahelian Population of Mali." *Annals of the American Academy of Political and Social Science* 648 (July 2013): 160–174.

Savadogo, Mahamadou. "Note d'analyse sur la situation sécuritaire au Burkina Faso." Unpublished analysis, April 2019.

Scheele, Judith. *Smugglers and Saints of the Sahara: Regional Connectivity in the Twentieth Century*. Cambridge: Cambridge University Press, 2012.

"Tribus, États et fraude: la région frontalière algéro-malienne." *études rurales* 184 (2009): 79–94.

Shapiro, Jacob. *The Terrorist's Dilemma: Managing Violent Covert Organizations*. Princeton, NJ: Princeton University Press, 2013.

Shesterinina, Anastasia. "Collective Threat Framing and Mobilization in Civil War." *American Political Science Review* 110:3 (August 2016): 411–427.

Singh, Naunihal. *Seizing Power: The Strategic Logic of Military Coups*. Baltimore: Johns Hopkins University Press, 2014.

Soares, Benjamin. "Family Law Reform in Mali: Contentious Debates and Elusive Outcomes." In *Gender and Islam in Africa: Rights, Sexuality, and Law*, edited by Margot Badran, 263–290. Washington, DC and Stanford, CA: Woodrow Wilson Center Press/Stanford University Press, 2011.

Islam and the Prayer Economy: History and Authority in a Malian Town. Ann Arbor: University of Michigan Press, 2005.

Staniland, Paul. "States, Insurgents, and Wartime Political Orders," *Perspectives on Politics* 10:2 (June 2012): 243–264.

Networks of Rebellion: Explaining Insurgent Cohesion and Collapse. Ithaca, NY: Cornell University Press, 2014.

Stenersen, Anne. *Al-Qaida in Afghanistan*. New York: Cambridge University Press, 2017.

Stone, Martin. *The Agony of Algeria*. New York: Columbia University Press, 1997.

Tankel, Stephen. *With Us and against Us: How America's Partners Help and Hinder the War on Terror*. New York: Columbia University Press, 2018.

Task Force on Extremism in Fragile States. "Preventing Extremism in Fragile States: A New Approach." United States Institute of Peace, February 2019.

Tawil, Camille. *Brothers in Arms: The Story of al-Qa'ida and the Arab Jihadists*. London: Saqi Books, 2011.

Tessler, Mark. "The Origins of Popular Support for Islamist Movements." In *Islam, Democracy, and the State in North Africa*, edited by John Entelis, 93–126. Bloomington: Indiana University Press, 1997.

Théroux-Bénoni, Lori-Anne et al. "Mali's Young 'Jihadists': Fuelled by Faith or Circumstance?" Institute for Security Studies, August 2016.

Thiam, Adam. "Centre du Mali: Enjeux et dangers d'une crise négligée." Centre pour le dialogue humanitaire/Institut du Macina, March 2019.

Thurston, Alexander. "Algeria's GIA: The First Major Armed Group to Fully Subordinate Salafism in Jihadism." *Islamic Law and Society* 24 (2017): 412–436.

  Boko Haram: The History of an African Jihadist Movement. Princeton, NJ: Princeton University Press, 2017.

"Escalating Conflicts in Burkina Faso." Rosa Luxemburg Foundation, September 2019.

"Political Settlements with Jihadists in Algeria and the Sahel." Organization for Economic Cooperation and Development, West African Papers Number 18 (October 2018).

"Timbuktu: A Laboratory for Jihadists Experimenting with Politics." War on the Rocks, January 23, 2019.

"Who Counts as Al-Qaeda: Lessons from Libya." Lawfare, May 7, 2017.

Tobie, Aurélien. "Central Mali: Violence, Local Perspectives and Diverging Narratives." SIPRI, December 2017.

Togola, Salif. "L'esclavage dans la region de Mopti." In *L'Esclavage au Mali*, edited by Naffet Keita, 47–77. Paris: L'Harmattan, 2012.

Topol, Sarah. "Guns and Poses." *Harper's Magazine* (December 2014).

United Nations Development Program. "Journey to Extremism in Africa: Drivers, Incentives and the Tipping Point for Recruitment." 2017.

United Nations Office for the Coordination of Humanitarian Affairs. "Burkina Faso: Armed Attacks in Arbinda, Flash Update." April 5, 2019.

"Niger – Diffa: Access, Insecurity and Population Movement." August 2017.

United Nations Panel of Experts on Mali. Final Report (August 2018).

United Nations Security Council. "Abderrahmane Ould El Amar." Version as of September 9, 2014

"Ansar Eddine." Version as of February 3, 2015.

"Report of the Secretary-General on the Situation in Mali." June 9, 2014.

"Report of the Secretary-General on the Situation in Mali." September 22, 2014.

"Report of the Secretary-General on the Situation in Mali." March 27, 2015.

"Security Council Al-Qaida Sanctions Committee Adds Ansar Eddine to Its Sanctions List." March 19, 2013.

"Security Council Al-Qaida Sanctions Committee Amends One Entry on Its Sanctions List." September 23, 2014.

"Situation in Mali: Report of the Secretary-General." March 26, 2019.

United States Department of State. "State Department Terrorist Designation of AQIM Operative Saleck Ould Cheikh Mohamedou." December 21, 2016.

"Terrorist Designations of Ansar al-Dine." March 21, 2013.

"Terrorist Designations of Iyad ag Ghali." February 26, 2013.

United States Department of the Treasury. "Treasury Targets Al Qaida-Affiliated Terror Group in Algeria." July 17, 2008.

United States Institute of Peace Task Force on Extremism in Fragile States. "Preventing Extremism in Fragile States: A New Approach." February 2019.

Vandewalle, Dirk. "Qadhafi's 'Perestroika': Economic and Political Liberalization in Libya." *Middle East Journal* 45:2 (Spring 1991): 216–231.

Volkov, Vadim. *Violent Entrepreneurs: The Use of Force in the Making of Russian Capitalism.* Ithaca, NY, and London: Cornell University Press, 2002.

Wagemakers, Joas. *A Quietist Jihadi: The Ideology and Influence of Abu Muhammad al-Maqdisi.* Cambridge: Cambridge University Press, 2012.

Wainscott, Ann Marie. *Bureaucratizing Islam: Morocco and the War on Terror.* Cambridge: Cambridge University Press, 2017.

Walter, Barbara. "The Extremist's Advantage in Civil Wars." *International Security* 42:2 (Fall 2017): 7–39.

Walther, Olivier and Dimitris Christopoulos. "Islamic Terrorism and the Malian Rebellion." *Terrorism and Political Violence* 27:3 (2015): 497–519.

Walther, Olivier and William Miles. "Introduction: States, Borders and Political Violence in Africa." In *African Border Disorders: Addressing Transnational Extremist Organizations*, edited by Olivier Walther and William Miles, 1–13. London and New York: Routledge, 2018.

Warner, Jason. "Sub-Saharan Africa's Three 'New' Islamic State Affiliates," Combating Terrorism Center *Sentinel* 10:1 (January 2017).

Wehrey, Frederic. "Control and Contain: Mauritania's Clerics and the Strategy against Violent Extremism." Carnegie Endowment for International Peace, March 29, 2019.

The Burning Shores: Inside the Battle for the New Libya. New York: Farrar, Straus and Giroux, 2018.

Wehrey, Frederic and Ala' Alrababa'h. "Rising Out of Chaos: The Islamic State in Libya." Carnegie Endowment *Diwan*, March 5, 2015.

"Splitting the Islamists: The Islamic State's Creeping Advance in Libya." Carnegie Endowment *Diwan*, June 19, 2015.

Wehrey, Frederic and Anouar Boukhars, eds. *Perilous Desert: Insecurity in the Sahara.* Washington: Carnegie Endowment, 2013.

Willis, Michael. *The Islamist Challenge in Algeria: A Political History.* New York: New York University Press, 1999.

Wojtanik, Andrew. "Mokhtar Belmokhtar: One-Eyed Firebrand of North Africa and the Sahel." Combating Terrorism Center Jihadi Bios Project, March 1, 2015.

Woldemariam, Michael. *Insurgent Fragmentation in the Horn of Africa: Rebellion and Its Discontents.* Cambridge: Cambridge University Press, 2018.

Wright, Lawrence. *The Looming Tower: Al-Qaeda and the Long Road to 9/11.* New York: Alfred A. Knopf, 2006.

Wright, Robin et al. "The Jihadi Threat: ISIS, Al Qaeda, and Beyond." United States Institute of Peace, December 2016.

Zelin, Aaron. "The Clairvoyant: The Guidelines: Measuring Zawahiri's Influence." Jihadology, March 9, 2014.

"The Islamic State's First Colony in Libya." Washington Institute for Near East Policy, October 10, 2014.

Your Sons Are at Your Service: Tunisia's Missionaries of Jihad. New York: Columbia University Press, 2019.

Zimmerman, Katherine. "Al Qaeda's Strengthening in the Shadows." Statement before the House Committee on Homeland Security Subcommittee on Counterterrorism and Intelligence on "The Persistent Threat: Al Qaeda's Evolution and Resilience," July 13, 2017.

Jihadist Documents and Sources

'Abd al-Hakim, 'Umar (Abu Mus'ab al-Suri). *Mukhtasar Shahadati 'ala al-Jihad fi al-Jaza'ir.* Self-published, June 2004.

'Abd al-Wadud, Abu Mus'ab ('Abd al-Malik Droukdel). "Hiwar ma'a Amir 'Al-Jama'a al-Salafiyya li-l-Da'wa wa-l-Qital'," Minbar al-Tawhid wa-l-Jihad, 2005.

Abu al-Zubayr, Mukhtar. "Letter About the Matter of the Islamic Maghreb." March 5, 2010. Recovered from Usama bin Laden's compound in

Abbottabad and declassified by the Office of the Director of National Intelligence.

'Aduww al-Murtaddin (pseudonymous questioner). "Hawla Hukm Radd al-Natija al-Sadira min al-Tahkim alladhi Radiya bihi al-Tarafan Idha Khalafa Shar' Allah." October 11, 2014.

Amin, Abu 'Abd al-Rahman [Djamel Zitouni]. *Hidayat Rabb al-'Alamin fi Tabyin Usul al-Salafiyyin wa-ma Yajib min al-'Ahd 'ala al-Mujahidin.* Self-published, 1996.

Al-'Anabi, Yusuf. "Fakku Hisar Banghazi," Ifriqiya al-Muslima, June 2016.

Ansardin, Katiba du Macina (Ansar al-Din, Katibat Masina). "Awwal Maqta' Fidiyu Yazhur Fihi Ahad Qadat al-Maydaniyyin li-Katibat Ansar al-Din bi-Mintaqat Masina." May 2016.

Al-Azdi, Abu Azuhayr. "Sal al-Husam li-Muwajahat Ahl al-Baghy wa-l-Ijram." May 4, 2015.

"Taslit al-Adwa' 'ala Ma Fa'alahu Tanzim al-Dawla bi-Masjid Fatimat al-Zahra'." May 5, 2015.

Belmokhtar, Mokhtar (Khalid Abu al-'Abbas). "Al-Muqaddima." In Al-Murabitun, *Tigentourine: Al-Harb 'ala Wukala' Faransa fi al-Jaza'ir.* Self-published, 2014.

Bin Ladin, Usama. "In Regard to the Money That Is in Sudan." Undated. Recovered from Usama bin Laden's compound in Abbottabad and declassified by the Office of the Director of National Intelligence.

Bin Nafi', Hafid 'Uqba [pseudonym]. "Irshad Dhawi al-Basa'ir hawla ma Ja'a fi Maqal al-Shaykh Majid al-Rashid 'an Jihad al-Jaza'ir." 2016.

Al-Bulaydi, Abu al-Hasan Rashid. *Nasa'ih wa-Tawjihat Shar'iyya min al-Shaykh Abi al-Hasan Rashid li-Mujahidi Nayjiriya.* Mu'assasat al-Andalus li-l-Intaj al-I'lami, 2017.

Droukdel, 'Abd al-Malik. "Bara'a min Af'al 'Hasan Hattab'." Minbar al-Tawhid wa-l-Jihad, February 10, 2005.

"Exclusive Interview with Shaykh al-Mujahid Hisham Abu Akram." *Al-Risalah*, January 2017.

"Gist of Conversation." Undated. Recovered from Usama bin Laden's compound in Abbottabad and declassified by the Office of the Director of National Intelligence.

Hisham, Abu Akram. "Al-Shaykh Abu Muhammad al-Yamani: Rihlatuhu ila al-Jaza'ir wa-Qissat Istishhadihi." Ifriqiya al-Muslima, December 2015.

"Hiwar ma'a Amir al-Jama'a al-Islamiyya al-Musallaha Abi Talha 'Antar Zuwabri [Zouabri]." *Al-Jama'a* 10 (September 1996): 5–16.

"Hiwar ma'a al-Qa'id Khalid Abi al-'Abbas – Amir al-Mintaqa al-Sahrawiyya li-l-Jama'a al-Salafiyya li-l-Da'wa wa-l-Qital." Minbar al-Tawhid wa-l-Jihad, May 25, 2006.

"Hiwar ma'a al-Shaykh 'Asim Abi Hayan: Mahattat min Tarikh al-Jihad fi al-Jaza'ir." Ifriqiya al-Muslima, September 2016.

Ibn al-Sadiqa. "Kalimat fi Ritha' al-Nabil/Abi al-Mughira al-Qahtani." January 5, 2016.

Islamic State. "Ba'd al-Hujum 'ala Ashadd al-Sujun Hirasa fi al-Nijar." *Al-Naba'* 182 (May 16, 2019): 9.

"Interview with Abul-Mughirah al-Qahtani." *Dabiq* 11 (August/September 2015): 60–63.

Islamic State of Iraq and Syria. "The End of Sykes-Picot." June 2014.

Al-Jama'a al-Islamiyya al-Musallaha [GIA]. "Al-Sawa'iq al-Hariqa fi Bayan Hukm al-Jaz'ara al-Mariqa." *Majallat al-Ansar* 131 (January 1996): 11–15.

Jama'at Nusrat al-Islam wa-l-Muslimin. "Bayan Tabannin li-l-Ghazwa al-Mubaraka 'ala al-Sifara al-Faransiyya wa-Mabna Hay'at al-Arkan al-Burkini." March 3, 2018.

"Hujum Kasih 'ala Qa'ida li-Quwwat G5 fi Jura." Mu'assasat al-Zallaqa, March 22, 2019.

"Infarru Hifafan wa-Thiqalan: Kalima Mar'iyya li-l-Shaykh al-Mujahid Muhammad Kufa Amir Mintaqat Masina." Mu'assasat al-Zallaqa, November 2018.

Al-Jama'a al-Salafiyya li-l-Da'wa wa-l-Qital [GSPC]. "Mithaq al-Jama'a al-Salafiyya li-l-Da'wa wa-l-Qital." Undated.

Al-Jaza'iri, Abu Muhammad Luqman. "Shadha al-Nasim fi Sirat al-Qa'id Mustafa Abi Ibrahim." Ifriqiya al-Muslima, January 2017.

Al-Jaza'iri, Abu Muslim. Fatwa in response to "Kayfa Tarawna al-Majlis al-Watani al-Intiqali fi Libiya?" Undated (likely April 2011).

Fatwa in response to "Hirasat Mustafa 'Abd al-Jalil 'Allamat Istifham fi Libiya." Undated (likely August 2014).

Al-Jaza'iri, Abu Shu'ayb. "Tanwir al-Basa'ir bi-Sirat al-Qa'id Abi Thumama Suwwan 'Abd al-Qadir." Ifriqiya al-Muslima, May 2017.

Katibat Shuhada' Abi Salim. "Kashf al-Shubuhat 'an Katibat Shuhada' Abi Salim." Facebook, April 2, 2015.

Al-Lajna al-I'lamiyya li-l-Jama'a al-Salafiyya li-l-Da'wa wa-l-Qital. "Hiwar ma'a Amir al-Jama'a al-Salafiyya," December 18, 2003.

Al-Lanja al-Shar'iyya li-Jama'at al-Tawhid wa-l-Jihad fi Gharb Ifriqiya. "Hadhihi 'Aqidatuna." Mu'assasat al-Murabitin, January 2013.

Letter from 'Abd al-Malik Droukdel to Saharan field commanders in al-Qa'ida in the Islamic Maghreb, 2012.

"Letter from Basir to the Brother in Command." Undated. Recovered from Usama bin Laden's compound in Abbottabad and declassified by the Office of the Director of National Intelligence.

Letter from the Shura Council of al-Qaʿida in the Islamic Maghreb to the Shura Council of the Veiled Men Battalian. October 3, 2012.

"Letter to Abu Basir." Undated. Recovered from Usama bin Laden's compound in Abbottabad and declassified by the Office of the Director of National Intelligence.

Majlis Shura Mujahidi Darna. "Al-Qasas Hayah." July 6, 2015.

Majlis Shura Mujahidi Darna wa-Dawahiha. "Al-Tahdhir al-Akhir li-Ghulat al-Takfir." May 6, 2015.

Al-Maqdisi, Abu Muhammad. "Hukm Hirasat al-Mustashar Mustafa ʿAbd al-Jalil wa-Ma Jara bi-Sabab Dhalik min Ikhtilaf wa-Fitan fi Libiya." Minbar al-Tawhid wa-l-Jihad, March 16, 2016.

"Li-l-ʿIbra min Dhakirat Afghanistan." Muʾassasat Bayan li-l-Iʿlam al-Islami, March 2, 2019.

"ʿAl-Masra' Tuhawir al-Shaykh Aba al-Fadl Iyad Ghali." *Al-Masra* 45, April 3, 2017.

Muʾassasat al-Zallaqa. "Wa-Ulaʾika Hum al-Kadhibun: Liqaʾ maʿa al-Shaykh al-Mujahid Muhammad Kufa Ithr Khabr Maqtalihi." February 2019.

Al-Muritani, Abu Hafs. *Al-ʿAmal al-Islami bayn Dawaʿi al-Ijtimaʿ wa-Duʿat al-Nizaʿ*. Self-published, undated.

Al-Qaʿida in the Arabian Peninsula. *Inspire* 8 (May 2015).

Al-Qaʿida in the Islamic Maghreb. "Bayan Hawla ʿGhazwat Burkina Fasu'." January 17, 2016.

Al-Qasrawi, Abu Rabbab Luqman Mustafa. "Safahat Matwiyya min Sirat al-Qaʾid al-Sayih ʿAttiya." Ifriqiya al-Muslimah, December 2016.

Al-Sahrawi, Adnan Abu al-Walid. "Announcing a New Amir and Giving Bayʿah to al-Baghdadi." May 13, 2015.

"Claiming the Kidnapping of the Romanian Hostages in Burkina Faso." May 19, 2015.

Al-Suri, Abu Musʿab. *Al-Thawra al-Islamiyya al-Jihadiyya fi Suriya*. Self-published, 1991.

Al-Wahrani, Abu Qatada al-Tayyib. "Ma Istafadtu min al-Shaykh Abi al-Hasan fi Ayyam al-Fitan." Ifriqiya al-Muslima, January/February 2016.

Al-Zawahiri, Ayman. *Al-Hisad al-Murr: Al-Ikhwan al-Muslimun fi Sittin Amm*. Self-published, 1991.

Al-Tabri'a. Self-published, 2008.

"Tawjihat ʿAmma li-l-ʿAmal al-Jihadi." Published online by Muʾassasat al-Sahab li-l-Intaj al-Iʿlami, 2013.

Shabakat Ansar al-Mujahidin, "Al-Liqaʾ al-Maftuh maʿa al-Shaykh Sanda Wuld Bu ʿAmama," 2012, 5–6, https://jihadology.net/wp-content/uploads/_pda/2012/08/ane1b9a3c481r-ad-dc4abn-open-meeting-with-sandah-c5abld-bc5ab-amc481mah.pdf.

Leaked US Government Cables

U.S. Embassy Algiers. "Mokhtar Belmokhtar and AQIM: Is One-Eye on His Last Leg?" 07ALGIERS904, June 27, 2007.

"New Armed Groups Joining the Old FIS?" 97ALGIERS952, March 12, 1997.

U.S. Embassy Bamako. "All in the Family: Legislative Politics in Kidal." 07BAMAKO594, June 1, 2007.

"AQIM Seeking Intermediary in Mauritania via Malian Government." 10BAMAKO17, January 12, 2010.

"Bahanga Releases Last Three Malian Soldiers." 09BAMAKO58, January 28, 2009.

"Berabiche and AQIM in Northern Mali." 08BAMAKO371, April 17, 2008.

"Dawa Meeting in Kidal Not Much to Talk about." 09BAMAKO822, December 21, 2009.

"Details on Recent Hostages Release and Next Steps for Mali-Tuareg Negotiations." 08BAMAKO712, August 7, 2008.

"Electoral Tensions in Tarkint: Where AQIM, Arab Militias, and Tuaregs Meet." 09BAMAKO280, May 8, 2009.

"A Familiar Name Surfaces in Search for Canadian Diplomts' Kidnappers." 09BAMAKO106, February 23, 2009.

"Follow Up on Tuareg Insurgents in Mali (C-AL8–00949)." 08BAMAKO824, October 3, 2008.

"The Liberation of AQIM's Austrian Hostages: An Inside View." 08BAMAKO888, November 14, 2008.

"Tribal Fault Lines within the Tuareg of Northern Mali." 08BAMAKO239, March 6, 2008.

"Tuareg Leaders from Gao and Timbuktu: Time for Peace Running Out." 08BAMAKO339, April 7, 2008.

U.S. Embassy Niamey. "More on Bultmeier Murder and GSPC." 06NIAMEY1296, December 4, 2006.

U.S. Embassy Nouakchott. "Ambassador's Luncheon with Anti-Coup Political Parties." 09NOUAKCHOTT323, May 11, 2009.

"Emerging Mauritanian 'Soft' Counterterrorism Strategy." 08NOUAKCHOTT365, July 13, 2008.

"GSPC Announces 'Names' of Five Members Killed in Attack on Mauritania." 05ALGIERS1525, July 19, 2005.

"GSPC Communique Extols Attack in Mauritania, Links it to Flintlock Exercise." 05ALGIERS1163, June 7, 2005.

"Mauritania: Layered Security Strategy." 09NOUAKCHOTT575, September 9, 2009.

"Mauritania: President Aziz on Terrorism and Extremism." 09NOUAK-CHOTT593, September 15, 2009.
"The Mayor of Tidjikja." 08NOUAKCHOTT629, October 27, 2008.
"The Post-Coup Al Qaeda Threat in Mauritania." 08NOUAK-CHOTT666, November 13, 2008.
U.S. Embassy Ouagadougou. "Burkina Faso: MOD Discusses Wide Range of Regional Security Issues with CDA." 09OUAGADOUGOU1136, December 8, 2009.
U.S. Embassy Paris. "Mauritania/France: Worries over AQIM Trump Search for a Perfect Democracy." 09PARIS483, April 2, 2009.
U.S. Embassy Tripoli. "Die Hard in Derna." 08TRIPOLI430, June 2, 2008.
"Extremism in Eastern Libya." 08TRIPOLI120, February 15, 2008.

News Sources and Online Forums

:24
Agence France-Presse (AFP)
Agence Nouakchott d'Information
Al-Ahram
Algeria Channel
Algeria Interface
Algérie 360
Al-Akhbar
Akhbar Libya 24
Alegcom
Anba'
Al Arabiya
Al-Araby
Al-Araby al-Jadid
Asharq al-Awsat
Assakina
The Associated Press
L'Aube
Azzaman
BBC News
BellewarMedia
Les Carnets du Sahel
CNN Arabic
Le Combat
La Dépêche (Mali)
La Dépêche de Kabylie

Der Spiegel
Deutsche Welle (DW)
Diaspora Saharaui
Echorouk Online
Ennahar
ESJ-Bamako Actu
Essirage
L'Express
Foreign Policy
France24
The Guardian
Al-Hayat
L'Humanité
L'Indépendant (Mali)
The Independent (UK)
L'Indicateur du Renouveau
The Intercept
Al Jazeera
Jeune Afrique
Le Journal du Dimanche
Journal du Mali
Kibaru
Kifa li-l-Anba'/Kiffa Info
Libération
The Libya New
The Long War Journal
Magharebia
Al-Majallah
Majallat Al-Akhbar
Mali Actu
Al-Masry Al-Youm
MENASTREAM
Le Monde
Al-Nahar
The New Humanitarian
The New York Times
The New Yorker
News24
Newsweek
Nomade Sahel
Nouvel Horizon
Paldf

Paris Match
Le Parisien
Le Point Afrique
Le Procès Verbal
Qanat Libiya
Al-Quds al-Arabi
Radiodiffusion Télévision du Burkina
Le Reporter
Le Républicain
Reuters
RFI
Sahara Medias
Sahelien
Sidwaya
Le Soir d'Algérie
Il Sole 24 Ore
Studio Tamani
Tahalil
The Telegraph
Time
Voice of America (VOA)
Vox
Al-Wasat
The Washington Post
Al-Yawm

Interviews (Alphabetically by First Name)

Aba Cissé. Bamako, January 24, 2018.
Abdoulaye Diallo. Ouagadougou, June 14, 2019.
Abu Hafs al-Muritani. Nouakchott, April 30, 2018.
Adam Thiam. Bamako, June 19, 2019.
Ahmad al-Wadi'a. Nouakchott, May 3, 2018.
Ahmada ag Bibi. Bamako, March 13, 2018.
Imam Ahmedou Ould Lemrabott. Nouakchott, April 28, 2018.
Alghabass ag Intalla. Washington, January 13, 2018.
Ali Tounkara. Bamako, June 20, 2019.
Amadou Mody Diall. Bamako, March 9, 2018.
Amadou Sall. Nouakchott, September 26, 2017.
Aminetou ag Bibi. Bamako, March 10, 2018.
Bilal ag Achérif. Bamako, June 21, 2019.

Boubacar Cissé. Bamako, January 25, 2018.

Boubacar Sangaré. Bamako, January 21, 2018 and June17, 2019.

Boukary Sangaré. Bamako, January 20, 2018.

Brema Ely Dicko. Bamako, January 22, 2018.

Colonel (ret.) El Boukhary Mohamed Mouemel. Nouakchott, April 30, 2018.

Burkinabè historian. Ouagadougou, June 2019.

Chrysogone Zougmoré. Ouagadougou, June 11, 2019.

Fahad ag Mohamed. Bamako, June 21, 2019.

Jamil Mansour. Nouakchott, September 27, 2017.

Koudbi Kaboré. Ouagadougou, June 11, 2019.

Luc Damiba. Ouagadougou, June 15, 2019.

Malian NGO official. Bamako, June 2019.

Manny Ansar. Bamako, March 13, 2018.

Marcelin Guenguéré. Bamako, June 22, 2019.

Modibo Galy Cissé. Bamako, June 17, 2019.

Mohamed ag Aharib. Bamako, January 24, 2018.

Mohamed Ould Mahmoud. Bamako, March 12, 2018.

Mohammed Mahmoud Abu al-Ma'ali. Nouakchott, April 28, 2018.

Imam Oumar Dia. Bamako, June 21, 2019.

Oumar Sow. Bamako, March 8, 2018.

Saïd Ben Bella. Nouakchott, October 2017.

Samir Abdulkarim. Ouagadougou, June 14, 2019.

Sidi Mohamed Ould Maham. Nouakchott, May 3, 2018.

Yoby Guindo. Bamako, March 8, 2018 and June 18, 2019.

Index

Made in United States
North Haven, CT
01 September 2022

23517038R00202